COMPUTER CONTROL AND AUDIT:
A TOTAL SYSTEMS APPROACH

COMPUTER CONTROL AND AUDIT
A TOTAL SYSTEMS APPROACH

JOHN G. BURCH, JR.
East Texas State University
Texarkana, Texas

JOSEPH L. SARDINAS, JR.
University of Massachusetts, Amherst

JOHN WILEY & SONS
New York   Chichester   Brisbane   Toronto

This book was set in 10 point
Aster by Imperial Litho/Graphics.
It was copyedited by Romayne
Ponleithner and illustrated by
Graphics Two. Sally Thompson
designed the text and the cover
was designed by Bud Thon.
Printing and binding was done by
Fairfield Graphics. Chuck Pendergast
supervised production.

Copyright © 1978 by John Wiley & Sons, Inc.

All rights reserved. Published simultaneously in Canada.

Reproduction or translation of any part of this work
beyond that permitted by Sections 107 or 108 of the 1976 United States
Copyright Act without the permission of the copyright owner is
unlawful. Requests for permission or further information should
be addressed to the Permissions Department, John Wiley & Sons, Inc.

Library of Congress Cataloging in Publication Data

Burch, John G.
  Computer control and audit.

  Includes index.
  1. Electronic data processing departments—
Auditing. 2. Auditing—Data processing.
I. Sardinas, Joseph L., joint author. II. Title.
HF5548.2.B778   658'.05'4   78-9093
ISBN 0-471-03491-6

Printed in the United States of America
10 9 8 7 6 5 4

To Mother for her help and inspiration
To my wife Ronnie and my son Michael

ABOUT THE AUTHORS

JOHN G. BURCH, JR. is a professor and head of accounting and information systems at East Texas State University in Texarkana. He has also taught at the University of Massachusetts and Louisiana State University. Dr. Burch has instructed graduate and undergraduate courses in accounting, administrative controls, computer auditing and control, computer programming, and information systems in his ten-year career. Prior to his academic career, he worked in general accounting and managerial positions in the construction and oil industry.

A native of Texas and Louisiana, Professor Burch earned his Ph.D. in business from the University of Alabama, and his undergraduate degree from Louisiana Tech. He is a member of several professional organizations and also holds memberships in Beta Alpha Psi, Beta Gamma Sigma, Phi Beta Phi, and Delta Sigma Pi. He has written a number of articles that have appeared in professional journals. He has presented a number of papers at several conferences. Dr. Burch is co-author of two texts, *Information Systems: A Case Workbook* and *Information Systems: Theory and Practice*.

JOSEPH L. SARDINAS, JR. is Assistant Professor of Accounting and Information Systems at the School of Business Administration, University of Massachusetts at Amherst. He is coordinator of the information systems program for the Department of Accounting. He received his Ph.D. degree from The Pennsylvania State University and his MBA and BS degrees from the University of Connecticut. He has done research in the areas of information systems and auditing EDP facilities. Prior to his academic career, Dr. Sardinas participated in the analysis, design, implementation, and evaluation of computer based information systems. Dr. Sardinas has presented several papers at accounting conferences and has coordinated and presented management training and development programs concerned with computer control and auditing. He has published several articles that have appeared in professional journals. He is an active member of the American Accounting Association (AAA), and is Northeast Regional Vice-Chairman of the Management Advisory Services (MAS) section of the AAA. He is also a member of the Association for Computing Machinery, and the Society for Management Information Systems.

PREFACE

INTRODUCTION

The growing use of computer-based information systems presents a number of challenges to the auditor as well as to management and systems personnel. The computer also gives the auditor a strong opportunity to become a complete auditor. Now that the increasing importance of computer systems to the auditor and accounting in general has been recognized by both academicians and practitioners, the need for a course that is supported by comprehensive material on computer control and auditing has become imperative.

Ultimately, the control and audit of computer systems are the responsibility of auditors as well as of computer and management personnel. All of these people are concerned with the control, integrity, accuracy, efficiency, and effectiveness of the computer system. This text deals with these concerns. Certainly, a proper system of controls and management of the computer system is not the exclusive concern of the auditor and accountant; they are also the concern of computer management, general management, controllers, systems analysts, programmers, and so forth.

This text brings together the practical experience of auditors and management, and many of the newer concepts in the field of computer control and auditing. Normally, the person taking this course is one of two types: (1) a practicing auditor or manager with a limited background in computer control and auditing, and (2) a student (usually of junior, senior, or graduating standing) who has had at least an introduction to accounting, computers, and programming.

We have tested this text material a number of times in three areas: (1) seminars for practicing accountants, auditors, and managers offered in continuing education; (2) training programs for auditors and examiners who work for the State of New York; and (3) a three-hour course in computer control and auditing at two universities.

OVERVIEW OF THE TEXT

One objective of Part I is to define and discuss in detail, both from a technical and an application viewpoint, the computer environment that the auditor works in. Today, a large part of the organization's accounting information flow is embedded in the logic of the computer system and its physical data base. To effectively perform control and audit tasks and meet his responsibilities, the auditor must become more knowledgeable about this computer environment. He must learn more about how to control and audit it and how to use it for his own needs.

Another objective of Part I is to discuss the concern of both the private and public sector about fraud and invasion of privacy. In addition to the need to understand the computer environment, these two areas may represent the biggest challenge to the auditor during the next decade.

Part II deals with a total system of controls. Strategic control points of a computer-based information system are defined. Each chapter then presents the control techniques applicable to each control point. Included at the end of each chapter is a control questionnaire that summarizes the material presented in that particular chapter. The final chapter in Part II deals with the cost/effectiveness analysis of a system of controls.

Part III presents techniques applicable to the examination and testing of the computer system. Like Part II, this part emphasizes the concept of a system of audit techniques. To perform a comprehensive audit, the use of one or two techniques is normally not sufficient, i.e., the auditor needs an array of techniques at his disposal. In Part III, use of the computer as an audit tool is emphasized. Online event processing systems are discussed in depth, and control and audit techniques that are especially applicable to these systems are presented.

ASSIGNMENT MATERIAL AND PROCEDURES

The assignment material at the end of each chapter (excluding Chapters 1 and 2) is divided as follows: (1) review questions that can be precisely answered upon completion of the chapter; (2) discussion questions that do not have neat, clear-cut answers but the chapter contains sufficient information to provide a basis for answering these questions; (3) exercises that are similar to review questions in that they usually require a specific solution; and (4) problems that may not have a solution per se but more than likely have an array of feasible "solutions."

Open discussion of the questions at the end of each chapter is one of the highlights of the seminars and course. In addition, students in the regular university course are divided into audit groups (four to six in a group). Each group undertakes an outside control and audit project in an organization of their choice with a computer-based system. Working with personnel such as the internal accountant and auditor, the manager of the computer system, and a systems analyst and/or programmer, each group actually applies some of the techniques presented in the text. They apply the system of controls questionnaires and investigate the controls employed in "their" system. After completing Part II, each group presents a "System of Controls Report" to their liaison in their organization and to the instructor. They also make an oral presentation of this report to other members of the class for debate and criticism. Four main ingredients of this report are: (1) completed questionnaires, (2) description of weaknesses, (3) recommendations for correcting weaknesses, and (4) cost/effectiveness analysis of the proposed system of controls.

After moving into Part III, the audit groups are assigned specific audit techniques to apply in their organizations. These techniques include: (1) test deck, (2) audit review of a simple program, (3) preparation and application of a simple audit program usually written in FORTRAN or COBOL, and (4) application of a canned program usually available at most universities via timesharing to analyze a sample of real or hypothesized data relative to their organization. Application of these techniques gives the student a good insight into effective use of the computer as an audit tool.

Application of other techniques discussed in Part III, which require a lot of planning and/or expense to apply, is simulated. Examples of these techniques are confirmations, generalized audit programs, computer vendor-supplied programs, hardware and software monitors, transaction logs, tagging and tracing, and integrated test facilities (ITF). Each audit group prepares formal recommendations as to how these techniques could be implemented in their organizations. On the basis of these recommendations, they garner replies from the people in their organization as to the feasibility of applying such techniques. A summary of their recommendations and replies is written up and included with the results from their application of other audit techniques (e.g., test deck). This total report is entitled "Audit Report." It is formally presented to appropriate personnel of their organization and to the instructor. It is also orally presented to other members of the class.

As stated earlier, both reports are discussed in class. The students enjoy this part of the course for two reasons: (1) the reports are based on real situations, and (2) the reports generate lively discussion and arguments. In gathering the material to prepare these reports, the audit groups must carry on pretty much as if they were full-fledged auditors, although they normally spend no more than twenty-five to forty hours in their organization during the semester. Moreover, the management personnel in the organizations are normally cooperative and appreciative of the results of the project.

The authors wish to express their gratitude to the reviewers who provided constructive advice during the revisions of the text. We would also like to acknowledge the assistance provided by Louise Barrett, David Callaghan, Richard Housman, Arthur Lash, and Gary Monroe. Special thanks go to Linda Parker and Fran Mitchell for their extra effort and pleasant attitude. Most importantly, we are grateful to our wives Glenda and Ronnie, who encouraged and inspired us during the preparation of this book.

CONTENTS

PART ONE: A PERSPECTIVE ON IMPLICATIONS OF COMPUTER BASED INFORMATION SYSTEMS ON CONTROL AND AUDITING

1	**The Computer Audit Environment**	**3**
1.1	Introduction	3
1.2	The Computer Environment and its Relation to Auditing	3
1.3	Components of the Computer Environment	5
1.4	An Increasingly Complex Environment	22
1.5	Summary	26
2	**Computer Abuse and its Impact Upon Auditing**	**29**
2.1	Introduction	29
2.2	Fraud	29
2.3	Invasion of Privacy	37
2.4	Challenges and Opportunities	46
2.5	Summary	49

PART TWO: SYSTEM OF CONTROLS

3	**Introduction to Controls**	**57**
3.1	Introduction	57
3.2	Need for Controls	57
3.3	Overview and Structure of Controls	60
3.4	Summary	66
4	**Administrative Controls**	**68**
4.1	Introduction	68
4.2	Implementation and Execution of Plans	69
4.3	Screening, Selecting, and Training Personnel	74
4.4	Personnel Administration	76

4.5	Establishment of Standards	79
4.6	Summary	82

5	**Operational Controls** ✓	**95**
5.1	Introduction	95
5.2	Input Controls	95
5.3	Operating System Controls	105
5.4	Processing Controls	112
5.5	Application Program Controls	117
5.6	Data Base Management System (DBMS) Controls	122
5.7	Built-in Computer Controls	128
5.8	Computer Operations Controls	131
5.9	Library and Data Base Controls	138
5.10	Output Controls	142
5.11	Summary	144

6	**Documentation Controls** ✓	**178**
6.1	Introduction	178
6.2	Purpose of Documentation	178
6.3	Consequences of Not Having Documentation	179
6.4	Basic Computer-Based Information Systems Documentation	180
6.5	Documentation Tools	185
6.6	Summary	196

7	**Security Controls** ✓	**214**
7.1	Introduction	214
7.2	Hazards	214
7.3	Physical Security Techniques	217
7.4	Procedural Security Techniques	221
7.5	Summary	230

8	**Cost/Effectiveness Analysis of Controls**	**247**
8.1	Introduction	247
8.2	Management's Responsibility in Regard to Controls	247
8.3	System of Controls Decision Model	249
8.4	Summary	257

PART THREE: COMPUTER AUDIT TECHNIQUES

9	**General Audit Considerations** ✓	**273**
9.1	Introduction	273
9.2	The Audit Function	273

9.3	The Computer Audit Environment	283
9.4	The Use of the Computer as an Audit Tool	288
9.5	Summary	291

10 Basic Computer Audit Techniques — 294
10.1	Introduction	294
10.2	Questionnaires	294
10.3	Auditing Around the Computer	301
10.4	Auditing Through the Computer	304
10.5	Test Deck	306
10.6	Audit Review of Application Programs	314
10.7	Summary	321

11 Computer-Assisted Audit Techniques — 340
11.1	Introduction	340
11.2	Overview of Using the Computer as an Audit Tool	340
11.3	Programs Written by Client's Programmer	354
11.4	Programs Written by the Auditor	356
11.5	Generalized Audit Programs	361
11.6	Utility Programs Supplied by Computer Vendors	369
11.7	Summary	369

12 Movement Toward Event-Processing Systems — 377
12.1	Introduction	377
12.2	Periodic Versus Event-Processing Systems	377
12.3	Computer Technology that Supports Event-Processing Systems	385
12.4	Information System Concepts that Require Event-Processing Systems	402
12.5	Controls Revisited	409
12.6	Summary	415

13 Event Auditing for Event-Processing Systems — 418
13.1	Introduction	418
13.2	Event Processing Revisited	418
13.3	Transaction Trail	421
13.4	Integrated Test Facility (ITF)	431
13.5	Parallel Test Facility (PTF)	441
13.6	Monitoring Systems	445
13.7	The Auditor's Involvement in Systems Development	456
13.8	Summary	460

14	**Final Comments**		**466**
14.1	Introduction		466
14.2	Anticipated Questions		466
14.3	Systems Approach to Auditing		472

GLOSSARY **483**

INDEX **489**

PART ONE

A PERSPECTIVE ON IMPLICATIONS OF COMPUTER BASED INFORMATION SYSTEMS

CHAPTER

1

THE COMPUTER AUDIT ENVIRONMENT

1.1 INTRODUCTION

If the experience of the early 1970's is a prediction for the late 1970's and 1980's in terms of the willingness of organizations to implement and use the newest computer technology and information systems concepts as the basis of their accounting systems, then we must plan for and tool up to meet the related auditing challenges and implications that will continue to confront the accounting and auditing profession. The purpose of this chapter is to discuss the computer environment and its relation to auditing, components of the computer's environment, and the increasing complexity of this environment.

1.2 THE COMPUTER ENVIRONMENT AND ITS RELATION TO AUDITING

New computer technology has provided an environment that is oriented to information processing and meeting the informational needs of users through the application of information systems concepts. These computer-based information systems are expanding beyond the limits of traditional accounting systems to encompass operational data to provide a broad range of information for planning, control, and decision making. Most of these systems are designed to capture and process all transactions and events that relate to the organization as soon as they occur.

These systems have not altered accounting methodology per se, but they have substantially altered the basic procedures of accounting. No longer are there clerks and bookkeepers to process accounting data who understand not only the procedures but also the overall accounting system. Conversely, computer-based information systems include personnel who are totally unfamiliar with the accounting system and its procedures. The accounting tasks, along with other activities, are embedded in the software of the computer. Also, the audit objectives, in and of themselves, are not changed by computer systems, but the tools and techniques used by auditors to achieve these audit objectives must change.

Advanced information systems require control and audit techniques that differ from those techniques applicable to manual systems and even, in some cases, computer batch-processing systems. The complexity of these systems also requires that the auditor become involved in the analysis, design, and testing of these systems before they are implemented to make sure that they contain a sound system of controls and that they are auditable. To accomplish these new demands, the auditor must increase his expertise. The obvious statement is: one must understand a system to audit it effectively. The American Institute of Certified Public Accountants (AICPA) supports this contention:

> . . . If a client uses EDP in its accounting system, whether the application is simple or complex, the auditor needs to understand the entire system sufficiently to enable him to identify and evaluate its essential accounting control features. . . .[1]

Moreover, if the accountant and auditor are to be able to deal with and audit the *accounting system,* they will have to understand computer-based information systems because they are effectively the same thing. Consequently, accountants and auditors can no longer afford to treat the computer as a "black box." Instead, they must get into the system itself and see to it that a good system of controls is in place and operating as planned. The auditor must also open "audit windows" in the "black box" to examine and test the program logic and data base. To do otherwise is to go around the computer (discussed later as auditing around the computer), but this method has little to offer the auditor. For example: "Equity Funding's management . . . preferred an audit-around approach. A newspaper reported that management rejected the idea of the external auditor bringing in a 'computer type' at one point."[2]

---

[1]Statement on Auditing Standards (SAS) No. 3, American Institute of Certified Public Accountants, December 1974, p. 2.
[2]Harold Weiss, "Rebuttal to 'Equity Funding Implications,'" *EDPACS*, October 1974, p. 11.

In all too many cases the computer and auditor are still relative strangers. There are two significant reasons for this. First, companies are trying to do today's work with yesterday's auditors, in terms of experience, education, and inclination. Second, many senior auditors and audit managers never really became involved with punched-card computer systems. Since they never had even a nodding acquaintance with the older systems, they now face a huge gap between the ledgers of the past and the integrated electronic data processing systems of today and tomorrow. Some computer systems of today operate in a fast-response, online, real-time mode and employ advanced input and output devices. This new environment requires new auditing techniques and auditing tools.[3]

The correct selection of auditing tools and techniques which can effectively deal with electronic data processing demands that the auditor have sufficient knowledge of the components of the computer environment. Insufficient knowledge of the computer environment places the auditor in an unacceptable position, according to statement on Accounting Standards No. 3 above.

1.3 COMPONENTS OF THE COMPUTER ENVIRONMENT

In Figure 1.1 the basic components of any computer-based information system are illustrated. At the center of this figure are the processing functions of input, transmission, processing, storage, and output. The four components of people, hardware, software, and data base drive these processing functions. Each of these four components is discussed below.

People

The success or failure of a computer-based information system, like that of any other system, rests primarily on the quality of its people. Probably the greatest challenge to management is to recruit, train, retain, and effectively manage qualified and loyal personnel. An additional problem from the auditor's viewpoint is that computer operators, programmers, systems analysts, and even the information systems manager are often not familiar with, and thus cannot relate to traditional conventions of accounting and auditing. These people do not normally

---

[3] Joe Wasserman, "Selecting a Computer Audit Package," *The Journal of Accountancy*, April 1974, p. 30.

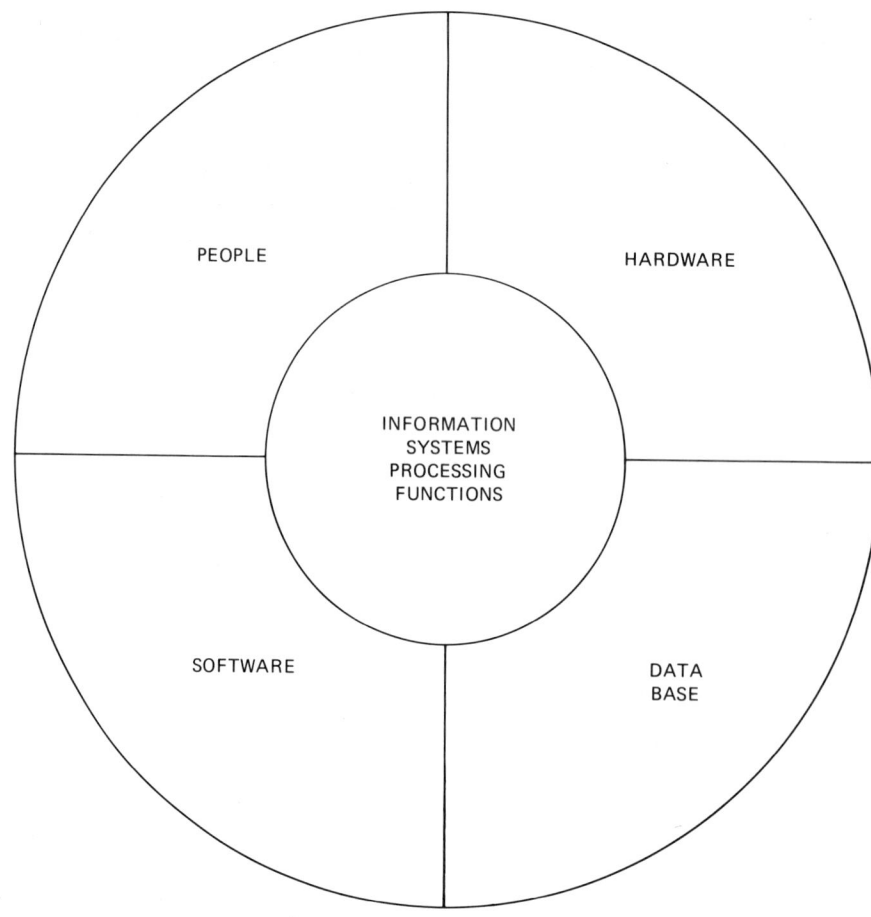

FIGURE 1.1.
Basic Components of a Computer-Based Information System.

place much significance on control and auditing. They may even view these activities as impinging upon their work. These people often have technical, computer science backgrounds but little appreciation for sound administrative principles.

Figure 1.2 presents an organization chart that illustrates the wide variety of job types that exist in a typical computer-based information system. The administration of the categories in this chart is the responsibility of (1) the information systems manager who is monitored by (2) a steering committee. The categories are: (3) systems development, (4) programming, (5) operations, (6) data center, and (7) security.

1. The manager of information systems must be able to unify the diverse and suboptimizing departments of the organization via an unbiased flow of information to all users. He normally has a vice-president's status, and he must have a strong administrative as well as technical background. His activities should be neutral and independent of those of other executives in the organization. He should not be an advocate of any department and should be responsible only to top management, directors, and/or owners of the organization.

Specifically, the duties of this person include:

a. Planning for and controlling all activities in the information system. This duty includes making long- and short-range plans for systems development projects, computer and software acquisition, and computer operations. It includes setting of standards, monitoring and evaluating computer operations, systems projects, hardware and software performance, and personnel activities. This duty should also include the development and management of a program of security designed to safeguard personnel, programs, data base, hardware, and peripheral facilities.

b. Acts as a liaison between the system and system users. This duty involves communicating and reporting to system users and top management concerning the plans and performance of the system. It also includes the development of an educational and training program for these users.

c. Performs personnel administration. This duty includes selecting, training, and managing information systems personnel.

d. General administration includes sound budgetary policies and cost/effectiveness analysis. This duty also includes setting priorities and charging system users for systems costs. This duty includes meeting and maintaining a proper relationship with vendors and suppliers and maintaining a system for evaluating acquisition of hardware, software, and other facilities.

2. The steering committee is comprised of top financial and operating management. Their function is to oversee and monitor the general activities of the information system, i.e., they apply general direction to the information systems manager. They interact with the information systems manager to establish and update the master plan. The members meet periodically to compare performance with milestones. They act as an advisory group to the information systems manager in setting priorities and acquiring resources.

Use of the steering committee helps to coordinate ideas and action. Different views can be unified and agreed-upon courses of action established. The committee can insulate the information systems manager from the crossfire of opinion and reduce the opportunity for a single

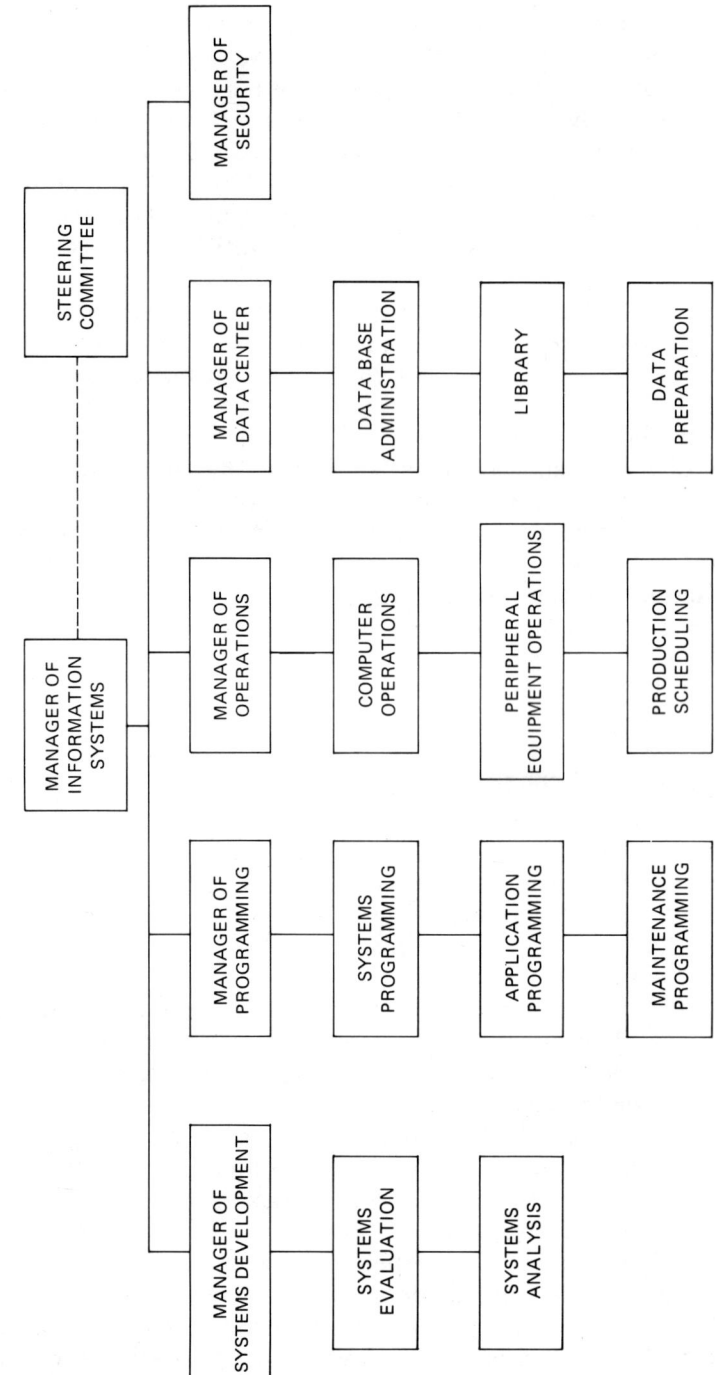

FIGURE 1.2.
Categories of Jobs in a Typical Computer-Based Information System.

person or group to exert too much clout. Using the steering committee encourages participation, which most people like and which is especially applicable to the administration of the information system, a system that is supposed to serve the entire organization. Moreover, each participant's viewpoint is broadened as he gains an appreciation of other departments' problems as well as those of the information system.

3. The systems development category includes the analysis, design, evaluation, and implementation of information systems for users in the organization. Planning for and evaluating present and proposed hardware and software systems results in recommendations for hardware and software modification or acquisition. In some systems, this category may be supported by data communications specialists, who design and implement data communications networks including telecommunications software, terminals, modems, and front-end processors. For more complicated logico-mathematical manipulation of data, operations research specialists apply mathematical models. The systems development category may also use the services of a methods and procedures analyst to develop improved clerical methods, procedures, and forms as part of the development of the new or improved system.

4. This manager supervises programming personnel who are responsible for the development and maintenance of the software logic. The three major areas of this category are:

    a. A systems programmer who develops and maintains the operating system and other technical systems software that control the basic functions of the computer. He or she is a highly trained person with a strong technical proficiency in hardware and software. The program instructions are written in machine or assembler language.

    b. An application programmer who designs, codes, tests, and implements computer programs for specific applications, e.g., accounts receivable application. The computer programs are usually written in a high-level language such as COBOL.

    c. Maintenance programmer who makes changes and corrections in existing application programs.

5. This manager supervises equipment operators and schedules jobs through the system. His job is analogous to that of a production foreman in a manufacturing process. The computer operator under his supervision monitors and controls the computer by operating the central computer console. Peripheral equipment operators assist the computer operator by setting up and operating tape and disk drives, printers, card reader and punch, and so forth. The production scheduler coordinates and controls the mix of data-processing jobs to achieve optimum equipment utilization and service to users. He also maintains records of job and equipment performance. Assisting the production scheduler's activ-

ity are job-setup clerks who assemble files and data-processing materials for various jobs in accordance with schedules. Also under his supervision are control clerks who review outputs to see that they satisfy job requirements and distribute them to authorized users.

6. The data center manager supervises the handling of data that are processed by the system. The three major areas of this category are:

a. The data base administrator, who designs and controls the data base of the system. He sets and enforces standards for the use, control, and security of all files comprising the data base.

b. The data library is a well-constructed (e.g., fireproof) structure used to house offline files, programs, documentation, and other sensitive material. It is under the control of a person, sometimes referred to as an operations librarian, who controls the receipt and issue of material contained in the library. This activity is similar to that of a librarian in a book library. Also under the supervision of the librarian is a supply clerk who maintains and issues data-processing supplies (e.g., printer paper and forms).

c. Data preparation requires devices to convert data into computer-processable form. This area includes data entry equipment operators who convert data on source documents into computer readable form by use of keypunches, key-to-tape or key-to-disk devices, point of sale terminals, CRT terminals, and so forth. Also, in more advanced systems, the users of the organization perform data entry without the aid of an operator. As we will see later in Part II, this area requires stringent access controls.

7. The security manager supervises a variety of security officers to provide overall safety to the system. In computer-based information systems the integration of processing functions in a concentrated system with a relatively small number of personnel (unlike old manual systems with a number of clerks and bookkeepers) increases the risk of unauthorized access, fraud, theft, sabotage, and destruction. Security against these hazards includes TV monitors, badge and check in/check out procedures, single door entry, and so forth. Security controls are discussed in depth in Part II.

Many of the individuals discussed above, including the auditor, must interact to some degree with computer hardware. The auditor must have a basic understanding of the functions of the individuals who interact with computers, as well as the computer hardware itself, if he is to perform his function in a manner consistent with the high degree of professionalism demanded of him.

Hardware

Hardware represents all of the equipment and devices comprising a computer configuration that inputs, transmits, processes, stores, and

CHAPTER ONE   THE COMPUTER AUDIT ENVIRONMENT   11

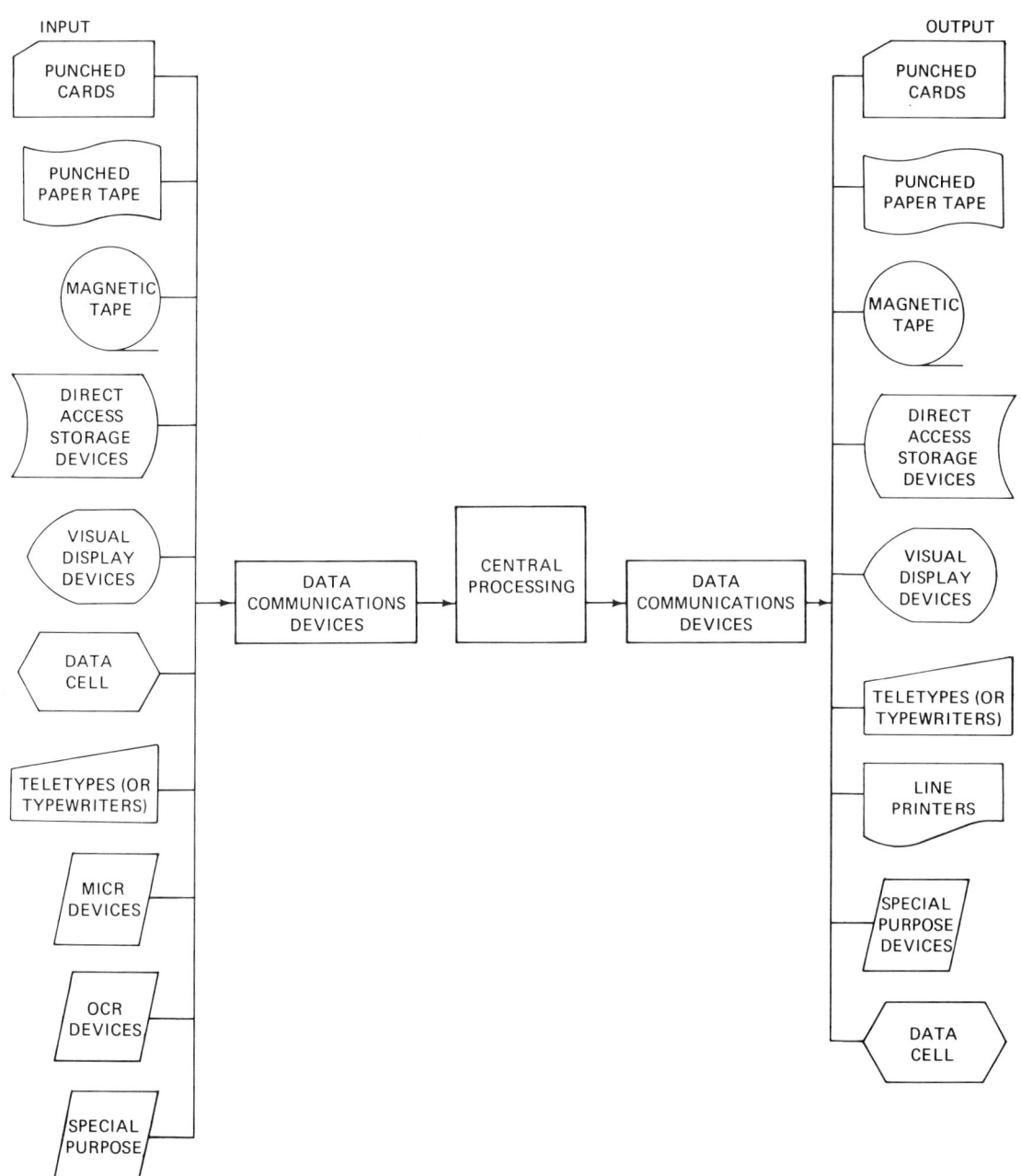

FIGURE 1.3.
Hardware Devices.

outputs data. Figure 1.3 illustrates the hardware that makes up a computer system. In this system the input of data is performed by different kinds of input devices that also frequently serve as output devices.

Typical input devices include those that accept punched cards, punched paper tape, magnetic tape, magnetic disk, magnetic ink, optically scanned data, keyed data, and special input derived from devices such as analog computers or voice recognition.

More and more information systems rely on data communication devices to transmit data from one or more locations to a central processing unit. Data communication devices are also being relied on to perform message switching functions and data transmission for organizations with widely separated plants, warehouses, and sales offices.

The central processing unit of the computer system is made up of three components. First, the control section directs and coordinates the entire computer system via programs (e.g., operating system) in residence. Second, the arithmetic-logic unit performs the operations of addition, subtraction, multiplication, division, shifting, storing, and comparisons. Third, the primary storage (often called core storage) provides space for input data, the program(s) that direct processing, and any files or tables of data needed for reference or additional processing.

Primary storage with the capacity to hold all data files and programs for an organization would be prohibitive in cost. Auxiliary storage devices, which are much cheaper, are used to store other programs and data, which are made available to the central processing unit when needed. Popular auxiliary storage devices that transfer data and program instructions rapidly between primary storage and input/output units are: magnetic tape, magnetic disk, magnetic drum, and data cells.

Output hardware in a computer system records, prints, or displays data as directed by the central processing unit. This output may be generated in a coded form such as punched cards, punched paper tape, magnetic tape, magnetic disk, or data cells. The output may be printed out via typewriters, impact printers, or high-speed laser and thermal printers. Data may be displayed on a visual display device such as a cathode-ray tube (CRT) or output pulses transformed to photographic patterns for computer output microfilm (COM).

Typical Equipment Configuration

To get a better feel for the computer audit environment, it is helpful to take a look at a typical equipment configuration for online and/or batch processing as illustrated in Figure 1.4. A computer configuration, per se, is not very complicated. The major challenges to the auditor are the kind of system of controls applied to the configuration, the evidential information extracted from it, and how he can use the computer configuration as an audit tool. With these objectives in mind, the auditor need not be confounded by numerous tape drives, terminals, and direct-access storage devices.

Hardware does not, in and of itself, represent the totality of a computer-based system. In fact, computer hardware is functionally dependent upon software which has been produced in order to control the data-processing function.

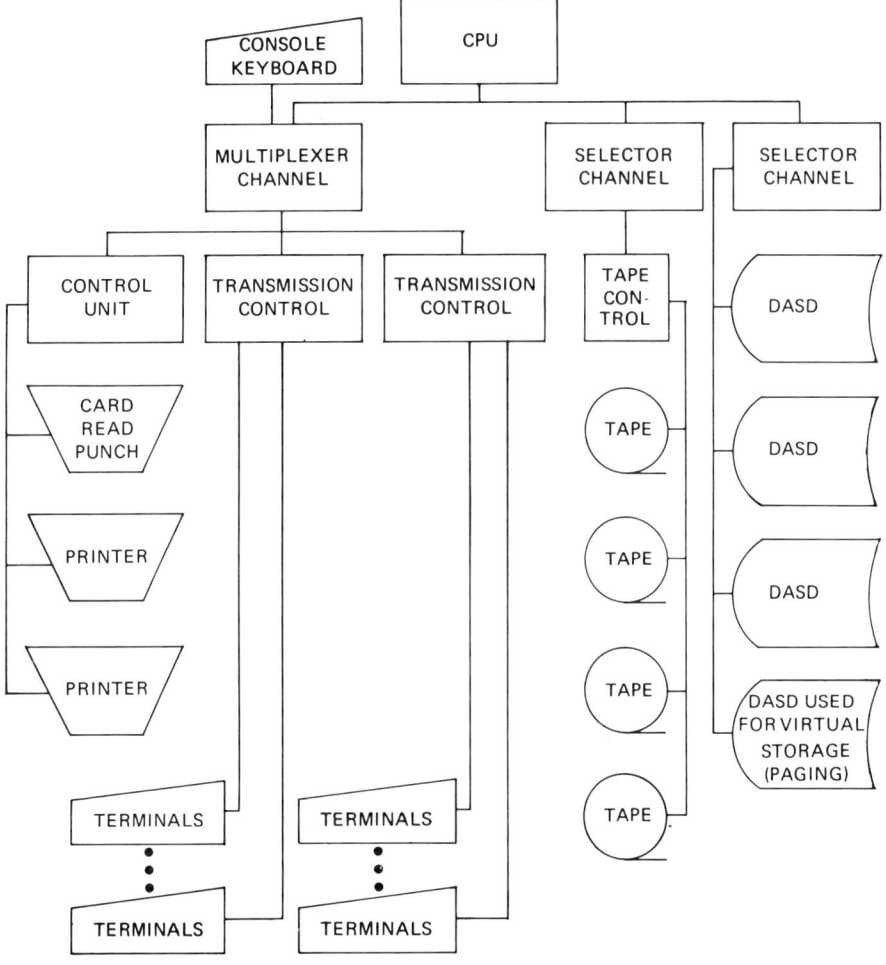

FIGURE 1.4.
Typical Computer Configuration For Online and/or Batch Processing.

Software

Software consists of the programs and routines that are used to make the hardware perform its data-processing functions. If the computer hardware is a tiger, the software represents the instructions given by the animal trainer. Included in software are manuals, documentation, and administrative policies.

Software refers to application programs (e.g., demand deposit accounting) that direct the processing functions of a particular application. It also refers to system software, such as control programs that are supplied by the computer manufacturers and independent software vendors to direct and control the operations of a computer system. We discuss software under four categories: (1) programming languages, (2) operating systems, (3) control programs, and (4) application and special service programs.

1. *Programming languages* Language or instructions that the computer can follow are of three types: (a) machine language, (b) assembler language, and (c) compiler language. Machine language is represented by and written in the binary code that the computer understands. This language is tedious for the human because in addition to remembering dozens of code numbers for instructions, the programmer is also forced to keep track of storage locations of data and instructions, all in the form of strings of 0's and 1's. It's efficient for the computer, but inefficient for the human.

Assembler languages were developed in the early 1950's to lessen the tedium and slow development process caused by writing programs in machine language. Assembler languages were made up of mnemonic instruction codes and symbolic addresses that the human could relate to. However, these instructions must be translated into a language that the computer understands, which is machine language. An assembler translator program converts the symbolic instructions, called a *source* program, into a machine language *object* program.

Compiler languages are also known as high-level, or people-oriented, languages, because the instructions resemble the English language or mathematical expressions used by people to communicate. However, the *source* program written by the human has to be compiled and translated into an *object* program that can be understood and executed by the computer. Compiler languages such as COBOL have many advantages over machine and assembler languages for writing application programs. For example, they are: computer independent, easier to write, more human efficient, easier to read and maintain, and universally understood. Some people include a fourth language used with data base systems.

2. *Operating systems* When a user acquires a computer, he is buying not only hardware but also an *interface* that will permit him to achieve his own needs through application programs without being too much concerned about the internal operations of the computer. This interface system, called an operating system, operates the computer in the most efficient manner. It is made up of an integrated system of complex, sophisticated programs (usually written in machine or assembler languages) which supervises the operations of the CPU, control I/O functions, translates assembler and compiler languages into machine language, and provides a host of support services. An operating system minimizes the amount of human intervention required during processing and maximizes the efficient utilization of hardware by performing many functions that were formerly the responsibility of the computer operator. It performs activities such as: loading and unloading input and output equipment, clearing central processor storage locations between jobs, or scheduling jobs stacked in a waiting queue. It also performs multiprogramming and paging functions.

3. *Control programs* The key components of the operating system are control programs that include a supervisor, an I/O control system, data communications control, initial program loader, and a job-control program.

The supervisor is similar to a traffic cop of the system in that it monitors I/O activities, handles interrupt conditions, job scheduling, program retrieval, and primary storage allocation. The I/O control system handles input/output scheduling, input/output error corrections, and other data management functions.

Data communications control programs are included in systems that use a network of data communication channels and remote terminals. It handles activities such as data input; automatic polling, queuing, and interruput for competing terminals; message switching; and inquiry and transaction processing.

The initial program loader is a small control program that loads the supervisor control program from a systems residence device (e.g., magnetic disk) into primary storage when the computer begins operation. The job control program's function is to prepare the computer system for the start of the next job by executing job-control language statements.

4. *Application and special service programs* Application programs are normally written by a programmer who works for the organization and performs tasks appropriate to specific applications, such as payroll, inventory, accounts receivable, and sales reporting programs.

Canned application programs have the same objectives, but these programs are supplied by computer manufacturers, independent software vendors, or other computer users. Normally these canned programs have wider application such as in the area of cash flow analysis, PERT, make or buy analysis, regression analysis, assignment and linear programming, depreciation schedules, and investment analysis.

Service programs include such aids as: (a) subroutines that consist of a set of instructions that perform some common, subordinate function within another program and that can be called by that program when needed; (b) librarian programs that catalog, control, and maintain a directory of programs and subroutines that are stored on the library (usually magnetic disk) of the computer system; (c) utilities that are a group of programs that perform various housekeeping functions such as sorts and merges and file and memory dumps; and (d) various other services and aids such as simulators, emulators, flowcharters, and debugging aids.

Some authorities have predicted that more than 20 percent of the software currently programmed into systems will be in hardware form (some people use the terms firmware, microprogram, or microcode) by the early 1980's, and more than 90 percent of all software functions will be found in firmware by 1990. This prediction assumes that a great deal of standardization and generality of business data-processing functions will occur among and between organizations in the future. For example, if every organization used the same kind of payroll system, then all payroll programs could be in firmware. This situation will probably never happen, but there will be more significant movement toward the use of microprogramming, especially in the operating systems area. The use of microprograms or firmware will have two noticeable impacts: (1) it will make computer systems significantly cheaper, and (2) it will enhance the control of the system from the auditor's viewpoint because firmware is prepared by the computer vendor and can normally only be changed by the computer vendor. One of the major problems in the area of controls today is the unauthorized change of software. Having microprograms installed in the circuitry of the equipment makes the logic of the system more "tamper free" than if it were written in the form of program instructions.

We have discussed three of the four basic components of a computer-based information system. They are people, hardware, and software. The final component provides the raw material that is "processed" into information. Specifically, it is data base.

Data Base

Data are defined as the representation of a fact or event. A data base is the entire accumulation of data to meet the data-processing and information requirements of the organization. The data base is not a formless mass of raw data. Rather, it is organized by records within files (also called data sets).

The creation and proper maintenance of a data base involve techniques for organizing the data elements in a manner to provide efficient, controlled access. In early systems, data were organized by logical records in a sequential manner (i.e., all the records for Customer No. 2 followed those for Customer No. 1 and preceded those for Customer No. 3). The records were grouped by application, e.g., accounts receivable balances as of a certain date or sales transactions for the month. Similar files were maintained for related systems, e.g., sales transactions might be organized by customer on one file for accounts receivable applications and organized by product, salesman, territory, etc., on a sales analysis file for marketing applications.

The modern data base concept involves defining and recording each data element only once for all applications, organizing information for efficient access and limiting access to authorized users, e.g., within a data base, customer payment information would be available only to credit department personnel, and sales product information would be available to marketing personnel. Therefore, the nature of user responsibility for each data base element should be considered.[4]

The technical reasons for moving toward a data base concept are: (1) to standardize record names and formats, (2) to interrelate common data elements, (3) to synchronize file updates, (4) to reduce data redundancy, (5) to separate logical from physical files, and (6) to reduce program maintenance.

The information reasons for implementing a data base are: (1) to logically relate and make the data consistent with the functional aspects of the organization's users; (2) to enhance multilevel and cross-functional flow of information; and (3) to permit users to zoom in on the data base and get quick, specific responses to inquiries.

From a systems designer's viewpoint, the reason for development of a data base is to increase accessibility of users from both local and remote locations. This access gives them the ability to add, change, delete, copy, or display information from the data base. From the auditor's viewpoint, he must make sure that the integrity, accuracy, and security of the data base are maintained and that it is free from unauthorized access through terminals, wire tapping, or other means. Another aspect that is becoming more critical every day is the confidentiality of the data base, the need to ensure that personal data are not misused; this, too, must be a concern of the auditor.

---

[4]Auditing Advanced EDP Systems Task Force of the AICPA's Computer Auditing Subcommittee, "Advanced EDP Systems and the Auditor's Concerns," *The Journal of Accountancy*, January 1975, p. 67.

The four basic components of a computer-based information system have been discussed on an individual or modular basis. Total information systems are dependent upon the proper interaction of the basic components. The auditor should have an understanding of these functional relationships in order to properly perform the audit function associated with a total information system.

Analysis of a Total System

One way to get a feel for the computer audit environment is to analyze a total information system, its elements, and its flow of information. Such a system is illustrated in Figure 1.5. We have previously discussed the components of a computer-based system. Now, we will put all these components together and discuss how various elements of these major components support a total information system and make it operative.

A computer-based total information system has the capability of batch processing by central equipment, and by installation of a data communications system, it has the capability of handling online processing and random information queries by a variety of remote users. In addition to a number of hardware elements, several levels of software support are required, along with an integrated data base, for total systems operation. It is the responsibility of the systems analyst and application programmer, along with other personnel, to combine these resources into a total system as depicted in Figure 1.5.

1. *Terminals* Terminals are communications-oriented input/output devices. They are normally installed at locations remote to the computer center. Ideally, they are located at the data source (e.g., sales office, branch bank, warehouse), where the personnel with the greatest knowledge and concern about certain activities are. These terminals give quick access to the data base for various queries, and they also permit various forms of data input, such as voice, laser-read bar codes, keyboard, cards, tape, and so forth. Output can be in the form of voice, video, paper, punched cards, and so forth. A terminal can range from a simple typewriter to a large computer.

2. *Modems* Modems are signal *mo*dulating-*dem*odulating units whose primary function in a communication system is to provide signal compatibility between the communication channel and the data communications equipment. Modems consist of the complex circuitry needed to change the digital-type signals used by the computer equipment to the analog-type signals used by the communication channel (e.g., telephone line), and back again.

3. *Communication channel* The communication channel is the medium for transmission of data between two remote locations. It can

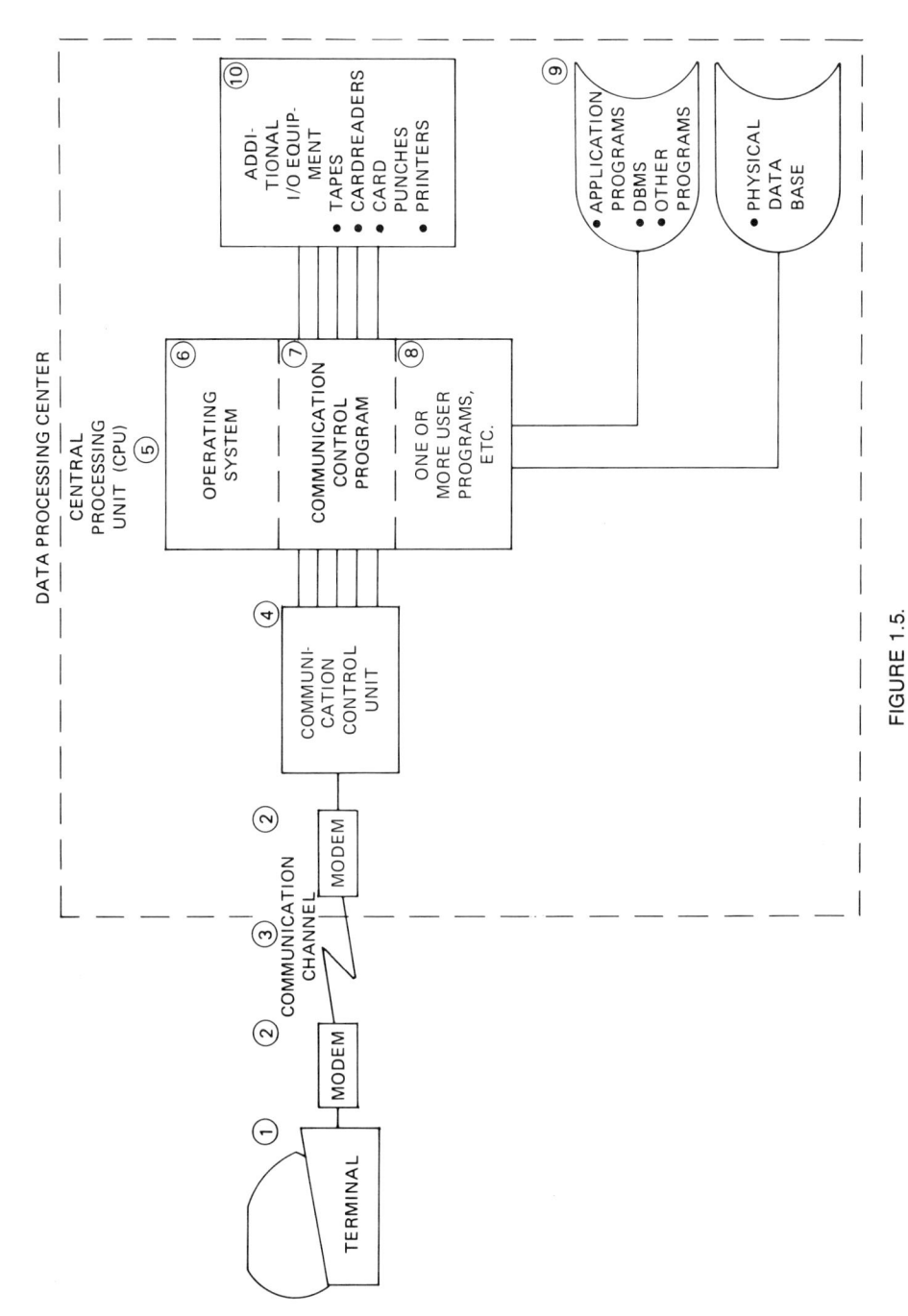

FIGURE 1.5.
Example of a Computer-Based Total Information System.

employ such transmission media as telephone or telegraph wires, microwave, radio frequencies, satellites, and so forth. The channels can be either privately owned or publicly accessible (e.g., the dial network).

4. *Communication control units* Communication control units are two-direction control units used for interfacing the communication network to the central processing unit (CPU). Thus, they provide the remote terminals with access to the system programming, data base, data base management systems (DBMS), application and other programs, and batched-type input/output resources at the data processing center. Some of these communication control units may be incorporated directly into the CPU, while others may be free-standing units. The latter type are connected by cable to a system channel at the CPU.

Communication control units can incorporate many optional features to adapt the data communications system to the wide variety of terminals and communication channels serviced by the communication control unit. They can be visualized logically as consisting of two sections. One section faces the CPU and performs control-type functions similar to other I/O control units. The other section faces the communication network, and controls and adapts the attached communication channels and terminals. Some of the new communication control units provide the ability for storing a network control program (NCP) in the control unit. This approach permits the communication controller to control the network via programmed action, substantially relieving the CPU of the network control task. This type of communications control unit is sometimes called a front-end programmable communications processor, and the central CPU is called the host computer. A minicomputer is normally used to implement a front-end system.

5. *Central processing unit (CPU)* The CPU serves as the primary logical and arithmetic control element of the system. When operating in a total information system, the CPU in conjunction with several levels of system control programs, will assemble and analyze information included in the messages received from the network. This task will determine what programmed action must be performed upon the received message. It will also pass the received message on to storage for future retrieval and processing. Any arithmetic and logical operations to be performed by the CPU are determined by a particular application program (e.g., COBOL) and/or a data base management system (DBMS) program to which the message is eventually routed. After the message is processed by a program, it is returned to its destination (e.g., a location in storage or a destination terminal), or possibly to some output-type I/O device (e.g., printer) at the data-processing center.

An element not shown in the schematic but one that is of concern to the auditor is the console. The console provides the computer operator/ system interface and provides the myriad of control-type messages depicting the status of the whole system. The console is used to alert the personnel at the central site to the ever changing operating circumstances in both the data-processing center and the farflung network. The console is also used, as in conventional operations, to initialize and generate the various resources of the system.

6. *Operating system* The total system, including both the communication system and the conventional data-processing system, requires the overall supervisory control provided by an operating system. The operating systems, which are available in several variations, are system control-type programs that are provided by the computer vendor. They are used to coordinate and schedule the work of the different application programs and access methods used by the various subsystems of the total system.

7. *Communication control program* This program element is normally the communications access method that operates in conjunction with the operating system. The communications access method provides the data access for the attached terminals.

8. *User programs* One or more application programs linked to a data base management system (DBMS) program may be required to provide the program code required for the processing of messages received from or to be transmitted to the remote terminals. Program instructions are designed, written, and input by the user (e.g., programmer or nonprogrammer) to perform the necessary arithmetic and logical manipulations on the data base that are required in day to day operations. Every computer system has a set of application programs, and, possibly a DBMS, that carry out the numerous online and batch processing functions that are unique to a particular organization.

9. *Direct-access storage devices (DASD)* DASD (e.g., magnetic disk files) represent the physical data base storage media that are used to provide online storage for both the voluminous data files and the numerous system programs (e.g., application, DBMS, utilities). Line and terminal, as well as process and message queues, frequently necessitate temporary storage in DASD. This need for temporary storage occurs as the processing and input/output loads on the system change from minute to minute and hour to hour during the day. DASD are also used as the temporary repository for any specialized routines, diagnostic routines, and so forth. Event processing systems must provide quick updates and a fast reply to the terminal user. The data required by application programs and DBMS must, therefore, be stored on DASD also to provide fast direct access to any portion of the data base. In addition, programs that cannot be held constantly in CPU storage but have a high frequency of use may be stored on DASD.

10. *Additional I/O equipment* In addition, to the above-mentioned equipment and program resources that are required in online event

processing systems, the following equipment (together with its programming requirements) will inevitably be found in a total information system. Magnetic tapes are frequently used for the storage of data received from a batch-type remote terminal. They can be used to store output data that are to be batch-transmitted to a remote terminal at a later time, and to log all messages received by or sent from the data-processing center. Magnetic tapes are frequently used to store historical data, i.e., material that is not required so often as operational and current financial data. Examples are closed orders, past accounting data, and so forth. Card-read/punch and printer equipment are used to perform such functions as the reading of program decks during assembly of the communication programs, the printing of various reports, and so forth.[5]

The computer environment is dynamic not static. Computer technology is advancing at ever increasing rates, and concepts that are considered theoretical possibilities today may be implemented as the "state of the art" tomorrow.

1.4 AN INCREASINGLY COMPLEX ENVIRONMENT

In the past, because computer technology and information systems concepts had not been fully exploited, the accountant and auditor with a traditional background were given a reprieve. This reprieve, however, was temporary, because today's systems do not depend on traditional manual or computer batch (periodic) processing systems. Yesterday's information systems concepts are today's realities.

Advances in data communications technology (e.g., microwave, satellites), the availability of online mass storage devices, implementation of the data base concept, and the integration of the information system into the functions of the organization have led to event processing systems in which all events that impact on the organization are captured and processed as they occur. For example, an airline or hotel reservation system interacts with the user and performs all necessary processing steps in a matter of seconds. An automatic teller system validates input transactions, transfers funds, and updates files via a terminal outside the bank.

In earlier systems, data input to the system were originally in paper (source document) form before being converted to computer-readable form. Today, in many systems, data are directly input via terminals such as badge readers and CRT's. For example, a badge reader is used to

---

[5]This section adapted from: *Introduction to Data Communications Systems* (White Plains, N. Y.: IBM Corporation, Data Processing Division, Pub. No. ZR20-4542-0), pp. 11-18.

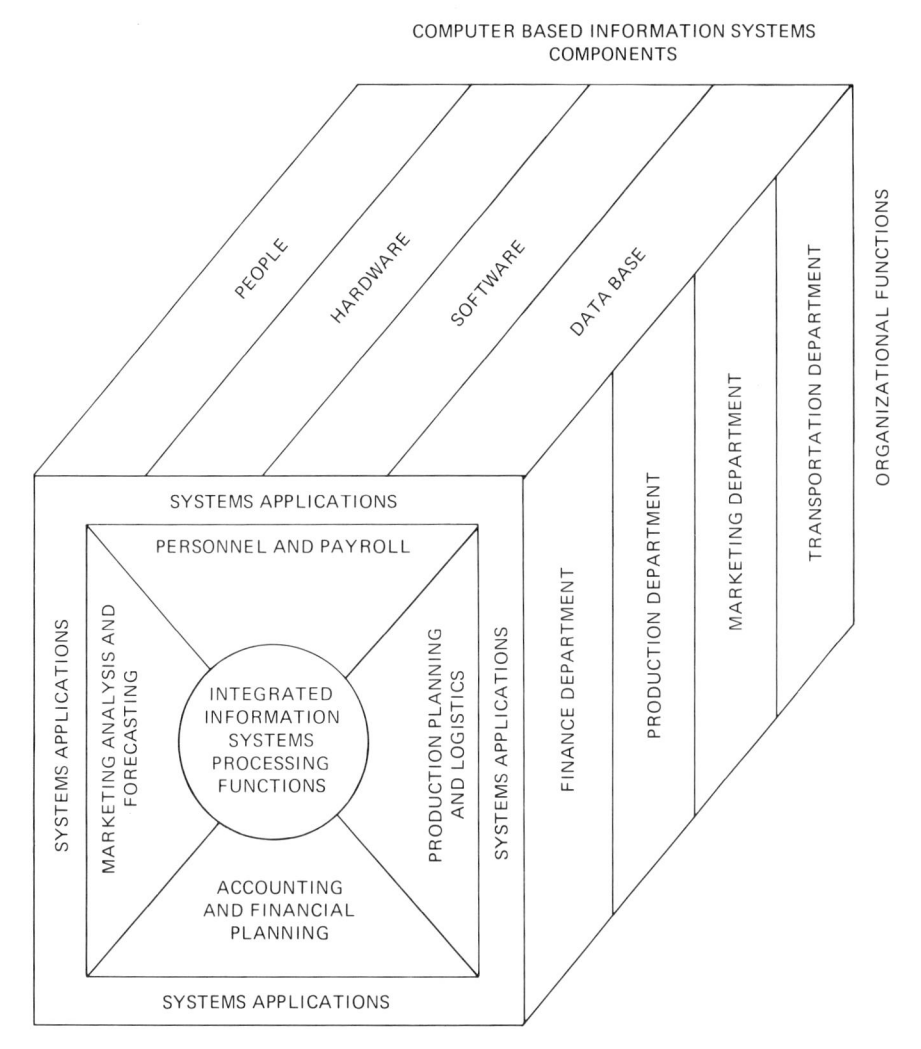

FIGURE 1.6.
Example of an Information System That Is an Integral Part of The Organization and In Sync With Its Operations.

record employee start and completion times by department and job. These inputs are used to automatically update appropriate files that are housed in a central data base. Or a CRT is used by an order clerk to enter sales order data into the system that in turn updates files and automatically generates decisions and other transactions. Data input can also occur without human intervention by sensor devices that directly interact with the system. For example, a laser scanning device reads a bar code on a railroad car as it passes a certain point, or a reader can read a

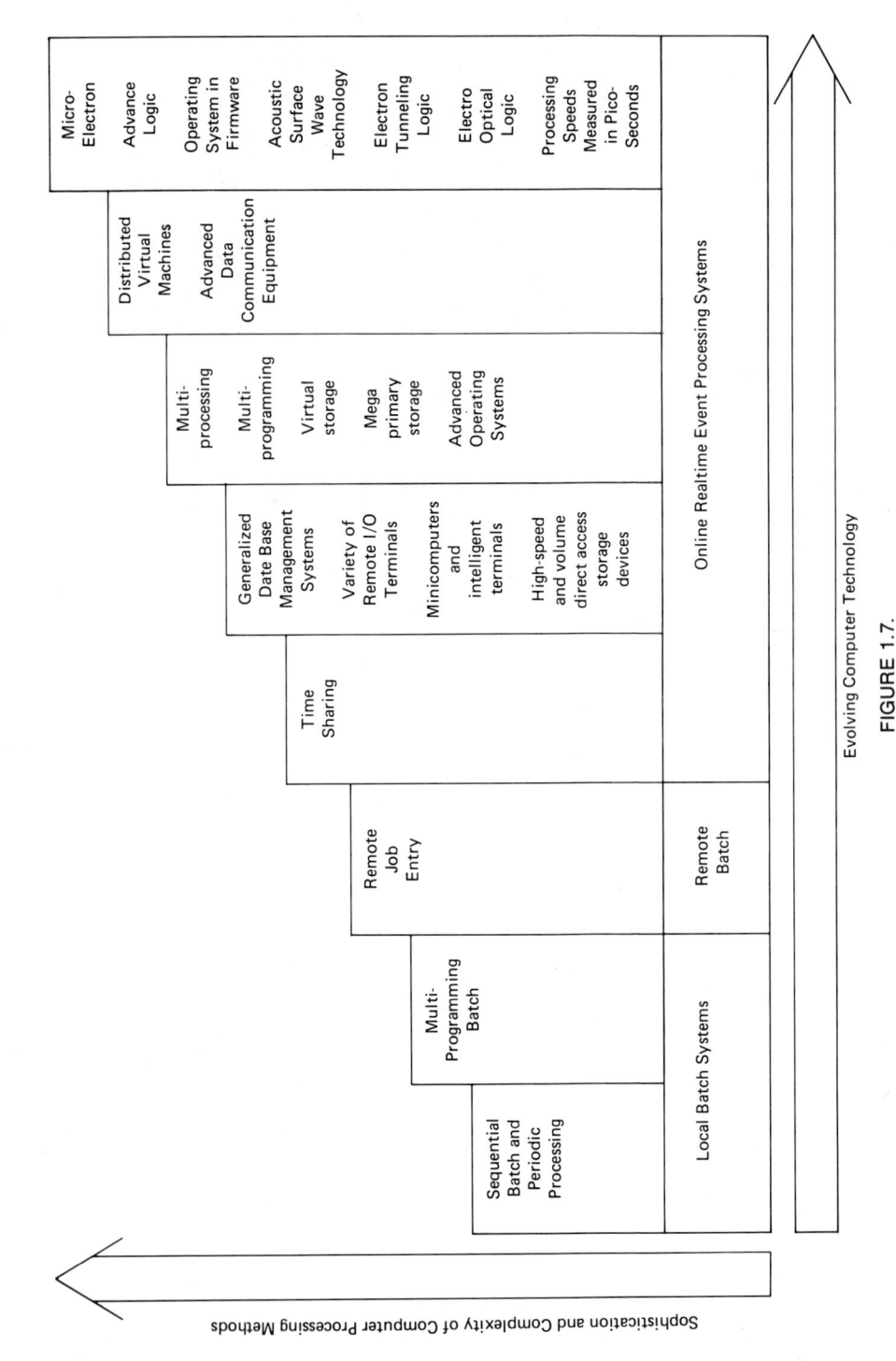

PART ONE IMPLICATIONS OF COMPUTER BASED INFORMATION SYSTEMS

FIGURE 1.7.
Example of the Increasing Sophistication and Complexity of Processing Methods.

similar code on a loaf of bread as it passes a point on the checkout counter. The result of these new ways of handling data-processing functions is an information system that is now an integral part of the organization and in sync with its operations, as shown in Figure 1.6.

Figure 1.7 depicts the evolution of computer technology. Several terms such as virtual machines, microelectronics, and advanced logic may not be familiar. These terms are discussed below.

Virtual machines is a systems program that permits a user to specify the machine configuration that he would like to use and run his choice of operating system simultaneously with other users on the same real machine. The virtual machine configurations can be different in storage size, number of I/O channels, and devices from any other user's virtual machine or from the real machine itself.

The virtual machine user communicates with the real machine via a terminal that serves as the control console of his simulated machine. With a set of simple instructions, the user can operate his virtual machine as though he had the same control facilities as the computer operator of a real machine.

Microelectronics will continue to play a major role in the development of computer technology. Semiconductor storage devices consist of microscopic integrated circuits such as large-scale integration (LSI) and metal oxide silicon field effect transistor (MOSFET) circuits. This circuitry is being used to replace core, thin film, and rod primary storage. These storage devices are small (a chip less than one-eighth of an inch square contains several thousand circuit elements), very fast (nanoseconds), shock and temperature resistant, and have a strong potential for low-cost mass production. Other storage devices that promise to be smaller and faster than semiconductor storage are also being developed. Cryogenic devices consist of materials that become superconductors at extremely low temperatures. Laser storage devices which use crystalline material to change the polarization of light are being developed. The laser has the capability of storing more than one million bits per square inch. Another promising storage device development for the future is magnetic bubbles or domains developed by Bell Telephone Laboratories. This technology takes advantage of the magnetic alignment properties of crystals grown from mixtures of iron oxides and rare earth metals.

Some more advanced concepts include acoustic surface wave technology which is based upon piezoelectric phenomena. It can be utilized to implement logic functions in addition to performing complex signal-processing operations. Electron-tunneling logic devices are based upon the Josephson junction phenomenon. At very low temperatures (1°K to 3°K), electrons are able to tunnel through a thin barrier separating two electrodes of a gate without a voltage drop, or the same action can take place and produce a voltage drop. Transition times in the laboratory have been less than 1 nanosecond. Electro-optical logic elements have been developed using fiber optics and injection laser elements, where the output beam of the injection laser is switched into different optical fibers under the control of other laser beams. For laser logic, operating times below 0.01 nanosecond can be expected. At present, the system operates at $-200°C$, and requires substantial power.[6]

In the area of advanced logic, more efficient compilers have been developed requiring smaller amounts of storage and providing more user-oriented instructions for the user. As stated earlier, many of the processing functions now performed by software will continue to be converted to firmware. This firmware will be in read-only memory (ROM) modules of the CPU which will enhance their control.

1.5 SUMMARY

As accounting systems became computerized and integrated with other systems, some accountants and auditors believed that they could deal with the system by going around it. Today, in many organizations, the accounting system has been transferred from the desks of accounting clerks and bookkeepers to the hardware, software, and data base of complex information systems. These systems are normally under the control of people with a limited accounting background and who, consequently, have little empathy and appreciation for a sound system of controls and auditing procedures.

The view that the auditor can continue to ignore the computer and go around it can no longer be defended. The trend toward computer-based systems will continue to grow. The auditor must understand these systems to audit them effectively. He must be involved in the system of controls and apply computer auditing techniques that will test these controls, extract data from the data base for review, and trace the flow of data from the point of event through the computer process to its final disposition.

More sophisticated information systems capture and process events as they occur. The time lapse between capture and processing of data during which errors might have been eliminated before impacting on the system has been substantially reduced, i.e., the principle of periodicity in accounting has been reduced, if not eliminated. The advent of these online real-time event processing systems is based on four system components: (1) people, (2) hardware, (3) software, and (4) data base.

There is a wide variety of job types in most computer systems. These

---

[6]Adapted from Rein Turn, *Computers in the 1980s* (New York: Columbia University Press, 1974), pp. 173–174.

personnel can typically be grouped into five categories: systems development, programming, computer operations, data center operations, and security. The number of different types of jobs in computer systems depends on the size and complexity of the system. Large systems permit more specialization of job assignments and thus create more types of jobs. Management of this wide variety of technical personnel is a major assignment equivalent to a vice-presidential level in most organizations. Since the information system is the nerve center that serves all departments of the organization, it is usually desirable to have a steering committee to monitor its management.

The introduction of hardware that is faster, smaller, and cheaper, has made it cost/effective for both small and large organizations to acquire and implement sophisticated information systems. With large-scale storage devices, a variety of terminals and data-capture techniques, and advanced data communications systems, the old information systems concepts are now realities for all organizations.

Computer software includes all programs that direct and control the hardware in the performance of information system processing functions. Systems software is prepared by writing programs in one of the following languages that are understandable to both people and computers: machine languages, assembler languages, and compiler languages. It has been predicted that within the next decade or so, most of what is now referred to as software will be in the form of firmware also referred to as microcode or microprogram.

The fourth component is the data base, the foundation of the information system. The data base concept centers around the idea of generating information for all functional areas of the organization including both accounting and operational information. Data events are entered when they occur, and they are interrelated to provide current, relevant information to all users.

The accounting profession has not kept pace with the present computer environment. Many accountants are confounded by the terminology, technology, and concepts currently employed by "computer types." If this trend is not reversed, then the future accountant may be faced with technological mysteries even more bewildering than those he must deal with today.

REVIEW QUESTIONS

1.1 Identify and describe the basic components of a computer system.
1.2 What are the major developments expected in the future concerning hardware and software?
1.3 Describe several activities that are involved in: (a) systems development, (b) programming, and (c) operations.

1.4 What three programming languages are used?
1.5 Explain the role of the steering committee.
1.6 Differentiate between the following terms: (a) operating system and application programs, (b) assembler language and compiler language, (c) control programs and special-purpose service programs, and (d) supervisor and canned programs.
1.7 List and define all the computer hardware elements.

DISCUSSION QUESTIONS

1.1 Discuss the audit implications of: (a) firmware, (b) data communications systems, (c) operating systems, (d) computer systems personnel, (e) microelectronics, (f) data base, (g) application programs, and (h) high-level programming languages.
1.2 Discuss efficiency, ease of development, maintainability, and availability of skills as they relate to the three programming languages.
1.3 If you were developing a system from scratch, what programming language would you use to write all of your application programs? Why?
1.4 Discuss the basic differences between manual accounting systems and computer-based event processing systems. What implications does the latter system have for auditors?
1.5 Why should auditors become more deeply involved in computer systems?
1.6 Explain why effective management is a critical requirement for an organization using computer systems.

CHAPTER
2

COMPUTER ABUSE AND ITS IMPACT UPON AUDITING

2.1 INTRODUCTION

A computer is a powerful, valuable tool that can make a significant contribution to organizations and society in general. But its potential for good can be twisted, because it can be used for fraudulent purposes. Moreover, massive amounts of data can be stored on data bases where sensitive, personal data can be cross-referenced, retrieved, and maliciously used.

The auditor on his own volition, or through the legal system, must become concerned with computer abuse, especially as it relates to fraud and invasion of privacy. Individuals and groups who have a special interest in the control of computer abuse are management, stockholders, creditors, consumers, and the government. They all want assurance that the computer system will not become a vehicle for abusive acts. The major person that they will be looking to for this assurance is the auditor.

There are a number of ways in which the computer can be misapplied, or abused itself, such as errors, poor management, sabotage, fire, and so forth. However, in this chapter, we are primarily concerned with two major abuses: fraud and invasion of privacy. These abuses, along with their impact upon auditing, are discussed below.

2.2 FRAUD

Fraud is the act of obtaining something or diverting assets through misrepresentation of the truth and cheating. On January 29, 1975, Equity Funding's trustee in bankruptcy filed suit on behalf of the corporation against all three accounting firms that participated in the audits of the parent company and its subsidiaries. Deliberation by the jury resulted in criminal convictions, prison sentences and fines, for three of Equity Funding's former independent auditors.

Eighteen officers and employees were convicted on an earlier trial, and the stiffest sentence, eight years, was given to the former chairman of the board, president, and organizer of the fraud.[1]

Auditors' Responsibility

The question is how the other auditors not believed to be connected with the fraud could have reviewed computer controls and audited computer files and outputs, but still missed the fraud. "If routine auditing procedures cannot detect 64,000 phony insurance policies, $25 million in counterfeit bonds, and $100 million in missing assets, what is the purpose of auditing?"[2] But there have been other cases besides Equity Funding that indicate that we have been spending too much time debating accounting principles and not enough time on auditing standards and techniques. For example, the Equity Funding fraud could easily have been uncovered as far back as 1971 or earlier if the auditors had used a simple statistical sampling and confirmation program. Such a program represents a classical and widely accepted audit technique. Presumably, the auditors failed to apply this technique because the president of the life insurance division protested that confirmation with policyholders would unnecessarily alarm the holders and embarrass the company's insurance agents. Failure by the auditors to perform a strong confirmation project after such a flimsy protestation represents either a milquetoast attitude or incompetency, or both.

> During the last half of the 1960's and the early years of this decade, the financial press has reported various management misdeeds that bankrupted a number of business institutions. These include Equity Funding, National Student Marketing, Continental Vending, Penn Central, Westec and U.S. Financial. Accountants, lawyers, underwriters and top management personnel associated with these enterprises have been implicated and in some cases legally sanctioned.[3]

---

[1] Summarized from: "Equity Funding Trustee Sues Auditors," *EDPACS*, March 1975, p. 19; "Equity Funding Auditors Convicted," *EDPACS*, June 1975, p. 17.
[2] Raymond L. Dirks and Leonard Gross, *The Great Wall Street Scandal* (New York: McGraw-Hill Book Company, 1974), quoted from *EDPACS*, July 1974, p. 13.
[3] Michael J. Barrett, Donald W. Baker, and Leon R. Radde, "Top Management Fraud: Definitional Problems, External Auditor Responsibilities, and Top Management Controls," *Collected Papers of the American Accounting Association's Annual Meeting* (Sarasota, Fla.: American Accounting Association, August 18–20, 1975), p. 33.

> ... I think these cases have indicated the fact that perhaps we've been overemphasizing too much accounting principles and overlooking the need to strengthen our auditing procedures. If you analyze the cases today, by and large they constitute auditing lapses rather than accounting and for that reason we need to really give consideration to the approach to auditing.[4]

The results of fraud have been corporate losses of billions of dollars. Some authorities estimate that losses from fraud are greater than from robbery, burglary, and shoplifting combined and that fraud is on the upswing. FBI authorities have noted that fraud and white collar crime have quadrupled since 1965! Moreover, a number of banks, insurance companies, and other organizations have been forced to close where significant fraud was committed. And there is still no strong statement from the auditing profession as to the auditor's responsibility relative to fraud, as the following quotation indicates.

> Some auditing experts contend that auditors who get a whiff of a fraud must take steps to fully resolve their suspicions, no matter how limited the specific job they were hired to do. If further investigation is blocked, or their findings ignored, the auditors should resign and possibly go to the authorities, it is argued. Others contend that such expectations are unrealistic, that auditors aren't detectives, and that no matter what an auditor does to resolve suspicions, in hindsight he might always have done more.[5]

The historical position of the auditor that fraud is not his responsibility is probably no longer tenable. "We have seen too many cases of management fraud where management has obscured the reality of the corporate activity from the auditor."[6] "There is no doubt that the auditor today is being expected to assume a greater role than he ever has and the question is whether or not the profession is going to live up to that demand."[7]

> I think we can see that the public is expecting more from the auditors than ever before and they will accept it readily if we restore the credibility that I think will certainly be restored after this purging storm through which we're passing. The SEC with its injunctive proceedings and class actions has more or less pointed up to the public the fact that we have this responsibility and it's been exposed to such an extent that we obviously need to react to it.[8]

---

[4]Philip L. Defliese, "Luncheon Address," *Collected Papers of the American Accounting Association's Annual Meeting* (Sarasota, Fla.: American Accounting Association, August 18–20, 1975), p. 406.

[5]G. Christian Hill, "Accountants Brought Equity Funding Fraud Almost to Surface in '71," *The Wall Street Journal*, Feb. 20, 1976, p. 1.

[6]John C. Burton, "The SEC and the World of Accounting,"*The Journal of Accountancy*, July 1974, p. 59.

[7]Defliese, *op. cit.*, p. 405.

[8]*Ibid.*, p. 407.

Auditors are backing themselves into a corner by continually thinking that many aspects of a computer-based information system including fraud are not their responsibility. These auditors continue to harp on the attestation of the financial statements as their only responsibility, failing to realize that the financial statements are the product of the computer and one cannot make a silk purse out of a sow's ear, or garbage in, garbage out. For example, the financial statements of Equity Fundings were distorted by the creation and inflation of assets, the failure to record liabilities for borrowed cash, and the creation of bogus insurance policies producing fictitious revenue. The financial statements looked beautiful with their "clean bill of health" auditor's opinions, and they impressed a lot of people, including stockholders. But they were phony.

Some auditors will have to change their "that's not my responsibility" attitude, take a broader, more professional view, and quit compartmentalizing their audit activities (e.g., internal versus external auditors).

> Whether a person is an operational or financial internal auditor would seem to be of little consequence. Rather than tell corporations what type of internal auditing should be done, it would be more profitable for these experienced external auditors to suggest how the internal audit functions can be further strengthened regardless of whether financial or operational internal audit examinations are routinely performed.[9]

All auditors must use audit and control techniques that are available. If they do not use them, they will be hard pressed to defend themselves in the event an organization falls victim to a fraud.[10]

The *Escott versus BarChris Construction Corporation* case was an action under the Securities Act of 1933 taken by purchasers of BarChris's registered debentures against the directors, underwriters, and independent auditors of BarChris. The plaintiffs claimed that the registration statement for the debentures contained false statements and significant omissions. The defendants pleaded "due diligence" defenses. The court found that the registration statement was false and misleading, and that the defendants had not established their due diligence defenses. It is probably safe to predict that under the Securities Acts of 1933 and 1934, the due diligence defense may not be available to auditors if a reasonable investigation would have disclosed the absence of an appropriate system of controls. This thinking makes sense because the auditor can work diligently, but be testing and investigating the wrong thing, or working hard but not knowing what he is doing. Therefore, the failure to acknowledge the absence of a system of controls, no matter

---

[9]Barrett, et al., *op. cit.*, p. 45.
[10]Robert L. Stone, "Who is Responsible for Computer Fraud?" *The Journal of Accountancy*, February 1975, pp. 35–39.

how industrious the auditor, will and should expose him to legal liability. Analogous to this situation is one in which a physician diligently and steadily treats a patient for pneumonia when, in fact, the patient has a serious heart condition. Due diligence in this case would probably not be a defense against malpractice.

There are several court decisions that indicate that due diligence also requires more than compliance with professional standards if those professional standards result in misleading results and statements. The *Continental Vending* case ruling showed that compliance with generally accepted accounting principles is not a conclusive defense to criminal fraud. The same conclusion was reached in a civil case, *Herzfeld versus Laventhal, Krekstein, Horwath and Horwath.* Similarly, in *Hochfelder versus Ernst and Ernst,* the court found that there was no defense because generally accepted auditing standards did not require particular investigation to be made and that judges are not constrained to accept faulty standards even if they are generally accepted and practiced within a profession or industry.

Responsibilities of auditors have increased greatly over the last twenty years. As a result of court decisions, federal securities laws, and public opinion, he is coming more and more to be looked upon as a safeguard or independent person between a highly mobile management and groups of constituents of the organization. "The auditor is swiftly moving into a new status of whistle-blower for the public interest. Past offenses which threaten the enterprise must be disclosed. Silence and failure to act on continuing irregularities can make the auditor liable as an aider and abettor by allowing the firm to trade on his reputation and credibility as an auditor."[11]

Ways to Commit Fraud

There are six basic ways in which fraud is committed in relation to the computer. These are:

1. Misappropriation of computer time or stealing computer resources.
2. Using the computer as a scapegoat.
3. Manipulation of input data or intentionally entering incorrect data.
4. Alteration of or copying data base records.
5. Modification of software or the substitution of invalid programs for valid ones.
6. Interception of transmitted data over communications systems.

[11]Denzil, Y. Causey, Jr., "Newly Emerging Standards of Auditor Responsibility," *The Accounting Review*, January 1976, p. 30.

Following is a compilation of summarized cases of computer abuse. These cases are examples of the fraudulent practices listed above.

Case 1: Man stole parts from Pacific Telephone and Telegraph Company by using a touch-tone phone.

Case 2: Attempt to sell computer programs to a brokerage firm stolen from an employee of a service bureau.

Case 3: Theft of computer equipment and computer time. Illegitimate service bureaus created were so successful that the organization had to acquire more computer equipment to keep pace.

Case 4: False advertising or laying blame on computer, e.g., "Fall in Love Through Computer Dating," or "The computer made me send you a duplicate invoice!"

Case 5: Wire tap with touch-tone phone to automated banks or order entry systems.

Case 6: Phony MICR deposit slips.

Case 7: Programmer altered the bank's demand deposit accounting program to ignore overdrafts in his checking account. He was caught by manual accounting only when the computer failed.

Case 8: The computer systems vice-president, senior computer operator, and three non-employees of a bank were charged with transferring money from infrequently used savings accounts to newly opened accounts.

Case 9: A bank vice-president and four others deposited checks designated as "cash deposits," which are recorded for immediate credit. This can be done by bank officials as an accommodation to known clients or when accepting the payroll checks of a local firm. Checks drawn on the account were therefore good until the deposit checks were found not to be covered by another bank. This clearance requires from four to seven days. The act was discovered when a bank messenger failed to deliver $440,000 worth of checks to the clearinghouse. The scheme had worked for four years with a total theft of $900,000.

Case 10: A computer operator pressed the "Repeat" button on the printer to print 200 extra copies of his own paycheck. He was caught when he cashed 37 checks all at the same bank.

Case 11: A programmer in a mail-order company created a sales commission account in the name of Zwana to be the last in order. He adjusted the commission program to collect commission round-downs in the last account. He was discovered after three years when the marketing department happened to choose the first and last accounts for a public relations project.

Case 12: A bank teller manipulated hundreds of accounts through his teller terminal into the computer system. He was caught when a raid on a bookie showed large bets placed by the suspect. He was prosecuted for embezzling $1.5 million by the Manhattan District Attorney's office.

Case 13: Alter program to send checks to fictitious accounts.

Case 14: Alter program to hide the theft of railroad cars.

Case 15: Computer programs for billing contained instructions that omitted printing of customer invoices on all bogus, "Department 99," policies. It is difficult to mail to and collect on invoices for which there are no clients.

Case 16: Vice-president of a brokerage firm stole more than $250,000 by punching new, fraudulent transaction cards over the weekends.

Case 17: Employee sold personnel files and preferred mailing lists.

Case 18: Communication lines tapped to gather data.

Case 19: A trio of criminals tapped the Bank of America for $600,000 by using a secret electronic code to authenticate fund transfer transactions.

Case 20: An EDP employee told the chief executive officer that unless all EDP salaries were doubled immediately, the 28,000 invoices which were about to be printed would be subject to an overall 5 percent markdown. The company complied and the invoices, at their proper amounts, were prepared and mailed. Later, the entire EDP staff was fired.

Case 21: A champion of sound computer controls in England gave a dramatic demonstration on television of how a hardware device could pick up signals processed at the Ministry of Defense computer installation. The sensitive data were printed out in the studio in full view of the television cameras. The advocate of computer controls is now being investigated on charges of having violated the Official Secrets Act.

Case 22: A young man in England manipulated data to cover a theft of 50,000 pounds. Later, when the fraud was discovered, the majority of the executives did not want to prosecute and thereby admit that they had been duped. A deal was made to give the defrauder a favorable written letter of recommendation. He moved on to another large organization. Nearly four years later, a 150,000-pound embezzlement was traced to the young computer wizard. Again, he asked for a letter of recommendation, and it was given. When he had the nerve to ask for 3,500 pounds in severance pay, however, management reacted by filing charges.

Case 23: A manager in a large manufacturing company had access to the company's online order entry system. He was able to place bogus orders that initiated the shipping of merchandise to a cover address. Then he initiated billing cancellation due to alleged loss, damage, or destruction of the shipment in transit.

Case 24: A systems analyst in a large department store used his knowledge of the sales-order processing system to place orders for expensive appliances and have them coded as "special pricing orders." He was then able to intercept these orders in data processing and change the price to only a few dollars. When the appliances were delivered, he paid his account and closed the loop.

Case 25: An employee in the data center at the welfare department of a large city entered fraudulent data into the payroll system and stole nearly $3 million over a nine-month period. He and several of his friends created a fictitious work force identified by fake social security numbers that were processed through the payroll system. The conspirators would intercept the checks and cash them.[12]

The list of cases above is by no means complete, yet it indicates the potential misuse of electronic data processing by unscrupulous individuals. Who are these individuals, and why do they commit fraud? The following section deals with these questions.

Who Commits Fraud and Why

The general conclusion by most authorities is that fraud is perpetrated by a person who is, typically, married, intelligent, young (25–40), and has two children, and fairly strong career aspirations. Fraud is usually uncovered by someone other than the auditor; it is usually detected by accident or because of a slip made by the defrauder. Some of the types of people who have committed fraud are: president, vice-president, loan officer, cashier, teller, accountant, systems analyst, programmer, auditor, and computer operator.[13]

People commit frauds for themselves, for their friends, or to impress someone. There is always a chance for great gain perceived by the perpetrator in terms of information, customers, assets, or cash. The thought of getting caught is usually suppressed. Some people feel that fraud is easier to perpetrate in a computer system because changes can be made to, or information copied from, the data base without leaving a trace.

---

[12]Additional cases may be found in Donn B. Parker, Susan Nycum, and S. Stephen Oura, *Computer Abuse* (Springfield, Va.: U.S. Department of Commerce, National Technical Information Service, Order No. PB-231-320, 1973).

[13]Treasury Department data included in: Donn B. Parker, "The New Criminal," *Datamation*, January 1974.

Some authorities believe that the so-called computer mystique has a lot to do with fraud. The computer is perceived by some people as omnipotent and any output generated by this all-knowing thing must, without question, be accurate. It could be that perpetrators at Equity Funding knew that people would have confidence in and be impressed by computer-generated reports. Dr. Carl Silver, Professor of Behavioral Sciences at Drexel University, says that one of the elements that contributes to prestige is the appearance of specialized knowledge or technical superiority. He also states that the mere appearance of information on a computer printout will generate a lot more credibility than would the same information in longhand.

Another outcome of the computer mystique crops up when management turns over the operation and control of the system to computer technocrats and then both auditors and management relax in a feeling of security that is unjustified. A good case in which liability was incurred because of excessive reliance on the accuracy of the computer is *Ford Motor Credit Company versus Swarens* (2 CLSR 347, 447 SW 2d. 533). In this case Swarens collected compensation and punitive damages because the computer reported that Swarens had not made payments, but actually he had.

Some authorities believe that a number of attempts at fraud are perpetrated by people taking up the challenge of beating the system manifested in the Robin Hood or Don Quixote syndrome. Everyone knows that Robin Hood was the chivalrous leader of an outlaw band in Sherwood Forest who robbed the rich and helped the poor. The present-day version of this syndrome, according to some authorities (Donn B. Parker), is to take from the rich and keep it. Don Quixotes are constantly doing things that they perceive as romantic thrills (Bonnie and Clyde escapades) and figuratively tilting at windmills of the system.

The Parker, Nycum, and Oura computer abuse study predicts that computer abuse will grow as the number of computer installations increases, and major frauds of the Equity Funding type will happen again, more computer crime will be committed via wiretapping, and the role of organized crime in computer fraud will increase.

Fraud is a major abuse of electronic data processing. The second major abuse of computer technology is invasion of privacy.

2.3 INVASION OF PRIVACY

The issue of individual privacy is nothing new. For a long time, people have been afraid of the specter of a faceless, bureaucratic Big Brother.[14] This concern is especially applicable in computer-based personal data

---

[14]Robert C. Goldstein and Richard L. Nolan, "Personal Privacy Versus the Corporate Computer," *Harvard Business Review*, March–April 1975, p. 62.

systems such as consumer credit, health, personnel, insurance, law enforcement,[15] and data bases maintained by a host of government agencies.

The Privacy Issue

The concern in regard to privacy is growing because: (1) computer systems, especially those using the massive online data bases and communications systems, have made information-processing functions more effective; (2) service companies, both public and private, require massive volumes of personal data to operate effectively; and (3) public opinion is beginning to demand more accountability by government and commercial organizations.

> It has been estimated that there are 800 separate federal data collection systems alone, containing one billion separate records on individuals, that only about 10 percent of these systems are authorized by law, that over 40 percent of the managers of these systems fail to inform individuals carried in their files that records are being kept on them, and that there is no provision in over half of these systems which would permit individuals to review their records and make applicable corrections to erroneous or obsolete data.[16]

Privacy of persons has become a sacrosanct legislative cause in Washington, as well as in the judiciary and state legislatures across the country.[17] This cause receives its impetus from the premise that people should be left alone and that if information is to be stored and processed about an individual by an organization, this information should be open for the individual's review. Furthermore, some public figures and groups believe that the maintenance and processing of certain data bases constitute an invasion of privacy and thus should be eliminated or severely restricted.

Alan Westin defines the privacy issue as: ". . . the claim of individuals, groups, or institutions to determine for themselves when, how, and to what extent information about them is communicated to others."[18] Ruth M. Davis views the issues of individual privacy as: (1) the desires of the individual to exercise control over the collection of information about himself; and (2) the desires of the individual to exercise some measure of control over the use of information about himself, once it is collected.[19]

[15]*Ibid.*
[16]John W. O. Williams, "Data Banks, A Cause for Concern," *Data Management*, July 1975, p. 25.
[17]Francis M. Gregory, Jr., and Wright H. Andrews, "The Privacy Debate, Business Must be Seen and Heard," *Data Management*, August 1975, p. 32.
[18]Alan Westin, *Privacy and Freedom* (New York: Atheneum, 1967), p. 7.
[19]Ruth M. Davis, "Privacy and Security in Data Systems," *Computers and People*, March 1974, p. 27.

A recent Louis Harris poll reported the following:

1. 75 percent of respondents favored legislation to spell out the kinds of personal information credit companies should be permitted to collect and hold in their files;

2. 83 percent believed that the individual included in a file should have the opportunity to review his file and correct inaccurate information;

3. 78 percent said that credit bureaus should be required to notify an individual in their files upon receipt of unfavorable data on him and should be further required to name the agency originally supplying the data;

4. 76 percent desired a law for prohibition of credit information disclosures to non-creditors, such as government agencies, without the individual's express permission;

5. 74 percent of respondents thought privacy legislation should contain procedures for removal of inaccurate/outdated information from the individual's credit file.[20]

Driving Forces Behind the Privacy Issue

The driving forces behind the privacy issue are consumer groups, legislatures, courts, agencies, and a variety of associations. The effects of the efforts of these groups are manifested in laws and rulings. Some of the more significant results are discussed below.

STATE AND LOCAL

The City of Wichita Falls, Texas, has enacted an ordinance designed to protect computerized personal data from misuse. The National Association of State Information Systems (NASIS) has been active in seeking to formulate model legislation in the privacy area. NASIS has reprimanded some state legislatures for their failure to act to protect individual privacy. NASIS states that the failure of states to provide control over and privacy for information-processing activities represents a "potential catastrophe of great magnitude."

The constitutions of several states include provisions to protect their citizens from unreasonable invasions of privacy and the right to recover damages if injured by computer abuse or error. The governor of the state of Massachusetts issued an Order on privacy which became effective on January 8, 1975 and which affects all state agencies except those dealing in criminal justice. The Order stipulates the rights of the individual and establishes strict rules with which information collection/processing agencies must conform. The state agencies and officials are to withhold Social Security account information on individuals involved in re-

[20]Williams, *op. cit.*, p. 28.

habilitation programs from federal agencies, specifically the Department of Health, Education and Welfare, to prevent the federal government from sharing, without the individual's permission, sensitive data on Massachusetts residents.[21]

JUDICIAL PROCESS

Although the U.S. Supreme Court has not accorded the right to privacy the status of a Constitutional right, it has recognized elements of this right. In a landmark case involving a state statute restricting the use of birth control, the Court found the right of privacy to be implicit in rights afforded by the First, Third, Fourth, and Fifth amendments to the Constitution. In *Griswold versus Connecticut*, it was held that the right to privacy was implied under the First, Third, Fourth, Fifth and Ninth amendments. The Court indicated that a person may have the protection of due process, the right to a fair hearing, and appeal to a higher authority with regard to the circulation of information about himself.

FEDERAL LEGISLATIVE PROCESS

One of the most significant legislative actions in regard to privacy has been the Fair Credit Reporting Act of 1970 (effective April 25, 1971). This was one of the first major acts of Congress affecting the private sector's collection and use of personal information. This Act is directed primarily to the problems allegedly associated with the collecting, maintaining, and reporting of credit, insurance, and employment information. Among its provisions, this Act gives the individual the right to be informed of what information is maintained about him by a credit bureau or investigatory reporting agency. Information that is challenged as inaccurate by the person about whom the information is maintained must be reinvestigated by the maintainer of the file and, if found in error, corrected.

The Privacy Act of 1974 places general restrictions and requirements on the processing and control of personal information handled by all government agencies. Although this act is directed to the public sector, there is a high probability that this act, or some of its provisions, will also cover the private sector. In any event, the impact of this act will be felt by managements, auditors, and information systems personnel for years to come. Many executives of commercial organizations have been actively monitoring privacy legislation and are aware of the potential extension of the Privacy Act of 1974 to the private sector. The general provisions of this Act are as follows:[22]

Sec. 2
(a) The Congress finds that—
(1) the privacy of an individual is directly affected by the collection,

---
[21]*Ibid.*, pp. 27–28.
[22]"The Privacy Act of 1974," *Data Management*, June 1975, p. 36.

maintenance, use, and dissemination of personal information by Federal agencies;

(2) the increasing use of computers and sophisticated information technology, while essential to the efficient operations of the Government, has greatly magnified the harm to individual privacy that can occur from any collection, maintenance, use, or dissemination of personal information;

(3) the opportunities for an individual to secure employment, insurance, and credit, and his right to due process, and other legal protections are endangered by the misuse of certain information systems;

(4) the right to privacy is a personal and fundamental right protected by the Constitution of the United States; and

(5) in order to protect the privacy of individuals identified in information systems maintained by Federal agencies, it is necessary and proper for the Congress to regulate the collection, maintenance, use, and dissemination of information by such agencies.

(b) The purpose of this Act is to provide certain safeguards for an individual against an invasion of personal privacy by requiring Federal agencies, except as otherwise provided by law, to—

(1) permit an individual to determine what records pertaining to him are collected, maintained, used, or disseminated by such agencies;

(2) permit an individual to prevent records pertaining to him obtained by such agencies for a particular purpose from being used or made available for another purpose without his consent;

(3) permit an individual to gain access to information pertaining to him in Federal agency records, to have a copy made of all or any portion thereof, and to correct or amend such records;

(4) collect, maintain, use, or disseminate any record of identifiable personal information in a manner that assures that such action is for a necessary and lawful purpose, that the information is current and accurate for its intended use, and that adequate safeguards are provided to prevent misuse of such information;

(5) permit exemptions from the requirements with respect to records provided in this Act only in those cases where there is an important public policy need for such exemption as has been determined by specific statutory authority; and

(6) be subject to civil suit for any damages which occur as a result of willful or intentional action which violates any individual's rights under this Act.

A new bill known as HR 1984 has been introduced by Congressmen Edward I. Koch* (D-N.Y.) and Barry Goldwater, Jr. (R-Calif.). This privacy bill involves both the governmental agencies at the state and local levels and the private sector. "The premise of this legislation is that a demonstrated need exists to sweep the private sector under the Privacy Act's umbrella and to impose substantial requirements to control and limit business collection and use of personal information."[23] Presum-

---
*Edward I. Koch is now Mayor of New York City. HR 1984 is presently in the Judiciary Committee.
[23]Gregory and Andrews, *op. cit.*, p. 33.

ably, it applies to everyone and everything that stores and processes records, not just computer systems.

The ten principles put forth by Congressmen Koch and Goldwater are:[24]

1. Permit any person to inspect his own file and have copies made at reasonable cost to him.
2. Permit any person to supplement the information in his file.
3. Permit the removal of erroneous or irrelevant information and provide that agencies (organizations) and persons to whom material had been previously transferred, be notified of its removal.
4. Prohibit the disclosure of information in the file to individuals in the agencies (organizations) other than those who need to examine the file in connection with the performance of their duties.
5. Require the maintenance of a record of all persons inspecting such files, and their identity and their purpose.
6. Insure that the information be maintained completely and competently with adequate security safeguards.
7. Require that when information is collected, the individual must be told if the request is mandatory or voluntary and what penalty or loss of benefit will result from noncompliance.
8. Require that the person involved in handling personal information act under a code of fair information practices, know the security procedures, and be subject to penalties for any breaches.
9. Permit anyone wishing to stop receiving mail because his name is on a mailing list to have that right.
10. Prohibit agencies or organizations from requiring individuals to give their social security number for any purpose not related to their social security account, or not mandated by federal statute.

There seems to be a marked difference of opinion as to whether or not this bill should be passed. Some public figures believe that a factual showing of the need for this bill has not been made. Other public officials, however, do not share this opinion and believe that businesses are infringing upon citizens' personal liberties. In any case, there is a high probability that some provisions or modifications of this bill will be passed in the near future.

Practical Aspects of the Privacy Issue

A number of complex, seemingly insoluble problems arise for organizations, consumers, computer personnel, and auditors when legislators and jurists move from the abstract philosophies and theories of invasion of privacy to specific and detailed statutory provisions and Constitutional interpretations.

[24]*Ibid.*, p. 34.

Certainly, the problem area which encompasses the privacy of individuals, the confidentiality of data and the security of computer systems is highly explosive and could, if not dealt with properly, trigger off negative chain-reactions as well as possibly damaging restrictive controls on many applications of technology.

At the same time, if the problem is treated lightly by the executive, judicial or legislative branches, if industry does not carry out its obligations to the public and if the scientific community disassociates itself from the technological underpinnings of the problem, then computer and communications technology could indeed victimize the individuals and intrude upon their rights as citizens and consumers.[25]

Thus, the problem of invasion of privacy is so complex that any progress towards resolution is dependent upon the coordinated efforts and cooperation of the judiciary; congressional and state legislatures; federal, state, and local government agencies; information service organizations (e.g., consumer credit); computer and software vendors; management; attorneys; and the auditing profession.[26]

The protection of the privacy of the individual is founded in laws, rulings, and interpretations that stem from the legislative and judiciary areas. It is the responsibility of attorneys to interpret and provide guidelines to management and the auditor in regard to the meanings of these laws and judicial interpretations and how to avoid conflict with them.

It is the responsibility of computer manufacturers, working with others in government and industry, to improve the security of computer technology and related devices. More effective reliability and security features must be incorporated into the hardware and software, especially in the operating system. Provisions for monitoring and adequately testing the system should be incorporated into the design. The complexity of operating systems prohibits comprehensive testing, and as a result, test procedures frequently indicate the existence of errors or misuse but not their absence. The operating system must insure that users cannot interfere with the system's operations, take control of the system, or circumvent or alter the built-in security safeguards. The operating system must insure that a user cannot gain unauthorized access to other users' data or interfere with other users' programs.

It is the responsibility of the auditor to make sure that a system of controls is in place to insure that the information system is in compliance with legislative and judicial requirements for privacy. Even without passage of additional privacy legislation or court decisions, the auditor must ascertain the effect of recent judicial interpretations and statutes already on the books. Every auditor should review the system of controls and management policies of his organization and decide what impact privacy legislation and rulings have had and will have.

[25]Davis, *op. cit.*, p. 20.
[26]For an insight into problems of privacy, see: "Privacy Briefing Washington D.C.," *Data Management*, July 1975, pp. 6–10.

The auditor must balance the purpose of the information system, which is to increase accessibility, against countervailing demands for accuracy, integrity, and confidentiality. One of the goals of information systems design is to give ready access to the system to a variety of users throughout the organization. Without proper control, this feature can present problems.

> ... One of the most dangerous (concerns) to individual privacy in computer data banks, is a remote terminal or computer console, combined with a clever, knowledgeable, unscrupulous individual. Such an individual, by obtaining key bits of information and knowledge of a system, can access those data files integral to that system with which the terminal/console is interconnected and obtain the contents for his/her own use and personal benefit.[27]

Confidentiality, as well as the accuracy and integrity of data, rest on the following controls:
1. Administrative controls, standards, and policies.
2. Input control of data.
3. Controlled access to the system and data base, and designation of authorized recipients of output.
4. Logs of accesses to the data base.
5. Processing and data communications controls.
6. Control from equipment and data base loss.

It is probably impossible to meet privacy requirements without a system of controls, but a sound system of controls does not guarantee privacy. Controlled access is both a systems and privacy problem. But one may be controlling access from a systems viewpoint without achieving privacy from a legal viewpoint. For example, a data base may be tightly controlled, but it may be standard operating procedure of an organization to sell preferred mailing lists made up of its customers to another organization. It is general practice today for both private companies and government agencies to sell lists of persons in their data bases to marketing organizations. Also, many of these same companies cross-reference data from each other's files to construct profiles (e.g., credit) of individuals. Therefore, a comprehensive system of controls must make sure that privacy requirements are met and that the system is operating in accordance with legislative and judicial actions.

Push for Certification

A licensed certified data processor (CDP) or similar certificate would indicate that the licensee has the credentials to certify the computer as

---

[27] Williams, *op. cit.*, p. 26.

to: (1) proper system of controls, (2) processing activities and their relationship to design objectives, (3) data base integrity and accuracy, and (4) compliance with privacy requirements.

Many legislators, both state and federal, are intent on regulating data-processing systems and people who are involved with them. They believe that consumers, taxpayers, investors, and businesses must be protected from fraud and invasion of privacy. They believe that licensing of computer systems people that play sensitive and key roles is not only socially desirable, but imperative.

The Society of Certified Data Processors (SCDP) has sent state legislators a sample draft of legislation that would declare data processing "a learned profession to be practiced and regulated as such." If such legislation is forthcoming, it would probably directly affect the auditor, especially if he is involved in any way with the control and audit of a computer-based information system. Presumably, regulations would be handled similar to those for lawyers, doctors, and CPA's.

The SCDP has circulated a draft of the licensing proposal to each of the fifty states, and hearings on the bill have already begun in several states. The reasons for this proposal are indicated in the following statement by Kenneth W. Lord, Jr., President of SCDP.

> Thieves, using a computer system, defraud the City of Los Angeles of $902,000 known, $2.5 million intercepted and potentially another $10 million. In a case destined to make the Equity Funding scandal a tale of fantasy, once again unethical practitioners have illegally used a computer to defraud and to commit grand theft. Clearly the time to regulate the computer and those who use the computer has arrived!
>
> Throughout the history of the data processing industry there has been potential for this type of occurrence. We're an industry which has grown in leaps and bounds in an uncontrolled fashion, insofar as the people themselves are concerned. Consent decrees and antitrust actions have regulated the vendor portion of the industry. Legislators are intent on regulating the data handled by the systems we produce. But not until the Society of Certified Data Processors (SCDP) produced its bill for the licensing of data processing professionals has anyone dared to darken the hallowed ground of people regulation.
>
> It would shed no new light to any reader to know of the instances where the computer has been used as a scapegoat for shoddy business practices. It would do no good to recount the more than 200 known "tip of the iceberg" incidents of computer-related fraud, as they are a matter of record. But now there is, with the advent of Los Angeles, a clear indication that the taxpayer is being bilked, via computer, in six-digit figures! Clearly that taxpayer, that consumer, has a right to be protected. That consumer needs, for his own confidence in our operations, the licensing legislation the SCDP has proposed.
>
> The Government, both Federal and local, needs this action. Taxpayers' revenue must be protected. Critical applications must be re-

viewed in the light of a currently non-existent "generally acceptable practice." There is need for a Uniform Code for Data Processing (UCDP), to permit Government to not only protect its own interests, but the interests of those whom it serves.

Business and industry need the protection this bill affords. Unless consumer-critical applications can be inspected by a person known to be professionally qualified and legally sanctioned to perform such inspections, then business and industry all face the frightening prospect of such a computer-related fraud as has occurred in Los Angeles. In addition, both business and industry must be put in a position of having to stop using the computer as a surrogate for acceptable customer service. A feature of this bill will require business and industry to do some long overdue education and systems inspection.

And finally, the practitioner himself needs licensing. It's about time that we really take the steps to becoming a true profession, with all the trappings of a profession. Only when the data processing professional has the legal sanction of a license, will many company practices cease. Only when we have taken the steps to make this a profession will the practitioner be required to upgrade his knowledge and his standard of practice. We will never have a profession until we have the means to keep an unethical or incompetent practitioner from the practice.

The SCDP has taken the steps to produce the nation's first data processing licensing bill because we feel that the time has come for this kind of practice to cease. We have taken the steps because we feel that unless the data processing profession begins to regulate itself, it most assuredly will be regulated by others. And we took the first step because important people and important associations in the industry didn't feel that it was very important. And we did. We felt it very important.[28]

Reacting to SCDP's licensing proposal, the Institute for Certification of Computer Professionals (ICCP) stated that the proposal was premature because at the present time the data-processing profession does not have generally accepted definitions of job functions which could be licensed, and it has not agreed upon the knowledge and skills that a given individual should have to practice in his job. Moreover, the profession does not have a complete set of validated tests to measure individual knowledge in those undefined areas.[29] Some aspects of the proposal, however, will probably be passed in a number of the states.

2.4 CHALLENGES AND OPPORTUNITIES

Undoubtedly, the auditor faces many new challenges brought about by computer-based information systems, new laws, data-processing per-

---

[28]"Licensing/Certification," *Infosystems*, April 1975, p. 45.
[29]*Ibid.*, p. 44.

sonnel, and changes in people's attitudes. These challenges also bring about opportunities.

The New System

Some auditors believe that event processing systems have eliminated what they call an audit trail (but they have not really done so, as we shall see later in this text). The old systems used to consist of documents, journals, ledgers, and worksheets that permitted the auditor to trace an original transaction forward to a summarized control total, or a summarized control total backward to an original transaction. These event processing systems have not only eliminated the so-called traditional audit trail but also rendered some of the traditional controls inapplicable.

But computers are predictable. Ten bookkeepers may do ten different things. Ten computers will all perform the same way every time, assuming the same program. Computers operate with great speed and are thus capable of extracting and processing large volumes of data faster and with fewer errors than these functions could be performed manually. This attribute makes the computer a strong control and audit tool. The computer can be used to test the information system more thoroughly than it could ever be checked without the computer. Through the use of test data, the auditor can test the logic of programs to see whether they are handling the processing functions properly. Further, audit programs can be used to analyze the data base, detect variances, and project trends which may help to prevent errors or abuse from occurring in the first place.

The New Auditor

The new auditor will have to move beyond the idea that periodically attesting to the financial statements of the organization is his only responsibility. He will have to begin to look at himself as the information system's doctor, interested in its proper operation and well-being. To meet these new requirements, the new auditor, must achieve the following:

1. *Expansion in scope* The auditor must become an information systems "doctor," one who practices preventive "medicine," that is, he must take a diagnostic/preventive approach to his work. The auditor must be more than the traditional financial auditor. He must be able to review and evaluate computer systems and their controls. Understanding of computer systems, controls, and computer auditing tech-

niques is fundamental, not optional or simply desirable, as it once was. The auditor must become involved in the development of systems to make sure that the system is properly controlled and that it is designed to provide the auditor with an audit interface to monitor, probe, and capture evidential information as it flows through the system. Involvement of the auditor in the development phase is most important, because, event processing systems are so complex that a retro-fitting of controls and audit interfaces would be extremely difficult, if not impracticable.

2. *Requirements from the auditor*   The auditor should have the right to apply computer audit techniques to retrieve any data in any format desirable from the data base without interference from computer systems personnel. He should have the authority to make sure that programmers use appropriate procedures, documentation, and programming aids. He should see to it that software changes are monitored and controlled. He should make sure that manufacturers' hardware and software contain standard control and security features. The auditor should be able to apply monitors (hardware/software) to collect and report operational data. He should have the authority to see that data base administrators and security officers are employed when and where he deems it necessary. At any time, the auditor should be able to report significant variances to top independent persons who have the responsibility and authority to take corrective action.

3. *Knowledge requirements for the auditor*   The auditor must have a firm knowledge of computer systems, system of controls, and computer audit techniques. He must understand flowcharts and decision tables. He must be able to write and debug moderately difficult computer application programs in at least one language (e.g., COBOL). He must be able to obtain independence from computer systems personnel by selecting and applying generalized audit programs. He must be able, when the need arises, to write his own audit programs. He should have no hesitancy in auditing computer operating performance and work flow. He should fully understand and be able to review and test a complete system of controls. He should know how to review computer programs. He should become involved in information systems development. He should be able to use the computer as an audit tool and apply sophisticated audit techniques such as integrated test facilities and tagging and tracing routines.

Major accounting firms have attempted to improve the qualifications of their auditors by requiring them to attend seminars concerning the audit of computer-based information systems. Generally, the training received is not sufficient to enable an individual to audit a relatively simple system, not to mention a sophisticated system. However, some have recognized the need for qualified auditors and have established more appropriate minimum knowledge requirements. For example, at a major corporation, an individual on the internal audit staff must be a Certified Public Accountant (CPA) and have a Certificate in Data Processing (CDP). These minimum requirements greatly enhance the quality of audits performed at this corporation.

When this knowledge is applied to computer-based systems, it can often provide better control and audit results than in a manual-based system. However, as someone once said: "To hit a moving target, you have to aim ahead of it. And if the target is accelerating, you must aim much farther ahead."

4. *Auditor attributes* Many people rely on the auditor to act as an independent party between them and the information system. Some of these people are management, consumers, investors, taxpayers, stockholders, government officials, customers, and so forth. If these people cannot rely on the auditor, then they must operate at their own risk. The auditor who acts as a guardian for these people must, first of all, be independent of data-processing personnel. He must be persistent and skeptical, and infuse both attributes with a good dose of common sense. And in addition to his expertise in the field of computer control and auditing, he must be creative and imaginative in order to adapt to dynamic conditions.

2.5 SUMMARY

Advancements in computer-based information systems do not occur in a vacuum. They are adapted and employed in organizations, both commercial and governmental, that affect the individual, management, auditors, political and judicial institutions, and society. Computers have had both beneficial and detrimental effects on the financial well-being of organizations and the privacy of individuals. Auditors must accept a large portion of the responsibility for the proper and beneficial use of computer systems.

The new auditor can face a challenging and rewarding future confidently if he plans and prepares for it. If the auditor is knowledgeable, computer systems are easier to control and audit than manual systems. The new auditor must be aggressive and knowledgeable about systems, and he must expand his audit scope to cover all aspects that impact upon the information system. If he is not aggressive in his work and knowledgeable about computer-based systems, lawsuits will continue to plague him (probably at an accelerating rate), just as they have the legal and medical professions. Auditors face ever-present hazards, not only in terms of civil liability but also in the threat of criminal activity. Several years ago, a number of authorities stated that we are entering into the "age of litigation." It appears that they were right.

REVIEW QUESTIONS

2.1 State the ways in which a computer can be misapplied. What are the two abuses discussed in this chapter?
2.2 Define fraud and its relationship to computers and the auditor.
2.3 As best you can, define the auditor's responsibility concerning fraud.
2.4 Explain the implications of the *Escott versus BarChris* case relative to auditing.
2.5 List and define the six basic ways in which fraud is committed in relation to the computer.
2.6 Why is fraud committed?
2.7 Define invasion of privacy and its relationship to computers and the auditor.
2.8 List and explain the driving forces behind the privacy issue.
2.9 What role does the auditor have to play in the privacy issue?
2.10 List the principles of HR 1984.
2.11 List the controls that confidentiality and integrity of data rest upon.
2.12 Explain the reasons behind the push for certification of personnel involved in computer data processing.

DISCUSSION QUESTIONS

2.1 What is the relationship of individuals, management, lawyers, computer manufacturers, legislators, jurists, professional groups, and auditors to computer-based information systems?
2.2 What changes do you see occurring in auditing?
2.3 What adverse affects could computers have on a democratic society? What positive affects can computers have?
2.4 Do computer systems increase or decrease the probability of fraud?
2.5 "Computer fraud is old wine in new bottles." Discuss the merit of this statement.
2.6 Discuss the impact of computers on society in terms of privacy.
2.7 The auditor must insist that privacy legislation and judicial rulings be considered when a computer-based information system is being developed. Explain how the auditor should do this.
2.8 The elimination of some adverse affects of computer usage may require more government control, one aspect of which may be certification of people involved in sensitive data-processing jobs. What affect, if any, would this type of certification have on the CPA?
2.9 Discuss audit ramifications of HR 1984.

2.10 "You can have a good system of controls but still not be meeting privacy requirements; however, there is no way to insure privacy without a system of controls." Discuss this statement and give an example.

2.11 Discuss the new auditor.

2.12 What knowledge should the new auditor have?

BIBLIOGRAPHY

Adams, Donald L. "The Accountant and the Computer," *The Journal of Accountancy*, January 1974.

_____. "Who is Responsible for Computer Fraud?" *The Journal of Accountancy*, February 1975.

Allen, Brandt R. "Computer Fraud," *Financial Executive*, May 1971.

_____. "Embezzler's Guide to the Computer," *Harvard Business Review*, July–August, 1975.

Auditing Advanced EDP Systems Task Force of the AICPA's Computer Auditing Subcommittee. "Advanced EDP Systems and the Auditor's Concerns," *The Journal of Accountancy*, January 1975.

Barrett, Michael J., Donald W. Baker, and Leon R. Radde. "Top Management Fraud: Definitional Problems, External Auditor Responsibilities and Top Management Controls," *Collected Papers of the American Accounting Association's Annual Meeting*. Sarasota, Fla.: American Accounting Association, August 18–20, 1975.

Bigelow, Robert P., and Susan H. Nycum. *Your Computer and the Law*. Englewood Cliffs, N.J.: Prentice-Hall, Inc., 1975.

Burton, John C. "The SEC and the World of Accounting," *The Journal of Accountancy*, July 1974.

Causey, Denzil Y., Jr. "Newly Emerging Standards of Auditor Responsibility," *The Accounting Review*, January 1976.

Croisdale, D. W. "DP People—Who Do They Think They Are?" *Datamation*, July 1975.

Davis, Ruth M. "Privacy and Security in Data Systems," *Computers and People*, March 1974.

Defliese, Philip L. "Luncheon Address," *Collected Papers of the American Accounting Association's Annual Meeting*. Sarasota, Fla.: American Accounting Association, August 18–19, 1975.

Dirks, Raymond L., and Leonard Gross. *The Great Wall Street Scandal.* New York: McGraw-Hill Book Company, 1974.

EDPACS. An excellent publication to help the auditor gain knowledge about computer control and auditing, and to keep current. The address of this publication is: Automation Training Center, 11250 Roger Bacon Drive, Suite 17, Reston, Virginia 22090.

"Equity Funding Auditors Convicted," *EDPACS,* June 1975.

"Equity Funding Trustee Sues Auditors," *EDPACS,* March 1975.

Frank, Ronald A. "Privacy Act Vagueness Rapped," *Computerworld,* April 30, 1975.

Goldstein, Robert C., and Richard L. Nolan. "Personal Privacy Versus the Corporate Computer," *Harvard Business Review,* March–April 1975.

Gregory, Francis M., Jr., and Wright H. Andrews. "The Privacy Debate, Business Must be Seen and Heard," *Data Management,* August 1975.

Gustafson, L. M. "Improving Relations Between Audit & EDP," *EDPACS,* September 1976.

Hill, Christian G. "Accountants Brought Equity Funding Fraud Almost to Surface in '71," *The Wall Street Journal,* Feb. 20, 1976.

Holmes, Edith. "New Hampshire Bill Would Keep Credit Files In-State," *Computerworld,* April 30, 1975.

Horvitz, Jerome S., and Joseph L. Sardinas, Jr. "Impeachment of Government Systems Documentation for Taxpayers Classified as Non-Filers," *Rutgers Journal of Computers and the Law,* Volume 6, Number 1, 1977.

International Business Machines Corporation. *The Considerations of Physical Security in a Computer Environment.* White Plains, N.Y.; IBM, 1972.

──────. *Introduction to Data Communications Systems.* Pub. No. ZR20-4542-0. White Plains, N.Y.: IBM, 1975.

──────. *Data Security and Data Processing.* White Plains, N.Y.: IBM, 1974. A six-volume work presenting the findings of an IBM study into specific aspects of data security. The study sites were MIT, the State of Illinois, TRW Systems, Inc., and the IBM Federal Systems Center.

"IRS Refund Case Shows How Courts Now View Computer Overbilling Suits," *Computer Law and Tax Report,* December 1975.

Kuong, Javier F. *Computer Security, Auditing and Controls.* Wellesley Hills, Mass.: Management Advisory Publications, 1974.

"Licensing/Certification," *Infosystems,* April 1975.

Mair, William C., Donald R. Wood, and Keagle W. Davis. *Computer Control & Audit.* Altamonte Springs, Fla.: The Institute of Internal Auditors, 1976.

McCusker, Tom. "The Industry in '76." *Datamation,* January 1976.

McKnight, Gerald. *Computer Crime.* New York: is available from Walker and Company, 1973. (According to *EDPACS* publication, January, 1976, page 8, this book is available from Publishers Central Bureau, 1 Champion Avenue, Avenel, New Jersey 07131. The book costs $1.00, but the minimum order is $3.00.)

Meigs, Walter B., E. John Larsen, and Robert F. Meigs. *Principles of Auditing* (Sixth edition). Homewood, Ill.: Richard D. Irwin, Inc., 1977.

Minsky, Naftaly. "Intentional Resolution of Privacy and Protection in Database Systems," *Communications of the ACM,* March 1976.

Myers, Edith. "The Taxing Question for Computers," *Datamation,* March 1976.

O'Brien, James A. *Computers in Business Management: An Introduction,* Homewood, Ill.: Richard D. Irwin, Inc., 1975.

Parker, Donn B. "The New Criminal," *Datamation,* January 1974.

_____. *Crime by Computer.* New York: Charles Scribner's Sons, 1976.

_____. Susan Nycum, and S. Stephen Oura. *Computer Abuse.* Springfield, Va.: U.S. Department of Commerce, National Technical Information Service, Order No. PB-231-320, 1973.

Perry, William E. "The State-of-the-art in EDP Auditing," *EDPACS* July 1976.

Privacy Briefing Washington, D.C.," *Data Management,* July 1975.

Review of all *EDPACS* publications since 1973. The address is: Automation Training Center, 11250 Roger Bacon Drive, Suite 17, Reston, Virginia 22090.

Rothman, Stanley, and Charles Mossmann. *Computers and Society.* Chicago: Science Research Associates, Inc., 1972.

Scannell, T. "Federal Systems Auditing in Bad Shape: GAO," *Computerworld,* November 28, 1977.

Standard Federal Tax Reports, 1975. Chicago: Commerce Clearing House, Inc.

Statement on Auditing Standards No. 3, "The Effects of EDP on the Auditor's Study and Evaluation of Internal Control," American Institute of Certified Public Accountants, December 1974.

Stone, Robert L. "Who is Responsible for Computer Fraud?" *The Journal of Accountancy,* February 1975.

Terry, George R. *Principles of Management,* Homewood, Ill.: Richard D. Irwin, Inc., 1968.

"The Privacy Act of 1974," *Data Management,* June 1975.

Thierauf, Robert J. *Data Processing for Business and Management.* New York: John Wiley and Sons, Inc., 1973.

Turn, Rein. *Computers in the 1980s.* New York: Columbia University Press, 1974.

Wasserman, Joe. "Selecting a Computer Audit Package," *The Journal of Accountancy,* April 1974.

Weiss, Harold. "Rebuttal to 'Equity Funding Implications,' " *EDPACS,* October 1974.

Westin, Alan. *Privacy and Freedom.* New York: Atheneum, 1967.

Williams, John W. O. "Data Banks, A Cause for Concern," *Data Management,* July 1975.

Yasaki, Edward K. "The 1970s: A Period of Pause and Appraisal," *Datamation,* December 1975.

PART TWO

SYSTEM OF CONTROLS

CHAPTER
3

INTRODUCTION TO CONTROLS

3.1 INTRODUCTION

Any system is subject to mismanagement, breakdown, error, and general abuse. Both the computer and human mind are marvelous instruments for great accomplishments; both also have the capacity to make mistakes. Because mistakes can occur in computer-based information systems, it is essential that a system of controls be implemented and maintained. In this chapter, we present a general discussion on controls. In subsequent chapters, these controls will be presented with more specification and detail.

3.2 NEED FOR CONTROLS

In manual systems and even to some extent in earlier computer systems, controls were effected by one person checking on the work of another. Today, many computers perform most of any data-processing job with little or no human intervention throughout the processing cycle. Moreover, the entire information system is in the hands of a relatively small number of people who communicate directly with the computer. Therefore, management and owners of organizations must have a greater concern for the integrity of both the computer system and the personnel who work with it. Some examples to show the need for controls follow.

Interconnected Subsystems

The idea of interconnecting subsystems by data communication networks and data bases is a good one, but it also has some drawbacks. One undetected error could have a serious impact by rippling throughout the system and causing many other errors to occur.

For example, assume that in a manufacturing organization an order for a number of X assemblies is incorrectly entered as an order for Y assemblies. This kind of error could cause the following inappropriate actions: (1) setting of wrong schedules, (2) incorrect ordering of raw materials, (3) missed delivery dates, and (4) incorrect budgeting.

In a manual system, because of the flow of informal information and the cross-checking of clerical work, such an error would probably be corrected before it was too late. However, today many people tend to follow the instructions of a computer system blindly.

Recent advances in data communications networks have had an impact upon the banking industry. Electronic Funds Transfer Systems (EFTS) are being widely employed by banks to handle customers transactions automatically.

Electronic Money

Some banks are beginning to use a currency dispensing machine that issues cash to customers without any involvement by personnel of the bank. The method is also referred to as an Electronic Funds Transfer System (EFTS). In any case, the system is almost completely automatic. Terminals are linked to computers of banks, credit unions, savings and loan, and other similar institutions that allow a customer to withdraw funds from his account, to transfer funds between savings and checking accounts, or to make a purchase on credit. Operation of the terminal is a step-through process in which instructions are displayed to guide the user through a specific transaction sequence. These automated teller terminals can even answer inquiries made by the customer about account balances, deposits, withdrawals, transfers, or payments. The idea behind these systems is to bring automated teller terminals to areas where members are concentrated and where business transactions are being made. The tellers are online to the computer twenty-four hours a day, i.e., they can transact business day or night on a self-service basis.

Because only a few people are involved in this kind of system, management is forced to place greater reliance on a system of controls to help insure that the system functions properly. "Management is faced with the problem of controlling the processing of transactions in a new technology. Management will have to make sure that new systems provide the ability to obtain the information needed to make management decisions and insure effective control."[1]

EFTS is a specific example of interconnecting subsystems by data communication networks and data bases, and it is currently in operation. Some have speculated regarding the future potential of these systems. One such suggestion is the Ultimate Corporation.

The Ultimate Corporation

Everett C. Johnson, CPA, Haskins and Sells, says that the Ultimate Corporation could exist by the year 2000, or perhaps tomorrow. Ultimate Corporation is a chemical corporation dealing only in liquid chemicals which it processes in vats. Automatic reorder points are designed into the system so that when the level of chemical in a vat falls below a certain point, a sensor automatically detects this situation. Thereupon Ultimate's computer communicates this information to a vendor's computer, which processes the order and starts pumping chemicals through a pipeline to Ultimate Corporation. Ultimate has a sensor on the pipeline which meters the receipt of this chemical, and as soon as it receives the amount that it ordered, it sends an electronic signal to the bank and the bank transfers the money from Ultimate's bank account to the vendors.[2]

The entire operation of Ultimate is efficient unless and until a mistake occurs (e.g., data communications error or an error in establishing vat capacity). For example, if a programmer made an unauthorized change to the capacity of one of the vats in excess of its limit, the same programmer, in collusion with others or by himself, could tap the tank and siphon off the excess capacity. Or worse, a data communications signal for one thousand gallons of chemical could be incorrectly transmitted and read by a vendor's computer as one million gallons. Not only would a mistake like this be financially costly, but it could also be dangerous if the vat were located in a congested area and the chemical was hydrocyanic acid.

One could think of many other things that could go wrong with any of the examples presented above. Think of at least five mistakes that could happen and attempt to devise a control(s) that would help to reduce the probability of their occurrence.

[1] American Institute of Certified Public Accountants, Computer Auditing Subcommittee, "Advanced EDP Systems and the Auditor's Concern," *The Journal of Accountancy*, January 1975, p. 68.
[2] Louise H. Dratler, "Tenth Annual AICPA Computer Conference," *Management Adviser*, July–August, 1974, p. 27.

3.3 OVERVIEW AND STRUCTURE OF CONTROLS

In everyday life, most of us attempt to increase the probability that good things will happen and reduce the probability that bad things will happen. Either way, there is no guarantee that good things will always happen. The same thing can be said about developing a system of controls, i.e., that it is an attempt to reduce the *probability* that bad things will happen; such a system of controls cannot *insure* that bad things will not happen. We will repeat this idea in several different ways throughout this book, because there is no such thing as a failsafe system. Moreover, there is a cost/effective and level of control consideration. One may acquire a cadre of armed troops to guard entrances to the computer center. Such a move would increase the probability that unauthorized persons would not be admitted, but it is doubtful that an expenditure to support this level of control would be cost/effective for most organizations.

Levels of Control

Theoretically, we will view any mishap or abuse that could impact upon any part of the system as a target. If the target is left without any form of protection, the probability is high that bad things will happen. In Figure 3.1, we illustrate how controls can be built around the target. The level of control at some of the exposure or threat gates may be at a lower level than at others because of cost/effective or technological considerations.

Generally speaking, as more money and resources are spent, the level of control goes up, and the level of risk that the target will be hit goes down. To design an optimum system of controls requires a great deal of judgment and an understanding of the kinds of exposures in a particular computer-based information system. For example, it would be foolish to spend $100,000 per year on encryption equipment for an information system if it transmitted a low volume of data that are unimportant to others. On the other hand, spending this much or more for encryption equipment may be a wise decision for an information system that transmits a high volume of sensitive data.

Another theoretical view of levels of control is illustrated in G. Scott Graham's rings of protection,[3] Figure 3.2. Essentially, Graham proposes a hierarchical structure for data and programs and that they be given a level of control commensurate with their level of sensitivity.

It may therefore be stated that whether the concept utilized be the level of control at threat gates, or Graham's rings of protection, the

---

[3]F. J. Corbato, H. J. Slatzer, and C. T. Clingen, "Multics: The First Seven Years," *Spring Joint Computer Conference*, Spring, 1972, p. 579.

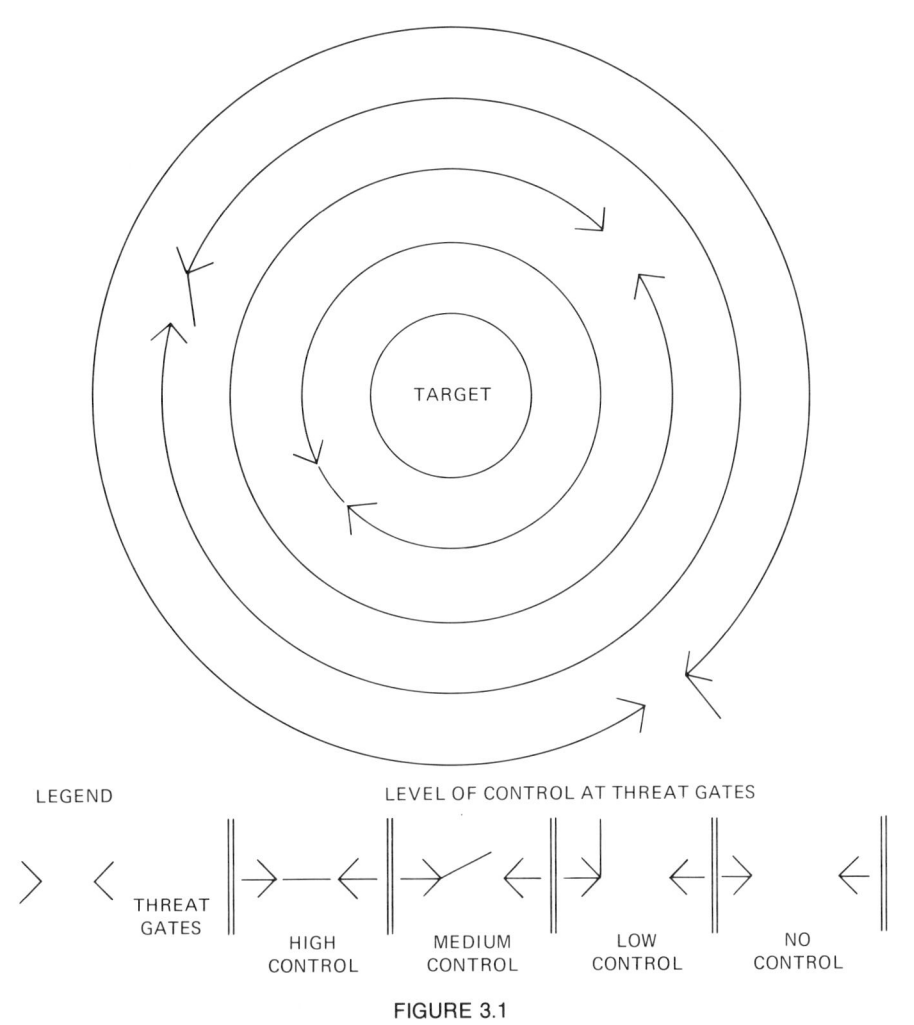

FIGURE 3.1
Control Maze with Different Levels of Control at Each Threat Gate for a Target.

scope and depth of controls selected for any given system should be directly proportional to the sensitivity of that system.

A system of controls presents to the auditor a dilemma or "tightrope" to walk. Too many controls, and controls that are too tight, can hamper processing. On the other hand, inadequate controls can make the processed data worthless. The implementation of more and more controls directly increases the accuracy, integrity, and protection (AIP) of the computer system, as well as its cost (C). More controls can also increase the effectiveness and efficiency (EE) of processing to an optimum point, after which the implementation of more controls can result in a disutility. The overall management objective is to achieve the optimum point as indicated in Figure 3.3. The installation of excessive controls decreases the efficiency and effectiveness (EE) curve to such a degree that at some point it has a tendency to pull the accuracy, integrity, and protection (AIP) curve with it.

Points of Control

The information system is a large and valuable resource to the organization. Insuring that this resource is performing as required, and protecting its operation from both internal and external misuse, begins in the design phase. There are four items that the auditor should consider.

1. Effective controls should be designed into the system, not tacked on afterwards.

2. In general, systems analysts and programmers have not devoted enough time to controls. In fact, many of these people are adverse to the establishment of controls.

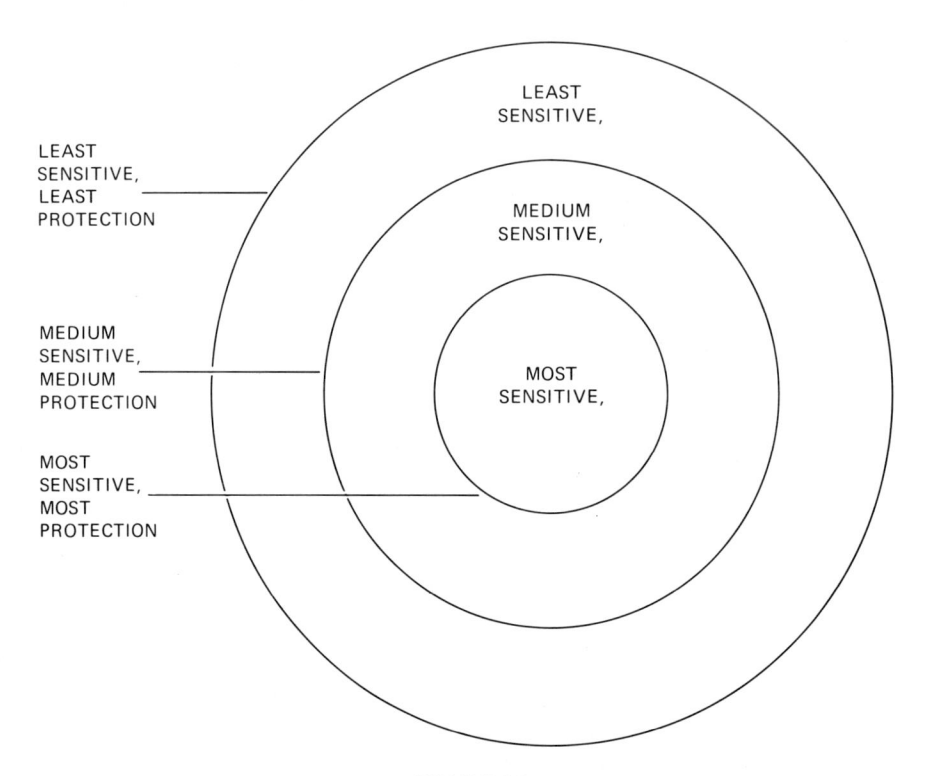

FIGURE 3.2
Graham's Rings of Protection.

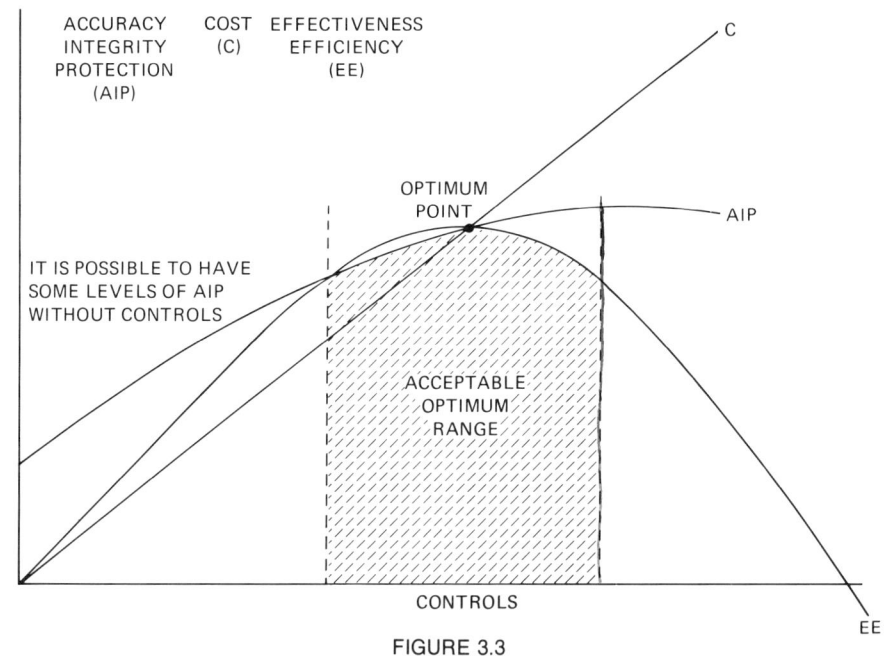

FIGURE 3.3
Example of an Optimum System of Controls.

3. Auditors should become more involved in systems development to help insure that appropriate controls are implemented.

4. Auditors must inform management that a system of controls not only serves the traditional accounting concept of internal control but also is important in achieving efficient operation of the information system. In other words the aim of a system of controls is stewardship of assets, reliability and accuracy of operations, integrity, completeness, and efficiency.

To carry on our general discussion about controls, we provide a schematic of the major control points of an information system in Figure 3.4. All of these major control points can be grouped into five general categories and defined as follows:

1. *External controls* These control functions emanate from, and are performed by, such groups as the auditing function and consultants, top management, special staff control groups, and various constituents of the organization. They help to establish an independent check on the overall activities of the information system through use of the system, observation, and feedback.

2. *Administrative controls* These controls are the responsibility of information systems management. They include traditional management functions, such as establishment of plans; screening, selection,

64 PART TWO SYSTEM OF CONTROLS

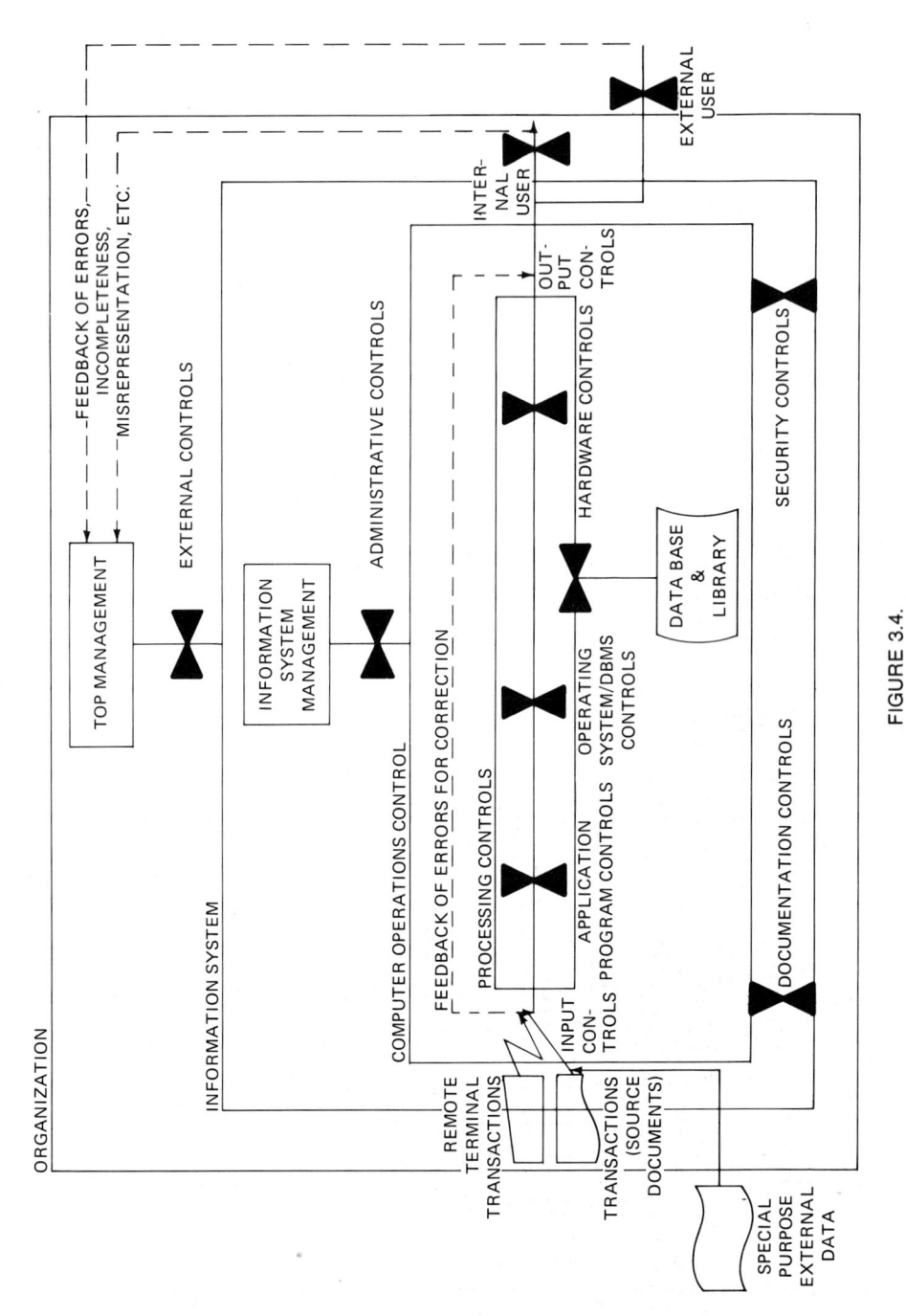

FIGURE 3.4.
Control Points Relative to the Information System.

assignment, and training of personnel; development and implementation of performance standards; and correction of deviations from standard.

3. *Operational controls.* These controls directly relate to the data-processing operations and consequently help to insure that transactions are handled properly and that data are accurately and reliably converted into information. These controls include the following:
    a. input controls
    b. processing controls
        1) program controls
        2) operating systems/DBMS controls
        3) hardware controls
    c. computer operations controls
    d. data base and library controls
    e. output controls

4. *Documentation controls* Documentation controls refer to all the communication and documents that tell how the system operates. Typical documentation contains: systems development reports; systems flowcharts; file, record, and report layouts; program flowcharts and decision tables; testing procedures; listings of source and object programs; and general manual procedures.

5. *Security controls* These controls include all of the physical and procedural operations used to help insure that the information system is not intentionally or unintentionally disrupted or misused by external or internal forces.

The concepts associated with proper internal controls is of paramount importance to the auditor. The American Institute of Certified Public Accountants has recently published an exposure draft concerning the evaluation of internal control in the computer environment.[4]

In this part dealing with system of controls, we devote our attention to: (1) administrative controls, (2) operational controls, (3) documentation controls, and (4) security controls. The last chapter of this Part will concentrate on the cost/effective analysis as it relates to controls. Rather than using a routine summary at the end of each chapter dealing with controls, we will use a questionnaire to summarize the material covered in that particular chapter.

---

[4]American Institute of Certified Public Accountants, Computer Auditing Subcommittee. *The Auditor's Study and Evaluation of Internal Control in EDP Systems*, Exposure Draft, March, 1976. Also see: Fitzgerald, Eason, and Russell. *Systems Auditability & Control Report: Data Processing Control Practices Report*, (Altamonte Springs, Florida: The Institute of Internal Auditors, Inc., 1977), and Computer Services Executive Committee. *The Auditor's Study and Evaluation of Internal Control in EDP Systems.* (New York: American Institute of Certified Public Accountants, 1977).

3.4 SUMMARY

In many computer-based information systems of today and in most of tomorrow, there will be little human intervention throughout the processing cycle. It is becoming increasingly important that extensive, cost/effective controls be designed into information systems to detect and, to the extent possible, prevent the processing of erroneous transactions and guard against mishap and abuse.

REVIEW QUESTIONS

3.1 Why is it important that a system of controls be implemented and maintained in a computer-based information system?

3.2 What is the basic difference between a manual-based and a computer-based system as far as processing functions are concerned?

3.3 In our theoretical discussion of controls, we used a term "threat gate." To the best of your ability, define "threat gate" and give an example of one.

3.4 From previous courses or from experience, it is assumed that you understand the division of duties among and between clerks in a manual-based system. How would a computer-based system affect this division of duties? Figuratively speaking, could the computer be looked upon as housing hundreds of electronic clerks?

3.5 What is the purpose of controls?

3.6 List the points of control in a computer-based information system. What are the five general categories that these controls are grouped in?

3.7 List the seven operational controls.

DISCUSSION QUESTIONS

3.1 Discuss at least five things that can "go wrong" in a computer-based information system.

3.2 Discuss the impact of a single error occurring in an integrated or interconnected system.

3.3 What would be the impact in an integrated system of assigning the wrong department number to a group of employees? What control(s) do you think might help reduce the probability of this kind of thing happening?

3.4 There seems to be a tendency for a large number of people to follow the instructions and accept as gospel the output of computer-based systems. Do you agree or disagree? Explain.

3.5 "Our system is under complete control." Discuss this comment.

3.6 Think of at least two situations in which too much control would reduce efficient operations.

3.7 Does an optimum system of controls mean implementation of maximum controls? Explain.

3.8 Let us assume that you are controller for Skipso Pen and you wish to send a TELEX message to your Dallas office. Further assume that for twenty dollars you can send a scrambled (or encrypted) message that supposedly can be read only by you and the authorized receiver of your message. Develop a situation in which it would be worth the expense of a scrambled message and one in which it would not.

3.9 Discuss the concepts of "control" in the classical auditing perspective and the concepts of "control" from an EDP perspective.

EXERCISES

3.1 List at least five threats to the information system of the Ultimate Corporation. Also, list at least five advantages of this kind of system.

3.2 Design a system of controls that would reduce the probability that your car and valuables in your house or apartment will be stolen or destroyed.

3.3 Contrast and compare the differences and similarities between the classical auditing concepts of control and the concepts of control discussed in this chapter.

PROBLEMS

3.1 Find out as much as you can about the Electronic Funds Transfer System (EFTS) used by some banks. Then attempt to imagine at least three exposures or hazards and develop appropriate controls to guard against them. At this stage, do the best you can and keep on file your response to this problem. When you have completed this part on system of controls, see if you would make any modifications to this response.

3.2 The great city of Metropolis was recently faced with a lottery scandal. Among the deficiencies of control cited as a contributing factor to the lottery problem was the lack of controls over unauthorized ticket printing. What controls should be established to insure proper control over lottery ticket printing? How should they be implemented? How should they be evaluated?

CHAPTER
4

ADMINISTRATIVE CONTROLS

4.1 INTRODUCTION

One of the basic concerns of an auditor is how well the information system is managed. In most organizations, the information system is a large, complex resource where good management is fundamental. Anything less could indicate a compromise in the integrity, reliability, and effectiveness of the system. Certainly, poor management would dictate that the auditor widen the scope of his auditing.

> The accounting profession's top rule-making group on auditing has proposed guidelines on the nature and limits of an outside auditor's responsibility for detecting fraud, embezzlement or other irregularities at a client company.
>
> The proposals reiterate traditional doctrine that a routine audit can't be relied on to bring out fraud or defalcations, especially where a company's management falsifies records or joins with third parties to fool the auditor. But in tone and detail, the proposals put new emphasis on an auditor's keeping aware that frauds do happen and can have an important impact on a company's financial statements.
>
> The guidelines are an "exposure draft" issued for public comment by the Auditing Standards Executive Committee of the American Institute of Certified Public Accountants, a 21-member rule-making group made up of partners from various accounting firms. The draft was issued along with previously reported similar proposals on an auditor's duty in detecting and reporting illegal acts by company management.

The draft on detecting fraud focuses on conditions or developments that should alert an auditor that something irregular may be going on. In particular, it stresses the importance of top management's integrity, inasmuch as such executives have the authority to order subordinates into what may be irregularities or concealment. According to the guidelines, an auditor should watch out if, for example, *a company's management doesn't seem to care about internal controls*, the company needs an internal audit staff but doesn't have one or key financial posts like controller have high turnover.

Generally, an auditor who develops such suspicions should extend his routine inquiry until the doubts are resolved and also inform the company's management at a high enough level for corrective steps to be taken. Where top management is implicated, this may mean informing the company's board, the exposure draft says.[1]

In this chapter, we discuss general administrative activities that help to insure effective management of the information system. These administrative activities are: (1) implementation and execution of plans; (2) screening, selecting, and training personnel; (3) personnel administration; and (4) establishment of standards.

4.2 IMPLEMENTATION AND EXECUTION OF PLANS

Six basic tasks are included in the planning activity. They are: (1) establish objectives, (2) identify the activities and events that must be performed to achieve the objectives, (3) determine the resources required to perform each activity, (4) define the duration of each activity identified, (5) determine in what sequence the activities are to be performed, and (6) see to it that the prescribed activities are carried out to achieve the objectives. In this chapter, we will discuss two kinds of plans that are especially applicable to the proper administration of an information system. These are: (1) master plan and (2) contingency plan.

Master Plan

For an information system to function effectively, it must be guided by a master plan, rather than a piecemeal or "brush fire" approach. A master plan outlines an overall framework of objectives for the total informa-

---

[1] "Guidelines Set for Friday Fraud By Outside Audits," *The Wall Street Journal*. May 6, 1976, p. 21. The document referred to is *The Auditor's Study and Evaluation of Internal Control in EDP Systems*, Exposure Draft, March 1976, developed by the AICPA Computer Auditing Subcommittee.

tion system and states general guidelines as to how to achieve these objectives.

Planning for information systems by involving management, other users of the service, technicians, and related clerical staff can save an enormous amount of backtracking, opposition, time, and expense. The full economic impact of charging ahead without planning can never be completely quantified. The costs of applications never completed, of other lost opportunities and poor decisions, however, are often painfully real. The more subtle effects of poor planning, on the other hand, usually lie hidden and manifest themselves only in general dissatisfaction and lack of steady progress.

... Never should individual major applications be started without a complete integrated plan. Above all, the matters of systems concepts, goals, and long-range planning must not be left to the discretion of the technical staff, but assumed entirely by top management.[2]

The overall benefit is one of corporate goal congruence. This concept implies the creation of and striving toward consistent goals by both management and other corporate employees. Specifically, this "overall" benefit may be subdivided into components. The benefits derived from establishing and carrying out a master plan for the total information system are the same as those derived from establishing a master plan for other endeavors. These benefits are:

1. It provides long-run and short-run guidelines that facilitate the smooth transition and implementation of subsequent applications. Personnel understand the overall administrative strategy relative to the information system. They know what should be taking place now and in the future.

2. It provides a sense of direction, and it reduces confusion and uncertainty. It is analogous to taking a trip in a car and using a road map as a master plan.

3. It establishes benchmarks. The personnel know how well they are progressing toward planned objectives.

4. It gives a means for controlling activities and projects. Any deviation from planned objectives is immediately highlighted for management action to correct the deviation or revise the plan.

5. It helps to insure a uniform basis for determining priorities and a sequence of continuing systems development. In nearly any system there is strong competition between projects for resources. A master plan allows management to get a better overview of the total system and therefore determines those projects that must be developed immediately and those that will have to wait or be postponed or scrapped.

6. It unifies and coordinates manpower and other resources. When

---

[2]Robert W. Holmes, "12 Areas to Investigate for Better MIS," *Financial Executive,* July 1970, p. 27.

priorities are set and everyone involved understands what projects are important, then a concerted effort can be made to complete these projects efficiently, and without divisiveness.

7. It reduces the number of isolated, noncompatible subsystems that might otherwise be developed, operated, and maintained. In a poorly managed system, one will often find everyone "doing their own thing" without a great deal being accomplished. Users' needs are seldom met, because the subsystems that are developed usually represent what the systems personnel are interested in rather than what the systems users need. Moreover, from a control standpoint, the development of isolated systems significantly increases the probability that mistakes and errors will occur.

As suggested in Part I, a steering committee should be formed to monitor, review, and ratify the overall information system program. Working with the manager of information systems and his staff, the steering committee should develop a master plan to identify projects that the different departmental users desire for the next N years (e.g., one, three, five, ten years), and to assign priorities to these projects. These plans also include people, hardware, software, and data base components needed to support the evolving information system.

The master plan can be comprised of the following elements:

1. *Strategic plan*   This plan gives a broad outline and direction over a long period (e.g., ten years) for the information system. It includes the objectives that management wants to develop and achieve in the long run. Some of these objectives may be: generalized data base management system; point of sale (POS) or point of transaction (POT) system; distribution of standalone and data base activities to remote users, installation of advanced data communications systems, development of more precise charging and pricing method for users; total conversion to high-level language using a top-down structural approach; and implementation of a complete array of system standards. This part of the master plan is subject to review and change. Overall, however, it should remain fairly stable.

2. *Specific projects plan*   This part of the master plan contains all of the projects that user and information systems management foresee for the next several years (e.g., two to five years). Projects may be divided into categories. Set projects have received total commitment and are firmly scheduled. Planned projects are tentatively scheduled. Intended projects are listed, but no schedule commitments are indicated. Users can make deletions, additions, or changes in the planned and intended projects. Every project must follow a standard systems development methodology with checkpoints and review at the end of each phase.

3. *Resources plan*   This part of the master plan lists the components —people, hardware, software, and data base—required to support the strategic and project plans. It also provides the projected costs needed to

acquire these components. This plan is reviewed and updated at least once every year, and in some instances more often.

The plans described above that make up the master plan are interrelated and give a good indication of what the auditor can expect from the system in subsequent engagements. Even though the plans are subject to change (e.g., first year firm, three years reasonably firm, five years general, and ten years rough estimate), the auditor can plan his work much better than he could otherwise. Certainly, with the master plan, the auditor can practice a stronger diagnostic/preventive approach to auditing. For example, the auditor can become involved in making sure that controls are designed into a system while it is being developed rather than trying to get them retro-fitted into the system after it has been implemented. He can also play a devil's advocate/consultant role and keep an eye open for trouble spots and to see to it that the system is planning for the right things.

Contingency Plan

A contingency plan is a set of procedures that instruct personnel what to do in the event of unforeseeable or uncertain circumstances. For example, if you were planning a trek across the Sahara you would carry supplies for every foreseeable contingency within the limits of specific constraints.

In a computer-based information system, what does management do if the computer goes down? If there is no backup system, or if management has not signed a contingency contract with another organization to use their computer as backup, then serious circumstances can develop if the computer is down for a long duration.

Management should make arrangements with another organization, if possible, to have access to its computer for backup. For this backup site, a provision should be negotiated to establish a reciprocal user agreement. Even with such an agreement, the auditor should confirm that there is in fact a compatible backup system available. There have been many cases where one organization has converted to another computer system that is incompatible with the other organization's computer. Worse than this situation is one in which a manager thinks he has a sound contingency plan when, in reality, there is none.

> ... when a senior executive of a major New England corporation was asked about the company's contingency plan, should its computer go down, he immediately replied that a nearby center could and would be used. A later interview with the manager of the center in question revealed that his center's equipment is not compatible with the company's; the nearest compatible equipment is located several

hundred miles away; and that equipment is busy 24 hours a day, 7 days a week![3]

Responsibilities and emergency procedures, in the event of disruption or disaster, should be clearly spelled out to all employees. Moreover, management should make sure that the systems personnel understand their responsibilities and can execute the procedures. For example, on an aperiodic basis, management should conduct a fire drill or a power outage simulation and observe what takes place. It might be added, that the term fire drill implies more than just having the employees file out of the computer center. Management should enter the computer facility and announce that all equipment and data at the present location have been destroyed. All relevant files should be identified and sealed with a red "destroyed" tape, thereby eliminating the possibility of using that particular file. The task at hand would be to reconstruct accounts receivable without utilizing any equipment or files at the present location. Much information may be ascertained in the ensuing melee. Exercises such as these can help insure that corrections are made prior to a real disruption or disaster.

To move quickly, efficiently, and effectively into emergency operations in the event of a disaster, a contingency plan should be prepared, published for all pertinent employees, and rehearsed periodically (e.g., fire drill, power failure of long duration). The more the plan is rehearsed, the less improvisation and confusion will occur if a real disaster happens. The following is a contingency plan outline.

   I. List of persons and their substitutes responsible for triggering and coordinating the contingency plan
      A. Include activities responsible for
      B. Include business and home addresses and telephone numbers
  II. Contingency plan activities
      A. Schematic or flowchart of all key activities plus instructions for carrying out activities
      B. Each activity should be assigned a person by name
      C. Rehearse activities
      D. Keep plan updated
 III. Include material that can be saved in certain disasters (e.g., fire)
      A. Set priorities with human life as no. 1 priority
      B. Checklist for disaster team
         1. Fire extinguishing and other procedures
         2. Include master files, programs, documents, and so forth

---

[3]"Computer Security: Backup and Recovery Methods," *EDP Analyzer*, January 1972, p. 9.

IV. Obtain and keep current contingency contracts (also called mutual assistance agreements)
   A. Major objective is to have ready access to comparable equipment
   B. Prepare for some level of degradation because it is impossible to switch to another company's system and maintain the same level of operations
      1. Identification of critical systems without which the company could not function
      2. Eliminate certain reports
      3. Define a minimum hardware configuration required to process a critical workload
   C. Search nearby service bureaus and private companies that have compatible equipment
   D. The contingency contract should stipulate the amount of computer time to be made available as well as the time of day during which the system will be provided
   E. Specify steps to invoke contract
   F. Signers of the contract should be constrained from making any changes to the contingency configuration without a thirty days' notice
   G. Provisions should be made to perform periodic tests of compatibility by running portions of the critical workload on the contingency configuration
V. Acquire critical backup equipment that is not covered in the contingency contract and store in an off-site location

4.3 SCREENING, SELECTING, AND TRAINING PERSONNEL

As in any other part of the organization, so in the information system effectiveness and operational success are functions of the quality of personnel hired to work in the system. All the abuses discussed in earlier chapters combined would not equal the amount of abuse and mishap caused by incompetency, simple human error, and greed. For example, computer fraud is perpetrated by people, not by the computer.

Screening and Selection Techniques

Good personnel control includes hiring the right people in the first place. The following aspects should be considered in the hiring of all personnel.
   1. Technical ability is fundamental. Certainly no one should be hired for a job unless he has the technical competency to perform required tasks.

2. Character and emotional stability are key personal factors. A person with dishonest tendencies is a real risk.

3. The past performance of the job applicant should be thoroughly investigated. If his past performance is inadequate or spotty, there is little chance it will be any different in a new job. The need to perform a thorough investigation into the prospective employee's background is emphasized by the following quote.

> Federal agents are less worried about lone-wolf operators than they are about the rising number of "gang jobs," or frauds and embezzlements planned and executed by rings. A common ploy involves getting a member of the ring a job in the bank. This insider then locates fat accounts and replaces the cards used to verify signatures for withdrawals on those accounts with duplicates made out in the handwriting of other gang members. The crooks then withdraw heavily from the accounts and everyone skips town before the next statement period.
> Federal authorities believe that lax hiring procedures and poor training are responsible for the success of some frauds and embezzlements....[4]

4. The ability of a person to handle his own affairs, especially financial affairs, helps to indicate the level of risk in hiring a particular person. Financial problems can cause many honest persons to commit fraud.

5. An investigation to determine whether or not an individual has been refused bonding may help to identify a potentially unreliable employee.

6. There has been a general movement in the profession to view the Certificate in Data Processing (CDP) as a minimum standard for individuals associated with EDP. If the CDP attains the stature of the Certified Public Accountant (CPA), such a requirement may be of some value.

Training Program

Without proper selection and training of personnel, it is difficult, if not impossible, to develop a viable, effective information system. It is, therefore, the responsibility of management of the information system to establish training programs for new employees. In no instance should a new employee be brought into an organization without some form of orientation and training. Moreover, management should establish a program not only to train new employees but also to update the expertise of all employees.

[4] Hal Lancaster, "Hit by Alarming Wave of Robbery and Fraud, Banks Take Elaborate Steps to Foil Criminals," *The Wall Street Journal*, February 18, 1976, p. 38.

Training approaches include: (1) universities and colleges, (2) special trade schools, (3) professional seminars and conferences, (4) inhouse training programs, and (5) special job assignments and on-the-job training.

Every company should have an inhouse training program. A good training program, properly structured and maintained, can be worth its weight in gold. First, the necessary skills will be supplied as the need arises, and a trained staff will generate higher-quality work within specified time frames. Second, a training program will broaden employees' viewpoints and increase their motivation as they begin to understand the more complex and challenging tasks that lie ahead. Third, it is easier for an organization to recruit new employees if it has a training program.

Every company should install a comprehensive technical library for its data processing staff. The library should include current industry publications, all system documentation, project controls manuals, standards manuals, and training and reference manuals. The list of contents will grow as the need for access to data grows.[5]

4.4 PERSONNEL ADMINISTRATION

Once personnel are hired and trained, they must be properly managed. Controlling a computer system is basically a matter of controlling computer personnel. They should be provided with a clear statement of responsibility and authority, and also be made aware of the goals of the organization. Traditional administrative methods should be established to determine if goals are being met. In the field of EDP, the concept that technical proficiency does not imply managerial ability applies most assuredly. The individual who can generate efficient program source code with a minimum of programming "bugs" does not imply that the same individual can manage an entire project. Administrative personnel should be selected for the ability to administer, although some technical knowledge is obviously required. A classic example of this concept may be found in the failure of the New York State Lottery.

> . . . As our work progressed, we examined areas of lottery operations in addition to those concerning the immediate problems described to us in order to place in better perspective the over-all environment within which the problems developed. In so doing, we uncovered a variety of problems of a very serious nature which raise grave concerns about the appropriateness of continuing the lottery without a major overhaul. Of critical concern is the current organizational frag-

---

[5]S. R. Mixon, *Handbook of Data Processing Administration, Operations, and Procedures,* (New York: AMACOM, a division of American Management Associations, 1976), p. 5.

mentation whereby a number of key functions are not under the immediate supervision of the Lottery Division including computer programming wherein the error we were originally asked to investigate occurred. It is essential that the lottery have all the resources necessary to discharge its responsibilities. As it is structured today, it is not clear who is responsible for what.[6]

Establishment of Goals and Policy

In the past, and to a great extent today, many intelligent and competent people have entered the computer field because they were attracted by the glamour, challenge, and mystique of the computer. Many of them have more loyalty and commitment to the computer than to the organization. Many of these people are disinterested in controls, budgets, management policy, and goals of the organization, all of which are viewed as interfering with their personal objectives and with using the latest fads, gimmicks, and equipment.

Goals of the organization should be made clear and methods set up to see that these goals are adhered to.

> ... Be sure your employees are kept well informed of company policy. Include your key employees in decisions that may affect their jobs. Set up a suggestion box and respond to the suggestions.
> ... Place larger posters in your computer facility informing employees that they are working with confidential information and that it is a criminal offense to remove anything from the computer room.[7]

Periodic performance reviews of personnel make a significant contribution to management's awareness of work that is going on and who is doing it.

Separate Functional Areas

A line should be drawn between personnel who authorize a transaction, those who produce the input, those who process the data, those who manage the data, and those who use the output.

> ... More than half the recent computer fraud cases involved collusion. This is a far greater incidence than in manual frauds. This may

---

[6]*Summary of Findings New York State Lottery*, (Cambridge, Mass.; Arthur D. Little, Inc., Nov. 26, 1975), p. 1. In September 1976, New York State introduced a new instant lottery. Additional lottery games will be phased-in by Mathematica, Inc. John P. Hebert, "New York Antes Up Revamped Lottery," *Computerworld*, Sept. 27, 1976, pp. 1, 4. It should be noted that the New York State Lottery has resumed operation with improved controls and procedures.

[7]Robert L. Stone, "Who is Responsible for Computer Fraud?" *The Journal of Accountancy*, February 1975, p. 371.

mean that computer fraud requires more skill, access, and knowledge than is possessed by one person. If this is true, then the need for separation of duties within a data center takes on greater meaning. . . . Segregation of duties was an important control in manual systems. In EDP systems it is vital.[8]

The functional areas that should be separated in the information system are: (1) systems analyst group; (2) programming group; (3) computer operators; (4) tape, disk, and document librarians; and (5) input and data conversion clerks. The preceding separation also properly segregates the operating and development activities. However, where people must work together, an attempt should be made to set up work groups of three. In groups of three, any wrongdoing is usually reported by the "third" person.

Other forms of separation of functional areas are: (1) rotation of personnel and (2) mandatory vacations. Rotation of personnel prevents any employees from dominating an area. Moreover, it not only provides a cross-check but it reduces the propensity to rely upon one employee where another can take over. At least two consecutive weeks of vacation should be required of all key personnel. A number of abuses and errors have surfaced during vacation periods, because the person perpetrating a fraud or some other abuse was not there to control it.

Exit Procedures

No matter how good the selection, screening, training, and administrative techniques used are, some employees prove unsatisfactory or others move on to better opportunities. In any case, businesses have been established on programs, information, trade secrets, and so forth stolen by departing employees. Also, some fired employees have destroyed valuable property.

> . . . We have all heard of the "war" stories of EDP employees venting their wrath on their employers when told they were fired. It is brutal, but the only safe thing to do is ask them to leave the premises immediately. You might ease the situation by giving them a month's pay to tide them over until they get a job.[9]

In addition to having terminal employees clear out their desks in the presence of security personnel and immediately leave the premises, management should also attempt to elicit information from the employee relating to the job and problems in general. In many instances, management can gather some straightforward information while conducting an exit interview in addition to creating goodwill.

[8]*Ibid.*, p. 371.
[9]*Ibid.*

4.5 ESTABLISHMENT OF STANDARDS

Not only should standards be established, but also a system should be set up to report to management any significant deviations from standards. Measurement bases for standards comprise procedures, quality, quantity, time, and money. These standard measurements relate to personnel, hardware, software, and data base.

Standard of Computer Operations

Managements and auditors rarely have the technical understanding to effectively control computer operations using traditional methods. Many organizations rely almost solely on budgetary control. However, computer operating budgets in many organizations have increased significantly year by year without a relative gain in effectiveness. Obviously, budgetary control is not sufficient if used by itself. In recent years, some managements have attempted to gain effective control by supplementary budgetary control with performance evaluation tools. These performance evaluation tools generate reports that reflect the trends in available capacity and the utilization of that capacity. Three performance evaluation tools that provide these kinds of reports are hardware monitors, software monitors, and accounting packages. These tools, especially the accounting package, also apply to auditing techniques (as does anything that relates to general management and administration), which are discussed in Part III.

Hardware monitors consist of probes, cables, logic plugboards, monitors, and data recorders. These all help to open up and show what the "black box" is doing. These monitors are used to measure the status of CPU, e.g., busy state or wait state; channel utilization; disk seek, transfer, and mount; tape mount, transfer, and rewind; and memory utilization.

Software monitors are programs that are part of the operating system or run as a high-priority problem program or systems task. This type of monitor provides accurate resource utilization statistics because it reads internal tables, operating system control blocks, status registers, memory maps, and so forth. It, however, can degrade the system it is measuring by as much as 10 percent because, unlike the hardware monitor, it is part of the system. However, as computer hardware technology improves, and the internal speed of the machines increases, it will be cost-justifiable to utilize software monitors. For example, an Amdahl 470V/6 is software- and hardware-compatible with an IBM 370/168, and it is approximately 100 percent faster.[10]

[10]Patrick Ward, "Amdahl Ends Silent Years With Unveiling of 470/V/6," *Computerworld*, November 1975, pp. 1, 3.

The objectives of using monitors are to reduce hardware cost and processing time, to prevent hardware overkill, and to defer unnecessary hardware acquisition and installation. These objectives can be achieved by determining productive and idle time. If used properly, they can also reduce shifts and improve response time. Most important for auditors is the fact that the various monitors can assist him or her to determine whether or not the systems being scrutinized are functioning properly. Some additional characteristics are listed in Table 4.1.

Another great benefit to the auditor and management of the computer system is to gain statistics on resources used by different jobs. IBM's System Management Facilities and Burrough's EDP-TABS are two accounting packages (part of operating systems) that capture and report a wealth of information. These packages (discussed in greater detail in Part III), for example, show elapsed time and CPU time percentages for each job and job step.[11]

TABLE 4.1

Characteristics of Hardware/Software Monitors[12]

Hardware Monitors	Software Monitors
Can be attached to any computer or peripheral through electrical probes	Runs as problem program
Requires no memory or other overhead and does not interfere with normal computer operation	Takes 6K to 12K bytes of memory
	Loading of program is generally trivial
Address obtainable with comparators	Consistent measures always possible once program is debugged
Sampling rate can be controlled independent of computer or tied to computer cycles	Overhead runs from 1% to 10%; typical overhead is 1% to 5%
	Easy to get program labels
Simultaneous multiple measures normal	Core storage address is easily obtained
	Sampling rate dependent on computer cycles
Can attach to IBM or non-IBM equipment	Can run only on machine for which programmed
Probes can be attached to wrong points giving misleading information	Can only measure information available through machine commands
Probe attachment takes time and skill for each measurement	Simultaneous measuring impossible—approach it by frequent sampling
Difficult to get program labels	Most software monitors available only for IBM 360/370's

[11] For more information on monitors and accounting packages, see *Computerworld*, April 30, 1975, pp. S/2–S/7, and Jerre D. Noe, "Acquiring and Using a Hardware Monitor," *Datamation*, April 1974, pp. 89–95.

[12] From Dr. Gary Carlson, Director, Computer Services, Brigham Young University, Provo, Utah, as cited in Louis J. Desiderio, Dennis Siloky, and Arnold Wasserman, *Measuring Computer Performance for Improvement and Savings*, (New York: Coopers & Lybrand, 1974), p. 14.

Standard of Systems and Programming Work

Understanding the management of systems and programming work requires a somewhat different approach than that used to evaluate the computer system. Basically, the reason for this difference is that computer operations are technical and fairly well defined, whereas systems and programming work are to a great extent creative in nature. However, a combination of two procedures will help to manage this work better. These are:

1. *Estimating time for project tasks* Once the systems analyst or programmer determines the tasks appropriate for the project, he should determine how much time is required to perform each one. For example, a systems task is interviewing, and the systems analyst may estimate that it will take six working days to complete this task. Or a programmer may estimate that it will take two days to test a particular program module.

2. *Scheduling and controlling the project tasks* Once the times for all the tasks for the project have been estimated, charting and/or network techniques should be used to help management allocate appropriate resources and control the systems and programming work. Two important techniques that can be effectively used for scheduling and controlling project tasks are Gantt charts and PERT networks.[13]

Standard Chargeback Techniques

Although in earlier years there was some debate about whether or not the information system should charge users for services rendered, we believe that this question is no longer debatable. We believe that some standard chargeback technique should be used in all organizations to charge the ultimate user, whether the information system is viewed as a profit center or service department. The real question relates to the kind of cost allocation technique or chargeback scheme to use.[14]

General Data-Processing Standards

The following general standards can substantially increase management and control of a computer-based information system.

---

[13] John G. Burch, Jr., and Felix R. Strater, Jr., *Information Systems: Theory and Practice* (Santa Barbara, Calif.: Hamilton Publishing Company, 1974), Chapter 15 and Appendix A.

[14] For a detailed discussion of this area, see Carol Schaller, "Survey of Computer Cost Allocation Techniques," *The Journal of Accountancy*, June 1974, pp. 41–46; and "Chargeback Schemes Allow Users to Evaluate Systems," *Computerworld*, April 30, 1975, p. S/5.

1. *Standard data definitions and names* Consistent data definitions and names help to make operations of the entire system more effective and harmonious. Inconsistency creates confusion. For example, if accounts receivable are called ACC-REC in one routine and ACCT-REC in another and these routines are used together in a job, to the computer the two names are as different as daylight and dark.

2. *Standard programming languages* There is no reason to spend thousands of manhours developing programs written in some obscure language only to find out later that it is not being maintained by the vendor or it is incompatible with new equipment. A standard language such as COBOL should be used. It is not totally machine-independent, but it is better than most languages.

3. *Modular and top-down structured programming* Modular programming is the art of breaking down a large program into modules that can be worked on and tested separately. Then, like those in a TV set, these modules can be linked together to form a large, sophisticated program package. This technique enhances control and management of programming, and the maintenance programmer can also change modules of a program much easier than he can the total program.

Top-down structured programming is a technique used by programmers to write programs that can be read from top to bottom without branching back to a preceding paragraph or instruction. In such programming, there is an attempt to have one entry point and one exit point and eliminate the GO TO statement. This technique increases the efficiency of programmers and simplifies maintenance.[15]

4.6 SUMMARY

A determination by the auditor as to the adequacy of administrative controls within the client's organization as a whole as well as the particular controls within the EDP area are fundamental. We have discussed the implementation and execution of plans, stressing the importance of master and contingency plans. We have also discussed the importance of proper screening, selecting, and training of personnel. These key individuals will have potential access to the most sensitive data and information the corporate entity possesses. Therefore, these

---

[15] For more information on program techniques, see Daniel D. McCracken, "Revolution in Programming: An Overview"; James R. Donaldson, "Structured Programming"; Edward F. Miller, Jr., and George E. Lindamood, "Structured Programming: Top-down Approach"; F. Terry Baker and Harlan D. Mills, "Chief Programmer Teams"; R. Lawrence Clark, "A Linguistic Contribution to GOTO-less Programming." All articles from *Datamation*, December 1973, pp. 51–63. See also Ned Chapin, et al.,"Structured Programming Simplified," *Computer Decisions*, June 1974, pp. 29–31: "The Advent of Structured Programming," *EDP Analyser*, June 1974; Clement L. McGowan and John R. Kelley, *Top-Down Structured Programming Techniques* (New York: Petrocelli/Charter, 1975).

individuals must be of the highest calibre, possessing honor and integrity. The importance of personnel administration cannot be sufficiently stressed. Unhappy employees with no direction or goal structure may engage in "gamesmanship" which could have a disasterous impact upon the corporation. Lastly, we discussed the need for the establishment of standards in the EDP function. The various standards should be developed, adhered to, and tested to assure compliance. To do less places the auditor and the client in untenable positions.

As stated earlier, each chapter on controls will contain a questionnaire containing questions that relate to material covered in that particular chapter. They are prepared to summarize, enhance, explain, and add to the points made in the chapter. The purpose of this arrangement is threefold: (1) the chapter discusses the points, (2) the questionnaire supports this discussion, and (3) the questionnaire can be used in a real world organization (when you perform your audit project).

ADMINISTRATIVE CONTROLS QUESTIONNAIRE

	ANSWER		ANSWERS BASED ON		
	Yes	No	Inquiry	Observation	Test

MASTER PLAN:

1. Do you have a master plan? ___ ___ ___ ___ ___

2. Is the master plan made up of a long-range strategy, planned projects, and resources required? ___ ___ ___ ___ ___

3. Are projects, schedule, and resources well defined? ___ ___ ___ ___ ___

4. Is the master plan subject to periodic review by information systems management, steering committee, and various user groups? ___ ___ ___ ___ ___

5. Are accepted budgetary procedures used to estimate costs for resources? ___ ___ ___ ___ ___

CONTINGENCY PLAN:

1. Is there a backup computer system available? ___ ___ ___ ___ ___

2. Is the backup system available on short notice? ___ ___ ___ ___ ___

3. Has a formal plan and agreement for use of the backup system been prepared? ___ ___ ___ ___ ___

ADMINISTRATIVE CONTROLS QUESTIONNAIRE
Page 2

4. Are backup procedures tested frequently?

5. Are contingency procedures assigned to specific individuals?

6. Are emergency provisions established for critical items such as files and programs?

7. Are emergency procedures established for fire, attack, sabotage, natural disasters, and power failure?

8. Are emergency drills frequently conducted?

PERSONNEL:

1. Are organization charts current?

2. Are manuals and operating procedures current?

3. Are personnel background reviews conducted before hiring?

4. Are personnel bonded?

5. Are established personnel reviewed occasionally?

6. Is there a formal indoctrination and training program?

ADMINISTRATIVE CONTROLS QUESTIONNAIRE
Page 3

7. Are personnel briefed on company goals?

8. Is there a discernible career path for personnel?

9. Is there a job rotation program?

10. Are provisions made for backup personnel in key positions?

11. Is there a separation of duties?

12. Is there a policy by which single-person access to the system is prohibited?

13. Are discharged personnel interviewed and immediately removed from sensitive areas?

14. Are transferred personnel required to turn in all keys, passwords, manuals, files, and programs signed out to them?

15. Is access to sensitive areas by maintenance personnel controlled?

16. Are maintenance tools and supplies removed from the computer room checked to prevent loss of vital programs or data?

ADMINISTRATIVE CONTROLS QUESTIONNAIRE
Page 4

17. Is there a current list of vendors' authorized service personnel? ___ ___ ___ ___ ___

18. Is there someone who checks this list for authorization? ___ ___ ___ ___ ___

19. Are vendor service personnel supervised? ___ ___ ___ ___ ___

20. Are all personnel required to take vacations? ___ ___ ___ ___ ___

STANDARDS:

1. Are monitors used to collect utilization statistics on computer usage? ___ ___ ___ ___ ___

2. Are systems analysts required to follow a prescribed systems development methodology? ___ ___ ___ ___ ___

3. Are programmers required to follow a prescribed program development methodology? ___ ___ ___ ___ ___

4. Are all projects set up on a scheduled basis? ___ ___ ___ ___ ___

5. Are standard data names used through the organization? ___ ___ ___ ___ ___

6. Have standardized programming techniques (e.g. program format, coding procedures, flowcharts,

ADMINISTRATIVE CONTROLS QUESTIONNAIRE
Page 5

labeling, use of programming aids) been compiled in a manual and is the manual current? ___ ___ ___ ___ ___

7. Is the procedure of modular and structured programming encouraged? ___ ___ ___ ___ ___

8. Have documentation procedures been established? ___ ___ ___ ___ ___

9. Is there a periodic review of documentation for completeness and current status? ___ ___ ___ ___ ___

10. Are there written procedures for:
    — start up of the system ___ ___ ___ ___ ___
    — shut down of the system ___ ___ ___ ___ ___
    — restarts ___ ___ ___ ___ ___
    — control of tapes, disks, cards, listings ___ ___ ___ ___ ___
    — software changes—application as well as systems software ___ ___ ___ ___ ___
    — change to security parameters ___ ___ ___ ___ ___
    — maintenance ___ ___ ___ ___ ___
    — control of jobs and job flow ___ ___ ___ ___ ___
    — systems tests ___ ___ ___ ___ ___

11. Is a chargeback method used to charge systems users for services rendered? ___ ___ ___ ___ ___

REVIEW QUESTIONS

4.1 List and briefly define the administrative activities discussed in this chapter.
4.2 List and briefly define the six basic tasks in planning.
4.3 Define master plan, its purpose, and its benefits.
4.4 Define contingency plan and its purpose.
4.5 As an auditor, list at least two things to look for when investigating contingency plans.
4.6 List the aspects one should consider when hiring personnel. Add at least two more to this list.
4.7 List the training approaches an organization can use to train its personnel.
4.8 What is the control purpose in separation of duties and functional areas?
4.9 Define and give the purpose of exit procedures.
4.10 Define and give the purpose of three performance evaluation tools.
4.11 Define and give the purpose of using a chargeback method.
4.12 What is top-down structured programming? Is it better than other methods used to program? Why?
4.13 Why is it important to use standard data definitions and names?
4.14 Why is it important to use a standard programming language?
4.15 How might a computer-based information system impact upon goal congruence within an organization?
4.16 Would a CDP insure that an individual was properly qualified to administer the development of a large system?

DISCUSSION QUESTIONS

4.1 Why would the evidence of poor management controls cause the auditor to widen his audit scope?
4.2 Are administrative controls in the purview of the audit function? In what way? If not, why not? Discuss.
4.3 As an auditor, what would your reaction be if you discovered that the computer system you were auditing had no contingency plan?
4.4 "Written procedures help to delineate responsibilities and effect administrative controls." Comment on this statement.
4.5 "Personnel are the most important part of the information system, but the trouble with personnel is people." Comment on this statement.
4.6 Do you believe that computer personnel have more loyalty to the computer system than the organization? Why? Why not?
4.7 Explain how rotation of personnel and mandatory vacation help to effect control.

4.8 If you were manager and one of your key people quit to move on to a better job, would you have him clean out his desk and immediately leave the premises? Why? Why not?

4.9 Discuss why systems and programming work are difficult to control.

4.10 As an auditor, you are desk-checking a program listing and you notice the use of a large number of GO TO statements. What is your reaction?

4.11 As an auditor, you have become aware that there are no written procedures available in the computer center. Everyone relies on Donnie Snowgrin to tell them what to do if something non-routine happens. What is your reaction?

4.12 You discover that in the organization that you are auditing, most of the application programs have been written in FAD I. What is your reaction?

4.13 During your visit to the computer room of a large bank's data-processing center, you notice a list of various batch systems which the center runs. Next to each system name is the name and home phone number of a member of the programming staff. As an auditor, you inquire as to the list's purpose. You are told that this represents the "on call" list if serious problems arise during a processing run. Corrections and instructions are frequently given over the phone. How could this be handled differently? Is there a need for it to be handled differently?

4.14 Discuss some of the potential problems which might be detected during the simulated destruction of all magnetic tapes, disks and other equipment.

EXERCISES

4.1 Visit an organization of your choice that has a computer-based system, (large or small) and using the questionnaire at the end of the summary, go over each question with the manager of data processing, controller, or internal auditor. Make a list of "no" answers. Are they significant? If you were engaged as an auditor of the organization you visited, at this point what effect would the results of your questionnaire have on your audit scope? (*Note:* We realize that audit techniques and other controls have not been discussed yet, but at this point we merely want you to anticipate and speculate.)

4.2 Ed French, programmer, has given the following time estimates to complete the coding of a payroll program:

    Optimistic: 9 days
    Most Likely: 14 days
    Pessimistic: 27 days

Using the PERT calculation technique, calculate expected time to complete coding.

4.3 Past experience has shown that a particular type of program has an expected time of completion equal to 200 manhours. Bob Malcolm is assigned to prepare this program. The plan provides the following tasks and related times for each task.

Design program logic	50 manhours
Code program	40 manhours
Test program	70 manhours
Document program	40 manhours

After reviewing the program and developing a flowchart, Bob begins to code. At the end of several days, he reports the following:

	Planned	Actual	Remaining
Design program logic	50	20	0
Code program	40	4	27
Test program	70	0	15
Document program	40	0	12

You are chief programmer. What is your reaction to Bob's revised plan? Does this kind of feedback help you in controlling the programming function? How? Does it help you to allocate personnel and resources? How?

4.4 Select one person to instruct a group of volunteers on how to do something, but before he has finished, have him leave the room. See if the volunteers can finish what you had in mind without him. For example, you want three chairs stacked, seat first, on the front edge of a desk. The chosen instructor tells the volunteers to pick up the chairs. As soon as they do, he leaves the room. Normally, the volunteers will not know what to do next, except put the chairs back in their original place, which is not the objective you had in mind. Try something like this and see what happens. What point is this simple exercise attempting to make?

4.5 Assume you are going on a hiking trip over the Rockies. Prepare a contingency plan. Do you feel that contingency plans are important? Why? Why not?

PROBLEMS

4.1 Roswell Steffen, who embezzled $1.5 million, says, "Anyone with a head on his shoulders could successfully embezzle funds from a bank. And many do."

He claims that, during the three years he took the money, the bank never seemed to miss a penny. An admitted compulsive gambler, he marvels at the fact he was ever hired to work in a bank. Banks seem to place complete trust in the honesty of their employees. When the police told the bank that Steffen was betting and losing $30,000 a day, officials were reluctant to believe the story.

Steffen took the money right after an audit, so he felt it would be some time before anyone noticed. Before that could happen, the 'loan' would be repaid.

... made it possible to withdraw funds from accounts and cover the activity by adjusting the daily proof sheets. Union Dime was completely online. Steffen does not feel that this made it easier to steal, but it did make it faster.

The theft from accounts began with those that had large balances, $100,000 or more, which had interest figured only once a quarter.

Corrections were made by moving funds from one account to another.

The Park Avenue branch where he worked had a high turnover among its tellers. Since most of the work force was inexperienced, the high volume of errors and corrections could be blamed on them. Whenever the auditors showed up to investigate an error, Steffen would look concerned, blame the new tellers for making a misposting, and enter a correction. Later another adjustment would be required to offset the correction.

Two-year certificate accounts were a good source of funds. If someone opened such an account, Steffen would issue all the paperwork to the customer, but he would not record the deposit on the books of the bank. He had two years to play with the money.

A supply of pre-numbered passbooks was always on hand for use in opening new accounts. This also proved to be a great help. When a large account was opened, Steffen would help himself to two passbooks. The account number from one book and the amount of the deposit were entered on the teller terminal and then the second book was inserted in the machine. After the transaction was recorded, the depositor got the second book. A correction would be put through eliminating the deposit, the first passbook was destroyed, and the money would go into Steffen's pocket.

Why wasn't he caught? He feels the bank placed too much authority in the hands of one person. For example, there should have been a strict control over new passbooks. More than one person should have been assigned to supervisory duties within the branch. Job functions should have been rotated (While Steffen was on his mandatory vacation, the branch officers would hold his problem transactions until he returned! After all, two weeks was not a long time to have to wait.) Steffen says proof sheets should be carefully checked. Large entries should be subjected to a special review. More accounts should be confirmed by auditors.[16]

Required On the basis of the material in this chapter, prepare a two-page report to management and stockholders of Union Dime, spelling out the administrative controls you recommend be implemented to guard against further abuses similar to those perpetrated by Steffen.

4.2 The checklist below lists some of the most common problems encountered in computer operations. If your organization reports some of these problems on a fairly regular basis, you can be sure it is time to look into the performance of your operations group.

There are regular delays in getting production work completed.
There is a high level of job reruns in the computer center.
There is a regular flow of requests for additional hardware components, or complaints about hardware inadequacy.
There appears to be a general lack of orderliness in physical plant, report flow, and internal procedures.
There is a relatively high rate of personnel turnover in the operation staff group.
There is no development program or route of advancement for operations personnel.
There is a relatively high, chronic level of keypunch or data entry errors.
There is a high level of reported hardware failure or hardware maintenance problems.
There are a limited number of internal performance measurement reports or procedures.[17]

Required Prepare a report specifically describing recommendations to help alleviate some of the problems above.

4.3 Following are some excerpts from a typical master plan: (1) Within the next five years, we plan to replace all existing application-oriented files with a data base system to serve multiple users. (2) During the next ten years, we plan to be involved in converting to an online event processing system to process transactions as they occur and provide fast response to user inquiries. (3) During the next seven years, we plan to move from an integrated toward a distributed system where hardware, software, and data base are

---

[16]Excerpts about Union Dime Savings Bank Fraud from *EDPACS*, January 1975, pp. 18–19.
[17]From: Bernard W. Romberg, "Eyeball Your Computer Operations Today," *Infosystems*, December 1972, p. 31.

moved to the point of origin of the transaction, and closer to the point of need.

Write a one- to two-page paper on how the foregoing information from a master plan would be helpful to you as an auditor. Indicate how this information would affect your audit strategy and how it would help you in planning your work. Also discuss how a master plan serves as a control element in the overall system of controls.

4.4 You have applied the Administrative Control Questionnaire and you notice that the answer to all contingency plan questions is "yes." For example, the respondent indicates that a backup compatible computer system is available on short notice for the company's use; that all individuals are aware of various contingency procedures; that emergency procedures are installed for recreating lost files and other critical items; that emergency procedures are established for fire, attack, sabotage, natural disasters, and power failure; and that emergency drills (e.g., fire) are frequently conducted.

Prepare a report for top management indicating how you would go about testing these contingency procedures to see if they are actually in place and working.

CHAPTER
5

OPERATIONAL CONTROLS

5.1 INTRODUCTION

Operational controls directly relate to daily computer data-processing operations. They include: (1) input controls, (2) operating system controls, (3) processing controls, (4) application program controls, (5) data base management system (DBMS) controls, (6) built-in computer controls, (7) computer operations controls, (8) library and data base controls, and (9) output controls.

5.2 INPUT CONTROLS

Input controls are divided into four areas: (1) input (or transaction) codes, (2) input preparation, (3) input verification, and (4) input completeness.

Input (or Transaction) Codes

Today's information systems cannot tolerate ambiguous meanings or input of erroneous data values in such computerized records as credit cards, personnel files, inventory files, tax forms, sales, airline reservations, or utility bills. Before accurate and authorized data input can occur, identification, classification, and definition of the data elements involved must be made.

In any organization, data elements (transaction documents, fields, records, files, etc.) represent people, events, assets, objects, and so forth.

All these individual elements provide potential data to be recorded and processed. For example, employees or goods on grocery shelves can be considered data to be captured, input into the system, and processed. It is important that all things processed by the computer be properly represented and uniquely identified.

Codes provide an abbreviated structure for uniquely classifying and identifying items in order to input, communicate, process, and/or retrieve these items. The use of computers has provided a strong impetus to the utilization of codes, especially numerical and bar codes for effective control and processing. Following are several of the more popular coding structures.

1. *Sequential codes* A sequential (or serial) code represents a consecutive assignment of numbers to such items as payroll checks, account numbers, inventory items, purchase orders, employees, and so on. For example, beginning with 0001, consecutive numbers are assigned to employees as they are hired. It is simple to use, it uniquely identifies, it is very useful in many control applications, and it can be used as part of a more specialized code structure. Basic documents such as checks, bonds, purchase orders, sales orders, and invoices should have preprinted sequential numbers. One of the tasks of data control is to account for all key documents, including voided ones, on a regular basis. These documents should be kept outside the computer center and released for processing personnel. After processing, any forms left over should be returned to the proper control area and accounted for. Any forms unaccounted for should be immediately followed up.

2. *Block codes* The block code classifies items into certain groups where blocks of numbers are assigned to particular classifications. The block representing a particular classification must be set up on the basis of an expected maximum utilization of that block. For example, review the block coding structure below.

If a data element is input into the system with a code of 421, it simply means that a typewriter which has been purchased is assigned to the accounting department.

CODE NUMBER \ CODE POSITION	1	2	3
1	DESK	LEASE	ACCOUNTING
2	CHAIR	PURCHASE	MARKETING
3	BOOKCASE	RENTAL	PRODUCTION
4	TYPEWRITER	—	—

Hierarchical block codes are developed on the basis of ascending significance (usually from left to right), i.e., special significance is attached to the location of the numbers within the code. For example, the clearing of checks through the Federal Reserve check clearing system uses a coding system developed by the American Bankers Association. This code uses a combination of standardized magnetic ink characters which include ten digits (0–9) and four special symbols. These characters are printed at the bottom of the check in three specific areas. The transit number code is printed near the left edge of the check. This classification uses eleven characters; four digits for the transit number, four digits for the American Bankers Association number, a separating dash symbol, and a beginning and ending transit number symbol. The next classification represents, in order, the transaction code (deposit or withdrawal) and the customer account number. The right-most characters, which are not part of the coding scheme per se, represent the dollar amount of the check.

The hierarchical scheme is also quite applicable to the area of accounting where the left-most digits represent the account classification. Subsequent digits represent the item identification, its location in the warehouse, user department, and so on.

3. *Bar codes* The different configurations shown in Figure 5.1 are called bar codes. The one at the bottom is used by the grocery industry and is a computer-language representation of the Universal Product Code (UPC), a voluntary ten-digit numbering system developed by the grocery industry to identify grocery manufacturers and their products. The symbols can be easily read by the computer and converted into numbers which represent the code. Therefore, the bars or symbols are not special codes of any kind; they merely represent number codes that we discussed earlier and symbols that can be quickly read by the computer.

Each participating manufacturer is permanently assigned the first five digits as its own number. This number is similar to the sequential code. The last set of digits are nothing more than five numbers that uniquely identify each of a particular manufacturer's products. For example, the manufacturer's number for Kellogg is 38000. Kellogg in turn assigns 01620 for Special K cereal in the 15 oz. box. Similarly, Hunt's tomato paste in the 6-oz. size is 2700038815, 27000 is the manufacturer's unique number, and 38815 is the product's unique number. By changing the bar widths and the spaces between the bars, all variations of products and sizes manufactured can be uniquely identified.

The use of bar codes requires the use of sophisticated equipment connected to a computer system. Items containing the bar code are passed by a laser scanner. (Some systems use a hand-held "wand.") The data are transmitted to the computer. If it is a supermarket application,

LITTON

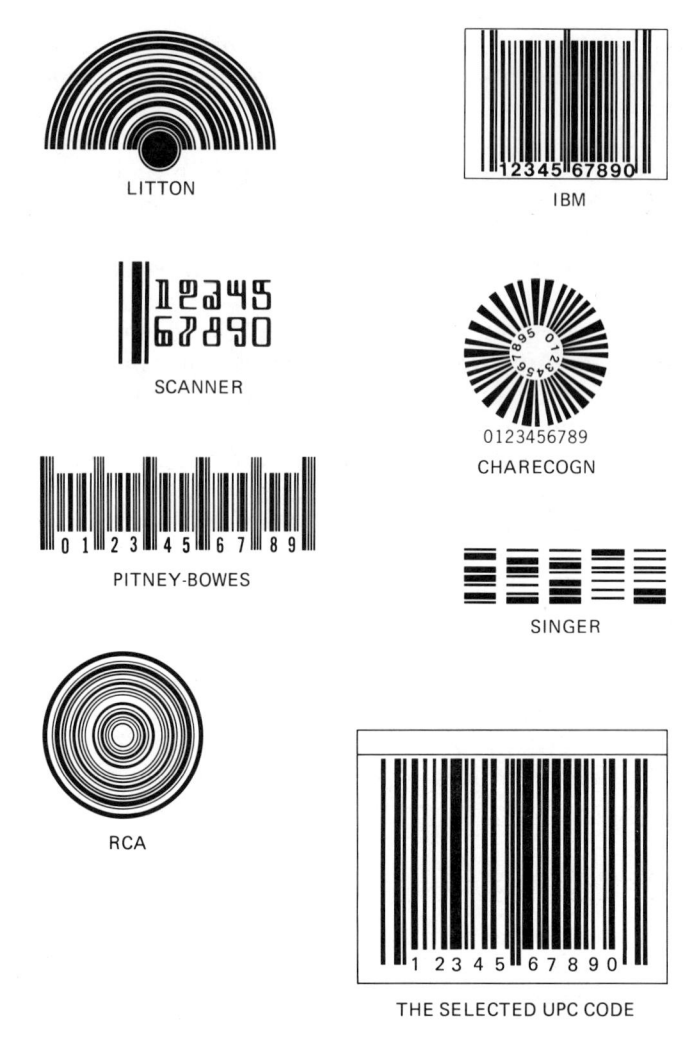

IBM 12345 67890

SCANNER 12345 67890

CHARECOGN 0123456789

PITNEY-BOWES 0 1 2 3 4 5 6 7 8 9

SINGER

RCA

THE SELECTED UPC CODE 1 2 3 4 5 6 7 8 9 0

FIGURE 5.1.
Examples of Bar Codes. (Notice that Some Have Human-Readable Characters Alongside.)

the computer matches the code to the correct price, product type, size, and other data already stored in the computer, where it is displayed on a screen and printed on a receipt at the same time. The process to enter and account for one item takes a split second.

In the grocery industry, this kind of point-of-sale (POS) or point-of-event (POE) system enables users to decrease checkout time; increase inventory control; eliminate price marking and price changing every item (prices along with other data will be stored in the computer system when allowed to do so by consumer law); improve communications between store, warehouse, and manufacturer; improve resource and shelf allocation; reduce the probability of human error, pilferage, and fraud through cash register manipulations; and generally produce a broader range of more timely information to a variety of decision-makers. It should be noted that the concepts associated with data capture through **POS** and **POE** have been attacked by consumer groups. The primary argument seems to be that an unscrupulous manager could alter the price for a given product by merely entering a change into the computer. Customers would then be charged unfairly for a particular product. For this reason, consumer advocates suggest the continued pricing of individual items. We think it unwise to discard such a valuable data capture method.

The typical sales receipt generated by a POS device clearly identifies items by name, and the associated price. (See Figure 5.2.) A consumer always has the option of looking at the sales receipt to determine if any improper transactions occurred. Improved consumer safeguards might be in order, but outlawing the use of **POS** or **POE** will do more harm than good.

There are a large number of other effective applications of bar codes. For example, materials control personnel are using bar-coded labels with scanners in an integrated, online, real-time scheduling production control system. Each representative bar code is attached to specific components and subassemblies and monitored as they pass through

```
           SUPER FOOD MART
             122 HIGH WAY
            ANYWHERE, USA

          STORE 00      03/30/76

          GRO    1.79F   CRISCO
          PRO     .69F   BROCCOLI
          GRO     .67F   V 8 JUICE
          GRX     .57X   NAPKINS
          PRO     .39F   LETTUCE

                  .03    TAX

                 4.14    TOTAL

                 5.00    CASH

                  .86    CHANGE

          0000   14 2    11.31AM
```

LEGEND: F = FOOD STAMPS MAY BE USED
         X = TAXABLE ITEM

FIGURE 5.2.
POS Sales Receipt.

production. These bar code labels also contain alphabetic characters and different colors for human reading and identification. Such a system provides an accurate count and control of materials. Moreover, it provides many timely reports containing assembly line performance, and improved planning, scheduling, control, and tracking information.

Bar code labels are attached to a window on the side of cars to identify authorized staff members for hospital parking lot control systems. Remote scanners are installed to read the bar code label to activate entry and exit gates. Similar to this application is the use of bar codes at toll booths. Bar code labels enable commuters who have purchased a pass to drive in express lanes equipped with scanners. This system can provide real-time input for the generation of up-to-the-minute scheduling and logistics information. Moreover, money is under stricter control. Using manual systems, a number of government employees working at toll booths have embezzled substantial amounts of toll fares. For example, in 1975, several toll booth employees in Florida allegedly embezzled more than $100,000 in a period of months. The use of bar codes would eliminate the exchange of money at the toll booth.

There are an endless number of applications for the bar code. For example libraries can use them for circulation control. The dispensing of valuable resources, such as tools, equipment, office supplies, drugs, and so forth can be more effectively accounted for and controlled using bar codes. We believe they show a great deal of promise, especially in the development of a system of controls.

Input Preparation

The preparation of input documents and transactions should always be handled by some authorized person outside of the computer center, i.e., a person working in the computer center should never be allowed to originate and input a transaction into the system. To help insure proper input preparation, the following procedures should be implemented.

1. All transactions should be coded (approval codes) by an authorized originating department.

2. Where possible, control totals should be prepared by the originating department and follow-up procedures instituted to compare these totals with totals produced by the computer system.

3. Sensitive forms such as passbooks, checks, stockholder registers, etc., should be prenumbered and controlled outside of the computer center.

4. Turnaround documents should be used where possible. Control involves using a machine-prepared document such as a billing statement which, when returned by the customer, is re-input into the system.

Use of these forms helps to eliminate improper changes and transcription errors and facilitates handling.

Input Verification

Input documents prepared by one clerk should be verified or proofread by another when dealing with data that require a high degree of accuracy. In a data conversion operation such as keypunch, key-to-tape, or key-to-disk, each document can be verified by a second operator or in the case of key-to-tape or key-to-disk systems, certain verification controls can be built into the minicomputer and terminals.[1]

Verification is a duplicate operation and, therefore, can substantially increase the cost of data input. To reduce this cost, it may be possible to: (1) verify only critical data fields such as dollar amounts and account numbers, while ignoring such fields as addresses, names, and so forth; (2) prepunch or machine duplicate constant data fields while keypunching only the variable field; and (3) use programming logic to provide verification. It must be clearly understood that verification does not imply the detection of all errors due to transcription. Indeed, errors are reduced, but they are not totally eliminated. In fact, it has been determined that for every 12.5 80-column cards punched and verified, one error will not be detected. See Figure 5.3.

Another important technique used to help verify input is the self-checking digit. This technique should be used for important codes such as: customer account numbers, charge account numbers, product numbers, employee numbers, and so forth. It is imperative that such num-

FIGURE 5.3
Data Collection and Conversion Technology with Representative Error Rates.[2]

Technology	Representative Cost per Kb*	Typical Undetected Errors per Kb
Handwriting	$1.00	1.00
Key-to-paper/card/tape/ disk/processor	$0.50	2.00
Optical scanning	$0.05	0.10
Direct sensing	$0.01	0.01

*Cost per Kb (Kilo-byte, or 1000 characters of data) includes hardware usage charge plus applicable operator costs.

[1] John G. Burch, Jr., and Felix R. Strater, Jr. *Information Systems: Theory and Practice* (Santa Barbara, Calif.: Hamilton Publishing Company, 1974), pp. 436–438.
[2] Chris Mader and Robert Hagin, *Information Systems: Technology, Economics, Applications*, (Chicago: Science Research Associates, Inc., 1974), p. 287.

bers be accurately transcribed and input into the system because they represent the key reference for subsequent processing.

The self-checking digit is generated when the code is initially assigned to a record or document, and, in fact, becomes part of the code itself. It is derived by performing a prescribed arithmetic operation on the code number itself. In subsequent processing, this same arithmetic operation is performed by the computer to insure that the code number has not been incorrectly recorded.[3]

Input Completeness

Input completeness simply means that all input that is supposed to be present and processed is, in fact, present and processed. To help insure that it is, all or a combination of the following controls should be used.

1. *Amount control total*   A selected series of numbers, for example, total of dollar amounts for all invoices, are summed. This total is recorded in the billing department. When the invoices are prepared for computer processing, the same figures are totaled. If this total is not equal to the total prepared by the billing department, the probability is that a document(s) has been lost, or some error has occurred. The control total is an efficient check when it is used to predetermine the results of calculations or the updating of a record. For example, when a payroll is to be processed, the total number of hours worked by all employees is predetermined from time clock or job-card records. This figure becomes the control total for payroll hours for all subsequent reports. Control totals are normally established for batches of convenient size, such as department, location, account, or division. When this approach is used, each batch of records may be balanced as it is processed. Corrective action, if needed, can be applied to small, easily checked batches rather than to one grand total.

2. *Record count control total*   This control simply involves adding up all input documents and having the computer do the same. If, for example, 1,000 time cards are to be processed, and only 999 are, then one time card has been lost. Similarly, if 1,000 time cards are supposed to be processed and, in fact, 1,010 are processed, further investigation is recommended. After records have been counted, the total number of records is carried as a control total at the end or the beginning of the file and is changed whenever records are added or deleted. Each time the file is processed, the records are recounted, and this new total is balanced against the original or adjusted total. If the recount agrees with

---

[3]For more information on self-checking digits, see Dr. Lane K. Anderson, et al., "Self-Checking Digit Concepts," *Journal of Systems Management*, September 1974, pp. 36–42.

the control total, it is accepted as proof that all records have been processed. Although the record count is useful as a proof of processing, it is difficult to determine the cause of error if the controls are out of balance. A failure to balance does not help to locate a missing record, nor does it indicate which record has been processed more than once. Therefore, some provision must be made to check the file against the source records, or a duplicate file of records may be maintained for comparison purposes. Still, the other control totals discussed here, when combined with record counts, provide a strong check to insure that all required data are received for processing and that all data leaving the system are complete.

3. *Line control counts* This control is applied where line items represent an important measure of volume.

4. *Hash control total* This control is applied to meaningless nonmonetary amounts. It is used for basically the same reason as document control totals; however, it adds an extra control feature, because no one in the computer center knows for sure what items are being added. For example, in payroll, it could be the numeric addition of employee numbers, social security numbers, or department numbers.

5. *Batch control total* This control is the same as an amount control total except the total applies to a specific batch or group of input documents.

6. *Batch serial numbers* Batches of input documents are numbered and accounted for consecutively, the same as in any numbering system (e.g., tickets, passbooks, payroll checks).

One large company established a control office known as the payroll bureau to prevent fraudulent or inaccurate processing by the computer center. All changes in payroll data, such as rate changes, new employees hired, terminations, and changes in 25 types of pay deductions, are routed through the payroll bureau. The changes are indicated on an authorization form prepared in duplicate in the originating department.

The original approved copy of this document is forwarded to the payroll bureau, where the change authorization forms are grouped by type of pay data affected. Adding-machine totals of numeric fields are accumulated, regardless of whether these fields represent dollar information or identification; in the case of new employees or terminations, the number of employees affected is also included in these control totals. Cards are then punched and key-verified for input to the computer.

The totals of the changes are accumulated weekly from the cards on a conventional punched-card accounting machine. These totals are checked with the adding-machine totals previously prepared. During one of the computer runs, normal pay and pay deductions are calculated. This sum is sent to the payroll bureau, where the totals are compared with those previously recorded. This control over payroll changes

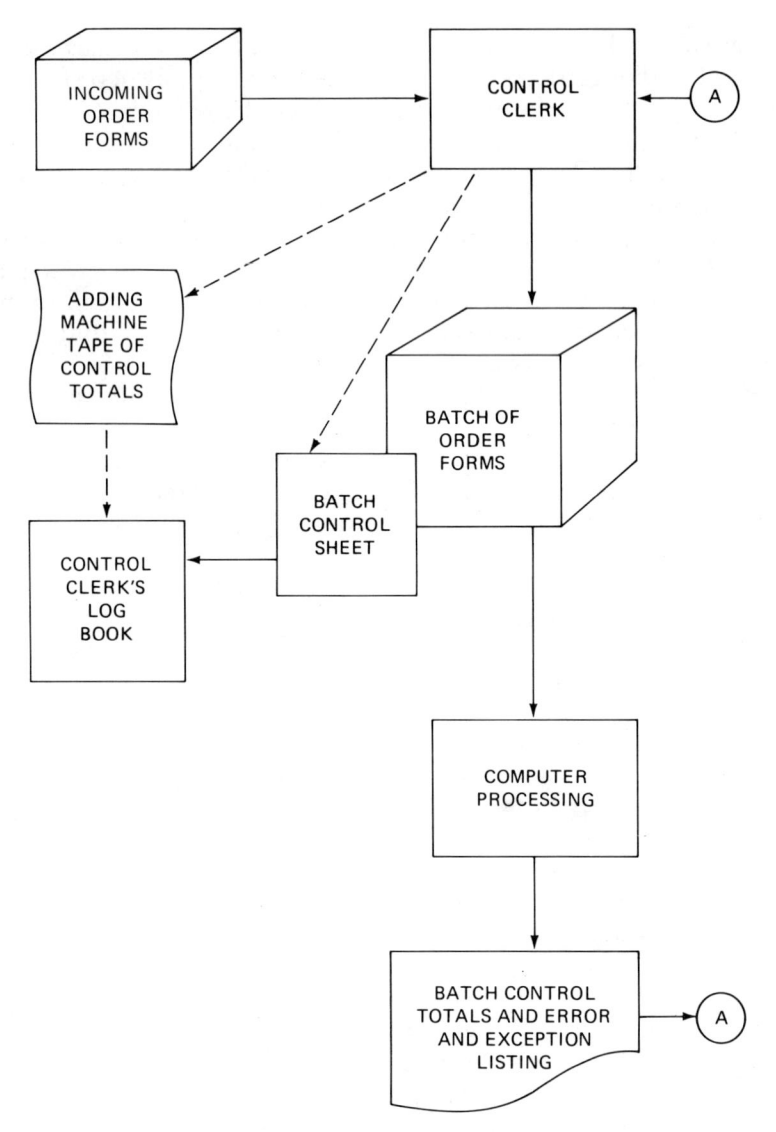

FIGURE 5.4.
Example of Controlling Batch Input by Control Totals.

not only incidentally checks the operation of the computer center's data processing system but also checks the clerical handling and accumulation of data as they enter the system.[4]

[4]*Introduction to IBM Data Processing Systems* (Poughkeepsie, N.Y.: IBM Corporation, Pub. No. GC20-1684-2), p. 97.

An example of how orders are handled in a typical batch processing order entry system follows. A data control clerk(s) is assigned the task of batching incoming orders, as shown in Figure 5.4. The control clerk divides incoming orders into manageable batches of a hundred or more. The control clerk then assigns a batch control number to the batch control sheet. Using an adding machine, the clerk adds up the desired elements in the batch of orders. The elements used are generally money fields, units ordered, number of orders, and customer numbers for a hash total. All of this control data plus a batch control number, date, and time of day are recorded in the control clerk's log book. The batch control sheet accompanying the batch of order forms should contain a batch number and any other identification data necessary. It should not, however, contain any control totals. Only the control clerk should know what the resulting control totals should be. The batch control sheet with a printout of batch control totals prepared by the computer plus any errors and exceptional conditions detected should be returned to the control clerk immediately after processing for comparison. Any errors are corrected by the control clerk. All exceptional conditions (e.g., customer over credit limit) are investigated and followed up.

The design of the batch control sheet is relatively simple. It should be a different color than the batch of input order forms it is controlling. Entries in this form should include the batch number (NNN), the date (DD/MM/YY), the time of day (HH:MM), and the number of input forms. Also on the batch control sheet should be a name (e.g., "order forms") for the input transactions being controlled, and any other documentation necessary. The control clerk should sign or initial his name and include his telephone extension number in each batch control sheet.

5.3 OPERATING SYSTEM CONTROLS

The auditor should have a basic understanding of the logical sequence of events that impact upon a user program. The primary interaction is between the user program and the operating system. In an attempt to acquaint the auditor with operating systems, the following operational descriptions are provided. The following operational procedures for operating systems are based upon conventions utilized by IBM. Most of the processing concepts are similar among the various mainframe manufacturers.

Operating System Processing

From the moment a source deck is read into a computer via the card reader until the output has finished printing, a series of integrated programs known as the operating system consistently interacts with the user program. The operating system is an integrated package of highly sophisticated and extremely complex programs. For example, a standard application program generally requires 140,000 bytes of core storage. Many large operating systems require approximately 1 million bytes or more of core storage. The operating system is perhaps the most powerful software package utilized by the computer.

The operating system controls the entire operation of the computer hardware and maintains control of all operations that occur within the machine. From an auditor's standpoint, it must be remembered that the operating system has the capability to suppress computer logs, insert modules in programs, bypass security routines, and modify computer audit packages. Indeed, properly modified, the operating system could render computer audit packages ineffective and still give the auditors the impression that the computer audit package is operating properly.

Generally, the procedure which an application program follows is straightforward. The source deck is read into the computer. The compiler is called and, after preprocessing, the source deck is translated into object code. The linkage editor or loader is invoked, and all unresolved external references are resolved. In addition, other load modules may be incorporated into the active load module. The load module is loaded into main memory, and execution begins. If the program needs data, an interrupt is caused, and service requested. The program then goes into a wait state.

While the program is waiting, the supervisor sets up a channel to the mass storage device where the data are according to the information on the Data Definition (DD) cards which is part of the Job Control Language (JCL). When the data have been located, they are moved into a buffer in core storage. The program is then notified that the data are available, and it returns to the execution state and accesses the data from the buffer. When the program is terminated, the output generated by the program is routed to an output device. Each of the steps described above will be discussed in detail.

A logical question is, why have no audit procedures been developed which could test the operating system? The primary reasons would have to include the extreme complexity and formidable size of the system itself. In addition, operating systems are generally written in a lower-level language, such as assembly language, which is more detailed than a high-level language such as COBOL or PL/1. Thus, it could be very difficult to comprehend.

Although no software packages have been specifically designed to audit the operating system, there are tools within the operating system itself which will assist the auditor in the conduct of an audit. It behooves the auditor to learn the tools that are discussed below and acquaint himself with the procedures for their proper utilization.

The processing phase involves a series of technical subfunctions. An auditor should have a working knowledge of the operations performed by each of the subfunctions, as well as the logical sequence in which these subfunctions are executed.

Applications Programs

An application program is a series of statements written in a programming language such as COBOL, PL/1, or FORTRAN. The program itself is generally designed to perform a task or solve a problem based upon an algorithm that has been conceived. Uncontrolled, programs may be designed to perform tasks that are fraudulent. Tight internal control must be present to insure the integrity of computer programs.

The operating system is clearly more complex and generally more powerful than an application program. The application programmer has the greatest potential, however, to create a disaster, intentionally or unintentionally, primarily because he or she understands computer technology, and, what is even more important, is intimately involved with the application. For example, there are many instances in which application programmers have written programs that perform tasks not in accordance with generally accepted accounting principles, unintentionally or intentionally.

Compile Time—Language Translation

Compile time may be generally defined as the time when a user's source program is translated into an executable object program. Ordinarily, changes may not be made to the source program at this time. With a programming language such as PL/1, however, the programmer does have some control over the source program at compile time.

PREPROCESSOR STAGE

During the preprocessor stage, the programmer can effectively perform three functions with regard to the source program before it is translated into the object module: (1) Any identifier appearing in the source program may be altered in part or in whole; this implies that the programmer may change the name of any variable that appears in the source listing. To the auditor, it means that any variable that he sees in a source listing may, in fact, not be the variable that is being used in the object module. (2) A conditional compilation may be requested, which would permit the programmer to identify those portions of the program that will not be compiled during language translation. To the auditor, this means that if a section of the source program contains a module that performs an audit function, the programmer could effectively deactivate that section by not including it in the object module simply by specifying that the audit section not be translated. (3) Strings of text residing in a user library or a system library may be incorporated into the source program so that they are translated into object code and become a fully operational segment of the translated program. To the auditor, this means that a programmer may include modules, in whole or in part, that perform any function that the programmer has determined to be necessary.

PROCESSOR STAGE

During the processor stage, the output from the preprocessor stage is compiled (translated) into an object module. The compiler may be considered to be a translator. Computers execute object code. Object code is very difficult for humans to utilize efficiently and easily. Therefore, programming languages, such as PL/1, or COBOL, have been developed so that humans can easily interact with the computer. The compiler translates the statements written in PL/1 or COBOL into object code, which is machine-readable. The object code is generally referred to as an object module, or if punched on cards, it is known as an object deck.

Language translators and service programs are essentially no different from other application programs. Therefore, there should be no mystery concerning language translators; they are simply programs, generally written in assembly language, which translate source programs written in a higher-level language such as PL/1 or COBOL into object code. Each of the language translators (COBOL, PL/1, and so on) generally produces object modules in a standard format. This generally permits the linkage editor to combine portions of a user program written in one language with portions of the same program written in another language. The result is a single program which is ready to be loaded into main storage for proper execution.

Linkage Editor

The work of the linkage editor is a necessary step that follows the source program translation of any problem-stage program. One of the major functions of the linkage editor is the resolution of all unresolved external references. The cross references between control sections in modules are obtained from an external symbol dictionary. In order to make these sections known to the present load module, the linkage editor calculates the new address of each expression in a control section. For example, an unresolved external reference may be a subroutine which the object module requires to perform some statistical task. Many statistical and other operations have already been programmed by IBM, and are located in IBM's Scientific Subroutine Package (SSP). The SSP is a collection of mathematical and statistical subroutines. It consists of input/output-free computational building blocks which may be applied to the solution of many problems in business, science, and engineering.

A programmer who wanted to calculate means, standard deviations, and correlations may perform all these operations without having to program the logic. CORRE is the name of a subroutine that has already been written and is a module of IBM's SSP. CORRE has been designed to calculate means, standard deviations, and correlations. The programmer need only CALL CORRE and all desired operations would be performed. When the source program is compiled, the CALL CORRE is considered an unresolved external reference. That implies that CORRE is a module that is external to the source program, and the operating system must find it and add the module to the source program. That action would "resolve" the external reference.

During link edit, the appropriate mass storage device, generally a disk, is scanned for the proper subroutine (CORRE). When the subroutine has been located, it is included in the object module. However, the programmer can override the standard search procedure by utilizing a JOBLIB or STEPLIB card. The JOBLIB or STEPLIB cards are Job Control Language statements that direct the system to search for a given module in a private library. The module stored in the private library may have any name assigned to it. The auditor should be acutely aware of the potential dangers associated with JOBLIB or STEPLIB cards. For example, an unauthorized module might be included in the job by utilizing the JOBLIB or STEPLIB capabilities. The unauthorized module could perform any task, fraudulent or not, and be easily removed by deleting the JOBLIB or STEPLIB cards.

The auditor should also be aware of the LET and NCAL options available during link edit. Among other capabilities, LET will mark a load module executable even if there are unresolved external references or a library module cannot be found. NCAL suppresses the "calling" of library members to resolve external references. The module is also marked executable. Clearly, auditors must consider the possibility that modules may not be included in the active load module and execution will still occur. The excluded module may be part of an audit procedure, or be an entire audit package.

When all unresolved external references have been resolved, which implies that all subroutines have been attached to the object module, or LET or NCAL has been invoked, this series of instructions is now called a load module. Generally, if no syntactic errors are detected after compilation, no logic errors exist within the program, and all necessary data are available and correct, the load module will be successfully executed.

A potential problem for the auditor is the fact that fraudulent tasks may be included in the program in the same manner. The programmer need only CALL the fraudulent module, and it will be included in the load module, and no listing of that subroutine will appear on the printout; only the CALL will appear.

The linkage editor performs many other tasks, e.g., it assigns storage hierarchies as directed by the control statements, and perhaps most important to auditors, it traces the processing history of a program.

Tracing the processing history of a program is simplified by the Control Section (CSECT) Identification records that are created and maintained by the linkage editor. A CSECT Identification record may contain data that describe: (1) the language translator utilized, its level, and the translation date for each control section; (2) the most recent processing performed by the linkage editor; and (3) modifications made to the executable code of any control section.

The processing history component of the linkage editor could be useful to the auditor. In effect, a form of internal control (within the computer) is automatic. Information that may assist the auditor to determine the last translation date of a given module may be helpful when determining whether a given module has been recompiled with authorization and why.

Supervisor

The supervisor provides resources that a problem-state program may need. The resources are allocated in such a manner as to maximize the efficient utilization of those resources. After a load module has been produced, the control program automatically brings it into main storage. If a program requires data, an interrupt is generated. The program then goes into a wait state. The program status word (PSW) is modified to indicate the wait state. The PSW contains the information required for proper program execution. The PSW is comprised of the instruction address, condition code, and other relevant fields. Generally, the PSW controls the sequencing of instructions and indicates the status of the system in relation to the currently executing program.

The control program then tries to access the device that contains the data the program is requesting. When the device has been located, the data are moved into a buffer. When the data are in the buffer, the PSW is modified so that the control program knows that the program in the wait state can now continue executing.

Upon termination of execution, the output is routed to the proper output device. Generally, this device is a printer. When the program has finished printing, the system is free of that particular program.

Observations Regarding Operating Systems

Improper modifications to operating systems may seriously impair processing. Discussions with individuals in accounting firms affirm that the unauthorized or improper changes to the operating system could deactivate their generalized audit software packages.

The pervasive power and vulnerability of the operating system are unquestionable. The auditor has at his disposal some knowledge and tools which will be of value during the performance of an audit, however. The use of JOBLIB or STEPLIB job control language statements should be scrutinized. Further, the LET and NCAL options could be improperly employed and highly desired portions of production programs deactivated as a result. The auditor can utilize the information in the Control Section (CSECT) Identification records as an effective tool to ascertain specific information pertaining to a specific program. Last, the auditor should require the utilization of a software package similar to IBM's System Modification Program (SMP).

SMP performs functions not unlike the capabilities of library packages. For example, SMP will create or update a control data set, verify and check program temporary fixes or user modifications, and put modifications into the operating system libraries. Most important to auditors is the generation of a log that places a time and date record of a change made to the operating system.[5] This audit trail will permit auditors the opportunity to determine when changes were made to the system. This knowledge, in conjunction with the auditor's understanding of the formal procedures required for a change to the operating system, will permit the auditor to more carefully scrutinize the operating system.

Thus far, the operating system has been presented as a highly powerful and vulnerable software package. The auditor, however, does have some salvation. The operating system is prepared by a vendor, generally the same vendor who manufactured the central processing unit. It would be proper to assume that the vendor supplying the operating system is not trying to gain access to the user's assets, or other sensitive information. In effect, there is a third-party nonconflict of interest situation.

Another factor in the auditor's favor is the fact that systems programmers are generally very knowledgeable in the area of systems programming. They generally lack knowledge concerning the business environment, however. A systems programmer may know "how" to make the computer do just about anything, but he doesn't know "what" to do.

---

[5]OS/VS System Modification Program (SMP) Logic, International Business Machines, Pub. SY28-0685-1, Sept. 1974. Also see OS/VS System Modification Program (SMP), GC28-0673, and SMP Reference Summary, GX28-0684.

Therefore, unless the systems programmer is well versed in the area of business, he or she may not be as great a threat as is sometimes perceived.

A final factor of benefit to the auditor is the trend toward the hardwiring of operating systems. The utilization of microcode will prevent individuals from modifying the operating system, since modifications require the replacement of firmware. The hardwired components will be available only from the vendor of the central processing unit.

The performance and productivity of a total system are clearly functions of the interaction of people, hardware, software, and data base. The operating system is designed to maximize the effectiveness of these resources and thus to improve performance and increase productivity.

Improper modifications to operating systems may seriously impair processing or result in performance of unauthorized operations.

In an effort to prevent such improper modifications, we suggest the utilization of a software package similar to SMP when updating the operating system. SMP will perform functions not unlike the capabilities of library packages. For example, if a change is made to the operating system, SMP will maintain a log of all updates to the system. This log will permit the auditor to verify any and all changes made to the operating system.

5.4 PROCESSING CONTROLS

Processing controls consist of a variety of techniques incorporated within application programs to help insure that only correct or valid data are being processed as prescribed by accounting and systems regulations. These controls are divided into two groups: (1) edit checks, and (2) program operating controls.

Edit Checks

Edit checks screen out undetected errors caused by omissions, invalid entries, and various inaccuracies. These checks are listed as follows:

1. *Numeric, alphabetic, and special character checks* These checks simply guard against the entry into processing of incorrect characters. For example, all department numbers are made up of digits, e.g., 12345. If, for some reason, a clerk transcribed a department number as 123B5, a numeric check would detect the mistake before processing was performed. Another example would be in handling customer names where JONES is input as JON75 or JO$ES. An alphabetic check would detect this error. And so forth.

2. *Sign checks* In a computer system there are three different sign conditions, positive, negative, and no sign. If the results of an arithmetic operation are negative, in some computer systems, without proper editing, this value would be converted to a no sign which, during further operations, would be converted to a positive value. With COBOL, for example, a PICTURE clause of 999V99 would not account for a negative value; but if this PICTURE were edited as S999V99, it would.

3. *Validity checks* Checks are made against predetermined transaction codes, tables, or other data to insure that input data are valid. For example, a table of valid vendors that the company does business with is set up on magnetic disk file under tight control. Every time a payment is made to a vendor, the number of the vendor must match a number in the table of valid vendors. This validity control helps to reduce the probability that payments will be made to bogus vendors. A code of 21 is assigned to Preventive Maintenance for all recording, processing, and recording purposes. If one or several time card codes from Preventive Maintenance did not agree with this predetermined code, then an error would be displayed and appropriate action be taken to correct this error. Another example would be where a chart of accounts may designate Current Assets with a number range of 100-199, where Cash is 100. If cash receipts are being processed, all cash credits or debits must contain the identifier number 100. Certain combinations of transactions are valid, and others are not. Some typical combinations are: (a) cash sales transaction debits cash account and credits sales account; (b) sales transaction debits accounts receivable and/or cash accounts and credits sales account; (c) purchase transaction debits inventory account and credits accounts payable and/or cash accounts. In limiting the number of transaction combinations, illogical combinations of valid account codes are rejected and deleted from the system. For example, a transaction coded as a debit to office expense and a credit to sales would be rejected by the system because of its illogical combination, and an error message would be displayed for corrective action. Let us assume, as a last example, that all warehouses that handle steel stock and pipe, code transfers with the number 74. If all issue and receipts transactions of steel and pipe inventory do not have the warehouse coded with the number 74, then either the transaction is being entered in the wrong location or there is a keying error.

4. *Limit and reasonableness checks* This control check is used to identify data having a value higher or lower than a predetermined limit. These standard high/low limits are determined and established before processing. This control detects only those data elements that fall outside these established limits. Examples of how this technique can be used are: (1) no employee can make over $999.99 per week; (2) no employee can work over 60 hours per week; (3) if the highest account num-

ber in a customer master file is 5897, but CUSTOMER-NUMBER 6582 is read, then CUSTOMER-NUMBER of this particular record is in error, or worse, a wrong file may have been mounted; (4) all customers with code of 3 cannot purchase any order over $1,000 on credit; (5) bank withdrawals from depositors' accounts over $2,500 need additional approval; (6) an exception notice is displayed if a customer order exceeds twice their average order; and (7) check for absence of pay for regular hours worked when sick pay is being paid. Another example is a data check of input records to insure that the record date is acceptable. The date is carried on records in various formats, such as YYMMDD, two digits for year, month, and day, respectively, or DDMMYY is often used. Calculations can be made that verify that the day is between 01 and 31, the month between 01 and 12, and the year is equal to the actual year. Also, limits are checked for dates in the future or in the past. A decision is made as to how far in the future a record may be dated, or how late the record may be on entering the system. An arbitrary length of time may be used, such as five days, thirty-one days, three months, or six months, in either direction. If these limits are exceeded, an error message is displayed for investigation and corrective action.

5. *Sequence checks* Files are often arranged in ascending or descending sequence, e.g., by employee number, account number, part number, and so forth. Instructions written in the processing program compare the sequential field in each record or transaction with the sequenced field of the preceding record or transaction. With this technique, any out of sequence record can be detected and the file will not be processed incorrectly. Typical reasons for occurrence of an out-of-sequence error are: (1) use of an incorrect file, (2) failure to perform a required sorting operation, (3) hardware malfunctions, and/or (4) incorrect merge operation.

6. *Arithmetic checks* Various computational routines can be designed into processing programs to validate the result of other computations, or the value of selected data fields. One method of arithmetic proof called crossfooting adds or subtracts two or more fields and zero balances this result against the original result. This control technique is applicable where total debits, total credits, and a balance forward amount are maintained for each account. For example, in the cash account, if the total debits equal $5,000 and the total credits equal $4,000, then the balance of cash should equal $1,000. Or during the processing of employee records in a payroll, calculations develop amounts of gross pay, taxes, deductions, and net pay. Normally, these amounts are accumulated by department or other convenient batch controls. The totals of gross pay at any point should be equal to the totals of net pay, deductions, and taxes. Other examples of the use of arithmetic checks are: (1) by division verification, in the first operation, 6/2 equals 3, then in an

arithmetic proof routine multiply the result by the divisor to see if this result equals the dividend, 3 × 2 equals 6; (2) if fairly homogeneous items such as steel or grain are shipped to a customer, the billable amount can be checked for appropriate accuracy. The average price for all steel stock may be $0.10 per pound. This rate is multiplied by the total weight of the shipment to derive an approximated billable amount. If this amount is, say, not within three percent of the billed amount, then a message is displayed for subsequent investigation to determine whether the billed amount is actually in error.

7. *Self-checking digit* When an account number is assigned to an individual, a self-checking digit is prepared by using an arithmetic operation and appended to the account number. Every time this account number is input for processing, the same calculation is performed by the computer. If the derived digit does not equal the one input into the system, then an error has occurred. A large number of methods are used to derive self-checking digits. A popular one is modulus 11 with prime number weighting. For example, if this method were used, a self-checking digit for account number 12314 would be calculated as follows:

Account number:	1	2	3	1	4
	×	×	×	×	×
Prime number weights:	17	13	7	5	3
Results of multiplication:	17	26	21	5	12

Add results of multiplication: 17 + 26 + 21 + 5 + 12 = 81
Subtract 81 from next higher multiple of 11, 88 − 81 = 7
Account number with appended self-checking digit is 12314 − 7.

8. *Overflow checks* This control technique guards against losing digits if an overflow condition arises during processing. For example, in COBOL, if a value of 1000.09 is moved to a PICTURE clause of 999V9, the result is 000.0, or plain zero. To prevent this kind of error from occurring, the ON SIZE ERROR option should be included in all arithmetic operations.

9. *Label checks* The header label, which includes at least file name, date created, and retention date, should be checked before processing begins. After processing, the trailer label, which includes at least a block count, record count, hash count, and end-of-reel or end-of-file condition, should be checked. Although tapes may have both a header and a trailer label located before and after the file data, respectively, disk labels can appear anywhere on the disk volume, as long as the user specifies where it is located.

10. *Control totals* All of the control totals, e.g., amount control totals, record counts, hash control totals, are calculated during processing and the results written out and returned to the originating department or a control clerk.

11. *Run-to-run total checks* Like links in a chain, this technique uses output control totals resulting from one process to establish input control totals over subsequent processing.

Program Operating Controls

In addition to routine processing and edit checks, there should also be other operating instructions in the programs. The programs should contain routines to display to the appropriate recipient all exceptional and error conditions resulting from all of the edit checks in addition to any error or invalid condition that gets through the edit screen. For example, a valid account number may be input, but for some reason it is not on the master file.

Besides the printing out of errors and invalid conditions, what else should the program do under different error conditions? Normally the system should continue to operate without interruption, and any error conditions should be written on an error file for subsequent correction. Only in rare circumstances would the program halt the job stream. Normally halts would occur in cases where subsequent corrections are impossible, for example, when a label check doesn't match which would indicate that a wrong file has been mounted. Instructions should be displayed to the operator as to what to do when these halts occur.

Another very important program operating control is referred to as checkpoint and restart procedures. A checkpoint procedure is a programmed checking routine performed at specific processing intervals or checkpoints. Its purpose is to determine that processing has been performed correctly up to some designated point. If processing is correct, the status of the job is recorded from core storage, usually by writing (dump, copied, taking a snapshot, etc.) this information on magnetic tape or disk. The normal processing of the job continues until the next checkpoint is reached.

Checkpoint procedures have the effect of breaking up a long job into a series of small ones. For example, the computer system is dedicated for long periods of time processing demand deposit accounting or a big payroll job. Defined smaller portions of the big job are run as a separate and independent part, and each part is checked after it is completed. If the check is correct, enough information is copied on magnetic tape or disk to make it possible to return to this last checkpoint with little difficulty if an error or breakdown occurs. The operator simply writes back into the computer, thus duplicating what existed at the previous checkpoint.

The restart procedure works as follows: (1) the operator backs up the entire computer system to the specified checkpoint in the job (e.g., tape files are backspaced or rewound, card limits and printers are manually adjusted); and (2) the computer storage is restored to its status at the preceding checkpoint; this process may include adjustment of accumulated totals, reloading the program itself, reestablishing switches and counters, restoring constant factors, and so forth.

The proper use of checkpoint and restart procedures in a program contributes to the overall operating efficiency of a computer system. If power failure or serious equipment malfunction occurs, these procedures provide a way of rerunning only a small part of a job without having to rework an entire job. Application of checkpoint and restart procedures may mean a saving of many equipment hours and much overtime pay.

Restart procedures also allow interruption of one job for the scheduling of other jobs that need immediate or emergency attention. Thus, any job may be interrupted intentionally by the operator and replaced with another job when necessary. Provision for restart is also convenient at the end of a shift or other work period when the operation of a job must be terminated without loss of production time. Finally, restart procedures provide interruption of computer operation for emergency repairs or unscheduled maintenance.[6]

5.5 APPLICATION PROGRAM CONTROLS

The need for program controls is obvious when one considers that the various software routines contain the processing and operating procedures for a significant portion of the activities carried out by an organization. Program controls consist of: (1) program development, (2) program documentation, (3) program changes, and (4) program aids.

Program Development

Programs in some organizations grow in a very haphazard manner. Programmers often follow no well-defined development methodology. Some try to start coding before the objectives are well understood, others tell systems analysts that they can do something when they aren't really sure what is needed, and so forth. The program development methodology that should be followed is outlined below.

1. *Logic design* Before any attempt to write program instructions is made, detail logic of the system to be programmed must be understood by the programmer and accepted by the user. This program logic is

---

[6]*Introduction to IBM Data Processing Systems, op. cit.*, p. 100.

usually prepared with the use of flowcharts, layout charts, and decision tables. This logic could also follow a top-down structured approach, as discussed in the previous chapter.

2. *Coding* The programmer must convert the logic prepared in the flow diagrams into the appropriate syntactic requirements of a programming language. The programming language most widely used for business purposes is COBOL. The programmer selects the appropriate program instructions and places them in logical sequence according to the logic described in the flowchart. When the logic has been coded then the program must be tested for both syntactic and logic errors.

3. *Testing* Difficult as it is to believe, some programmers spend little time testing their programs. And, when the programs are tested, the testing is usually performed with a high degree of programmer bias. The program is generally tested to see whether the error routines built into the program function properly. The implicit, and erroneous, assumption is that no other conditions are possible. Consequently, what will work under certain conditions won't work under others. When this happens, disruption of processing results. Mistakes by the programmer are more difficult to avoid than might be expected. It is, in fact, a rare program that works correctly the first time it is tried with test data. In most cases, several test runs must be made before all mistakes are found and corrected. The program compiler itself finds most of the obvious mistakes during compilation. After successful compilation, however, the real test is to make sure that the program does not have logical errors and that it is capable of producing correct output. Management should require that the programmer thoroughly test his program, and then someone other than the one who wrote the program should test it before placing the program in operation.

4. *Implementing* After the first three steps have been completed, the JCL (job control language that acts as an interface between the program and the computer) is prepared, and the program is turned over to the operations group for production.

5. *Cataloging* The last step in the development cycle is to catalog the program in the library under tight control. No access and change to the program should be permitted without proper authorization.

Program Documentation

Program documentation serves as a reference that describes all aspects of a particular program. Minimum documentation should include the following.

1. *Narrative description* This description provides a broad overview of what the program does and what its purpose is.

2. *Identification number and name*   This designation is simply for program identification purposes; it provides a way to retrieve the program from the library.

3. *Program logic*   Includes all flowcharts (systems, macro, and micro) plus decision tables, if used.

4. *Program listings*   This listing is a duplicate copy of all the instructions used by the programmer in coding the program.

5. *Date of testing and final approval*   In addition, the names of the person who tested and the person who approved the testing should be included.

6. *Test deck*   A deck or listing of the test transactions should be included in the documentation package.

7. *File and record layouts*   These forms specifically describe all the input and output.

8. *Operating instructions*   These instructions are displayed to the computer operator, for example, "MOUNT A/R MASTER FILE."

9. *Output distribution instructions*   These instructions tell the operating personnel just who is authorized to receive various reports.

10. *Self-documented program*   It is, perhaps, most important that a program be written in a manner that permits ease of understanding; that is, variable names that have a logical relationship to the data that are being manipulated should be used. It is easier to understand AC-COUNTS-RECEIVABLE as a variable name than it would be to understand X43J1B. Also, a liberal use of NOTES at strategic points in the same listing is a helpful documentation aid.

Program Changes

Unauthorized program changes represent one of the most significant threats to the computer-based information system. However, from time to time programs must be changed to meet the diverse needs of systems users. It is imperative that any change to a program be made in accordance with strict procedures for approval of program changes and supervision of changes, if they are approved. If authorized changes are made to programs, the programs must be tested to make sure that the program does what it is supposed to do. Deviation from this procedure may result in errors, as New York State learned.

> The computer programmer responsible for the Lottery's programming had to make several changes to the existing computer program to properly consider the reduction in the number of tickets from five million tickets to only four million tickets. The computer programmer made certain assumptions about the computer files which subsequently proved to be incorrect and he did not adequately test the

changes to the computer program. The programmer also informed us that the EDP Section does not retain testing data. Therefore we could not determine if the computer program used to print tickets for the Colossus Halloween Special drawing was actually tested. Furthermore, changes to the computer program were not reviewed by the Director of the EDP Section who is responsible for the supervision of the computer programmers. Accepted EDP standards and procedures require that adequate testing of new computer programs and program changes be done and that an independent supervisor review and approve the changes.[7]

The discovery that lottery tickets for the Colossus Halloween Special had been printed incorrectly was the main reason that the governor of New York suspended all lottery operations in 1975. The auditors' review of computer operations showed that there had been inadequate supervision over computer program changes and new computer programs. The review also showed that there was a lack of quality control techniques that resulted in the printing, distribution, and sale of some lottery tickets that had duplicate and erroneous ticket numbers.

The inadequacy of the computer program-testing procedures and lack of supervisory controls by the EDP Section also caused the printing of one million erroneous tickets for a proposed Christmas Holiday Special because the same basic computer program was used for both the Christmas Special and the Colossus Halloween Special. The Christmas tickets were never distributed and were eventually destroyed.

Program Aids

Aids that not only help to increase the efficiency of the programming function, but also increase controls are listed below.

1. *Shorthand* These aids help to reduce cumbersome and verbose characteristics included in high-level programming languages, such as COBOL. For example, rather than writing PICTURE each time, the programmer can write PIC, and W-S stands for WORKING-STORAGE SECTION, and so forth.

2. *Decision tables* Decision tables support modular program design and help to make the program logic clear to users and maintenance programmers. In addition, there are decision table preprocessors which provide a means for automatically converting decision tables into source code. This aid not only helps reduce errors, but also reduces coding by 30 or more percent.[8]

---

[7]*Special Audit Report on the Financial and Operating Practices of the Racing and Wagering Board, Division of the Lottery* (Albany, N.Y.: Office of the State Comptroller, Division of Audits and Accounts, Report No. AL-St-3576, Nov. 14, 1975), p. 11.

[8]R. N. Dean. "A Comparison of Decision Tables Against Conventional COBOL as a Programming Tool for Commercial Applications," *Software World*, Spring 1971, pp. 26–30. "COBOL Aid Packages," *EDP Analyzer*, May 1972.

3. *Test data generators* It is difficult to manually prepare a comprehensive series of test transactions that include a sufficient combination of test conditions. Test data generators, which are computer driven, can produce an infinite number of combinations and permutations of test conditions. and, thereby, substantially aid testing.

4. *Librarian* Programs should never be stored in the computer center using card decks. These program decks can be changed easily, and imagine what would happen if several cards were lost or stolen. Librarian packages get rid of programs and decks by storing programs on magnetic tape or disk. This aid provides better controls by indicating status of program (e.g., test or active state), library control codes, directory system, and reports of who has used what programs. Program maintenance is more easily performed because documentation is better. Moreover, librarians help save storage by compressing data to a 3 to 1 or better ratio, e.g., no blanks are stored.

> ... control over unauthorized ticket printing should be established both by appropriate stock control and by keeping critical programs on magnetic tapes and/or disks which are removed by the lottery from the computer room when not in planned use.[9]

Librarian packages should not be restricted to application program use. Software packages have been developed to aid in the handling of the highly vulnerable operating system. The System Modification Program (SMP) was developed by IBM to "log" or journalize any changes made to the operating system on an IBM machine. In effect, it generates an audit trail which IBM's engineers could analyze if the system should fail. In addition, SMP would prevent improper updating to the operating system. For example, if a given change is put on the system, an earlier change cannot be placed on the system if it would deactivate the new change.

The ability to trace all changes to the operating system is one that an auditor could use to see whether any unauthorized changes had been made to the operating system. Internal auditors have revealed much apprehension in regard to the potential modification of operating systems by unscrupulous programmers.

SMP, or its equivalent, is a highly technical tool, one that requires substantial knowledge of systems programming. However, an auditor could require that SMP be utilized by systems programmers as standard procedure. Should any questions arise, the auditor could then contact an EDP specialist.

The use of a package similar to SMP will improve internal control within the computer. Although SMP was not specifically designed for

---

[9]*Summary of Findings New York State Lottery* (Cambridge, Mass.: Arthur D. Little, Inc., Nov. 26, 1975), p. 7.

auditors, its capabilities clearly make it a most acceptable EDP audit tool. The auditor should require the use of SMP as an internal control procedure.

5. *Flowcharters* These program aids prepare computer-generated flowcharts. This aid can reduce the tedious chore of manually preparing flowcharts. In some instances, these packages produce better results than manually prepared flowcharts by reducing off-page connections and including page/line/statement number references to the source programs.

5.6 DATA BASE MANAGEMENT SYSTEM (DBMS) CONTROLS

Data base management systems (DBMS) are rapidly becoming an integral part of the data-processing scene. The effective auditor must have a basic understanding of these sophisticated software packages.

The concepts of data base management systems range from the relatively simple to the most complex. Data base has been defined in simple terms to be "... an orderly collection of business facts stored to serve information requirements."[10] At the other end of the spectrum,

> A data base then can be viewed as more than an ordinary collection of data for several related applications. The data base must be viewed as a generalized, common, integrated collection of company or installation-owned data which fulfills the data requirements of all applications which access it. In addition, the data within the data base must be structured to model the natural data relationships which exist in a company.[11]

The data base management system spectrum is clearly subject to differing opinions.

> There is such a wide range of prepared programs in use that the selection of the best one for any given application becomes a challenging problem.... One large class of programs stores and retrieves records and requires that any record to be stored or retrieved be uniquely identified by a key or address location. ... Another large class ... (offers) a complete file handling service, allowing users to specify desired record structures and then allowing for retrieval or maintenance based on any fields within a record rather than key or address only.[12]

The notions of data base and data base management systems may be appropriately defined and discussed on an individual basis. It is our

---

[10]Gerald Price, "The Ten Commandments of Data Base," *Data Management,* May 1972, pp. 14–23.

[11]Richard Schubert, "Basic Concepts in Data Base Management Systems," *Datamation,* July 1972, pp. 42–47.

[12]Charles T. Meadow. *The Analysis of Information Systems.* (2nd Ed.) (Los Angeles, Calif.: Melville Publishing Company, 1973), pp. 314–315.

opinion however, that a functional relationship exists between a data base and its associated data base management system which demands that the two concepts also be considered in conjunction with one another.

Data within a data base are generally stored with specified techniques, that is, the size of the items or records, the specific formats of those records which may or may not include pointers for linked lists, and so on. The data base management that operates a particular data base must be so constructed as to permit operation upon that data base. For example, a data base that has been created using the DM-6700 data base management system cannot be updated by the IMS data base management system.

In addition to the obvious hardware incompatibility, e.g., Burroughs and IBM, the DM-6700 data base itself is constructed in a manner that is not consistent with the methods of data base management utilized by IMS. A substantial cost is associated with the creation of a complex integrated data base. An organization would not allocate substantial sums of money for the creation of a data base with no data base management system to operate upon the data base.

The reverse argument is also applicable. An organization would not spend great sums of money to develop a data base management system without a data base for that system to operate upon. Meadow has concisely stated this functional relationship,

> Deciding upon a basic approach to file organization and search is only the first step on the user's way to an operational information retrieval system. The method chosen must be embodied in a computer program and the program must handle not only file searching, but maintenance as well.[13]

The key word in the statement above is "embodied"—the observation that the data base is embodied in the data base management system. The clear implication is that the two concepts have functional relationships with one another. However, a high degree of standardization is recommended for data base concepts which will reduce, indeed eliminate, the functional relationship between a data base and its associated data base management system.

Data Base Management Systems (DBMS)

The "software graveyard" is filled with data base management systems. Unfortunately, many new data base management systems are based upon the rubble of previous disasters. Data base management systems are emerging with little, if any, common base of operation. The CODASYL Report emphasizes this problem of incompatibility and states

---

[13]Meadows, *op cit.*, p. 314.

that at this point in the development of data base management systems, COBOL source programs can be transferred from one machine to another more easily than the files upon which the program operates.[14] The primary reason for this situation is that COBOL and CODASYL do not concern themselves with the methods of data storage techniques external to the executing program. Therefore, the data stored on mass storage devices have incompatibilities similar to those described above for DM-6700 and IMS. Clearly, this problem of data base incompatibility must not be permitted to continue.

The CODASYL Report identifies two basic types of systems which are associated with data base. They are (1) systems with host language capabilities, and (2) systems with self-contained capabilities. Host language implies the necessity to use a procedural language, and self-contained capabilities implies no connection with a host (procedural) language.

HOST LANGUAGE CAPABILITY

A system with host language capability is built upon the facilities of a procedural language such as COBOL, PL/1, or assembly language. The interface between the host language and the host language capabilities is usually through the CALL statement in the former.

"Built upon" used in this context must not be confused with "built with," as, in general, the host language and its associated compiler usually remain intact. Briefly, the host language capabilities may be identified simply as new tools for the application programmer.

SELF-CONTAINED CAPABILITIES

The self-contained capabilities have evolved from various origins. They are aimed at handling a certain set of data base functions in such a way as to negate the necessity of conventional procedural programming. In systems offering self-contained capabilities, the definitions of the data on item, record, and file levels reside in some encoded form with the data. In fact, they may be stored either in a catalog of several such data definitions or with the data file (namely, on the same volume).

> A self-contained system provides data base access and data display capabilities through the use of a simplified, high-level language, designed to be used by nonprogrammers. The language provides considerably less flexibility than a language such as COBOL, but is easier to learn and use.[15]

Briefly, the self-contained capabilities are tools for the non-programmer as well as for the programmer.

[14]CODASYL Systems Committee Technical Report, *Feature Analysis of Generalized Data Base Management Systems*, (New York: Association of Computing Machinery, 1971).
[15]Schubert, *op. cit.*, p. 42.

Data Base Management Systems Subfunctions

A data base management system, as it exists today, is comprised of one or more of the following subfunctions: (1) file management, (2) query, and (3) program generators.

FILE MANAGEMENT

The concept of file management connotes the operations of data base creation, deletion, and update. However, we contend that data independence, data relatability, data non-redundancy, data integrity, data compression, data security, and system auditability are also file management functions.

1. *Data independence*   Data independence implies the ability to store and retrieve data without concern for a specific data format. Currently, data items must be formatted when they are stored or accessed. For example, in FORTRAN, a character variable twenty bytes long would have the following format: A20.

The Joint GUIDE-SHARE Report discusses the tremendous cost involved in making a seemingly trivial change, owing to the present dependence of application logic on physical data format and structuring.[16] The application program should be insensitive to a change from packed decimal to fixed binary, character to numeric (if appropriate), or the movement of a data element from one physical location to another. PL/1 has begun to approach the problem at the programming language level. Unlike FORTRAN, PL/1 permits the automatic conversion of numbers stored in character form to a numeric value in either binary or decimal. The character representation of the number will automatically be converted to a numerical value by simply assigning a variable with the desired attributes to the character variable.

It is evident that when true data independence is attained, the costly trend described above will be reversed. This, of course, assumes that the cost of data independence will be less than the cost to make a change. In addition to the assumed positive cost factor, there will be the added benefit of substantial flexibility for the many programs that will access the data. A standardization of file techniques will greatly broaden the positive effect of enhanced program flexibility, and CODASYL and others have started in the right direction.

2. *Data relatability*   Data relatability implies construction of a data base with logical relationships among data items intra-record, as well as logically consistent inter-record associations. Intra-record relationships may best be explained with the following example. It is logical to have the information concerning an individual within a given record arranged in a consistent manner as follows:

[16]Joint GUIDE-SHARE Data Base Requirements Group, *Data Base Management System Requirements*, November 11, 1970.

byte positions 1–25   name (first, middle initial, last)
byte positions 26–50   street address
byte positions 51–73   city
byte positions 74–75   state
byte positions 81–n   other relevant data

It would not be logically consistent to have "name" in byte position 1–25, "street address" in byte positions 100–125, "city" in byte positions 321–343, and so on.

Inter-record relatability means the use of addressing techniques such as chaining or inverted files so that records with similar types of information may be accessed without the necessity of scanning the entire file.

Relationships may exist among data that are in the data base and must therefore be clearly specified so that the desired associations may be derived. Improved data relatability may improve program efficiency and thereby reduce execution time.

3. *Data non-redundancy*   Data redundancy implies the storage of the same data in more than one location on a mass storage device. Usually, this technique is a wasteful procedure. In order to improve efficient storage utilization, any given item of data should be stored only once. This procedure would eliminate the negative impact of redundant data.

As increasing amounts of information are merged to form integrated data bases, a great potential exists for the presence of redundant data. For example, if the payroll file was merged with the personnel data file, names, addresses, and social security numbers, among other potentially redundant data, would be duplicated on the newly created file. The duplication or redundancy of data is costly, not only from the standpoint of inefficient utilization of storage space, but from a processing standpoint as well, since more irrelevant information must be passed during processing. Therefore, from the standpoint of storage cost and access time, the data base should strive for data non-redundancy.

4. *Data integrity*   Perfect data integrity would imply error-free data. A data base implies many users, and it is of the utmost importance that the system be able to prevent "pollution" of data at time of capture. Errors will occur when data are captured and transcribed into machine-readable form. What is most important to remember is that errors are made on new data captured, as well as on data that will update existing data. Therefore, it is within the realm of possibility (if carried to its extreme) that the data base could be completely "polluted" by erroneous data. Numerous techniques to reduce error are available.* These include the use of check digits, validation of field size and composition, control totals, and others, as described earlier in the chapter.

*See E. A. Gentile and J. R. Grimes. "Maintaining Internal Integrity of On-Line Data Bases," *EDPACS*, February 1977, pp. 1–14.

5. *Data compression* A compressor is hardware or software that shortens the length of the string of bits or characters of data that are its input. A decompressor is hardware or software that expands the shortened string back to its original form. The result is more efficient utilization of mass storage devices.

For example, in a character string that has the last name of an individual, the variable that contains the name may be declared to be twenty characters long. If the name being stored is SARDINAS, only eight of the twenty characters contain relevant information. The other twelve characters are blanks, and occupy storage space with blanks. A compressor might take the character string and determine that there are twelve blanks. A new character string might be formed with 'SARDINAS12.' The number of blanks in the original string has been incorporated into the new string, and only ten characters (instead of twenty) are stored. In this particular example, there has been a 50 percent savings of space. This technique could have a substantial effect upon cost. In fact, a computer facility realized clear savings of $10,000 per month as a result of utilizing data compression techniques.[17]

The example above illustrates the concept of data compression. However, data compressors are highly sophisticated algorithms which may operate at the "bit" level instead of the character level described above. Bit manipulation will permit more efficient utilization of storage space.

6. *Data security* The difficulty of gaining access to data should be a function of the sensitivity of the data referenced and the authority of the user. Security must be provided at the most elemental level. Combinations of elements will also require proper security when necessary.

Prevention of unauthorized access to data is but one of the many facets of data security. The probability of loss of data due to fire, theft, etc., is greater than zero, and must also be considered in the total security system. However, it must be clearly recognized that no security system can absolutely *guarantee* data safety.

> In current practice security measures in information systems are neither elaborate, flexible, nor impenetrable. . . . The best prospects for enhancement of security would seem to lie in the more recent generalized data management systems. These systems offer a controlled environment and impose sufficient restraint upon user activity to enforce reasonable general security conditions.[18]

Obviously, software technology (especially concerning security systems) requires substantial improvement, and it would appear that generalized data base management systems hold the most promise for this task.

---

[17]Stephen Ruth and Paul Kreutzer, "Data Compression for Large Business Files," *Datamation*, September 1972.

[18]R. W. Conway, W. L. Maxwell, and H. L. Morgan. "On the Implementation of Security Measures in Information Systems," *Communications of the ACM*, April 1972, p. 220.

7. *System auditability* System auditability is becoming an extremely important aspect of data base management systems, since auditors must verify that all transactions are being properly received as input and that the data residing in the data base are properly modified.

Although no specific software packages exist to insure system auditability of the data base management systems, these systems generally have built into them auditing capabilities that auditors can utilize effectively. The basic rationale is that when the systems were designed, one of the major considerations was the ability to restore the data base in the event of a computer malfunction or other disaster that destroyed the data base. Therefore, elaborate logging or journaling procedures are built into these data base management systems.

For example, IMS (an IBM DBMS) has procedures that log all input, all output, and log before and after images of the data base record modified. For batch programs, a utility is provided which uses log records created during the original run to back out from the data base any changes to a specified user checkpoint. Clearly, a continuous audit is being performed, and an auditor can use the log tapes and the computer itself to scan those tapes to insure that all operations have been performed properly.

5.7 BUILT-IN COMPUTER CONTROLS

Most vendors provide computers with a variety of built-in automatic control features to help insure proper operation. These controls consist of: (1) built-in hardware controls, and (2) vendor software controls. Many control features are standard in many computers; where they are not, management should require that they be incorporated in the computer system by the vendor before it is installed.

Built-In Hardware Controls

These controls are built into the circuitry for detection of errors that might result from the manipulation, calculation, or transmission of data by various components of the computer system. These equipment controls are required to make sure that only one electronic pulse is transmitted through a channel during any single phase, that data are encoded and decoded accurately, that specific devices are activated, and that data received in one location are the same as those that were transmitted from another location. Examples of some of these internal equipment control features follow:

1. *Parity checks* To insure that the data initially read into the system have been transmitted correctly, an internal self-checking feature is

incorporated in most computer systems. In addition to the set of bits (e.g., byte) used to represent data, the computer uses one additional bit for each storage position. These bits, called parity bits or check bits, are used to detect errors in the circuitry which would result in the loss, addition, or destruction of a bit due to an equipment malfunction. The parity bit makes the number of bits in a binary code either even or odd, depending on whether the computer uses even or odd parity. Either system requires an additional bit location associated with each coded set.

2. *Validity check* Numbers and characters are represented by specified combinations of binary digits. Representation of these data symbols is accomplished by various coding schemes handled by the circuitry of the computer system. In a single computer system several different coding schemes can be used to represent data at various stages of processing. For example, the Hollerith characters of an input card are converted to Binary Coded Decimal (BCD), or Extended Binary Coded Decimal Interchange Code (EBCDIC), or to U.S.A. Standard Code for Information Interchange (USASCII). If output is written on a printer, for example, the data will have to be converted to yet another code. Therefore, a message being transmitted or received goes through an automatic encoding and decoding operation that is acceptable to the sending or receiving device in question.

3. *Duplication check* This control check requires that two independent components perform the same operation and compare results. If there is any difference between the two operations, an error condition is indicated. For example, cards being read by a card reader pass through two read stations where data are read by the second read station and compared back to the first read station. If the two readings do not equal, an error is indicated. The same principle of duplication is used in nearly all of the computer system components. For example, much of the circuitry of the arithmetic-logic unit (ALU) of the central processing unit (CPU) is duplicated where calculations are carried out twice to increase the probability of accurate results.

4. *Echo check* This control feature authenticates the transmission of data to and from components of the computer system. The data transmission is verified by echoing back the signals received by the component and comparing it with source data for agreement. For example, the CPU transmits a message to a card punch to perform an operation. The card punch sends a message back to the CPU, where it is automatically checked to see if the correct device has been activated.

5. *Miscellaneous error checks* In addition to the control checks discussed above, the computer system should also contain controls to detect various invalid computer instructions, data overflows, lost signs, zero division, and defective components.

6. *Firmware controls* Firmware or hardwiring implies the use of solid state techniques to represent instructions. Unlike programming instructions, a hardwired instruction cannot be modified. In the early years, boards were hardwired. Different operations could be performed when an individual would plug various wires into different holes in the board. However, new technology permits many hardwired instructions to be placed on a single chip. For example, hand calculators that perform functions like square root have the logic for the calculation permanently placed on a chip. The logic cannot be modified with conventional software techniques, but the chip itself may be physically altered or replaced.

The concept of firmware is extremely important, because it removes from the programmer the ability to alter programs, including the highly vulnerable operating system. Furthermore, owing to the increased complexity and sophistication of computer systems, greater reliance for internal control must be placed upon the computer itself.

Hardwiring a compiler or an entire operating system might seem to be a devastatingly difficult task, but it has already been accomplished. IMS Associates has combined multiple Intel 8080 microprocessors into a configuration called the Hypercube. The Hypercube operating system resides entirely in firmware.[19]

As technology advances, more efficient methods of transferring algorithms to integrated circuits are making hardwired programs inevitable. Auditors should require that audit procedures within computers be hardwired. When computers are hardwired, internal control within them will be greatly improved.

Unfortunately, not all computer equipment installed today has a total complement of built-in hardware controls. In making equipment selection, the one charged with this responsibility must evaluate the completeness of the control features incorporated in a particular component. If equipment is selected with a limited number of these controls, the probability of errors occurring as a result of equipment malfunction is much greater.

Vendor Software Controls

These controls, which are designed into the operating system, deal to a great extent with the routine input/output operations of the system. These controls are as follows:

1. *Read or write error* In the event of a read/write error, the machine will halt the program and allow the operator to investigate the error.

---

[19] Ronald A. Frank, "Imsai Arrays Micros for Low-Cost Power," *Computerworld*, Oct. 29, 1975, p. 3.

For example, a writing operation may be attempted on dirty tape, or the system will stop if the printer runs out of paper.

2. *Record length checks*   In some instances, blocks of records are set up that are too long for the input buffer area of the computer. This control feature, therefore, insures that data records read into the computer from tape or disk are the correct length.

3. *Label checking routines*   There are two kinds of labels: header and trailer. At a minimum, the header label should contain: file serial number, reel serial number, file name, creation date, and retention date. The trailer label should contain the block count, record count, control totals, and end-of-reel or end-of-file condition. If it is an input file, the header label is used to check that the file is the one specified by the program. The trailer label is used to determine whether all data on the file were processed correctly and whether there is an end of physical or logical files. For output the header label is used to check whether the file may be written on or destroyed, e.g., file retention date. For example, an old master file may be erased and used for something else if the old data are no longer relevant.

4. *Access control*   An error condition occurs when reference is made to a storage device that is not in a "ready" status.

5. *Address compare control*   An error condition occurs when a storage address referenced by one component does not compare with the component's address that is referenced. For example, the core storage address does not agree with the address referenced by a disk drive.

Whether the original equipment manufacturer's software control program is used or the installation writes its own software control packages, the auditor should satisfy himself as to the adequacy of these verification and error-handling techniques.

5.8 COMPUTER OPERATIONS CONTROLS

The computer is one of the key components in the information system. It is, therefore, important that it be properly maintained and controlled. Moreover, it is imperative that the personnel who operate computer equipment be subjected to the same stringent controls. This area of controls is divided into two groups: (1) physical controls, and (2) procedural controls.

Physical Controls

These controls pertain to the environment that the computer system is housed in. Common sense and the establishment of simple physical controls can help prevent many errors and mishaps.

COMPUTER SITE

The location of the computer system and site construction is fundamental. Some computer systems have been housed next to steam boilers, experimental wind tunnels, jet aircraft take-off and landing flight paths, radio stations, carpentry shop, radar towers, on the first floor next to a busy street and in view of all passers-by, and so forth. The construction of the site should be of high quality, fire-proof material.

ENVIRONMENTAL CONTROL

Adequate and separate air conditioning, dehumidification, and humidification systems should be installed. Regardless of what the vendors say, computer systems still need a great deal of air conditioning to operate properly. For example, although equipment manufacturers often suggest that their equipment will operate in a temperature range from 50° to 95° F, a stricter guideline of 72° F ± 2° is advised to avoid malfunctions. Similarly, with regard to relative humidity (RH), the manufacturers cite the range of 20% to 90% RH, but here again a much stricter guide is given as 50% RH ± 5%. Semiconductors in the logic and memory of computers are very sensitive to temperature fluctuations. High RH levels (e.g., 80% and above) can cause problems in computer systems in various ways, including the corrosion of electrical contacts or the expansion of paper. The latter effect can be felt in the malfunctioning of printers and card readers or any equipment that uses paper. Low RH, on the other hand, can build up charges of static electricity, causing paper to stick and jam. Today, because of more sensitive technology, an almost surgically clean environment is necessary.

UNINTERRUPTIBLE POWER SYSTEMS

In many areas, power supply is erratic during extreme weather conditions. It may be cost/effective to acquire and install an emergency power source. An emergency power shutoff should also be installed in the event of fire or other disaster. Computers, like most highly sophisticated systems, depend on the uninterrupted operation of their functionally contributive subsystems. One obviously important subsystem is electric power.

It is generally acknowledged that the quality and quantity of utility power are diminishing daily. In some geographical areas, brownouts (a sustained reduction of electrical power) have become expected occurrences during peak demands, and total power loss is not unthinkable. Nonetheless, increased sophistication of computer systems requires the utilization of "clean" electric power. "Dirty" electric power implies short-term transients and line instability, i.e., fluctuations in voltage and/or frequency of the electricity.

In order to insure the continuous availability of "clean" electric power, uninterruptible power systems (UPS) have been developed. A UPS generally consists of a rectifier/charger, a battery, and an inverter. The rectifier/charger normally converts AC utility power to DC, and maintains a full charge on the battery. Should utility power fail, the battery provides DC to the inverter, which converts the DC power into clean and continuous AC power. Transfer of the critical load from the utility power source to the battery and back is generally accomplished by a static bypass switch. A static switch is electronic (unlike a mechanical switch) and therefore permits critical load transfer within four milliseconds, which is within the acceptable tolerances required by most mainframes and peripherals.

Although the power support time available from batteries is clearly a function of the number and size of batteries utilized, the recommended maximum support time is five minutes. Although this figure may be increased, calculations should be performed to determine whether it is cost effective to do so. If computer installations are of a highly sensitive nature, it might be appropriate to consider the addition of emergency motor generators to supplement utility power for extended power outages.

Procedural Controls

Procedural controls relate to the performance of tasks in the system. Management must establish how the tasks are to be performed, and close supervision must be effected to see to it that those tasks are being performed accordingly.

SUPERVISION OF COMPUTER ROOM

All computer center staff, especially operators, should be under direct supervision. Supervisors should establish job priorities and run schedules for every working day, and all computer operators should be required to sign the computer operating log (run log) at the beginning and end of their shifts. Overtime computer usage should be limited.

Supervisors should demand equipment utilization reports and maintain accurate job cost records of all computer time, including production, program listing, rerun, idle, and downtime. On an aperiodic basis, the auditor should review these reports.

No transactions should be initiated by any computer center staff. Only computer operators should operate the computer, but operator intervention in processing should be limited. Moreover, access of computer operators to sensitive tapes, disks, programs, and documentation should be tightly controlled.

> Public confidence in the New York State Lottery was impaired ... when a Department of Taxation and Finance computer operator printed and cashed a winning lottery ticket after the drawing had been held. The computer operator confessed and was convicted of forgery after the holder of the bona fide ticket attempted to cash her ticket a short time later.
>
> A possible reoccurrence of the forgery was eliminated when the Tax Department's EDP Bureau implemented a procedure whereby a programmer would "lock out" the computer file that generates ticket numbers so as to prevent unauthorized use of the file after the lottery tickets have been completely prepared for distribution.[20]

Access to the computer room facilities should be restricted to authorized personnel only. Any authorized visitors should wear badges and be closely supervised. Even information systems personnel should not be allowed in the computer room without approval by supervisors. For example, many programmers request "hands-on" testing. Any "hands-on" use of the computer by programmers should be limited and closely supervised.

Good housekeeping procedures are fundamental to any system, especially a computer system. Along with good housekeeping, preventive maintenance procedures should be established. These procedures help to forestall a deterioration in performance, or a failure of the various computer components, by an on-going system of detection, adjustment, and repairs. Basic to preventive maintenance is an inventory of spare parts. It is foolish to cease operations of a million dollar system for want of a one-dollar part. All service of equipment should be performed by qualified and authorized service engineers.

Supervisors should make reviews of work in process and completed work to insure quality and correct disposition of output. Spoiled printouts of confidential or sensitive information should be destroyed by shredders or other appropriate means. They should never be thrown in waste containers for disposal.

All computer operating logs should be reviewed daily by supervisors. Operating logs include all messages to and from the computer via the computer console, a device used by the computer operator to monitor and control the operations of the computer. The computer console usually consists of a control panel and a console typewriter, although a number of computers are replacing one or both of these units with a CRT unit plus a keyboard. The console control panel of a computer appears to most observers as a confusing array of lights, switches, and buttons. Some new computer systems are reducing the number of these components as the internal operations of the computer are becoming more automatic and, thus, require less operator intervention.

---

[20]*Special Audit Report on the Financial and Operating Practices of the Racing and Wagering Board, Division of the Lottery, op. cit.,* p. 13.

The console terminal, either typewriter or CRT, and the switches and buttons on the console control panel enable the computer operator to enter messages or commands into and receive information directly from the storage unit of the CPU. Using keys, switches, audible tone signals, and display lights on the console unit, the computer operator can: (1) start, stop, or change the operation of all or part of the computer system; (2) manually enter and display data from internal storage; (3) determine the status of internal electronic switches; (4) determine the contents of certain internal registers; (5) alter the mode of operation so that when an unusual condition or malfunction occurs, the computer will either stop or indicate the condition (e.g., card jam in card reader or wrong tape file mounted) and proceed after the condition or malfunction has been corrected; (6) change the selection of input/output devices; (7) load programs and various routines; and (8) alter the data content of specific storage locations.

The operating log (also called a console log) includes all messages and instructions to and from the computer. It can be in the form of continuous paper printout either from the console typewriter, or in some large installations, a printer may be dedicated to printing out the operating log because the console typewriter is not fast enough to handle high-volume output. In some installations, the operating log (or console log) may be written out on magnetic media such as magnetic tape, especially if a CRT is used instead of a console typewriter. In any case, the operating log is a valuable control document because it gives a running account of all the messages generated by the computer and all of the instructions and entries made by the computer operator. In addition, it can indicate the beginning or end of various stages of processing and intermediate or final results of processing.

A point of concern to the auditor is that the computer operator can bypass program and other controls. He has the ability to interrupt a program run and introduce data manually into the CPU through the CRT or console typewriter. With proper separation of the programming function from the computer operating function, and with computer operators having access to *object* programs rather than *source* programs, it is unlikely that an operator will have enough knowledge of the program statements and its purpose to make any successful manipulations for fraudulent or improper purposes. Normally, computer operators are not adept programmers anyway. But the possibility of unauthorized intervention and manipulation by the computer operator should be reduced by using several control techniques.

Since, for example, the console typewriter (or printer) is used to print-out interventions (both authorized and unauthorized) by the computer operator plus the results of operations during a definite period (most computers have a tamper-proof twenty-four hour clock built into the system) of both time and date, paper sheets in the typewriter can be prenumbered and periodically reviewed by computer center management and the auditor. The computer operator must account for all computer operating time throughout his shift. Compared to the speed of the computer (e.g., thousands of instructions within a micro-second), manual intervention by the computer operator is slow, and manipulation can therefore result in processing times that are significantly different from standard for affected jobs. Additional administrative control techniques include proper background checks, required vacations, rotating shifts, and rotating duties of all computer operators.

CONTROL OF THE PROGRAMMER/DATA BASE INTERFACE

A general objective of good procedural controls is to insulate "live" data from programmers, thereby reducing the probability of unauthorized access to or modification of the data. At present, this task may be accomplished by utilizing one or both of the following techniques: (1) compile-time facilities, and (2) job control language (JCL).

Each of the methods identified above requires the employment of a precisely defined organizational procedure. Further, the employment of a data base administrator or similar individual is suggested.

In the currently accepted course of events, an application programmer receives an assignment to generate a program that will perform a specified task. Upon completion of that task, and any subsequent testing to assure that proper processing functions are performed, the programmer places the finished product in the program library on the computer system.

The procedure described above should be modified to the extent that internal control is strengthened by using the classical concept of separation of duties. For example, the programmer should not be the individual to place the final copy of the program on the system; the data base administrator should. In fact, any subsequent modifications to a program should be written by programmers, but always placed on the system by the data base administrator.

The data base administrator has at his disposal two general techniques to widen the "narrow gap" between programmer and data. Both will be discussed.

1. *Compile-time facilities* If a company is utilizing a data base management system, the auditor should consider the steps that occur during program compilation. As discussed previously, there is a preprocessor stage where the source program is scanned for any modifications to the source code or inclusion of partitioned data set modules. The use of a data base management system with host language capabilities permits access to the data base through a CALL. The preprocessor step will permit a procedure to be developed to insure, to some degree, the security of data.

When a programmer has completed his program, including tests using test data, it is time to have a final compilation of the program so that it may be stored in load module form on a direct access storage device (DASD). However, instead of the programmer submitting his source deck to the computer operator, he should submit the source program to the data base administrator.

The data base administrator should know what the purpose of the program is, as well as the data that the program is permitted to access from the data base. Using the preprocessor function of the compiler, the data base administrator has the ability to insure that only those relevant data are being accessed.

The data base administrator places in front of the source deck a series of commands that will change only those standard variable names into some coded representation which the data base management system can accept. In this manner, if the programmer tried to access data that were not part of his program, during the preprocessor stage, that variable would not be converted into a recognizable value. Such a condition should prevent the program from executing. It is obviously important to insure that the programmers not have access to the conversion deck. If a compromise did occur, it would be important to make any necessary changes to the system.

This procedure places a substantial amount of responsibility upon the data base administrator. Therefore, this individual must be selected carefully, and sufficient internal control procedures established to insure that the system will operate properly. Such controls might include provisions that (1) the data base administrator is not permitted to write computer programs, and (2) programmers may not submit programs for final compilation to the computer operators.

This procedure would tend to discourage individuals from attempting to gain access to unauthorized data. Also, it would prevent an individual from writing an unauthorized program to access sensitive data, since without the preprocessor conversion, no program could access any data from the data base.

The procedure would help to discourage: (1) unauthorized program changes to existing programs which would permit access to sensitive data, and (2) unauthorized new programs that are written to access sensitive data. An attempted compilation of a source deck could not be accomplished without the preprocessor deck. Further, the described procedure above has been developed with, and is consistent with, existing hardware and software technology.

2. *Job control language (JCL)* A concept similar to the one described above could be applied in an environment where no data base management system is in operation.

At present, data definition (DD) cards are a component of Job Control Language (JCL). The DD cards act as an interface between the user program and the operating system. The DD cards have information on them pertaining to the name of the data set, the type of storage device (disk, tape, etc.), the volume serial number of the disk or tape, and other vital information.

The data base administrator could develop an organization procedure that would prohibit programmers from developing the final DD cards used for a production program. This procedure would effectively insulate programmers from data, since the programmers would not know where the data are, or any other vital information about the data set or file.

Granted, the procedure may be burdensome and require information to be transmitted from the programmer to the individual creating the DD cards. If the program is of a highly sensitive nature, however, or has access to highly sensitive data, or the situation warrants such a procedure, it should be established.

ELIMINATION OF REPLACEMENT CARDS

Computer programs are continually modified, updated, and otherwise maintained in order to reflect the changing needs of a dynamic organization. Generally, program modifications are made to the source program itself. However, utilization of a Replacement (REP) Card permits changes to be made to object decks! A number of potential problems manifest themselves as a result of utilizing REP cards; therefore, procedural controls should be instituted to prevent utilization of REP cards.

First, modification of the object module does not imply a concomitant updating of the source program. The result, observed in numerous instances, is that when the source program must be recompiled, many "bugs" corrected or changes made with REP cards suddenly revert to their original state. The obvious reason is that the "bug" was corrected with a REP card, and the source program retained the improper logic.

The utilization of REP cards is usually limited to installations that use assembly language as the main programming language, primarily because, in many instances, there is a one-for-one relationship between an assembly instruction utilized, and object code generated. However, care should be taken to insure that no installation utilizes REP cards, even if high-level languages are used for application programs.

5.9 LIBRARY AND DATA BASE CONTROLS

The library and data base represent the foundation of the information system. These key components must be controlled with great care. If loss or destruction does occur, then preplanned procedures should be established to recreate any lost data or other vital documents. We divide library and data base controls into two groups: (1) physical controls, and (2) procedural controls.

Physical Controls

To withstand stresses and disasters (e.g., fire), a strongly constructed storage vault should be available to store files and documents when not in use. In addition, all backup files, programs, and other vital documents should be stored in secure facilities off-site. Fire, flood, theft, disgruntled employees, riot, vermin, or even nuclear attack represent hazards to an organization's vital records. The secure storage of these vital records is of utmost importance for the continued operation of any business. There are several sites available to management that guarantee safekeeping of records.[21] Some of these storage centers are in mountains. One is in a 500-acre limestone cave that is 175 feet underground. This installation provides a dirt-free environment and year-round temperature of 70°F with 35% relative humidity. In addition to secure storage, many off-site installations provide services such as: microfilming, telecopier long-line transmission of stored paper documents, copying and shipment of stored paper records, 24-hour TWX service, and 24-hour emergency shipment of stored documents. Records may be sent to an installation by truck, express, courier service, or United States Postal Service.

File-protection devices (e.g., file protect rings for magnetic tape), should be used to prevent accidental erasure. All storage devices, especially magnetic tape and disk, should be kept free of air pollutants. Also, temperature and humidity conditions should be strictly controlled.

Procedural Controls

Again, all files should be stored in the library (sensitive files in vault) when not in use. The librarian's function should be independent and segregated from other functions, e.g., programmers and computer operators. The librarian should maintain a complete record of all files and documents such as an inventory list, the individual to whom files are assigned, the status of the files, and when they are due back. All files should contain external labels for identification, but these labels should be coded and understandable only by authorized personnel. For exam-

---

[21]For example, Inland Vital Records Center, 6500 Inland Drive, P.O. Box 2249, Kansas City, Kansas 66110.

ple, it would be unwise to label a file as CUSTOMER-ACCOUNTS-RECEIVABLE; it would be better to use some code, e.g., 14927.

The librarian should make sure that all backup copies are properly maintained off-premises. Unusable magnetic tapes and disks should be segregated until they can be cleaned, repaired, or replaced. Cleaning and repairing should be done on a regular basis. Such a procedure minimizes read/write errors, and insures an adequate supply of usable storage media. It should be noted that in many computer installations which operate on a twenty-four hour basis, the librarian is present for only eight of those hours. During the remaining sixteen hours, the tape vault is unattended, and therefore subject to abuse. It appears that security that is adequate for the first shift, is reduced for the second shift, and quite often nonexistent during the third shift. Computer installations are vulnerable twenty-four hours a day. Is it worth the risk not to have a librarian on duty twenty-four hours a day?

A simple yet important file reconstruction procedure that is recommended for important sequential files such as magnetic tape is explained and illustrated in Figure 5.5. This backup system is normally referred to as the grandfather-father-son file reconstruction procedure. With this procedure, three versions of a file are available at any one time. File A (father) in Update Cycle I produces File B (son). In Update Cycle II, File B (now a father) produces File C (son of B). During this cycle, File A becomes the grandfather.

The advantage of this control procedure is that recovery is always possible. For example, if File C contained errors or was damaged during processing, the job could be repeated using File B again with transaction data from transaction File 2. If both File B and File C are damaged or destroyed, File A (stored off-premises) is still available, along with transaction File 1, to create File B, which can then be used to create a new File C.

With direct access storage devices (DASD) such as magnetic disk, it is recommended that the contents be periodically written (dumped or copied) on a backup file, e.g., magnetic tape and stored at another location. In addition, a transaction log should be maintained for two reasons: (1) because transactions are occurring constantly, the transaction log provides a link from one backup file to the next; and (2) writing on magnetic disk or any DASD occurs by overlay, i.e., a write command erases the previous value and puts the new value in its place. The transaction log contains a record of all transactions that caused a change to the direct access file.

If the system goes down and/or a file(s) in the data base is destroyed or incorrectly modified, there must be a method available to reconstruct the file. In Figure 5.6, a file reconstruction plan for direct access files is illustrated. In this example, assume that the online direct access file (master file) is destroyed sometime during Period II. With Backup File A,

UPDATE CYCLE I:

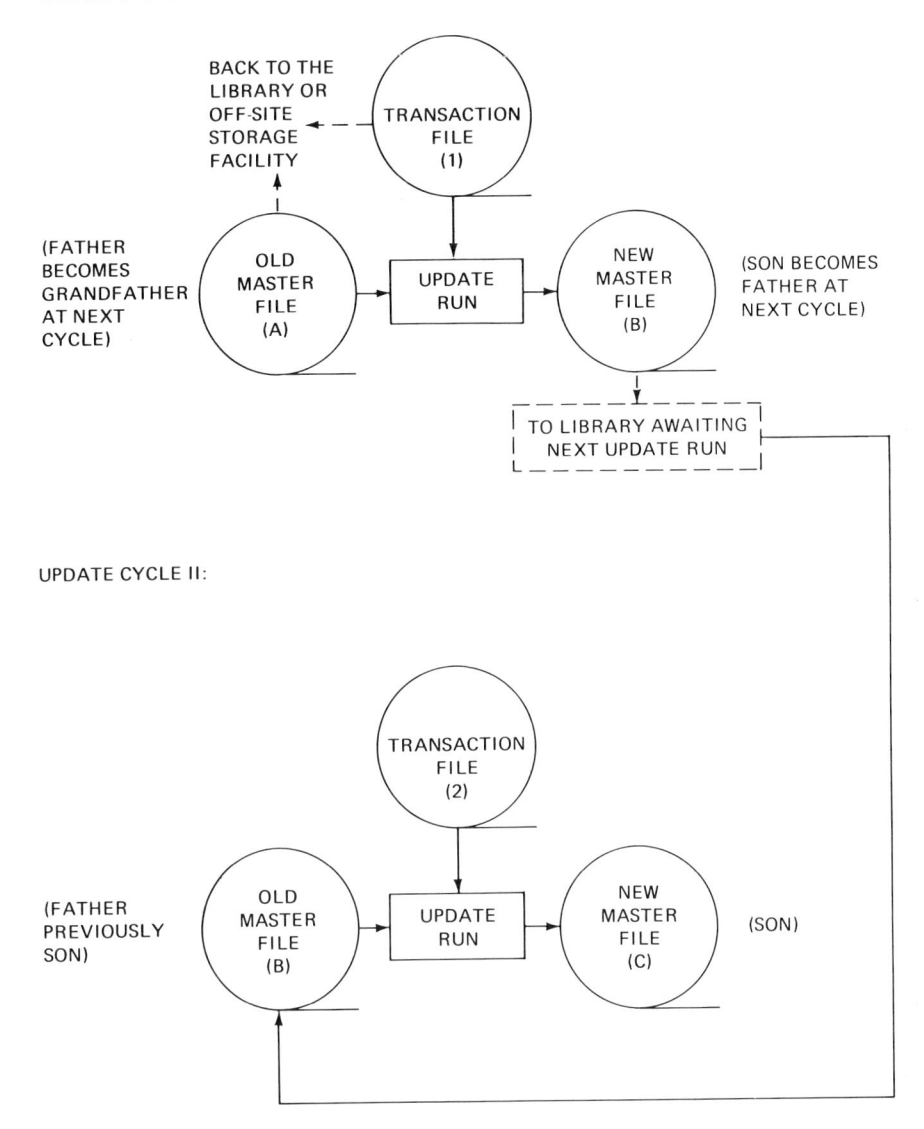

FIGURE 5.5.
Example of Grandfather-Father-Son File Reconstruction for Sequential Files.

which is a copy of the online master file as of the end of Period I, and Transaction Log 2, which recorded all transactions during Period II up until destruction of the online master file, a new online master disk file can be reconstructed. First, all master file data from Backup File A are written on the new master disk file. Then, all transactions from Trans-

PERIOD I:

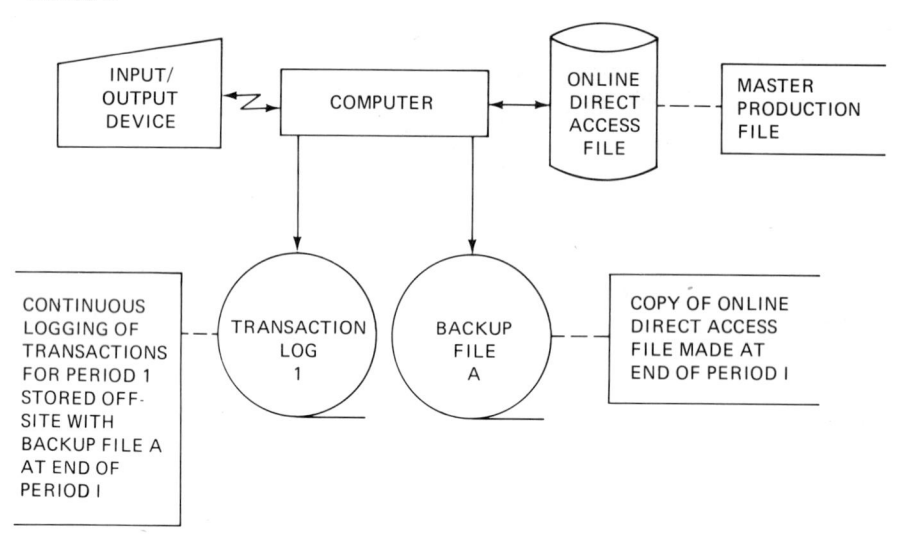

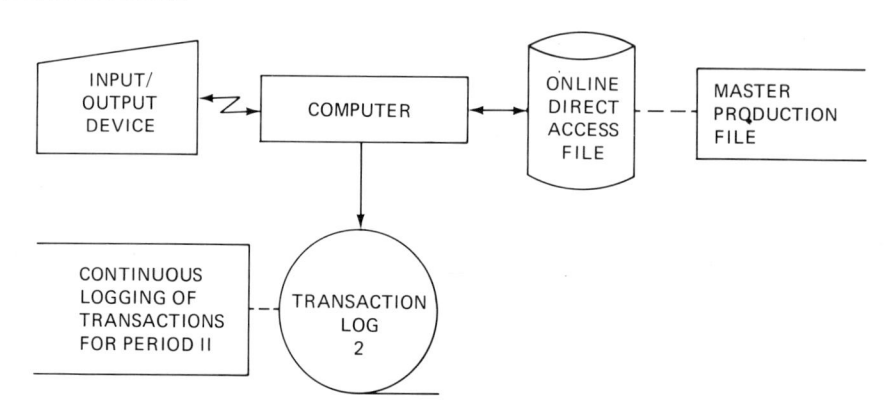

FIGURE 5.6.
Example of a File Reconstruction Plan for Direct Access Files.

action Log 2 are properly recorded, thus bringing the master file to a correct present state.

5.10 OUTPUT CONTROLS

Output controls are established as final checks on the accuracy and completeness of the processed information. These procedures are:

1. An initial screening should be conducted to detect obvious errors, as the following quote indicates.

> Errors which occur in printing lottery tickets should be detected before the tickets are distributed for sale. Most printing errors should be detected either by the EDP Control Unit at the Department of Taxation and Finance where the lottery tickets are printed or by the Materials Handling Section of the Division of the Lottery where the lottery tickets are cut and packaged for distribution.
>
> There are no written procedures for these two units that require them to review the lottery tickets. We believe that the duplicate, missing or erroneously numbered tickets printed for the Colossus Halloween Special could have been detected before distribution if the computer programmer had previously provided the two units with some written procedures and specifications as to the format for the tickets. For example, in Box A of the ticket, the single digit corresponds to the number of million tickets issued (series). The computer program was only supposed to print four million tickets; thus, any number in Box A other than one, two, three, or four is an erroneously numbered ticket and is indicative of faulty programming. Also, the sheets of tickets were supposed to be printed in such a way that the numbers one through four should have run down each page of the tickets sequentially one through four and should have repeated in this manner. Visual observation by the EDP Control Unit and by those wrapping the tickets would detect any deviations from the established pattern.[22]

2. Output should be immediately routed to a controlled area and distributed only to authorized persons by authorized persons.

3. Output control totals should be reconciled back to input control totals for agreement to insure that no data have been lost or added during processing or transmission. For example, the number of input records delivered for processing should equal the number of records that are processed, or hash totals should agree, or financial totals, such as net pay, should agree.

4. All vital forms (e.g., paychecks, stockholder registry forms, passbooks, etc.) should be prenumbered and accounted for.

5. Any highly sensitive output that should not be accessible by computer center personnel should be generated via an output device, e.g., printer in a secure location outside the computer room.

6. In spite of all the precautions taken, errors do slip through. The major detection control point for detecting such errors is, of course, the user. Therefore, procedures should be established by the auditor to set up a channel between the user and the control group for the systematic reporting of occurrences of errors or improprieties. Such a systems design would employ a feedback loop where users would report all errors

---

[22]*Special Audit Report on the Financial and Operating Practices of the Racing and Wagering Board, Division of the Lottery, op. cit.,* p. 12.

to the control group, and the control group, in turn, would take action to correct any inaccuracies or inconsistencies that might be revealed.

There are other output controls, such as systematic manual checks, statistical sampling, physical counts of inventories, and analysis of reports. Many methods can be devised for output controls, but the level of control should be a function of the sensitivity of the output. For example, departmental statistical reports probably would require little control.

5.11 SUMMARY

We have discussed operational controls and the importance and composition of input controls, operating system controls, processing controls, application program controls, data base management system (DBMS) controls, built-in computer controls, computer operations controls, library and data base controls, and output controls. Each of these controls is designed to assure the proper functioning of the total system. Specifically, to maintain the effectiveness and proper interaction of people, hardware, software, and data base.

Perhaps the best summary to this chapter comes from a report to the Congress of the United States by the Comptroller General of the United States.

> In our three reports we pointed out that Government computer systems and their applications and data were not being properly protected because many installations lacked important security and control measures and/or recovery procedures for continuity of operation.
>
> Some effects that have occurred because computer systems were not properly protected include:
> —Dollar losses;
> —Building, equipment, software, and data losses;
> —Personnel injuries; and
> —A loss of life.

Some of these losses were minimal, while others were catastrophic.[23] Each of the above described controls is important to maintain the total system. Degradation of one of the controls may cause the compromise of the entire system. Therefore, the auditor must be alert and carefully assess each of the operational controls. The following questionnaires help to summarize and enhance the material presented in this chapter.

[23]*Report to the Congress by the Comptroller General of the United States,* "Problems Found with Government Acquisition and Use of Computers From November 1965 to December 1976," FGMSD-77-14, March 15, 1976, pp. 34–35. Also see the following reports: *Criminal Actions* FGMSD-76-27, *Inadequate Physical Security Protection* FGMSD-76-40, and *Inadequate Controls over Automated Transactions* FGMSD-76-5.

INPUT CONTROL QUESTIONNAIRE

	ANSWER		ANSWERS BASED ON		
	Yes	No	Inquiry	Observation	Test

INPUT (OR TRANSACTION) CODES:

1. Are all items input to the system assigned codes? ___ ___ ___ ___ ___

2. Are the designation and approval of codes tightly controlled? ___ ___ ___ ___ ___

3. List code structures used:

   _____
   _____
   _____
   _____

4. Explain the purpose of these codes.

   _____
   _____
   _____
   _____

5. Are responsibilities clearly established for initiation, review and/or proper authorization of transactions? ___ ___ ___ ___ ___

INPUT PREPARATION:

1. Is input reviewed for acceptability? If so, by whom? ___ ___ ___ ___ ___

INPUT CONTROL QUESTIONNAIRE
Page 2

2. Are input documents prenumbered?

3. Are all prenumbered documents accounted for by a control group?

4. Are signatures verified on customers' checks or debit orders?

5. Are approval initials required on internal entries and on all adjusting entries, and are they checked and verified.

6. Is approval authority for changes to sensitive records carefully restricted, and are these restrictions observed?

7. If checks or other negotiable forms are printed by the computer, do the procedures for requisitioning and accounting for blank stock provide adequate control?

INPUT VERIFICATION:

1. Are key-punching and key-verifying instructions documented?

INPUT CONTROL QUESTIONNAIRE
Page 3

2. Are procedures established to sight-verify documents for reasonableness?

3. Is responsibility fixed, and are adequate procedures in effect, for tracing and correcting input errors?

INPUT COMPLETENESS:

1. Are predetermined control totals established independently of the EDP department?

2. Are batches serially numbered, and are these numbers associated with each transaction amount throughout processing?

3. Are batch control totals passed from run to run to insure that all transactions received are processed throughout the entire system?

4. Is a control total log maintained and reconciled to computer totals?

INPUT CONTROL QUESTIONNAIRE
Page 4

5. If online transmission is used, are message counts, character counts, and dual transmission performed to insure that transmission is correct and no messages are lost? ____ ____ ____   ____ ____

6. Are self-checking digits prepared for account numbers? ____ ____ ____   ____ ____

OPERATING SYSTEM CONTROL QUESTIONNAIRE

	ANSWER		ANSWERS BASED ON		
	Yes	No	Inquiry	Observation	Test
1. Is there a definite procedure for operating system generation?	___	___	___	___	___
2. Are there written procedures for operating system maintenance that provide for:					
a. formal request for program change?	___	___	___	___	___
b. approval by authorized person?	___	___	___	___	___
c. test of change?	___	___	___	___	___
3. Is the utilization of SMP or similar software packages a required procedure?	___	___	___	___	___
4. Are all security aspects of the vendor-supplied operating system active?	___	___	___	___	___

PROCESSING CONTROL QUESTIONNAIRE

	ANSWER		ANSWERS BASED ON		
	Yes	No	Inquiry	Observation	Test
1. Are input records edited for:					
a. character checks?	___	___	___	___	___
b. sign checks?	___	___	___	___	___
c. validity checks?	___	___	___	___	___
d. limit and reasonableness checks?	___	___	___	___	___
e. sequence checks?	___	___	___	___	___
f. arithmetic checks?	___	___	___	___	___
g. self-checking digit checks?	___	___	___	___	___
h. control total checks?	___	___	___	___	___
i. run-to-run total checks?	___	___	___	___	___
j. overflow checks?	___	___	___	___	___
k. logical relationships checks?	___	___	___	___	___
2. Do programs identify data as type and date?	___	___	___	___	___
3. Are program checks provided to detect loss or nonprocessing of data?	___	___	___	___	___
4. Do programs test for valid codes in input data, and are halts or error messages printed out when invalid codes are detected?	___	___	___	___	___
5. Is there a follow-up procedure to determine whether corrections are made in errors found by the computer?	___	___	___	___	___

PROCESSING CONTROL QUESTIONNAIRE
Page 2

6. Are all halts and error conditions printed out in exception report form and retained for audit?

7. Do programs test for header and trailer labels?

8. Are checkpoint and restart conditions provided for?

PROGRAM CONTROL QUESTIONNAIRE

	ANSWER		ANSWERS BASED ON		
	Yes	No	Inquiry	Observation	Test

1. Is there a definite procedure for program development? ___ ___ ___ ___ ___

2. Does the current documentation for each computer program contain:
   a. self-documentation? ___ ___ ___ ___ ___
   b. narrative description? ___ ___ ___ ___ ___
   c. standard identification? ___ ___ ___ ___ ___
   d. testing dates, procedures, and approval? ___ ___ ___ ___ ___
   e. flowcharts and decision tables? ___ ___ ___ ___ ___
   f. program listing? ___ ___ ___ ___ ___
   g. description of input and output? ___ ___ ___ ___ ___
   h. console run book? ___ ___ ___ ___ ___
   i. instructions for distribution of output? ___ ___ ___ ___ ___

3. Does the console run book contain:
   a. set-up instructions? ___ ___ ___ ___ ___
   b. operating messages for halts and errors? ___ ___ ___ ___ ___
   c. procedures for distribution of input and output? ___ ___ ___ ___ ___

4. If instructions for distribution of output are not handled through the console

PROGRAM CONTROL QUESTIONNAIRE
Page 2

    run book, is a control clerk charged with the responsibility of distributing output to authorized recipients and is he/she provided with a distribution list?

5. Are there written procedures for program maintenance that provide for:
   a. formal request for program change?
   b. approval by authorized person?
   c. test of change?

6. Are programming aids used, such as:
   a. shorthand?
   b. automatic decision tables?
   c. test data generators?
   d. librarian packages?
   e. flowcharters?

DATA BASE MANAGEMENT SYSTEM (DBMS) CONTROLS QUESTIONNAIRE

	ANSWER		ANSWERS BASED ON	
	Yes No	Inquiry	Observation	Test

1. Is a data base management system being utilized? ____ ____ ____ ____ ____

2. Does the data base management system have procedures to restrict unauthorized access to data? ____ ____ ____ ____ ____

3. Are the logging or journaling procedures within the data base management system operational? ____ ____ ____ ____ ____

COMPUTER OPERATIONS CONTROL QUESTIONNAIRE

	ANSWER		ANSWERS BASED ON		
	Yes	No	Inquiry	Observation	Test

PHYSICAL CONTROLS:

1. Is computer housed in an area that provides safeguards against fire, smoke, flood, etc.?
2. Is computer isolated from other equipment, water pipes, etc.?
3. Are manufacturer's temperature and humidity requirements maintained?
4. Is equipment serviced by qualified engineers on a regular basis?
5. Is an inventory of critical spare parts maintained?

PROCEDURAL CONTROLS:

1. Are adequate measures provided to restrict unauthorized access to the computer room facilities?
2. Has a policy been established regarding visitors, neatness, smoking, eating, drinking, etc. in the computer room?
3. Is there a procedure by which service personnel are verified?

COMPUTER OPERATIONS CONTROL QUESTIONNAIRE
Page 2

4. Is there a schedule of daily computer operations with priority listings?

5. Are material schedule deviations followed up by a supervisor?

6. Is a daily report of the jobs processed reviewed by a responsible person? If so, by whom?

   _____

7. List the types of prenumbered forms, such as checks or invoices, that are processed by the computer center.

   _____

   _____

8. Are these prenumbered forms controlled?

9. Is a record of halts and error messages retained for review by someone independent of the operating staff? If so, by whom?

   _____

10. Is supervision of console operators sufficient to prevent unauthorized program changes or entry of data through the console?

COMPUTER OPERATIONS CONTROL QUESTIONNAIRE
Page 3

11. Is the use of external switches held to a minimum, and are the instructions for their use set forth in writing? ____ ____ ____ ____ ____

12. Are console printouts controlled and reviewed? ____ ____ ____ ____ ____

13. Are console printouts labeled so as to be intelligible? ____ ____ ____ ____ ____

14. Is the console typewriter paper two-ply? ____ ____ ____ ____ ____

15. If so, does the original serve as the permanent record of activity? ____ ____ ____ ____ ____

16. Is the console typewriter paper serially numbered and are the numbers accounted for at the end of each shift? ____ ____ ____ ____ ____

17. If the console terminal is a CRT rather than a typewriter, are messages from and instructions to the computer captured in hardcopy (permanent) form via a diskette, magnetic tape, or dedicated printer? (Note: Although a system employs a CRT for its console terminal, there is no reason

COMPUTER OPERATIONS CONTROL QUESTIONNAIRE
Page 4

    why a permanent console log cannot be produced for review by the auditor and/or computer system management.) ____ ____ ____ ____ ____

18. Is the console log, or a copy thereof, produced via a device (e.g., printer) that is located outside the computer center and under the control of the internal auditor? ____ ____ ____ ____ ____

19. Is the machine utilization log maintained? ____ ____ ____ ____ ____

20. If so, is it signed by the operator? ____ ____ ____ ____ ____

21. Does it contain:
    a. program identification? ____ ____ ____ ____ ____
    b. start time? ____ ____ ____ ____ ____
    c. stop time? ____ ____ ____ ____ ____
    d. unusual conditions? ____ ____ ____ ____ ____
    e. down time? ____ ____ ____ ____ ____
    f. production time? ____ ____ ____ ____ ____
    g. test time? ____ ____ ____ ____ ____

22. Do operator instructions for each job contain:
    a. identification of all equipment components used? ____ ____ ____ ____ ____
    b. identification of all input and output used? ____ ____ ____ ____ ____

COMPUTER OPERATIONS CONTROL QUESTIONNAIRE
Page 5

    c. detailed set-up and end of run instructions?
    d. identification of all manual switch settings?
    e. identification of all possible programmed halts and prescribed restart instructions?

23. Are reasons determined and corrective action taken for rerun hours?

24. Are equipment utilization reports produced to aid in planning and justifying continued use of equipment?

25. Are physical inventories taken periodically and reconciled to computer equipment records, e.g., invoices?

26. Are replacement (REP) cards utilized to make program changes?

27. Are "live" data insulated from programmers?

LIBRARY AND DATA BASE CONTROL QUESTIONNAIRE

	ANSWER		ANSWERS BASED ON		
	Yes	No	Inquiry	Observation	Test

PHYSICAL CONTROLS:

1. Are there physical controls to prevent inadvertent erasure of tapes? ___ ___ ___ ___ ___

2. Is the library adequately protected against fire, smoke, and water? ___ ___ ___ ___ ___

3. Are files environmentally controlled? ___ ___ ___ ___ ___

PROCEDURAL CONTROLS:

1. Are at least two previous generations of files maintained in order to reconstruct the records if necessary (grandfather, father, son)? ___ ___ ___ ___ ___

2. Is at least one generation maintained in a location away from the storage area? ___ ___ ___ ___ ___

3. Is a library maintained under the supervision of a librarian. If so, by whom?
   _____ ___ ___ ___ ___ ___

4. Is the library adequately controlled during all shifts? ___ ___ ___ ___ ___

5. Are codes or serial numbers used for external labels? ___ ___ ___ ___ ___

LIBRARY AND DATA BASE CONTROL QUESTIONNAIRE
Page 2

6. Are internal header labels prepared for all magnetic tapes or disks?

7. Are internal header labels tested by program instructions to determine whether proper input data are being used?

8. Are internal trailer labels containing control totals generated for all magnetic tapes or disks?

9. Are internal labels tested by program instructions to determine whether all records were processed?

10. Has a policy been established for the retirement of tape reels which had excessive read or write errors?

11. Are magnetic reels stored according to manufacturer's specifications?

12. Are files released from the library to operator returned to the library promptly upon the completion of processing?

LIBRARY AND DATA BASE CONTROL QUESTIONNAIRE
Page 3

13. Are tape files checked periodically for quality? Are tapes to be discarded degaussed before leaving library control?

14. Is access to the off-site storage adequately restricted?

15. Does the librarian maintain and regularly reconcile a schedule of all company tapes showing Master, Confidential, On Loan, Scratch, and Testing tapes received and disbursed and to whom they are disbursed?

16. Is a separate access log maintained for recording confidential tape use?

17. Are transaction logs maintained for direct access storage devices?

18. Is the content of direct access storages devices periodically written on backup files?

19. Are these backup files stored at another location or in a secure vault?

OUTPUT CONTROL QUESTIONNAIRE

	ANSWER		ANSWERS BASED ON	
	Yes No	Inquiry	Observation	Test

1. Are output values screened for abnormal and inconsistent amounts? ⎯⎯ ⎯⎯ ⎯⎯ ⎯⎯ ⎯⎯

2. Are sensitive reports controlled and routed to authorized recipients? ⎯⎯ ⎯⎯ ⎯⎯ ⎯⎯ ⎯⎯

3. Is output returned to operations control area? ⎯⎯ ⎯⎯ ⎯⎯ ⎯⎯ ⎯⎯

4. Are output totals reconciled to input totals? ⎯⎯ ⎯⎯ ⎯⎯ ⎯⎯ ⎯⎯

5. Is the completed job logged out in a log book and the output routed to the authorized recipient? ⎯⎯ ⎯⎯ ⎯⎯ ⎯⎯ ⎯⎯

6. Are couriers verified? ⎯⎯ ⎯⎯ ⎯⎯ ⎯⎯ ⎯⎯

7. Are vital forms (e.g., payroll checks) controlled from unauthorized access? ⎯⎯ ⎯⎯ ⎯⎯ ⎯⎯ ⎯⎯

8. Are exception conditions recognized by the program and are such conditions printed out and routed to authorized personnel? ⎯⎯ ⎯⎯ ⎯⎯ ⎯⎯ ⎯⎯

9. Is sensitive output that should not be viewed or handled by data processing per-

OUTPUT CONTROL QUESTIONNAIRE
Page 2

sonnel generated via an output device located in a secure area outside the computer room?

10. Do reports include understandable and proper headings?

11. Are output values properly aligned?

12. Are all numeric fields sign-controlled?

13. Are cents or units positions zero-suppressed?

14. If page headings change on control break, are headings corrent where page overflow occurs during total break?

15. Is page number sequence correct?

16. Is page numbering based on page number of total number?

17. Is the end-of-report printout obvious?

18. Are both "Date of Report" and "Date of Run" dates on the report?

19. Are checks "check protected" by editing in asterisks preceding money amounts?

OUTPUT CONTROL QUESTIONNAIRE
Page 3

20. Are unused checks or damaged checks properly voided?

21. Are vital documents counted and the ending number maintained by a control clerk, outside of the computer room?

REVIEW QUESTIONS

5.1 List the operational controls.
5.2 Define and give the purpose of input controls. Give an example.
5.3 Explain how the use of control totals helps insure input completeness.
5.4 Define and give the purpose of processing controls. Give an example.
5.5 At a minimum, what should header and trailer labels contain? What is the purpose of these labels?
5.6 Explain the checkpoint and restart procedure. When should it be used?
5.7 Define and give the purpose of program controls. Give an example.
5.8 Define program methodology or development cycle. What is its purpose?
5.9 How can control be increased by having someone other than the one who wrote a computer program test it?
5.10 Why should computer program changes be controlled?
5.11 At a minimum, what items should be included in program documentation?
5.12 List and describe program aids. How do they increase control?
5.13 Define and give the purpose of built-in computer controls. Give an example.
5.14 Define and give the purpose of computer operations controls. Give an example.
5.15 What is preventive maintenance?
5.16 Define and give the purpose of library and data base controls. Give an example.
5.17 Define and give the purpose of output controls. Give an example.
5.18 Explain why a POS or POE device reduces input data error.
5.19 Why doesn't verification of key-punched cards detect all errors?
5.20 Explain the advantages of a UPS.
5.21 Define a LET statement in the linkage editor.
5.22 Why should REP cards be prohibited from use?
5.23 Following are some questions taken from AICPA exams.
    1. A technique for controlling identification numbers (part number, man number, etc.) is (check one)
       a. self-checking digits ✓
       b. sequence checks
       c. parity control
       d. file protection
    2. Echo checks and dual heads are both control devices for checking the transmission of recorded information. The major advantage of dual heads over echo checks is that (check one)

a. the cost is less.
   b. they require less time.
   c. they check the recorded information.
   d. they also check overflow.
3. If a trailer label is used on a magnetic tape file, it is the last record and summarizes the file. Which of the following is information not typically found on a trailer label?
   a. record count.
   b. identification number.
   c. control totals for one or more fields.
   d. end-of-file or end-of-reel code.
4. (T or F) A hash total is obtained by counting all documents or records to be processed.
5. (T or F) A limit check in a computer program is comparable to a decision that an individual makes in a manual system to judge a transaction's reasonableness.
6. (T or F) When they are not in use, tapes, disks, and card files should be stored apart from the computer room under the control of a librarian.
7. The night shift computer operator understood more about programming than anyone realized. Working through the console, he made a change in a payroll program to alter the rate of pay for an accomplice in another department. The fraud was discovered accidentally after it had been going on for several months. The best control procedure would be
   a. review of console log for unauthorized intervention.
   b. payroll review and distribution controls outside of data processing.
   c. audit trail use of payroll journal output.
   d. control total review.
8. Computer department functions have not been properly separated. Under existing procedures, one employee completely controls programming and operations. What are your recommendations to overcome this weakness?
9. Physical control over computer operations is not adequate. All computer department employees have access to the computer. What are your recommendations to overcome this weakness?

DISCUSSION QUESTIONS

5.1 Why should computer personnel be prevented from originating and inputing transactions?

5.2 Relate the old acronym GIGO (garbage in, garbage out) to input controls.

5.3 "Duplication is a key concept in establishing control techniques." Discuss this comment.

5.4 Give at least two examples (not in the text) of how control totals can be used to insure input completeness.

5.5 Give at least five examples (not in the text) of how edit checks can be used to help insure the accuracy of data processing.

5.6 Give examples of control totals that can be used in preparation of a payroll.

5.7 A master inventory file was destroyed when it was inadvertently written over by another processing run. What elementary control procedure(s) was not used to prevent incorrect mounting of the file? What elementary control technique(s) was not used to prevent the computer from writing on the wrong file? If a file is destroyed, how can it be recreated?

5.8 "My computer operator can mount the correct files by reading the external label, so why should it be necessary to also have internal header and trailer labels?" Comment.

5.9 "Built-in equipment checks are more effective in insuring the accuracy of processing than programmed control checks." Discuss the merits of this statement.

5.10 "We verify everything that is input to our computer. Keypunching is cheap compared to rerunning jobs because of bad input." Evaluate this comment.

5.11 "Many users have become disenchanted with the computer because systems designers often fail to insure the reliability of systems performance with adequate control procedures." Discuss.

5.12 "One sign that managements have become more control oriented is that computers are no longer installed behind viewing windows next to the street." Comment.

5.13 "Why is it that my programmers always want to start coding before they understand the problem?" Comment on this statement by a frustrated programming supervisor.

5.14 "Computer programs represent the way business and activities are carried on in organizations; therefore, everything about them should be stringently controlled." Comment.

5.15 Identify at least two applications of bar codes that would help to increase control. Discuss the advantages and disadvantages.

5.16 "If an organization uses a computer-based information system, the computer will take the place of a number of employees who formerly handled the data-processing operations. Consequently, there will be no system of internal control for the auditor to review. Therefore, it will be impossible for the auditor to follow the auditing standards required for an unqualified opinion on the fairness of financial statements."

Discuss the merits of this statement, if any. Do you agree? Disagree? Why?

5.17 "Auditors should be involved very early in the development cycle of any major DP project to make sure good controls are in place, but the auditor has to tread a very narrow line and must not get emotionally involved in the project."[24] Discuss the merits of this statement. What is meant by ". . . but the auditor has to tread a very narrow line and must not get emotionally involved in the project"?

5.18 If an external auditing firm advises a client on the development of an information system, as well as advice on the scope and depth of auditing procedures built into the system, discuss the potential problems associated with independence.

5.19 While reviewing a particular computer program, you notice a CALL statement. It references a module which is not present within the existing program. What should you do? Why?

EXERCISES

5.1 Calculate a self-checking digit for a hypothetical account number. Simulate what would happen if the account number was transcribed incorrectly and input for processing.

5.2 In a programming language of your choice (e.g., COBOL, FORTRAN), write several examples of the processing controls given in the text.

5.3 Recently, several employees of a car manufacturing plant set up a fictitious vendor for molding sand. For several years, until this fraud was accidentally uncovered, the company paid, along with other invoices for molding sand, the fictitious one. As a consulting, independent auditor, what controls would you suggest be implemented to prevent this kind of fraud from occurring again?

5.4 In an organization of your choice that has a computer based information system, use some of the questionnaires at the end of the chapter to help management in the review of their operational controls.

5.5 The I.C. Cream Company manufactures ice cream, toppings, and other food items that are sold in company-owned outlets. Orders are made at a designated time once a week to the central computer located at the main warehouse via a keyboard pad attached to the telephone. The manager keys in a product code (e.g., 14632—Double Chippy Chocolate) and the quantity (5 tons) he wants delivered

---

[24]Don Leavitt, "Auditors Should Be Involved Early in Project Development Cycle," *Computerworld*, May 28, 1975, p. 13.

the next week. Following completion of the entire order, a tone is transmitted back to the manager. A high tone signifies some type of error in the format of the order, and another attempt should be made.

You have been asked to prepare a list of controls that are to be considered for implementation with the order entry system—both at the individual stores and within the central computer system.

5.6 Prepare a list of controls for the system described in 5.5 above. However, make revisions to the system that you feel would enhance the control aspects of the system. Assume that there are no monetary constraints, so a different system configuration is possible.

5.7 Indicate the nature of the *validity* check a computer editing program would have to perform in the following situations. Describe the type of information required by the system in order to perform such a check.
   1. Insurance company—Payment of an automobile claim where a deductible is applicable.
   2. Manufacturing company—A factory data collection system in which workers enter the time they started and finished a particular job. Paychecks and performance bonuses are calculated from this data.
   3. Internal Revenue Service—Preparation of personal income tax rebate checks.
   4. University—Production of semester bills.
   5. Retail Credit Verification System—Credit authorizations made via terminals located in individual retail stores.
   6. Commercial Bank—Online audio responses for cashing customers' checks.
   7. Personal Products Distributor—Bonus merchandise is shipped for ordering specific items in minimum quantities. One bonus is allowed per customer during the promotional period.
   8. Timesharing Company—Users wanting to "sign on" to the system.
   9. State Government—Preparation of welfare checks.
   10. Paper Manufacturer—Overtime paychecks for employees in authorized departments. Certain employees are exempt from earning overtime, and others have restrictions on the amount of time allowable.

5.8 Describe the *reasonableness* checks that might be implemented in a computerized editing process in the situations described below. Indicate what information would be necessary for these checks to be accomplished.
   1. Public Utilities—Production of monthly bills with the meters being read every other month.

2. Automotive Parts Distributor—An online order entry system that generates all supporting invoices, shipping documents, and packing slips.
3. Health Insurance Company—Policyholder's application for maternity benefits.
4. Municipal Government—Initial inputing of real property ownership into the master tax file.
5. Custom Metalworking Company—Paychecks and bonus checks produced from time records produced by an in-shop data collection system.
6. Sporting Goods Manufacturer—Computerized ordering of golf club component parts handled by an inventory management system based on desired stock levels. The desired levels are inputed by the regional sales officer.
7. Large University—Textbook ordering for the next semester.
8. State Government—Motor vehicle registration. (Look at your own registration—whether it is computer produced or not—for some ideas.)
9. International Airline—A system that consists of terminals located in travel agent's offices is employed. Flight information is keyed into the terminal, and the system responds with a printed ticket.
10. Internal Revenue Service—Processing of personal income tax returns.

5.9 Calculate:
1. The cost to keypunch and verify 250,000 cards with an average 75 characters per card.
2. The total number of errors expected for the 250,000 cards described above with verification.
3. Assuming that 100,000 cards are updated each year, and 50,000 new cards are added each year, calculate the cost and total number of expected errors within the data base for five years.

PROBLEMS

5.1 Following is a data center audit performed by Mark Tick, Auditor Extraordinaire. Write a critique of this audit.

Driving up to headquarters, Mark could sense he was close to his destination, probably because of the neon sign on the roof indicating that the division's data center was located in the basement of the main building on the river side, which was four inches below flood level.

Mark donned his dark glasses, adjusted his CIA-emblazoned belt buckle, checked his supply of red and blue dual-pointed pencils, and, approaching the receptionist, asked for the data center manager. Without questioning Mark's identity or reason for being there, she informed him that the manager was away from the data center for a few minutes and told him to wait in the computer room.

"We have all our visitors wait there. They seem to be infatuated with the twinkling little lights on the console," she crooned.

"What's a console?" asked Mark.

"It's the thing next to the 10-gallon gas-fired coffee urn," was her reply.

Mark walked toward the data center, down a hallway crowded with employees on their way to the cafeteria. On both sides of the hall he noticed, without interest, open racks of magnetic tapes labeled neatly with such titles as "Accounts Receivable Master File," "YTD Payroll Master," "Stockholder Records," "General Ledger Summary," etc. He paused for a moment to watch a pick-up game of ring toss, noting that the lunch crowd had obtained the rings from the sides of magnetic tape reels.

"Ingenious people," he thought, "finding use for those worthless little rings."

As Mark walked through the keypunch room, he noticed employees drifting into the room and dumping loose source documents into a box labeled "Input." The keypunch operators were taking out handfuls of the documents for punching. Mark, ever alert, recognized that documents were selected in conformity with the generally accepted "Random LIFO" method.

Entering the computer room, Mark waved to the sole occupant, a machine operator who was hastily punching up cards and inserting them in a deck labeled "Payroll Source Code."

"Obviously, a valuable employee," mused Mark. "It's good to see someone putting forth some extra effort."

Mark poured a cup of coffee, and, as he started to count the petty cash, placed it on top of the 4-foot high stack of dust-covered disk packs. He wondered if the small amount of coffee he spilled would stain the floor as it drained through the disks. Noticing that the hot cup was causing the plastic top of the disk to bend a bit, he pulled a few cards from a deck labeled "Daily Sales Update," which was lying on the console, to use for a coaster.

Mark noticed that the machine operator, having run the unnumbered payroll checks through the check signer, was separating the carbons from the checks. The fourth copy of the checks passed neatly into the fiberboard wastebasket as the machine hummed smoothly, giving the operator a chance to have a smoke and discuss with two mailboys who had just entered how much the various vice-presidents were being paid. Mark was impressed with the operator's concern for neatness, displayed by his having run the console log sheets through the shredder as soon as he finished the payroll run. Mark drew an appreciative smile from the operator as he quipped,

"Nobody could make anything out of the gobbledygook the typewriter just printed, so better to destroy it than get buried under it."

Mark saw a box in the corner labeled "To Disaster File" and inquired, "What's this for?"

The operator explained that the maintenance department's foreman allowed the data center to store copies of important programs in the bottom of his locker.

"What type of programs?" asked Mark.

"Well, as far as I know, the only program over there is the one which causes the printer to use millions of little x's to form a nude girl saying "Merry Christmas!" was the reply.

Mark glanced at the bulletin board and immediately got an indication as to how well organized the data center manager was and that he was nobody's fool. The three signs that impressed him the most read:

—"Fairness is our motto. All input is processed on a first-come, first-served basis."

—"This is a data processing operation, not a delivery service. All output for the current week will be placed on the big table in the cafeteria before 4 p.m. each Friday. Help yourself."

—"To expedite processing and cut down on unnecessary paper shuffling, all documents rejected by the computer because of out-of-balance controls or invalid data will be immediately corrected and re-entered by the machine operators."

The data center manager came in and introduced himself to Mark. He apologized for being away so long. He explained that he had had a hard time finding a garden hose long enough to reach into the data center through a hole in the plywood partition separating it from the adjacent boiler room.

"Good idea," Mark said approvingly. "A lot cheaper than buying fire extinguishers for the data center."

"Well, how does the place look?" the manager asked, perspiring slightly in the 90-degree heat.

"Great!" said Mark. "There will be only one item in my report. There is the serious matter of the 47-cent unexplained shortage in your $5 petty cash fund. Now, as soon as you buy me lunch, I can be off on my next adventure."[25]

[25] Paul D. Johnson, "Mark Tick's Data Center Audit," *EDPACS*, June 1974, pp. 16–17.

5.2 I. Seymore Buggs, auditor, found tape reels stored at various unprotected locations and various computer output scattered around the computer room.

Buggs told N. Burr Cruncher of his concern. Cruncher was irate. "I don't need you telling me about my files and stuff. I know where everything is."

As Buggs, what is your response?

5.3 A. Introduction

In order to maintain tight control over the computer center intervention into production runs being performed by the computers with console typewriters, certain procedures must be followed.

If these rules are followed without deviation, the control will serve as a protection for both the computer center personnel and programmers. Any changes to the audit system either by the computer center, data processing, or auditing personnel must be approved by the auditor. All requests for changes to control procedure should be routed through the auditing data processing staff.

B. Computer Center Requirements

1. All runs (production, test, rerun) must have a start and stop time.
2. Any run that is not identified as test or rerun will be considered an original production run.
3. Prior date reruns (rerun of a previous day's production) will have both today's date and the original run date on the log.
4. The original part of the console typewriter log should not be broken into segments but must remain continuous between the hours of 0001 and 2400. Only one forms break, with the exception of end-of-forms, should occur during the day. Only the auditing staff may break the forms.
5. When the end of the console typewriter forms occurs, make sure the next box of forms used is in correct numerical sequence.
6. If a program is charged to a number other than that of the program, both numbers are to be displayed, and the one to be charged with the run time indicated. Log example: PROG 95200 CHG TO 45070.
7. For a production run, console alterations into the program area must be initialed by the shift supervisor. The assistant supervisor or senior computer operator can initial the alterations if the supervisor is absent.
8. Decisions to bypass label errors on production runs are to be made by the shift supervisor. All bypassed label halts must be initialed.
9. The requirements above will also be in force on the weekends.

C. Data Processing Control Section Requirements
1. Each morning, go immediately to the various computers, and detach and take control of the previous day's logs.
2. Make sure the logs are intact and account for all logs used. The page sequence numbers should be continuous.
3. Check the logs for alterations and label errors. If any are found, determine whether they are properly initialed.
4. If there was a prior rerun, check the original production against the rerun. Check into the reason for the rerun.
5. Members of the data-processing group may ask to take possession of the logs relating to their runs. Deliver the logs, but record the numbers distributed on the sequence number makeup sheet.
6. Balance the demand deposit master posting final total against the statement posting total.
7. On Friday's logs only, pick up the savings interest figures.
8. When new program numbers appear and the logs are not labeled test, try to determine in which category (test or production) the program belongs.
9. Tag each days' logs with the date and file them in the binders. Retain logs for approximately one and one-half months.
10. All exceptions must be followed through, and a satisfactory conclusion must be reached.[26]

D. **Required:** Critique the control procedures above. Prepare a list of additional controls you would recommend.

5.4 I. Seymore Buggs, auditor, approached N. Burr Cruncher, manager of data processing, and said, "I noted that your programmers sometimes operate computer equipment."

"So what?" asked Cruncher.

"A situation like that is counter to good control procedures," said Buggs, "and it really opens up the possibility of improper manipulation by programmers."

"Do you have any evidence that there has been any improper manipulation?" asked Cruncher.

"No," answered Buggs, "and I don't need any. When organizational controls are unsound, and I consider then unsound if programmers can operate equipment, then I'm going to say so."

"But this system is new, the programs are complex, we haven't fully defined users' needs, and I've got to let the programmers in here for testing," responded Cruncher.

Write a short response to this case. Assume that you are Buggs' supervisor.

[26]From Bank Administration Institute, *Auditing Bank EDP Systems*, Park Ridge, Ill.: Bank Administration Institute, 1968), pp. 120–122.

5.5 "The EDP function ran in a mode that courted disaster but left the EDP staff apparently isolated from knowledge of the fraud. An open shop functioned where a central staff developed and ran the primary programs for the business, but programmers in other departments such as actuarial could also write and run their own programs that had access to the live data base of insurance policies. The special processing required to carry out the fraud could have been done, and, it is claimed, was done by the programmers outside of the central EDP staff."

"It is also claimed that EDP management had proposed on numerous occasions the establishment of an internal audit group for the EDP environment, but it was always rejected by top management."

"The EDP staff also observed the external auditors from a revealing point of view. The auditors were apparently handed EDP listings of policy records printed from the master files and accepted them as documents of record since they had no capability or skills to directly access the master files in the system themselves. When the auditors happened to select a fake policy for confirmation, they were told that policy folder was in use by somebody in the company and would be available the next day."

"The way it worked as the Equity's head, Stanley Goldblum, set standards for growth in income, assets, and earnings. The desired quarterly and annual profits were relayed to Alan Green through Lewis and another executive. . . . Green would then go on to the computer and crank out the necessary fictitious policies."[27]

As auditor of Equity Funding, how would you have reacted to the case above?

5.6 In late March, a programmer made a minor change in the program that was used to update the New York City Welfare Department's master file. Because the revision was "trivial," the program was not tested. In the ensuing months welfare recipients died, moved away, or lost their eligibility to receive further payments. Delete transactions were prepared in each case and processed as part of the normal master file update.

The update program received both batch and online updates. Because of the program change, however, it no longer was able to handle both transactions. The "trivial" change caused the update program to ignore batch-entered deletions to the master file, so closed cases remained open.

During April, May, and June, the printers on the system kept spewing out checks. After the checks were burst and stuffed into envelopes, they went winging on their way to dead men, people

---

[27]Donn B. Parker, *Further Comment on the Equity Funding Insurance Fraud Case,* quoted from *EDPACS,* January 1975, p. 16.

who were long gone from the city, and those no longer entitled to receive payments. Finally, field workers started to report payments on closed cases. By this time, $7,500,000 had been disbursed to people who should have been deleted from the files.

Now it is possible to go back and find which checks should not have been written. Getting the money back is a different question. Most of the checks are in the low three figures. It costs $150 to file legal papers to bring suit for recovery of the funds. Collecting the $7,500,000 might end up costing $7,500,000 . . . Oh well, it wasn't real money! It came out of the taxpayers' pockets![28]

List the controls that would have prevented this fiasco from happening.

5.7 A young man opened an account at a large bank in the Midwest. A week or two later, after an electronic communication from a California bank authorized a payment of $2.5 million into his account, the young man absconded with the money. When the bank went to collect from its West Coast correspondent, it found that there had been no authorization for such a payment.

The security manager for the California bank's computer manufacturer was called in to investigate. His first question was, "Who's recently left your data-processing department?" The reply was, "Oh, only Jenny who's going to be married next week."

The security manager went to see Jenny immediately, and found her waiting for her young man to take her to Mexico for their honeymoon. When shown a photograph of the absconder, Jenny said that it was her fiance. She was asked if her fiance had told her to do anything in particular with the computer console she operated. "Yes," she replied, "he told me he had a buddy in some Midwest bank and asked me to please type in some funny little numbers so they could say hello to each other."

So Jenny typed in those funny little numbers and the bank was $2.5 million the loser.

List the controls that would reduce the probability that this kind of problem could happen again.[29] (Hint: Also refer to the previous chapter.)

---

[28]Donald L. Adams, "We Didn't Test the System But How Much Could We Lose? Would You Believe $7,500,000?" *EDPACS*, August 1974, p. 6.

[29]Alan F. Westin, "Privacy, Security and Related Managerial Concerns," *Senior Management and the Data Processing Function* (New York: The Conference Board, Inc., 1974), p. 117.

CHAPTER
6

DOCUMENTATION CONTROLS

6.1 INTRODUCTION

Documentation is a collection of written or printed matter that provides information about a given subject. In computer systems there is hardware and software. The only thing for people is documentation. Documentation is an invaluable part of the review of all the controls in a system. The auditor should review all facets of the systems documentation to ascertain that it conforms to his understanding of the system. Failure to provide necessary documentation seriously impairs the system's auditability.

6.2 PURPOSE OF DOCUMENTATION

The overall control feature of documentation is that it shows the human, in our case, the auditor, what the system is supposed to be and how it should perform. Besides improving overall operating, management, and auditing controls, documentation also serves the following specific purposes.

1. It serves as a starting point for an audit engagement. Simply stated, documentation, in human-readable form, states what the system is and how it is supposed to perform. It gives the auditor something to compare to. It also serves as a roadmap of the system.

2. It improves communication. Nothing is more confusing than to try to find out about a complex system by word of mouth from uninformed personnel or to be told, "Jim takes care of that, but he's not in today."

The New York State Lottery realized too late the importance of documentation.

> ... the order to print the tickets was apparently given informally by the programmer acting under the instructions of his supervisor. There was not, nor is there now, any formal documentation to trace who gave what order to whom on programming and ticket production. Apparently this system in this area depends upon informal word of mouth instructions.[1]
>
> There is a general absence of written instructions for initiating computer actions as well as any formal review to insure that the instructions are properly implemented. Formal procedures are essential to any business, but especially critical in a lottery, and especially to the documentation of the computer programs themselves. It is no exaggeration to say that there is only one individual who currently understands all the computer programs used for the Lottery. If this individual were to resign or be incapacitated, it could be certainly weeks and possibly even months before all the programs were sufficiently documented so that changes, if desired, could be made.[2]

3. It provides reference material for what has happened in the past. This aspect is invaluable in serving as a guide to systems development.

4. It serves systems maintenance, modification, and recovery. Having documentation that shows what the system is supposed to be and how it performs makes systems maintenance and modification much easier. However, the control feature is that it helps to *minimize unauthorized changes*, especially program changes. If a system has good documentation, and a change in some item must be made, such a change is noted and properly recorded. In the event of a disaster or mishap, complete, up-to-date documentation has a direct effect on the organization's ability to recover.

5. It serves as a valuable tool for training and educating personnel.

6. It reduces the impact of key personnel turnover. If the "documentation" is in Jim's head, then this "documentation" leaves when Jim leaves. For example, we know of a company that has spent several hundred dollars in long distance telephone calls to their ex-programmer, who now resides in Florida, and untold sums on headaches because documentation is spotty and no one knows what is going on.

6.3 CONSEQUENCES OF NOT HAVING DOCUMENTATION

As many systems and auditing authorities have said, the documentation area is really the "Achilles' heel" of information systems. Some of the

---

[1]*Summary of Findings, New York State Lottery*, (Cambridge, Mass.: Arthur D. Little, Inc., Nov. 26, 1975), p. 3.
[2]*Ibid.*, p. 9.

consequences of not having appropriate documentation are listed below.

1. It increases the "fog index." Most of the systems personnel and auditors are walking around in a fog, confused about what the system is really doing. Poor control is the result.

2. Lack of good documentation creates inefficient and uncoordinated operations. The left hand never knows what the right hand is doing, so to speak. This situation increases systems costs and wastes manhours. As a matter of fact, an inefficient and uncoordinated system is usually characterized by a lack of good documentation.

3. A lot of work may have to be repeated. All developing systems work should be documented as it is being done rather than afterwards. "A data processing manager who just lost his first programmer will readily testify to the costs which he has incurred in 'taking over' the inherited program.... The language used may be highly individual ... the abbreviations and mnemonics absolutely not understandable. If changes to these programs are required, the problems to be faced are so severe that many programs are completely rewritten after the resignation of their authors."[3]

4. Systems personnel and users become disillusioned and discouraged when they do not know what is going on.

6.4 BASIC COMPUTER-BASED INFORMATION SYSTEMS DOCUMENTATION

The documentation that directly relates to the computer-based information system and its operation is made up of general, systems, and program manuals. These manuals should be developed and organized in a global to detail (general to specific) fashion. They should be maintained in loose-leaf binders and be expandable so they can grow with operations and kept current.

General Systems Documentation

This documentation provides guidance and operating rules to information systems users when interfacing with the system. This part of the systems documentation is listed below.

1. *Users' manual* This manual provides information to the users in the organization as to what the system is and how to receive services from it. It provides names of key personnel to contact, chargeback methods (if used), and overall objectives.

[3] Dick H. Brandon, *Management Standards for Data Processing* (New York: Van Nostrand Company, 1963), p. 29.

2. *Procedures manual* This is a general manual which introduces to all operating, programming, and systems staff the following information: (1) master plan of the system; (2) computer operating standards, controls, and procedures; (3) programming standards and procedures; and (4) systems standards and procedures.

3. *Guidelines* Some people view guidelines (memoranda, etc.) as documentation. In a classical sense, they are not. Manuals are preferred to guidelines. They should contain well-defined information systems policies, standards, controls, and procedures of a permanent and semipermanent nature. Guidelines should be used only for: (1) subject matter that is advisory or directional in nature, with a temporary life span, e.g., 60 days; (2) procedure or policy guides that lead to a known or definite conclusion for a particular problem, and not intended for longstanding information; and (3) other policy and procedure guides of general interest but not considered suitable for documentation manual material.[4]

Systems Development Documentation

Unfortunately, a number of systems projects are developed in a haphazard manner. Common sense should dictate that systems be developed in accordance with a standard methodology. Such an approach informs everyone concerned of what is going on and the exact progress of a project. Moreover, it requires that documentation be prepared as the work progresses rather than afterwards. A typical systems development methodology is shown in Figure 6.1. Each phase of this methodology is described below.[5]

SYSTEMS ANALYSIS

The systems analysis phase represents the first phase in the development methodology. Its purpose is to ascertain the needs and objectives of the users. This phase produces two reports.

1. *Proposal to conduct systems analysis report* This report defines the reason for conducting the analysis. It deals with the technical, economic, operational, and schedule-feasible aspects of the proposed systems analysis. In addition, it is used to disclose systems performance requirements, systems scope, study facts needed, sources of study facts, and schedule of major events.

2. *Systems analysis completion report* This report is very important. It is designed to insure that everyone involved in a systems project

---

[4]William L. Harper, *Data Processing Documentation: Standards, Procedures and Applications* (Englewood Cliffs, N.J.: Prentice-Hall, 1973), p. 99.

[5]For further information, see John G. Burch, Jr. and Nathan Hod, *Information Systems Development: A Case/Workbook Approach* (Santa Barbara, Calif.: Wiley-Hamilton, 1975).

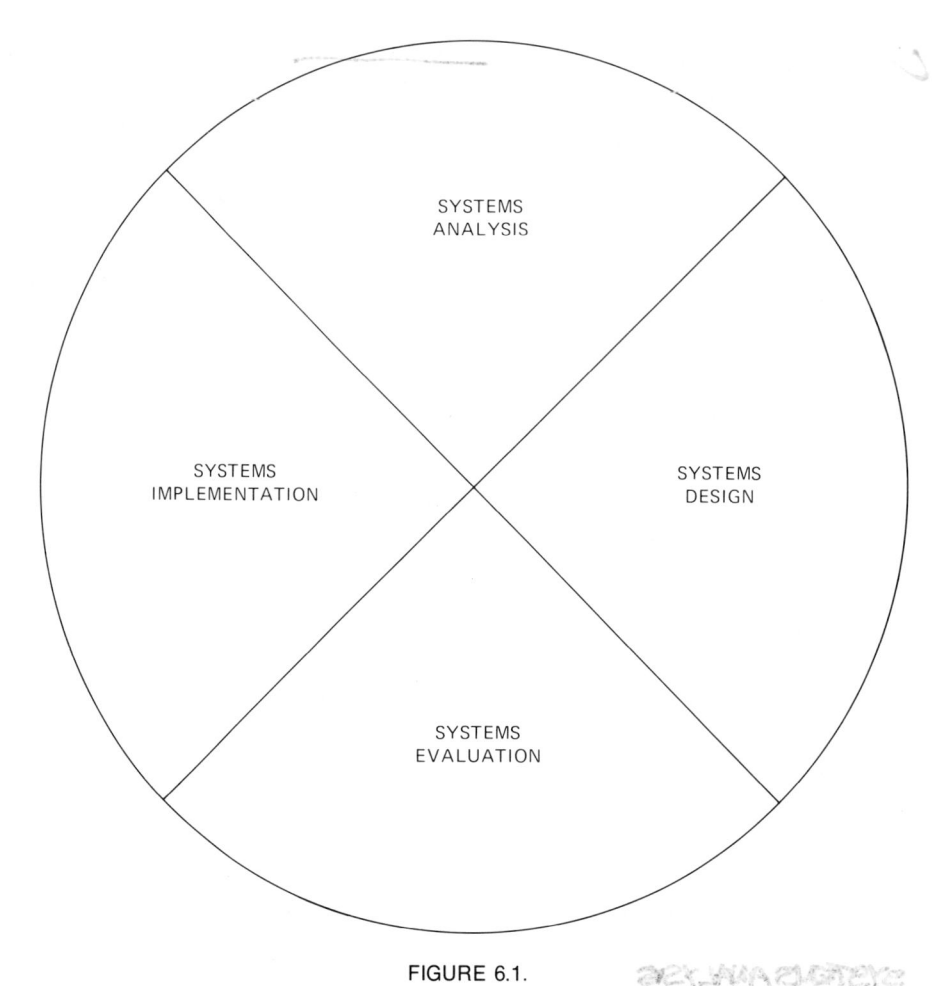

FIGURE 6.1.
Systems Development Methodology.

understands the objectives and overview of the project before the next phase is undertaken. It identifies major problem areas and makes critical assumptions and general recommendations. Agreement should be obtained at this stage before further systems work is performed.

SYSTEMS DESIGN

The systems design phase produces the general systems design proposal report. It defines and/or reiterates agreed-upon systems performance requirements. It then provides general alternative feasible designs based upon (1) outputs, (2) inputs, (3) data base organization, (4) processing procedures, and (5) systems controls.

SYSTEMS EVALUATION

The systems evaluation phase produces the final systems design report. This report contains specific detail and evaluation of a design that is to be implemented. Systems evaluation is based upon employee impact, cost/effectiveness analysis, and implementation plan and schedule. Specific details of the chosen systems alternative include: (1) detail output layouts and reports; (2) detail input layouts and forms design; (3) systems flowcharts, decision tables, and document flow diagrams; (4) equipment specifications; (5) processing module definitions; (6) file organization and labels; (7) controls and backup procedures; (8) standard program requirements; (9) operating system requirements (e.g., job stream assembly and job control language); and (10) programming schedule. This report becomes a permanent part of systems documentation until the system is scrapped or modified.

SYSTEMS IMPLEMENTATION

The systems implementation phase produces the systems implementation report. This report, which also becomes part of permanent systems documentation, includes the following:

1. *Systems training and educating*   This part contains a user training checklist, i.e., those personnel who are to be trained and their job responsibilities. A training plan and schedule are included to prevent wasted manhours. All training procedures and aids used are described.

2. *Systems testing*   This part consists of a hierarchy or increments of testing, which are: (1) components, (2) modules, (3) subsystem, and (4) total system. Also included at each tested level are systems test acceptance and approval.

3. *Systems conversion*   In this step, the operations group accepts the system from the development group. Conversion can be: (1) direct, (2) parallel, (3) modular, and (4) phase-in.

4. *Post-implementation review*   This component permits feedback concerning systems analysis, design, evaluation, and implementation for the system under development. This feedback makes it possible to identify areas that may be improved for the present system, if possible, and certainly for the next system. If we do not learn from our mistakes, we are doomed to repeat them.

Program Documentation

Program documentation consists of all documents, diagrams, and layouts that explain all aspects of the program that supports a particular systems design. We alluded to program documentation and presented a minimum package in the previous chapter. Below we describe what should comprise a typical program documentation package.

1. The program package or manual should start with a general narrative describing the system. Also, a general systems flowchart should be included. This material links the program manual to the systems manual.

2. Program flowcharts showing the input/output areas, source and mainflow of data, entrance and exit of subroutines and program modules, and sequence of program operations should be clearly illustrated. Also, notes, narratives, and decisions tables should be included if they enhance understanding of the program.

3. The job control language (JCL) used to interface the program with the computer should be included with a complete explanation of the purpose of each job-control statement. Without this explanation, many JCL statements are difficult to understand.

4. All programming aids used should be described. These aids (e.g. librarians) were discussed in the previous chapter.

5. Program listings of both the source and object program should be included.

6. Program-testing procedures should be described.

7. Sample printouts of all reports generated by the program should be included.

PROGRAM NAME AR Update	PROGRAM NO. 178 AR
CARD READER	SWITCHES
Trans AR cards	None
CARD PUNCH	HALTS
Not Used	99999 EOJ
PRINTER	DISPOSITION OF OUTPUT
Standard 11 × 14 paper — 3 part	Original to accounting department
	Carbon 1 to sales department
PARAMETER VALUE	Carbon 2 to production department
Upon request from console, input today's date via card reader	DISPOSITION OF INPUT
	Hold for Program 189 AR

FIGURE 6.2
Example of Operating Instructions Contained in a Console Run Book.

8. All controls (as explained in the previous chapter) written into the program should be clearly noted.

9. All operating instructions, operator console commands, and type-in of parameter values should be spelled out. Computer operator instructions are contained in what is normally called a console run book (also called operator's manual, etc.). This book should contain: (a) flowchart and decision tables relative to the part of the system to which the program applies, (b) identification of file media required for input/output, (c) all console switch settings, (d) list of program halts and required action, (e) description of any exceptions to standard routines and input of parameter values (e.g., current date, titles, constants), and (f) authorized disposition of output. An example of operating instructions is illustrated in Figure 6.2.

10. Approval and change sheet should be included and kept current. See Figure 6.3.

6.5 DOCUMENTATION TOOLS

In some instances, the auditor may have to develop a roadmap and documentation of the system for himself. Why? Because, as stated earlier, many information systems contain poor to nonexistent documentation. Tools that will aid the auditor to develop his own documentation are: (1) organization charts, (2) flowcharts, and (3) decision tables.

Organization Charts

These charts give an overview of the personnel and their responsibilities in the organization. These charts are: (1) traditional organization chart, (2) organization chart with narratives, and (3) linear organization chart. An example of each chart is illustrated in Figures 6.4, 6.5, and 6.6, respectively.

To gain an overview of the computer system, the auditor should draw a physical layout chart if one is not available. An example of this chart is depicted in Figure 6.7.

Flowcharts

Flowcharts are made up of standard symbols that show the logical flow, processes, and operations of systems and programs. Figure 6.8 illustrates these symbols.

```
┌─────────────────────────────────────────────────────────────┐
│  TO _____  DATE _____        │
│                                                              │
│  Description of change requested:                            │
│                                                              │
│                                                              │
│  Date desired: _____                                   │
│                                                              │
│  Requested by:   Name _____ Title _____ Phone _____   │
│                  Department _____  │
│                                                              │
│                                                              │
│             SPACE BELOW FOR DATA PROCESSING USE ONLY         │
│                                                              │
│  Program Name _____ Program Number _____   │
│  Changed approved by _____ Date _____   │
│                                                              │
│  Estimated starting date_____ DOCUMENTATION    BY DATE  │
│  Estimated completion date _____  1. Source deck corrected _│
│  Assigned to _____   2. New program listing  _ │
│  Program change number _____   3. New program tested   _ │
│  _____ Patched _____ Recompiled  4. Results approved     _ │
│  Released to operations _____  5. Flowcharts corrected _ │
│  By _____  6. Other manuals changed _│
│  Department notified _____  7. Operating instructions │
│                                       changed             _  │
│  By _____  8. Old listing destroyed _│
│  Effective date of change _____  9. Old object deck        │
│  Change reviewed and                  destroyed           _  │
│  Accepted by _____ 10. Accepted by librarian _│
└─────────────────────────────────────────────────────────────┘
```

FIGURE 6.3

Example of Program Approval and Change Sheet Included in Program Documentation Manual.

FLOWCHART SYMBOL USAGE[6]

Following are some guidelines on the use of flowchart symbols.

    1. *Flowline* Normal direction of flow is from left to right and top to bottom. When the flow direction is not left to right or top to bottom, open arrowheads should be placed on reverse-direction flowlines. When increased clarity is desired, open arrowheads can be placed on normal direction flowlines. When flowlines are broken because of page lim-

[6]William L. Harper, *op. cit.*, pp. 63–67.

CHAPTER SIX DOCUMENTATION CONTROLS **187**

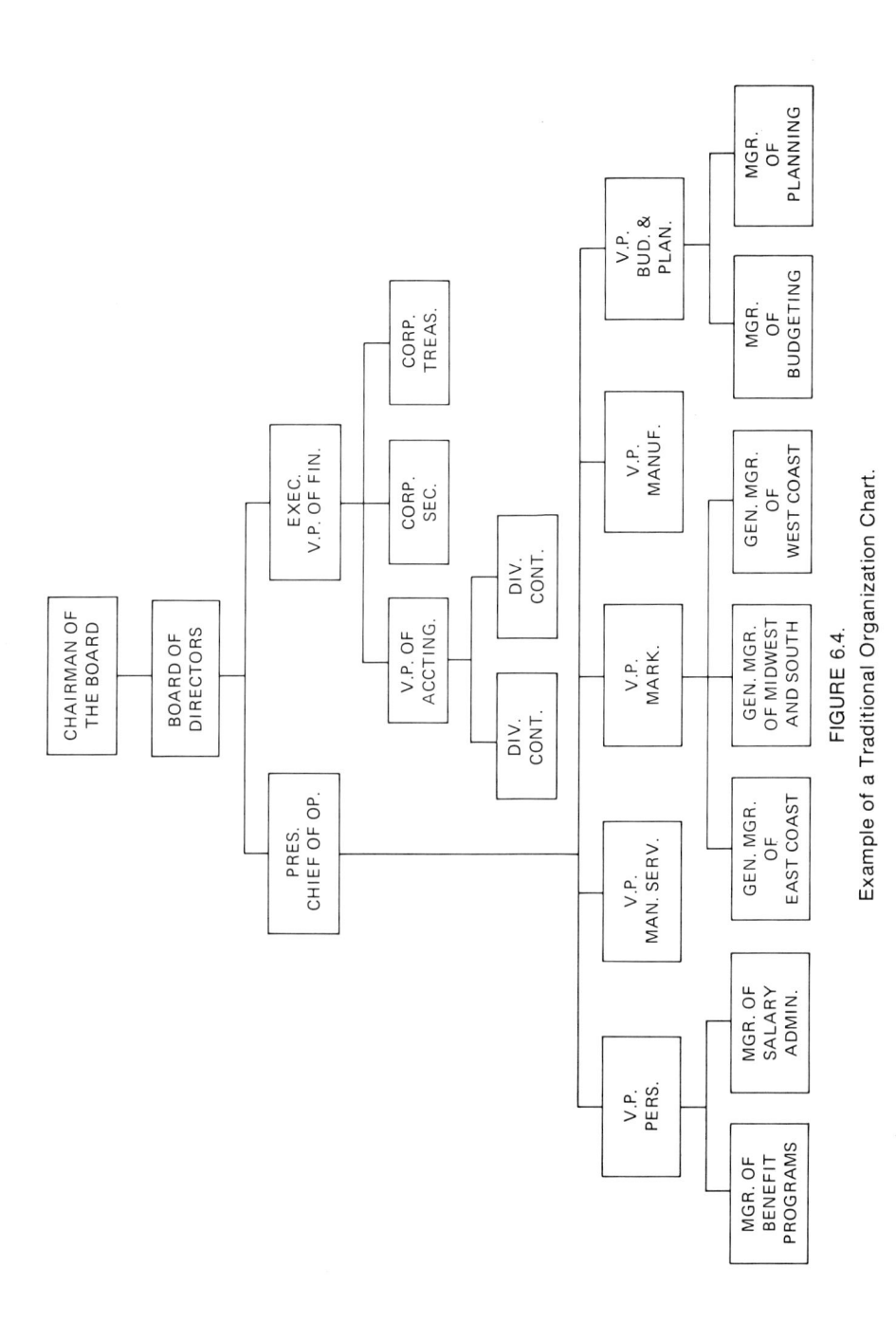

FIGURE 6.4.
Example of a Traditional Organization Chart.

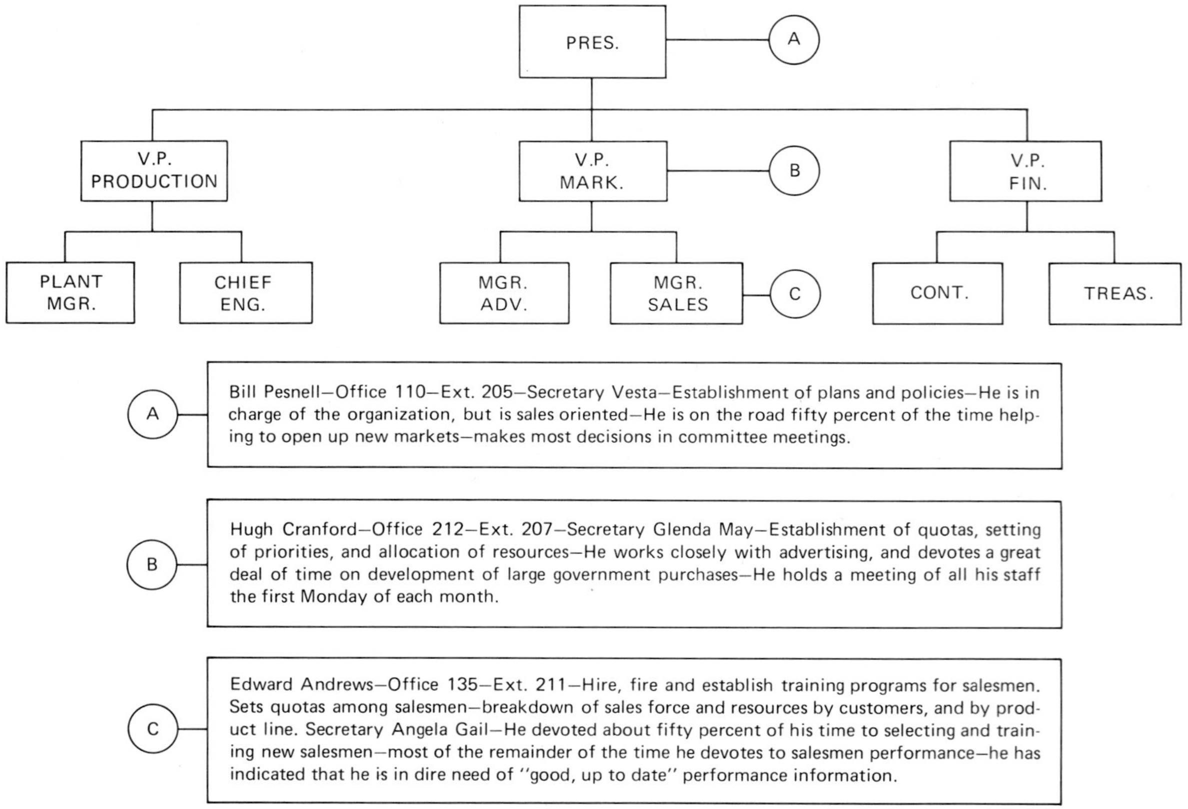

188 PART TWO SYSTEM OF CONTROLS

```
                        PRES.
                          │
        ┌─────────────────┼─────────────────┐
        │                 │                 │
      V.P.              V.P.              V.P.
   PRODUCTION          MARK.              FIN.
        │                 │                 │
    ┌───┴───┐       ┌─────┴─────┐       ┌───┴───┐
  PLANT  CHIEF    MGR.        MGR.    CONT.  TREAS.
   MGR.   ENG.    ADV.        SALES
```

(A) — attached to PRES.
(B) — attached to V.P. MARK.
(C) — attached to MGR. SALES

(A) Bill Pesnell—Office 110—Ext. 205—Secretary Vesta—Establishment of plans and policies—He is in charge of the organization, but is sales oriented—He is on the road fifty percent of the time helping to open up new markets—makes most decisions in committee meetings.

(B) Hugh Cranford—Office 212—Ext. 207—Secretary Glenda May—Establishment of quotas, setting of priorities, and allocation of resources—He works closely with advertising, and devotes a great deal of time on development of large government purchases—He holds a meeting of all his staff the first Monday of each month.

(C) Edward Andrews—Office 135—Ext. 211—Hire, fire and establish training programs for salesmen. Sets quotas among salesmen—breakdown of sales force and resources by customers, and by product line. Secretary Angela Gail—He devoted about fifty percent of his time to selecting and training new salesmen—most of the remainder of the time he devotes to salesmen performance—he has indicated that he is in dire need of "good, up to date" performance information.

FIGURE 6.5.
Example of an Organization Chart with Narratives.

FIGURE 6.6.
Example of Linear Organization Chart (LOC).

	New Products	New Markets	Training	Salary and Commission
President	A			A
Vice President—Marketing	A	A		A
General Manager—Sales	C	A	A	AP
Regional Manager—Sales	C	P	AP	C
Manager—Product Planning	PC	P		
Vice President—Personnel				A
Manager—Supply and Transportation	O	O		
Manager—Product Engineering	APC			
Manager—Manufacturing	O			
Salesmen	O	O	PO	
Manager—Research and Development	P			
Controller				PC
Manager—Information Systems	O	O	O	PO

Legend: A—Approval; C—Control; P—Planning; O—Operation

itation, connection symbols should be used to indicate the break. When flow is bidirectional, it can be shown by either single or double lines, but open arrowheads should be used to indicate both normal-direction flow and reverse direction flow.

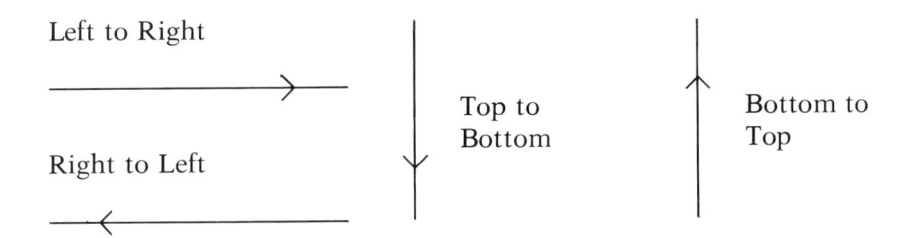

Left to Right

Right to Left

Top to Bottom

Bottom to Top

2. *Multiple logic paths* Each exit from a symbol should be identified to show the logic path it represents. The logic paths may be represented

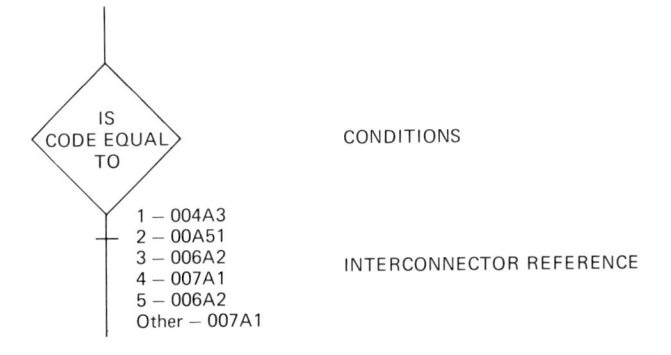

IS CODE EQUAL TO

1 — 004A3
2 — 00A51
3 — 006A2
4 — 007A1
5 — 006A2
Other — 007A1

CONDITIONS

INTERCONNECTOR REFERENCE

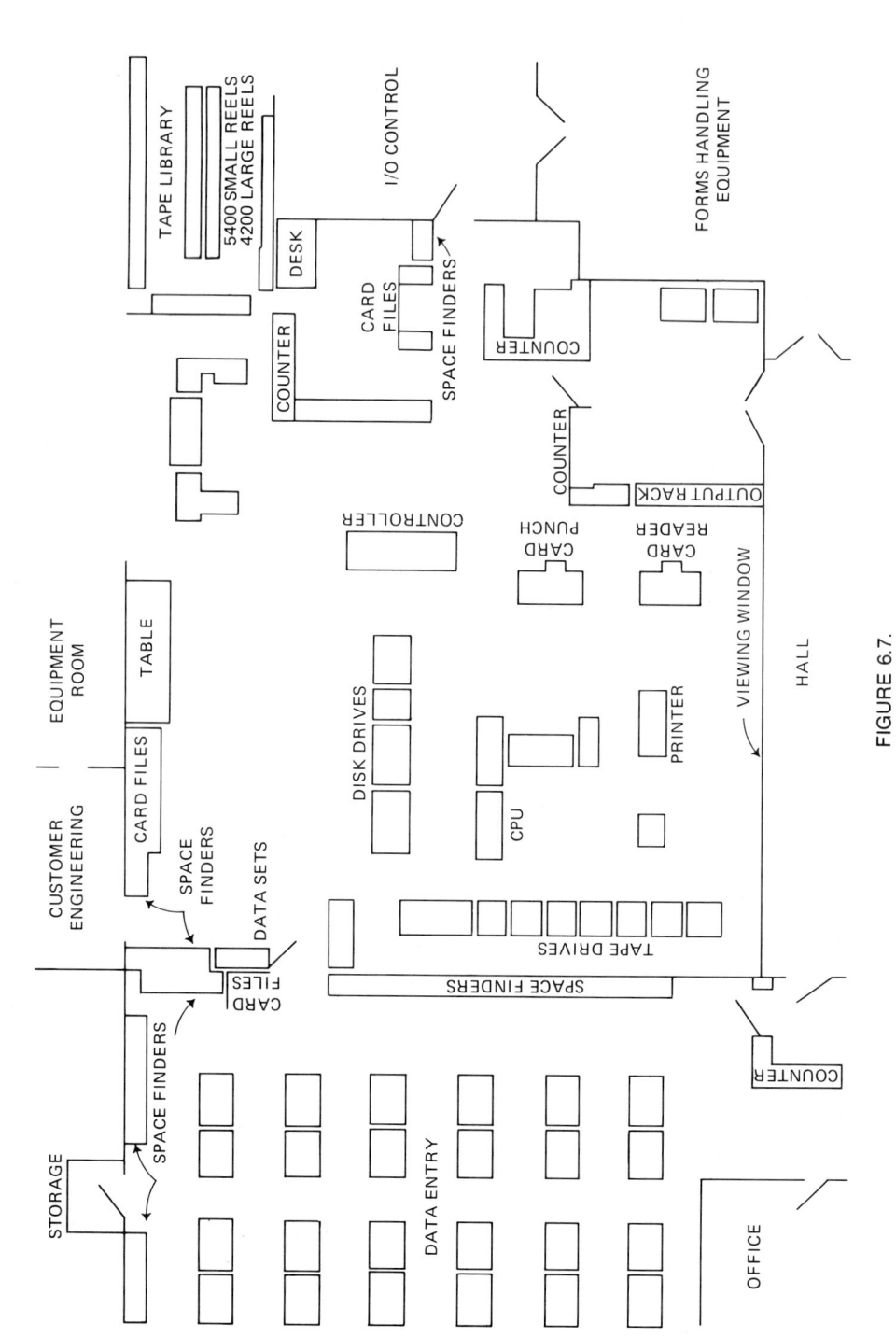

FIGURE 6.7.
Example of a Computer System Physical Layout Chart.

CHAPTER SIX   DOCUMENTATION CONTROLS   **191**

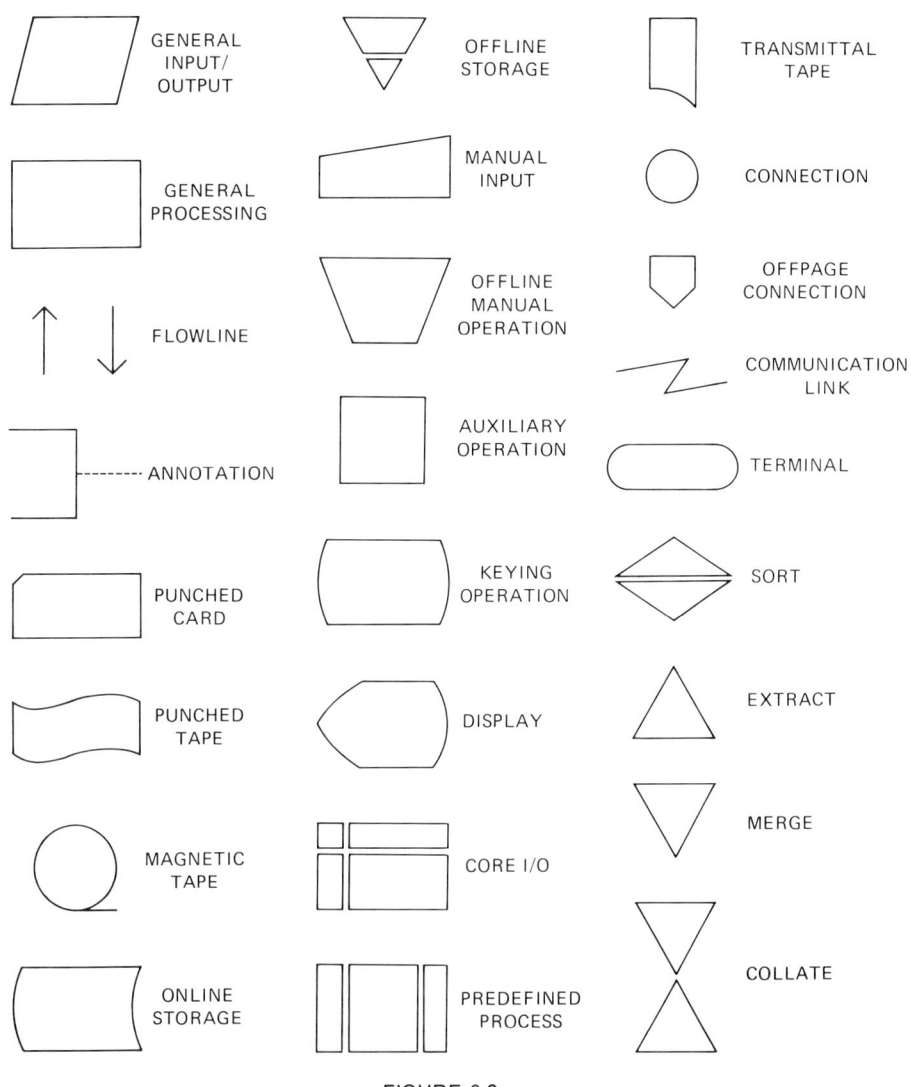

FIGURE 6.8.
Summary of Flowchart Symbols.

by a table that indicates their associated conditions and the interconnector references.

3. *Branching table* A branching table may be used in lieu of a decision symbol to depict a decision function. The table is composed of a statement of the decision to be made, a list of the conditions that can occur, and the path to be followed for each condition. The terms "Decision Statement" and "Paths" are not part of the standard. The "Go To" section contains either an inconnector reference or a single flowline exiting to another symbol. Examples of branching table formats are shown below.

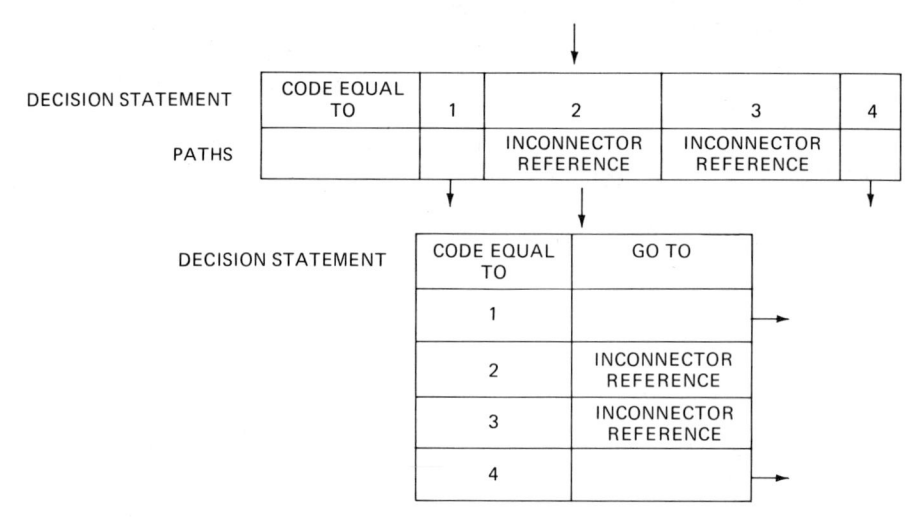

DECISION STATEMENT	CODE EQUAL TO	1	2	3	4
PATHS			INCONNECTOR REFERENCE	INCONNECTOR REFERENCE	

DECISION STATEMENT	CODE EQUAL TO	GO TO
	1	
	2	INCONNECTOR REFERENCE
	3	INCONNECTOR REFERENCE
	4	

4. *Multiple symbols* As an alternative to a single symbol with appropriate text, the same input/output symbols may be shown in an overlay pattern to illustrate their use or creation of multiple media or files; for example, number of copies, types of printed reports, types of punched-card formats, multiple magnetic tape reels.

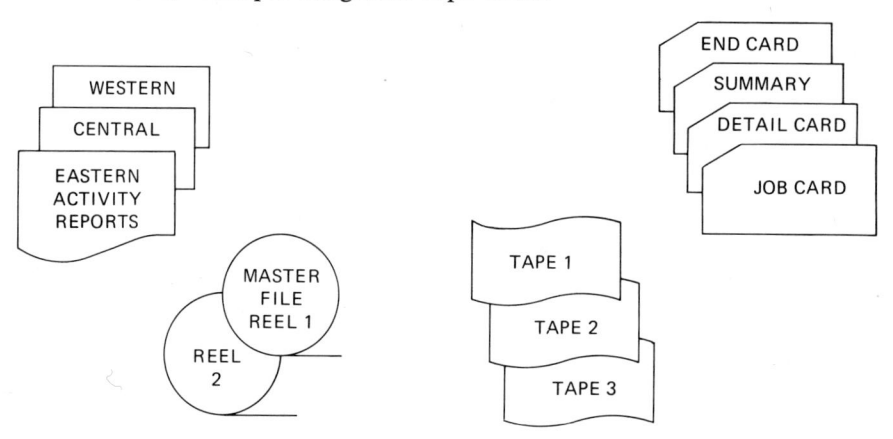

5. *Communication link* Unless otherwise indicated, the direction of communication link flow is left to right and top to bottom. Open arrowheads are necessary on symbols for flow that are not in the conventional direction. An open arrowhead may also be used on any line when increased clarity will result.

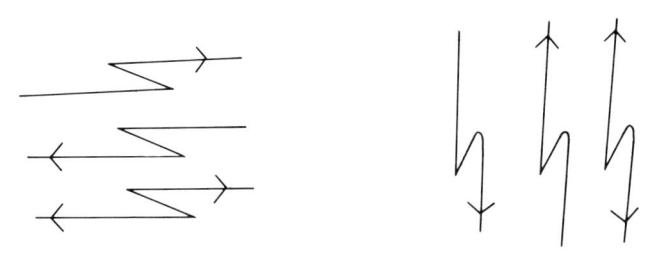

6. *Flowchart texts* Descriptive information with each symbol should be presented so as to read from left to right and top to bottom regardless of flow direction.

7. *Symbol identifications* The identifying notation assigned to a symbol, other than a connector, should be placed above the symbol and to the right of its vertical bisector.

8. *Symbol cross references* Identifying notation(s) of other elements of documentation (including this set of flowchart(s) should be placed above the symbol and to the left of its vertical bisector.

9. *Connector common identification* A common identifier, such as an alphabetic character, number, or mnemonic label, is placed within the outconnector and its associated inconnector.

10. *Cross reference connectors* Additional cross referencing between associated connectors is achieved by placing the chart page(s), coordinates, or other identifier(s) of the associated connectors above and to the left of the vertical bisector of each connector.

OUT CONNECTOR

10
A
CHART PAGE 2

INCONNECTOR

2
A
CHART PAGE 10

11. *Symbol striping* Striping is a means of indicating that a more detailed presentation of a function is to be found elsewhere in the same set of flowcharts. This representation differs from a predefined process symbol, which need not be represented in detail in the same set of flowcharts.

12. *Striped symbols* A horizontal line is drawn within, completely across, and near the top of the symbol, and a reference to the detailed representation is placed between that line and the top of the symbol.

13. *First symbol of detailed representation* The terminal symbol should be used as the first and last symbols of the detailed representation. The first terminal symbol contains an identification which also appears in the striped symbol, as indicated in the paragraph above.

14. *Cross referencing of striped symbol and detailed representation* A reference to the location of the detailed representation within the flowchart is placed above and to the left of the vertical bisector of the striped symbol. A reference to the striped symbol is placed above and to the left of the vertical bisector of its associated terminal symbol.

Example: Striped Symbol and Detailed Representation

STRIPED SYMBOL

DETAILED REPRESENTATION ON PAGE 10

10
X B4

CHART PAGE 1

COMMON IDENTIFIER

DETAILED REPRESENTATION

STRIPED SYMBOL ON PAGE 1

1
X B4

CHART PAGE 10

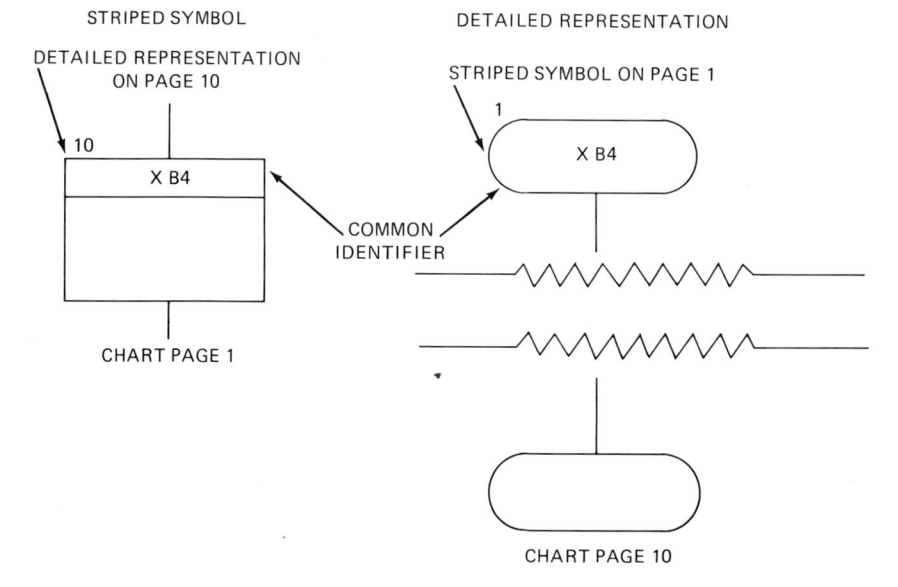

15. *Multiple exits* Multiple exits from a symbol should be shown by several flowlines from the symbol to other symbols or by a single flowline from the symbol which branches into the appropriate number of flowlines.

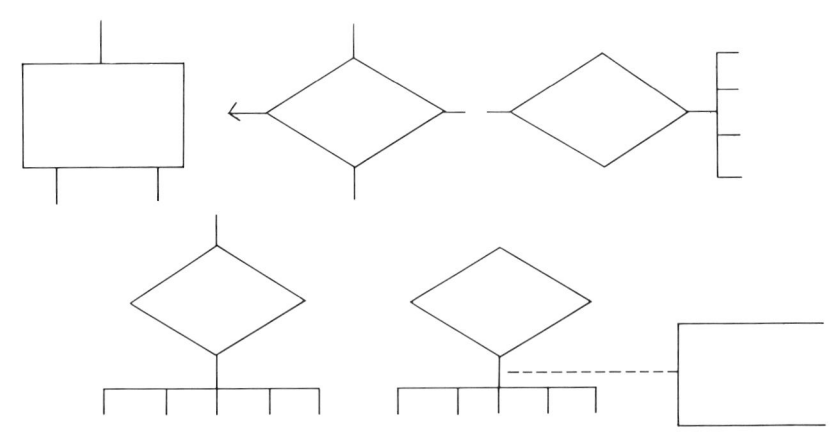

16. *Overlay pattern* The overlay pattern must be drawn from front to back with the first symbol as the entire I/O symbol. The center line of the second symbol must be offset up or down from the horizontal center line and to the right or left of the vertical center line of the first symbol. Similarly, the third symbol must be offset in the same direction from the second symbol, the fourth from the third, and so on for any remaining symbols.

17. *Priority representation* When the multiple symbols represent an ordered set, the ordering shall be from front (first) to back (last).

18. *Flowlines with repetitive symbols* Flowlines may enter or leave from any point on the overlay symbols. The priority or sequential order of the multiple symbols is not altered by the point at which the flowline(s) enters or leaves.

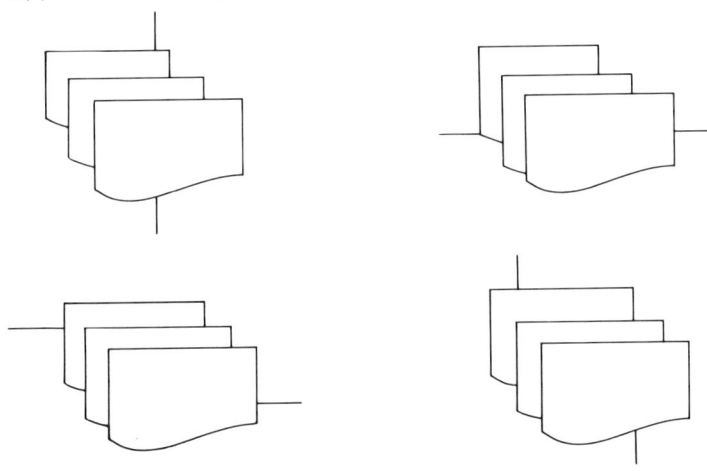

EXAMPLE OF SYSTEMS, MACRO, AND MICRO FLOWCHARTS

In Figure 6.9 is an example of a systems flowchart for a payroll application. In Figures 6.10 and 6.11 the macro flowchart describes the earnings calculation routine. In Figure 6.12, the micro flowchart describes in detail the subroutine to derive the standard deductions for the earnings calculation routine.

EXAMPLE OF DOCUMENT FLOWCHART

To perform an effective audit in many situations, the auditor must gain a full understanding of the flow of paper documents and reports in the organization. An ideal tool to gain this understanding is called a document flowchart. Symbols used to construct this type of flowchart are listed in Figure 6.13. In Figure 6.14, an example of how to develop a document flowchart is given. This particular flowchart was developed by the major accounting firm of Ernst and Ernst.

DECISION TABLES

Decision tables help to explain the if-then relationships that exist within a system. They help to cut through verbose narratives and complexities. Examples of both limited and extended entry decision tables are represented in Figure 6.15 and 6.16, respectively.

6.6 SUMMARY

Following the series of figures is a questionnaire that is used to summarize and help clarify the material in this chapter.

CHAPTER SIX DOCUMENTATION CONTROLS 197

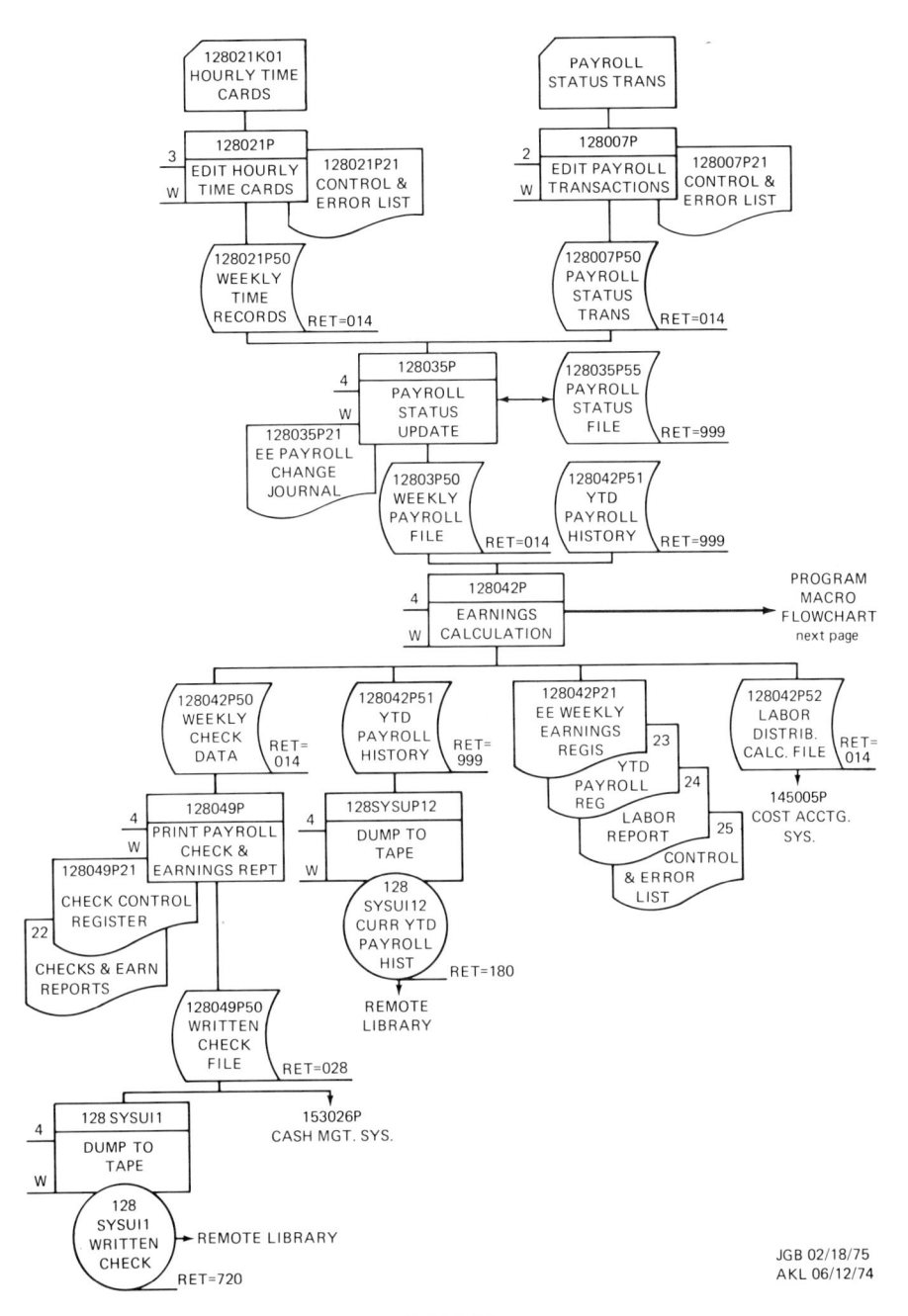

FIGURE 6.9.
Example of a Systems Flowchart for a Payroll Application.

198 PART TWO SYSTEM OF CONTROLS

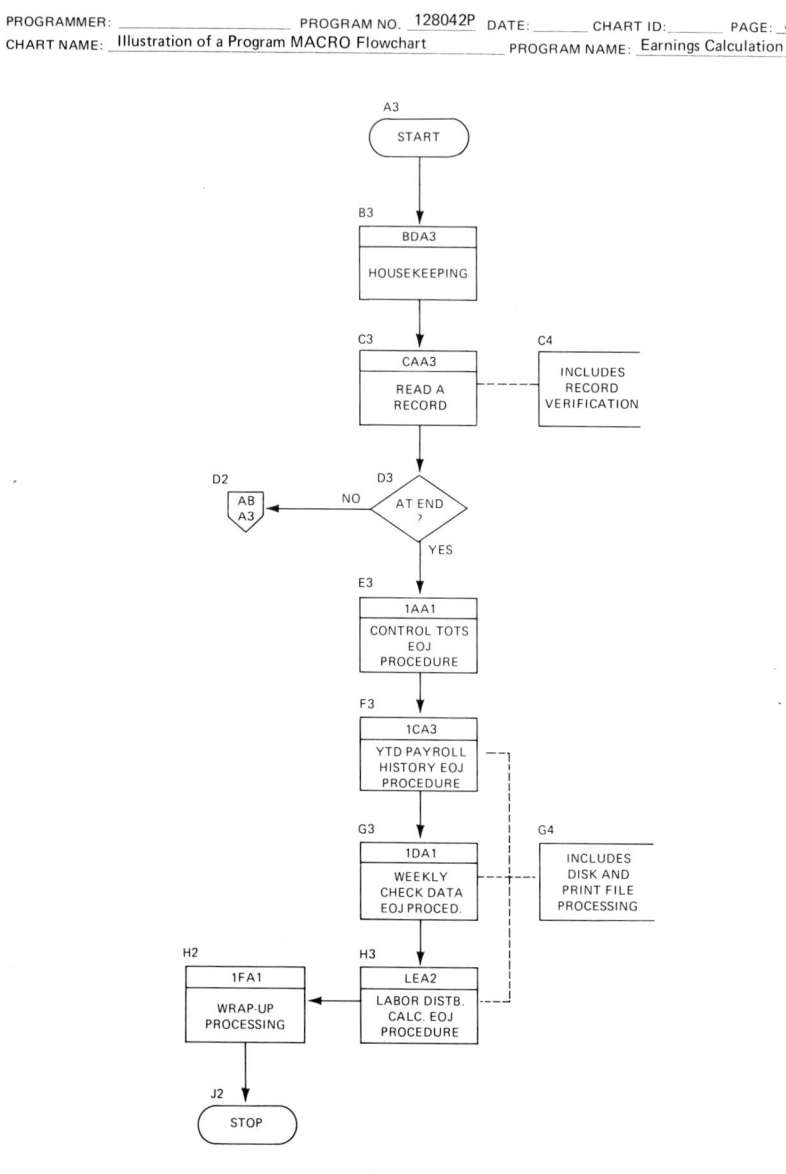

PROGRAMMER: _____ PROGRAM NO. 128042P DATE: _____ CHART ID: _____ PAGE: AA
CHART NAME: Illustration of a Program MACRO Flowchart PROGRAM NAME: Earnings Calculation

```
                          A3
                        ( START )
                            │
                          B3│
                        ┌───▼────┐
                        │ BDA3   │
                        │HOUSE-  │
                        │KEEPING │
                        └───┬────┘
                          C3│                    C4
                        ┌───▼────┐          ┌──────────┐
                        │ CAA3   │          │ INCLUDES │
                        │ READ A │ ─ ─ ─ ─ ─│ RECORD   │
                        │ RECORD │          │VERIFICA- │
                        └───┬────┘          │ TION     │
                            │               └──────────┘
          D2              D3│
        ┌─────┐          ╱──▼──╲
        │ AB  │   NO    ╱ AT END╲
        │ A3  │◄───────╱    ?    ╲
        └─────┘         ╲        ╱
                         ╲──┬──╱
                         YES │
                          E3▼
                        ┌────────┐
                        │ 1AA1   │
                        │CONTROL │
                        │TOTS EOJ│
                        │PROCED. │
                        └───┬────┘
                          F3│
                        ┌───▼────┐
                        │ 1CA3   │
                        │YTD PAY-│
                        │ROLL    │─ ─ ─ ┐
                        │HIST EOJ│      │
                        │PROCED. │      │
                        └───┬────┘      │
                          G3│          G4
                        ┌───▼────┐  ┌──────────┐
                        │ 1DA1   │  │ INCLUDES │
                        │ WEEKLY │  │ DISK AND │
                        │ CHECK  │─ ┤PRINT FILE│
                        │DATA EOJ│  │PROCESSING│
                        │ PROCED │  └──────────┘
                        └───┬────┘
        H2                H3│
     ┌──────┐          ┌────▼───┐
     │ 1FA1 │          │ LEA2   │
     │WRAP- │          │LABOR   │
     │ UP   │◄─────────│DISTB.  │
     │PROC. │          │CALC EOJ│─ ─ ─ ┘
     └──┬───┘          │PROCED. │
        │              └────────┘
      J2▼
    ( STOP )
```

FIGURE 6.10.
Example of a Macro Flowchart for an Earnings Calculation Routine (continued).

CHAPTER SIX DOCUMENTATION CONTROLS **199**

FIGURE 6.11.
Example of a Macro Flowchart for an Earnings Calculation Routine.

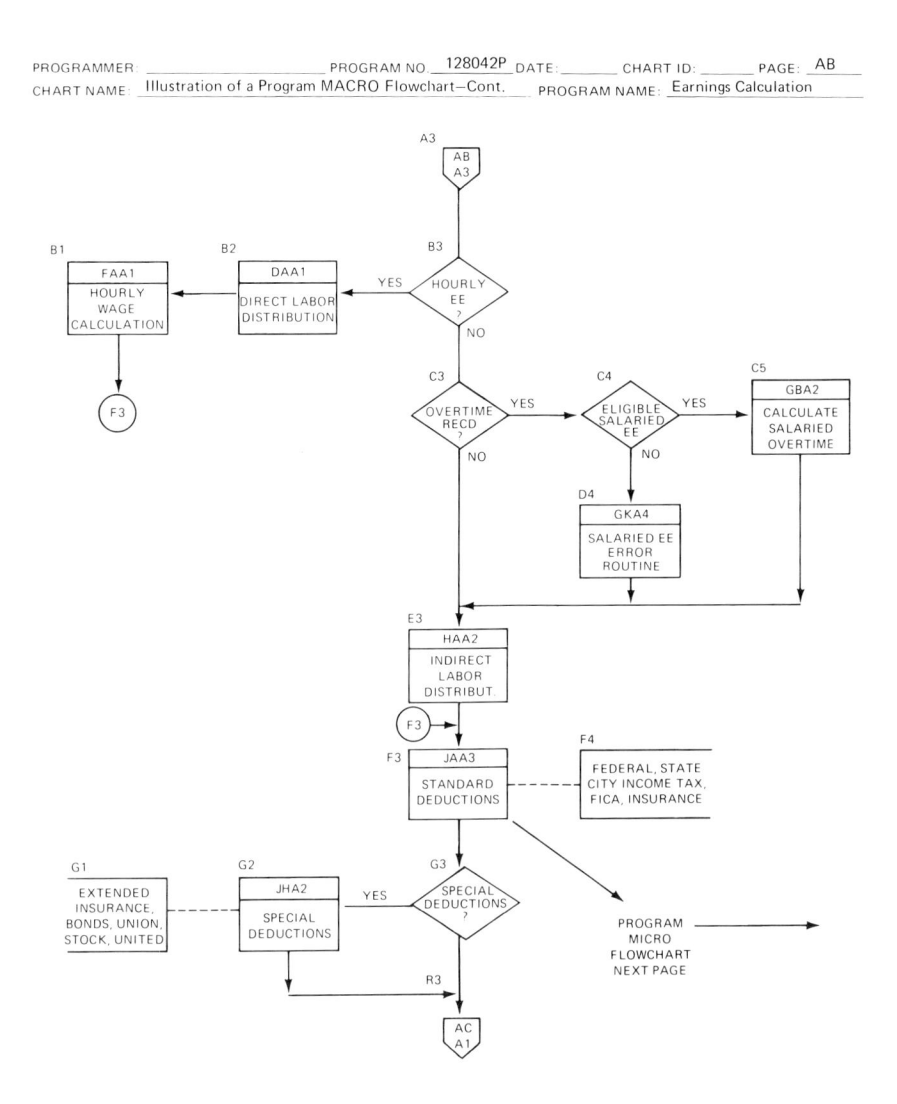

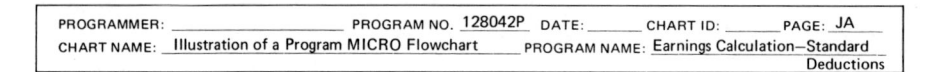

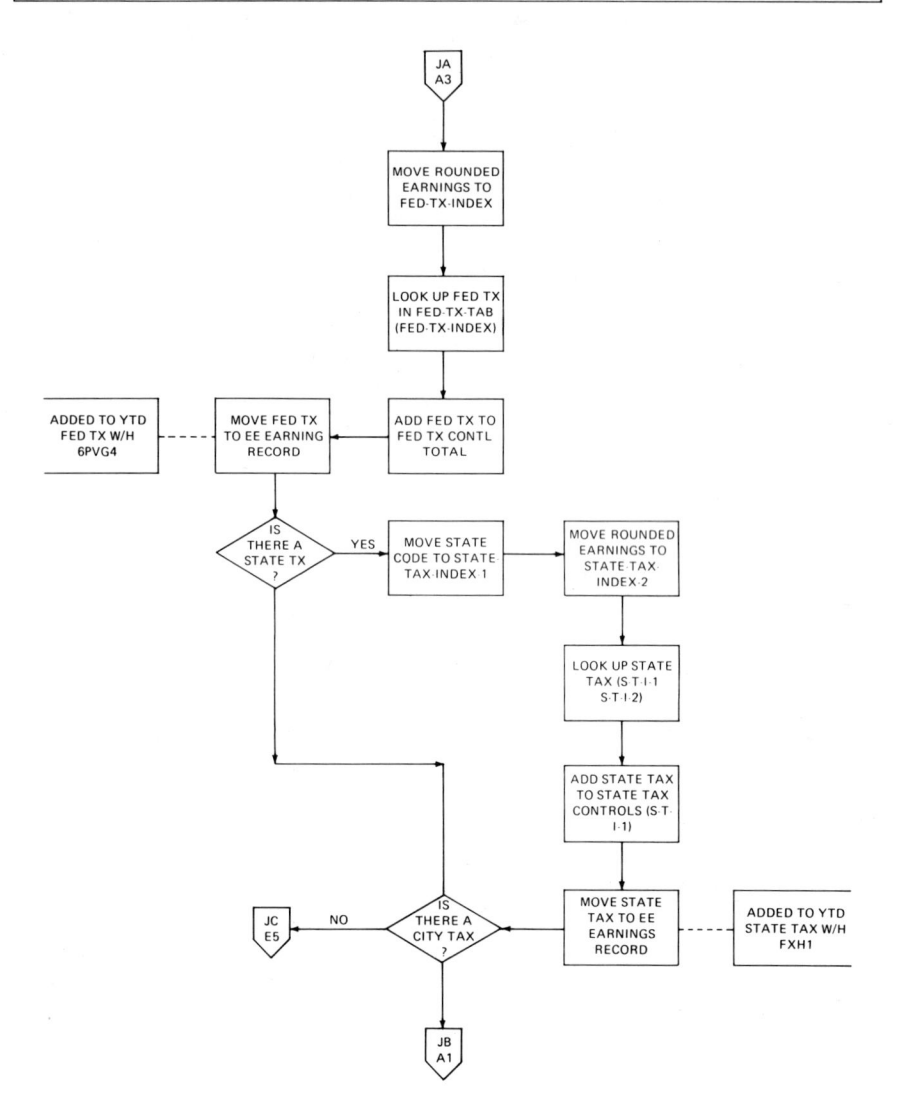

FIGURE 6.12.
Example of a Micro Flowchart for the Standard Deductions Subroutine.

CHAPTER SIX DOCUMENTATION CONTROLS 201

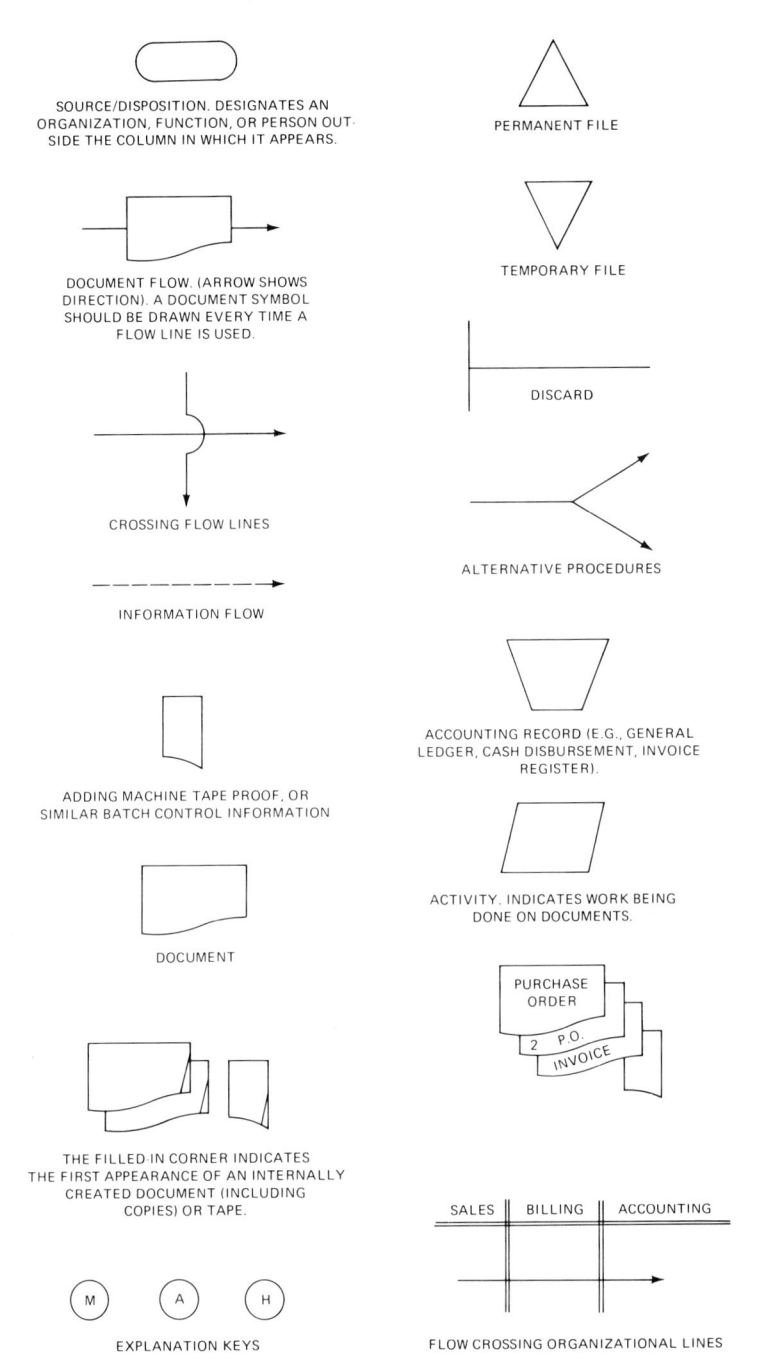

SOURCE/DISPOSITION. DESIGNATES AN ORGANIZATION, FUNCTION, OR PERSON OUTSIDE THE COLUMN IN WHICH IT APPEARS.

PERMANENT FILE

DOCUMENT FLOW. (ARROW SHOWS DIRECTION). A DOCUMENT SYMBOL SHOULD BE DRAWN EVERY TIME A FLOW LINE IS USED.

TEMPORARY FILE

DISCARD

CROSSING FLOW LINES

ALTERNATIVE PROCEDURES

INFORMATION FLOW

ACCOUNTING RECORD (E.G., GENERAL LEDGER, CASH DISBURSEMENT, INVOICE REGISTER).

ADDING MACHINE TAPE PROOF, OR SIMILAR BATCH CONTROL INFORMATION

ACTIVITY. INDICATES WORK BEING DONE ON DOCUMENTS.

DOCUMENT

PURCHASE ORDER
2 P.O.
INVOICE

THE FILLED-IN CORNER INDICATES THE FIRST APPEARANCE OF AN INTERNALLY CREATED DOCUMENT (INCLUDING COPIES) OR TAPE.

SALES | BILLING | ACCOUNTING

M A H

EXPLANATION KEYS

FLOW CROSSING ORGANIZATIONAL LINES

FIGURE 6.13.
Document Flowcharting Symbols.

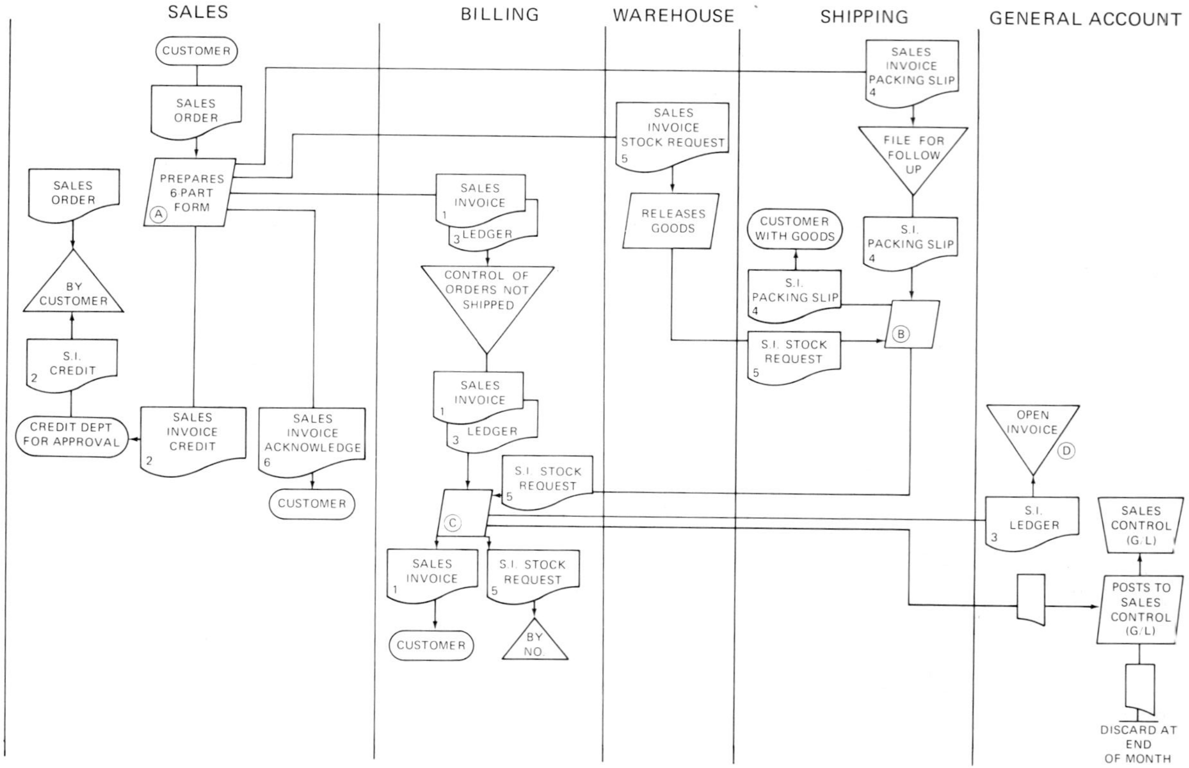

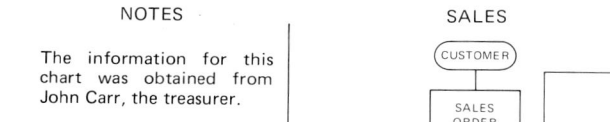

FIGURE 6.14.
Example of a Document Flowchart.

NOTES

The information for this chart was obtained from John Carr, the treasurer.

A— The remaining five parts are held until the credit copy is returned, marked OK.

B— The goods are compared with descriptions on stock request. Items shipped are marked on the stock request and the packing slip is placed with the goods.

C— Items shipped are entered on the sales invoice and ledger copy, extensions are made and checked, prices are compared to price lists, and an adding machine tape is run from the ledger copy. The numerical sequence of invoices is accounted for when the stock request copy is filed.

D— Open invoices file is balanced monthly with the sales control.

CHAPTER SIX   DOCUMENTATION CONTROLS   203

| | DECISION TABLE TITLE | RULES |||||||
		1	2	3	4	5	...	N
A								
B	CONDITION STUB							
C								
D								
E								
F								
G								

I								
J								
K	ACTION STUB							
L								
M								
N								
O								

LIMITED ENTRY DECISION TABLE

	MONTHLY SERVICE CHARGE	1	2	3	4
A	BUSINESS ACCOUNT	Y	N	N	Y
B	PERSONAL ACCOUNT	N	Y	Y	N
C	MINIMUM BALANCE < $100	N	Y	N	N
D	MINIMUM BALANCE > $500	Y	N	N	N
E	NO MONTHLY SERVICE CHARGE	X		X	
F	CHARGE 10¢/CHECK		X		
G	CHARGE 02¢/CHECK				X

FIGURE 6.15.
A Limited Entry Decision Table.

LIMITED ENTRY DECISION TABLE

	MONTHLY SERVICE CHARGE	1	2	3	4
A	BUSINESS ACCOUNT	Y	N	N	Y
B	PERSONAL ACCOUNT	N	Y	Y	N
C	MINIMUM BALANCE < $100	N	Y	N	N
D	MINIMUM BALANCE > $500	Y	N	N	N

		1	2	3	4
E	NO MONTHLY SERVICE CHARGE	X		X	
F	CHARGE 10¢/CHECK		X		
G	CHARGE 02¢/CHECK				X

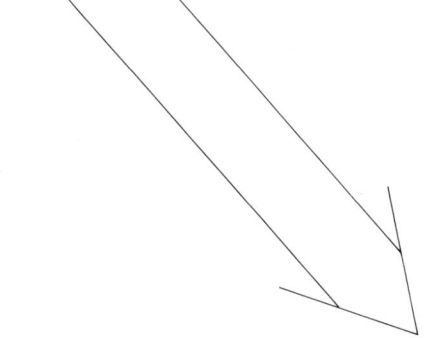

EXTENDED ENTRY DECISION TABLE

	MONTHLY SERVICE CHARGE	1	2	3	4
A	BUSINESS ACCOUNT	Y	Y		
B	PERSONAL ACCOUNT			Y	Y
C	MINIMUM BALANCE	< $5,000	$5,000	< $100	$100

		1	2	3	4
D	NO MONTHLY SERVICE CHARGE		X		X
E	CHARGE/CHECK	.02/check		.10/check	

FIGURE 6.16.
An Extended Entry Decision Table.

DOCUMENTATION QUESTIONNAIRE

	ANSWER		ANSWERS BASED ON		
	Yes	No	Inquiry	Observation	Test

1. Does the current documentation for each computer program contain:
   a. a narrative description?
   b. flowcharts and decision tables?
   c. JCL?
   d. program listing?
   e. description of programming aids?
   f. controls used?
   g. description of input/output?
   h. testing procedures used?
   i. console run book?
   j. approval and change sheet?

2. Does the console run book contain:
   a. flowchart of specific application?
   b. set-up instructions
   c. description of input/output layouts?
   d. console switch settings?
   e. operating messages (errors, halts, etc.)?
   f. procedures for labeling and disposition of input?

Documentation Questionnaire
Page 2

    g. procedures for labeling and disposition of output? ___ ___ ___ ___ ___

3. Are there written procedures for program maintenance which provide for:
   a. a formal request for a program change? ___ ___ ___ ___ ___
   b. approval by a responsible individual for a change? ___ ___ ___ ___ ___
   c. a test of the change prior to acceptance? ___ ___ ___ ___ ___

4. Are duplicate copies of either the source decks, object decks, or program listings maintained away from the EDP premises as protection against loss? ___ ___ ___ ___ ___

5. Is there a definable systems development methodology? ___ ___ ___ ___ ___

6. If so, describe it below:

REVIEW QUESTIONS

6.1 Define documentation and give its purpose.
6.2 How does documentation affect control?
6.3 List the consequences of not having documentation.
6.4 Define and list the ingredients of a program manual.
6.5 What role do guidelines play in documentation?
6.6 Why is it important to have systems analysts follow a systems development methodology?
6.7 List the phases of a systems development methodology and briefly describe the results of each phase.
6.8 List and illustrate documentation development tools as discussed in this text. What purpose do they serve?
6.9 Explain the purpose of a post-implementation review.

DISCUSSION QUESTIONS

6.1 "Documentation reduces the impact of key personnel turnover." Elucidate.
6.2 "Preparing documentation is a waste of time and money." Comment on the merits of this statement.
6.3 Discuss three examples of how the lack of documentation could create management and control problems.
6.4 Why should documentation be kept current? Discuss three examples in which out-of-date documentation could cause control problems.
6.5 "It is a good idea to keep operator instructions to a minimum, i.e., design a program with little or no interaction with the computer operator." Comment on this statement.
6.6 "As I see it, unauthorized program changes and computer operator intervention are two of the biggest control problems." Comment on this statement.
6.7 How could an auditor determine whether or not the documentation he has been provided depicts the system actually being run?

EXERCISES

6.1 In an organization of your choice, apply the questionnaire included at the end of this chapter.
6.2 Develop a decision table based on the following narrative: "These procedures relate to handling an order request. When an order is placed and this order is greater than or equal to the discount quantity, we check to see if credit is acceptable. If credit is acceptable and quantity ordered is available, we prepare an invoice

at the discount rate and ship the quantity ordered. If quantity on hand is less than ordered, we prepare an invoice at the discount rate, ship the quantity we have available, and backorder the balance of the order.

Some customers may place an order greater than or equal to our discount quantity for goods that we have available, but their credit rating may be unacceptable. In this case, we simply send a letter disapproving of the order.

On the other hand, many of our customers do not order discount quantities. If their credit is OK and we have the stock on hand, we prepare an invoice at the regular rate and ship quantity ordered. If we do not have the necessary stock on hand, we ship what is available and backorder the rest. A regular rate invoice is also prepared for this kind of order."

Does your decision table help to explain in a clearer and more precise manner how orders are processed?

6.3 The water department of a medium-size city has computerized its water meter reading and billing function. A systems flowchart for a portion of this procedure is presented below. How are the meter readings entered into the system? Does this system keep track of unpaid water bills? What medium are the files stored on? What type of information is probably stored on the meter file? What type of clerical procedures would you expect the water department to be executing in relation to this system? Follow the system flowchart on the next page and determine whether there are any missing pieces. How would you evaluate this type of flowchart? What is helpful about it? What additional information would you want to ascertain about this system?

PROBLEMS

6.1 You are reviewing audit workpapers containing a narrative description of the Milestone Corporation's factory payroll system. A portion of that narrative is as follows:[7]

Factory employees punch time clock cards each day when entering or leaving the shop. At the end of each week the timekeeping department collects the time cards and prepares duplicate batch-control slips by department showing total hours and number of employees. The time cards and original batch-control slips are sent to the payroll accounting section. The second copies of the batch-control slips are filed by date.

---

[7]Adapted with permission from the Uniform CPA Examination, copyright by the American Institute of Certified Public Accountants.

CHAPTER SIX DOCUMENTATION CONTROLS 209

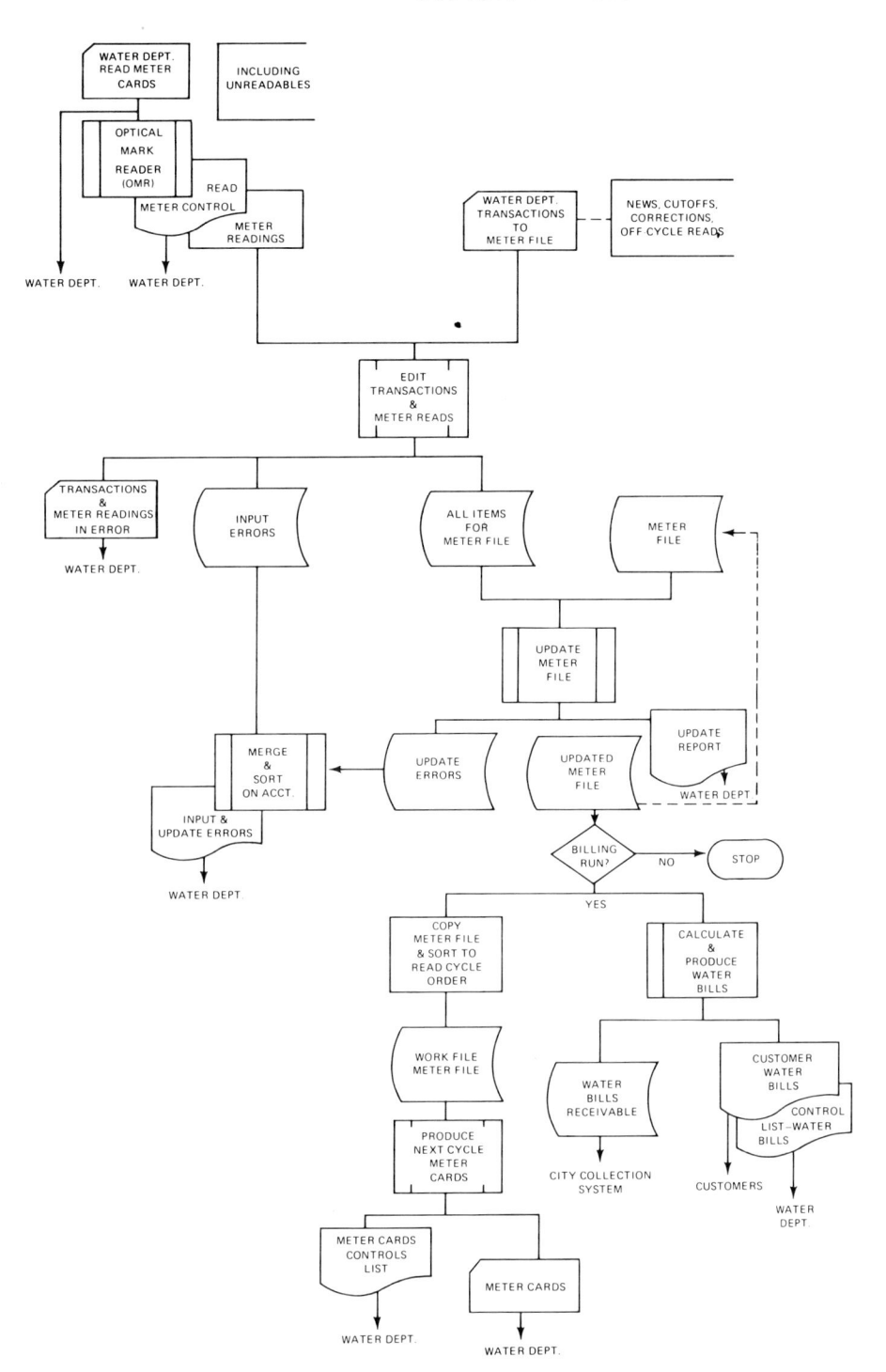

FIGURE 6.3.
System Flowchart.

In the payroll accounting section payroll transaction cards are keypunched from the information on the time cards, and a batch total card for each batch is keypunched from the batch-control slip. The time cards and batch-control slips are then filed by batch for possible reference. The payroll transaction cards and batch total card are sent to data processing where they are sorted by employee number within batch. Each batch is edited by a computer program which checks the validity of employee number against a master employee tape file and the total hours and number of employees against the batch total card. A detail printout by batch and employee number is produced which indicates batches that do not balance and invalid employee numbers. This printout is returned to payroll accounting to resolve all differences.

In searching for documentation, you found a flowchart of the payroll system which included all appropriate symbols (American National Standards Institute, Inc.) but was only partially labeled. The portion of this flowchart described in the narrative above appears on the next page.

Required:

a. Number your answer 1 through 17. Next to the corresponding number of your answer, supply the appropriate labeling (document names, process description, or file order) applicable to each numbered symbol on the flowchart.

b. Flowcharts are one of the aids an auditor may use to determine and evaluate a client's internal control system. List advantages of using flowcharts in this context.

6.2 As an internal auditor for a large insurance company, you have been assigned to audit the department that converts individual life insurance policies into cash at policyholder request. Since no user's manual exists, you decide that some form of flowchart documentation would be a good starting point for your audit. Following observations, discussions with department personnel, and reviews of various job descriptions, you have assembled a series of steps that pertain to the redemption for cash value of the individual policies.

1. Mail is opened in the central mailroom. Correspondence for the Cash Value Department is forwarded via messenger to the department. The correspondence falls into two categories:
   a) Requests for redemption of cash value in a letter or on a company-produced form, or
   b) Requests for further information concerning redemption and the current cash value of a policy.
2. Once the mail is delivered to the department, a "correspondence clerk" stamps the letters on a time clock.

CHAPTER SIX   DOCUMENTATION CONTROLS   211

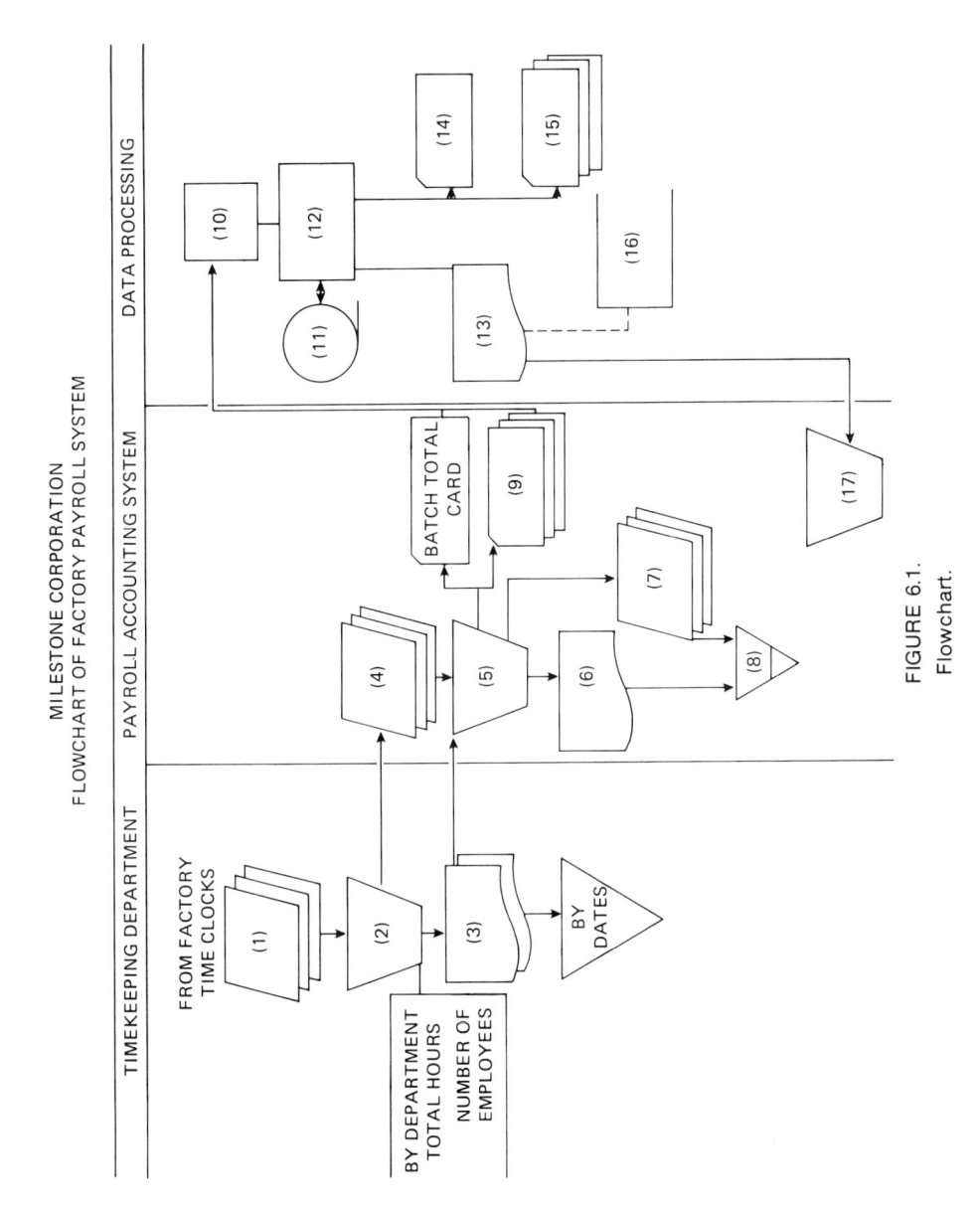

MILESTONE CORPORATION
FLOWCHART OF FACTORY PAYROLL SYSTEM

FIGURE 6.1. Flowchart.

3. The "correspondence clerk" then separates the letters into the two categories detailed in Step (1).
4. Letters in the first category are divided into two batches. The division is alphabetic on the individual's last name with A–K in one batch and L–Z in the second. Letters in the second category are kept by the correspondence clerk (see Step 11 for further processing).
5. Each batch is given to a "transaction clerk." This individual codes a transaction form for those requests in the form of letters. Some codes are entered on the requests originating on company-prepared forms.
6. Each letter or form is scanned for obvious errors or omissions, such as policy number, name, address, date of request, correct department, etc. Transactions that fail these visual edits are pulled from those that appear to be correct. The clerk than "researches" the erroneous transactions utilizing a microfiche copy of the company's policy master file, the envelope in which the letter was sent, and, if necessary, refers it back to the correspondence clerk for communication with the policyholder.
7. Each transaction clerk takes the transactions that have passed the visual edits and places them in batches of not more than 50. Batching is determined by a two-character state abbreviation contained in the policy number. A "batch header record" is completed which contains the number of items in the batch, date of the batch, special type of transactions (e.g., re-entry transactions), transaction clerk ID number, and a unique batch number.
8. The clerk then takes each batch to a microfilming machine. Each batch is fed into the machine, which films each transaction and imprints the batch number, date of batch (which the clerk presets), and a sequence number (which the machine does automatically).
9. The transaction clerk then notes the batch header record information and total number of items in the batch on a control sheet. All the batches for one day are then filed in a cabinet.
10. The batches are then given, via messenger, to the data-processing "I/O clerk." This individual records the various batch header record numbers that are to be inputed at the company's data-processing center.
11. The correspondence clerk, having kept the letters requesting information about cash values and current cash values of policies, is responsible for two types of processing. Letters requesting additional information are answered as completely

as possible. For the current value of a policy, the clerk looks up the policy master microfiche, where this information is updated monthly. Then a response can be made to types of inquiries.

12. The following day, a computer printout of the previous day's cash value transactions is delivered to the Department. The transaction clerks review this "daily transaction report," which identifies the source of rejection ("no such policy number," "bad character in position X"). The transactions that were not accepted by the system are pulled from the filing cabinet, corrected, batched, and then go through steps 7–10. The clerk also compares the control sheet with the control totals produced on the transaction report for missing transactions or batches.
13. For transactions that were accepted by the system, a check register is produced. A correspondence clerk, after receiving a phone call from the I/O clerk, goes to the data-processing center to pick up the check register and the corresponding checks.
14. The checks and the register are compared by the correspondence clerks for omissions.
15. The checks and the register are then given to a transaction clerk, who verifies them against the daily transaction report. Again, checking for omissions and obvious errors (unreasonable dollar amounts, missing addresses) is completed.
16. A form letter and the checks are inserted into window envelopes by the correspondence clerk. The checks are then delivered to the mailroom for stamping and mailing.
17. The department supervisor is contacted if any of the control checks fail during any processing step. If the problem cannot be resolved within the department, and it is probably due to a computer program error, the supervisor contacts a liaison officer for the division. This individual conducts further investigation. If necessary, this documentation and requests for program changes are carried out by the liaison officer.

    Prepare graphical documentation of this procedure.

6.3 Prepare a decision table, document flowchart, or systems flowchart of a system, or component, you regularly interact with. These systems could include writing a check, registering for classes, hiring an employee, ordering an item from a catalog house, servicing your car. If you do not have complete information on the workings of the system, imagine what type of processing must take place (or should take place). What type of controls do *you* put on your interaction with these systems?

CHAPTER

7

SECURITY CONTROLS

7.1 INTRODUCTION

Ordinarily, security controls do not affect the proper and accurate processing of transactions as much as the controls discussed earlier. Conceptually, a secure system is one that is hazard-proof. Security controls help to assure high systems standard and performance by protecting against hardware, software, and people (humanware?) failure. Absence of security controls can increase the probability of foul-ups, such as: (1) degraded operations, (2) compromised system, (3) loss of services, (4) loss of assets, and (5) loss or unauthorized disclosure of sensitive information.

Security controls, as well as all of the controls discussed so far, apply to small computer centers; large, sophisticated computer systems; and outside computer services. Because security controls are a key ingredient in the system of controls, they cannot be neglected by the auditor.

In this chapter, our discussion of security controls is divided into three categories: (1) hazards, (2) physical security techniques, and (3) procedural security techniques. The summary contains examples of security checklists and a security questionnaire.

7.2 HAZARDS

A hazard represents a risk of loss or a chance of harm, i.e., a danger, threat, or peril. For example, a fighting soldier's life is full of hazards.

The antonym of hazard is security. In information systems (as in other systems), there is usually a hierarchy of hazards. We will discuss this hierarchy of hazards and the goals of security controls against it.

Hierarchy of Hazards

Following are the classic hazards of a computer-based information system arranged in accordance with their probability of occurrence and their impact on the system. No. 1 is greater than No. 2, and so forth. This hierarchy is based on research, intuition, and generalizations. It cannot be proved or disproved, so it is subject to debate. Furthermore, in any particular system, the arrangement of these hazards may be quite different. In any case, the following hierarchy gives us a vehicle for discussion and analysis.

1. *Malfunctions* People, software, and hardware error or malfunction cause the biggest problems. In this area, humans are the culprits by virtue of acts of omission, neglect, and incompetency. Some authorities have said that simple human error causes more damage than all other areas combined. We read of one incident where a disk pack was dropped; the warped pack was mounted on a disk drive, thus damaging the access mechanism. The same pack was moved to another drive, and a different pack was mounted in the first drive, and so on, and more drives were damaged and disk packs rendered unusable.

2. *Fraud and unauthorized access* This hazard or threat is the attainment of something through dishonesty, cheating, or deceit. Fraud can occur by: (a) infiltration and industrisl espionage, (b) tapping data communication lines, (c) emanation pickup from parabolic receivers (the computer and its peripherals are transmitters), (d) unauthorized browsing through files via online terminals, (e) masquerading as an authorized user, (f) physical confiscation of files and other sensitive documents, and (g) installation of Trojan horses (things that aren't what they appear to be).

3. *Power and communication failures* In some locations, this hazard may occur with greater frequency than other hazards. To a great extent, the availability and reliability of power and communication facilities is a function of location. In heavily populated areas, brownouts occur frequently, especially during the summer. Conversely, in some instances, power surges have occurred, burning out sensitive components of a computer. Of course, this hazard can be easily controlled with a power regulator. Also, during each working day, communication channels are sometimes busy and/or noisy.

4. *Fires* Fires occur with greater frequency than some people think, and they can be one of the worst single disasters. For example, in July 1973, in the Army Records Center in St. Louis, Missouri, a very large fire

caused extensive damage in a gigantic computer center. This fire was set by an arsonist. In 1975, extensive fires caused untold damage to a computer telephone switching center in New York City.

> A three-alarm fire of undetermined origin ripped through First Data Corp's computer installation and knocked out normal service to most of the time-sharing vendor's 500 customers for at least four days. Some were down almost a week.
> Damage to First Data was estimated at $3.5 million, with about $2 million directly attributed to mainframe destruction. The firm lost all or part of three of its seven large Digital Equipment Corp. Decsystem-10s, several front ends, a dozen disk drives, six tape drives and two line printers as a result of heat and water.
> 'Saves' of customer disk files completed only hours earlier and awaiting transportation to the company's fail-safe storage area in a nearby building were in the computer room when the fire broke out. However, after reading a random sample of the reels pulled out of the computer room, Frezen indicated more than 90% suffered no damage. The remaining 10% sustained data losses ranging from one block to an entire file. Additional backups, made as recently as a week or at most a month before the fire, depending on the backup system customers elected to use, were in the other building.[1]

5. *Sabotage and riot* There have been a number of instances where computer centers installed in or close to decaying urban areas have been damaged. But location is not always the key factor. In 1975, a sponge rubber plant in Shelton, Connecticut was bombed. The fire that resulted caused more than $10 million in damages and the loss of more than 900 jobs.

6. *Natural disasters* Relatively speaking, natural disasters do not occur that often, but when they do, the results can be devastating. These disasters, termed acts of God, include earthquakes, tornadoes, floods, and lightning. Common sense and preplanning will help to reduce their impact. For example, an organization once installed its computer center in a suburban center only to discover later that the center was constructed on a lot beneath the flood plain. However, there is no sure safeguard against acts of God, only probabilistic ones.

7. *General hazards* This category covers a number of random hazards that are difficult to define and anticipate. Normally, common sense and general safeguards will lessen the likelihood of their occurrence. For example, one Sunday morning, a vice-president arrived at his organization to find a fully loaded gasoline truck with brakes on fire parked next to the computer center. Better site planning would have prevented such an occurrence.

---

[1] "$3 Million in CPUs Damaged As Fire Ravages Installation," *Computerworld*, April 19, 1976, pp. 1 and 4.

Goals of Security Controls Against Hazards

Goals of security controls against hazards can be viewed as a series of levels of controls. That is, if one level fails, then another level takes over, and so forth, and thus the overall impact on the system is reduced.

1. *Deter* At this level, the goal is to prevent any loss or disaster from occurring.

2. *Detect* Total deterrence cannot normally be achieved. Therefore, the goal at this level is to establish methods of monitoring and watching for hazards and reporting them to people and equipment for corrective action.

3. *Minimize impact of disaster and loss* If an accident or mishap does occur there should be established procedures and facilities that help reduce the loss. For example, a backup master file would help reduce the destruction of the mainline master file.

4. *Investigate* If a loss occurs, an investigation should be started immediately to determine what happened. Information gained from this investigation can be used for future security planning.

5. *Recovery* There should be a plan of action to recover from the loss and begin operations again as soon as possible. For example, if the data-processing operation for a financial institution could not operate for a week or two, the results would probably be bankruptcy, because a financial institution's lifeblood is processing data. Recovery procedures can range from backup facilities to insurance coverage.

7.3 PHYSICAL SECURITY TECHNIQUES

Physical security techniques include devices and physical placement of computer facilities that help to guard against hazards. These techniques are: (1) physical controlled access, (2) physical location, and (3) physical protection devices.

Physical Controlled Access

Access control protection is basic to a workable security system. If unauthorized personnel cannot gain entry to the computer facilities, then the chance for harm is considerably reduced. The following items help to control access.

1. *Guards and special escorts* Guards should be placed at strategic entry points of the computer facility. All visitors who are given permission to tour the computer center should be accompanied by a designated escort.

2. *Sign-in/sign-out registers* All persons should be required to sign a register indicating time of sign-in, purpose, and time of departure. An improvement upon the standard signature register is the utilization of devices that analyze signatures as a function of time and pressure. Thus, an individual may be able to duplicate the outward appearances of a signature, but the duplication of time and pressure during the signing of an individual's name is highly improbable.

3. *Badges* Color-coded (e.g., red for programmers, blue for systems analysts) badges, with picture of holder where possible, can be used to identify authorized personnel and visitors.

4. *Cards* Card control entry equipment, used alone or in conjunction with other measures, is probably the most popular access control device. Doors can be opened by either optical or magnetic coded cards. Authorization for entry can be dynamically controlled by individual doors, time of day, day of week, and security classification of individuals to whom the card was issued. Authorizations can be easily added or deleted, and entry activity logs and reports can be prepared and displayed to a control officer. Open or closed status of all doors can be monitored, and attempts at unauthorized entry can be immediately detected and an alarm sounded.

5. *Closed-circuit monitors* Devices such as closed-circuit television monitors, cameras, and intercom systems connected to a control panel manned by security guards are becoming more popular. These devices are very effective in controlling a large area rather than concentrating only on entry and exit points.

6. *Paper shredders* Sensitive reports should never be thrown in waste paper baskets for disposal. In a number of cases, thieves were able to steal confidential information by gaining access to waste disposal facilities. Any sensitive reports should be shredded before being thrown away. A destruct system that works better than shredders is a disintegration system that converts an end product into unclassified waste or micro-confetti that cannot be reconstructed.[2] These machines will disintegrate bound manuals, computer printouts, carbons, microfilms and microfiches, EDP cards, plastic binders, printer circuits, mylar computer tape, and so forth.

The New York State Lottery was apprised of the value of document disintegration.

> The treatment of returned tickets poses problems. There is an intent to mutilate returned tickets so as to preclude their later use to claim prizes. This practice is not uniformly carried out and we found a situation where the unsold tickets are locked up but not mutilated. We have no firm idea as to the security of this arrangement but the very

[2] For more information, contact: Security Engineered Machinery, 5 Walkup Drive, Westboro, Mass. 01581.

existence of unmutilated tickets does pose a risk for as long as such tickets may still be used to claim prizes on past lotteries.[3]

7. *Double-door entry* Entry through the first door leads to a man-trap area which is sealed off from the computer facilities. A second door has to be opened to enter the computer room.

8. *One-way emergency doors* These doors are for exit only and are used in case of emergency situations such as fire.

9. *Combination of control devices* The devices above can be combined along with other safeguards that we will be discussing in following sections to increase security. Card systems can be combined with a hand geometry identifier. Or, for another example, entry could be through one door equipped with a card reader and thence into a man-trap area that is sealed off from the computer system by bullet-proof glass. To get through the second door, which leads into the computer room, a valid card would have to be used and identification made over an intercom and television monitoring system.

Physical Location

Location of the computer system is an important consideration in security planning. Note the following guidelines.

1. *Remote location* The computer site should be located well away from airports, electrical equipment (e.g. radar, microwave), decaying urban areas, heavy traffic, steam boilers, and so forth. The farther removed the computer system is from these kinds of hazards, the better. If the site cannot be as remote as desirable, some degree of remoteness can be achieved by clearing a 200- or 300-foot radius around the site and installing floodlights and a perimeter fence.

2. *Separate building* Many security specialists recommend that the computer system be housed in a separate building. When the computer system occupies a separate building access control is easier, and there is less risk from general hazards. For example, there would be less risk from water damage or from fire caused by flammable products used by other occupants. The disadvantage of a separate building is that a deliberate attack on power source, communication lines, air intake, and water supply could be made easier because the computer system is housed in a specific structure. If the computer system is not housed in a separate building, then the computer system should be in the center of the building away from walls and not on the top floor or in the basement. It should not be made a showcase.

---

[3]*Summary of Findings New York State Lottery*, (Cambridge, Mass.: Arthur D. Little, Inc., Nov. 26, 1975), p. 12.

3. *Identification* The computer site should not contain any signs that identify it to outsiders.

4. *Carrier control* Power and communication lines should be placed underground. Air intake devices, compressors, and cooling towers should be protected by fences and/or placed at heights that cannot be easily reached. Manhole covers should be locked.

5. *Backup facilities location* Backup plays a major role in many areas of a total system of control. Backup is the key element to recovery. As far as location is concerned, backup facilities should be far enough away from the main facility to be safe from the same hazards, but close enough to provide quick recovery and service. When possible, the backup facility should be located in a place that uses different power sources. Its location should be kept confidential.

Physical Protection

Additional protective devices should be considered for an overall protection plan. These items are:

1. *Drains and pumps* Sometimes water pipes burst or water from a fire or flood threatens a computer system. To help reduce the impact of these mishaps, drains and pumps should be installed.

2. *Emergency power* Again, backup plays an important part in control. Uninterruptible power systems (UPS) should be installed for power backup to provide continuous processing. The need for an uninterruptible power source UPS (also called an uninterruptible power system and uninterruptible power supply) depends upon the frequency and nature of the power disturbances and the effect they have on the computer system. Power failure or disturbance can range anywhere from transients of a few milliseconds to long-term power outages. These power fluctuations can result in loss of data, processing errors, downtime, equipment malfunction and damage, and so forth.

A complete study of power failures should be made to determine the causes of any disturbances. For example, a study may reveal a number of short-term transients and line instability rather than real power outage. Power fluctuations may be caused by extreme load changes (e.g., air conditioning, elevators) within the building; such fluctuations are beyond the control of the utility. In such cases, an approach less expensive than UPS, such as a motor generator set (also referred to as a M-G set) or a voltage regulator may be more applicable. The primary objective of the UPS and other power control devices is to supply precise, smooth, steady, clean power to the computer system at all times. Any power interruption to the critical load may produce a variety of harmful effects. Although a UPS may not be justified today in some sparsely populated areas, it may be in the future. However, as utility power becomes less reliable and the number of outages increases, downtime costs rise. Therefore, it behooves the conscientious auditor to keep an eye on this area, because what may not be needed today may be essential tomorrow.

3. *Coverings* All equipment should be covered with plastic covers when not in use. In several cases water damage to computer equipment was reduced during a fire because some alert individual covered the equipment.

4. *Fire control* Basically, there are three kinds of fire: Class A—cellulosis, Class B—Flammable liquid, and Class C—electrical. Fire department personnel and fire control equipment vendors should be consulted in order to determine the appropriate fire and smoke detectors and extinguishing methods to use. Normally, recommended methods include: (1) portable fire extinguishers, (2) fluoride gas, (3) Halon (causes no permanent damage, good for office material and equipment), (4) CO_2 (carbon dioxide, good for electrical fires, but it can suffocate personnel), (5) water sprinklers, and (6) smoke exhaust systems. We added a smoke exhaust system to this list of fire control methods because smoke, in many instances, is a bigger problem than fire, especially where there is a preponderance of vinyl and other plastic material.

Insurance companies say that there are more insurance claims from water and flooding from putting out the fire than from the fire itself, a statement that reinforces the need for drains, pumps, and coverings.

When various detection and extinguishing systems are used, it is important that the detectors not release a fire-extinguishing agent immediately. To do so is wasteful, and in the case of CO_2, it can be hazardous to personnel in the area. The detectors should trigger an audible and visible alarm locally and at appropriate fire or guard stations. There should be a control panel available to indicate which detector(s) has triggered the alarm. By zeroing in on the fire, some designated individuals (no one should be sent alone) can go directly to the source of trouble, determine the extent of the fire, and put it out with a portable fire extinguisher if it is small.

5. *General building safeguards* Walls of the building should be constructed from slab to slab. Walls and ceilings should have at least a one-hour fire rating. The number of doors should be limited, and there should be no windows. All ducts should be filtered and contain fire dampers.

7.4 PROCEDURAL SECURITY TECHNIQUES

It is difficult to draw a precise line between physical and procedural security techniques, because there is a great deal of overlap between the two. Both, for example, control access by unauthorized penetrators. One technique can work in conjunction with, and enhance the effectiveness of, the other. One is more device-oriented; the other is more logic-oriented. In many instances, a procedural security technique is nothing more than the use of a physical security technique. To think in terms of one instead of the other will not lead to a good security control system. For example, the following quotation implies that a bank can be physically secure against access to its information system but still vulnerable to unauthorized access.

> Recently, many banks have opened the floodgates to theft of confidential financial information through the information systems designed to give bank tellers real-time access to customer accounts. In many cases, virtually no safeguards have been erected to prevent unauthorized access to these files. Many of these systems use ordinary touch-tone telephones and automatic dial cards provided by the telephone company to gain access to the central files of all depositor accounts. It is not even necessary for the information thief to acquire one of these automatic-dialing devices. All he needs is an ordinary touch-tone telephone. The dial codes employed are generally the most obvious and straight-forward; anyone watching a bank teller's operation for about ten minutes can learn them. Once they are learned a simple telephone tap anywhere within the bank's telephone system is all that is needed to read (and in a limited way, modify) any account in the bank, to ascertain whether an account is being used or not (for purposes of forgery or kiting), and to gain detailed information as to deposits and withdrawals in that account. All this can be done without ever setting foot in the bank.[4]

Whereas physical security techniques deal with a number of hazards including fire, natural disaster, and so forth, procedural security techniques deal almost exclusively with access control. In some cases, a procedural technique will require the application of a physical technique.

Our discussion on procedural security techniques will cover six concepts: (1) integrity, (2) isolation, (3) identification, (4) authorization, (5) authentication, and (6) monitoring.

Integrity

Integrity means that the system is honest and dependable. As a concept of security controls, integrity is basically the assurance that the system is functionally correct and complete. The absence of integrity will render all the other concepts ineffective.

---

[4]Stephen W. Leibholz and Louis D. Wilson, *User's Guide to Computer Crime: Its Commission, Detection and Prevention* (Radnor, Pa.: Chilton Book Company, 1974), p. 27.

If a user is authorized to retrieve Item A from a file, then the system can be depended upon to provide Item A, and only Item A, to the user. Analogous to this idea of integrity is a situation in which an authorized user is given a key to unlock Door A, but not Doors B, C, and D. Therefore, the locking mechanism system should guarantee that the key does, in fact, unlock only Door A. For another example, if a user is supposed to be in read-only mode, then the system should guarantee that the user cannot do something else, e.g., write.

Another aspect of the application of integrity procedures is during simultaneous job processing. The greatest exposure occurs while the information resides either within main storage or within working files. The system should make sure that after one authorized job is completed, information from that job is sanitized (e.g., erased, scrubbed), so that unauthorized penetrators cannot read it by browsing. Without sanitizing procedures, confidential information would be exposed to unauthorized access at various points during processing.

Isolation

In any system where a high level of security is to be maintained, no individual or part of the organization should be in a position to have available all the components or subsystems that, put together, make a whole. This concept sometimes referred to as interface isolation or compartmentalization, and is a concept used in the design and construction of secret weapons. In computer-based information systems, this isolation should be maintained between users and information as well as between hardware and software resources and processes.

This concept recognizes and deals with the increased simultaneous sharing of facilities and processes and the extensive use of data communication networks in today's computer systems. The concurrent processing of many different users requires the separation and protection of each individual's information and job processes. The increased use of data communication networks has opened up other exposures that must be protected. Several protective procedures that affect isolation are listed below.

1. *Disconnection and separation* One form of isolation is achieved by geographical or logical distribution in which there are no connections between certain elements of the system. For example, Terminal 1 is not connected to Computer A.

In most situations there has to be some connection or interfacing between elements to make the total system operative. Several examples of key interface points that require logical separation procedures and tight control are: (1) computer operator/console, (2) computer operator/

programs, (3) computer operator/data base library, (4) programmer/computer, (5) systems analyst/programs, and (6) user/terminal.

Like traditional accounting internal control, separation procedures, mean, for example, that no single individual should have access to computer programs *and* operation of the computer *and* the design of the system. Also, it means that individuals who input transactions into the system should not be those who have access to programs.

2. *Least privilege access* To make a system operative, certain privileged states and instruction sets must be assigned to appropriate users. This assigned privilege should be the minimum access authority necessary to perform the required process. For example, an order clerk is given the privilege to access only quantity on hand and price of items in an inventory file. He cannot access cost, vendor, vendor performance, and so forth. Another example of least privilege access occurs when programmers are required to use high-level languages such as COBOL which automatically isolate them from the computer equipment and operating system. With the use of a high-level language, there is no need to have direct access to or "hands on" use of the computer system.

3. *Obfuscation* This procedure means to isolate by confusing, bewildering, obscuring, or hiding something from a potential penetrator. For example, a simple method of hiding the computer system from would-be penetrators is to omit the listing of the computer system in the building directory. For another example, when authorized users are given user numbers and codes (also called lockwords) to gain entry to the computer system via terminals, a procedure should be installed to inhibit the display of these user number/codes to unauthorized users. Obviously, if a user inputs his number/code via a teletype and it is printed, the probability is increased that someone else will gain access to it. Even if the number/code is struck over by extraneous keys, there is still no guarantee that others will not obtain it.

Data communication systems, like voice communication systems, are vulnerable to wiretapping. The number of users of data communication networks is growing, and, by the same token, common carriers are increasing capacity through telephone channels, microwave, satellite systems, and so forth. Paralleling this growth in data communications are: (1) increasing domestic and international competition; (2) rising international conflict over resources and business policy; (3) increasing crime, fraud, and espionage; and (4) increasing availability of wiretapping and snooping devices. A procedure that helps to reduce vulnerabilities inherent in data communications is commonly referred to as encryption or cryptography, a word based on Greek terms meaning "hidden" and "writing."

Common cryptographic systems involve: (1) substitution, which is the replacement of message characters with other characters in a one-for-one manner, or replacement of characters with other characters using a table-lookup process, (2) transformation, which is the conversion of characters in a message by an arithmetic process, and (3) transposition, which changes the order of characters in a message.

A useful data transformation method is one in which the encoding and decoding processes are the inverse of another as follows:

Data	=	100110	
Key	=	111011	Encoded Message
Cipher	=	011101	
Cipher	=	011101	
Key	=	111011	Decoded Message
Data	=	100110	

This cryptographic method involves adding a bit to each bit transmitted. The same bit string is then subtracted from the transmitted text to get back to the original message. Obviously, if the penetrator or tapper is aware of what is going on, he can do the same thing.

Management can develop their own cryptographic methods using one or a combination of the methods above, or they can acquire automatic encryption devices from vendors. These devices, called cryptoboxes, are installed between the terminal and modem. Binary digits, the computer language, are converted into English characters for business processing operations. The cryptoboxes put the binary digits of a message through a series of alterations and substitutions. The result is to eliminate tell-tale combination of digits which, repeated even once in a cipher, might betray a pattern to an alert wiretapper. Many other less effective cryptographic devices assign substitute characters for alphabetic letters and digits in the original message. Any simple one-for-one substitution can easily be broken by frequency analysis. For example, if the letter Y occurs more frequently than any other in a fairly long message, it is likely that the cipher Y stands for E, the most frequently occurring letter in the English language, and so forth.

The main disadvantages of using cryptographic methods, besides increased overhead, are: (1) many encrypted methods can be broken, and (2) all cryptographic methods require the use of a key, and if one person has access to the key, then it is possible for another person to gain access to it.

Identification

If a system installs isolation procedures, then the system must also have the ability to identify authorized and proper interfaces. The system must have the ability to distinguish between those users to whom access is permissible, and those to whom it is not. Depending on the level of security required, either the person, the terminal, the file, and/or the program must be identified, so that the right to use the system can be verified, and the user can be held accountable. Methods to effect identification are listed below:

1. *Something user has* A user is identified by something he has in his possession. Identification items can consist of: (1) codes (also called passwords, lockwords), (2) keys to locks, (3) badges, (4) magnetic stripe or optical cards, (5) phone numbers, (6) terminal ID numbers, and (7) encryption keys. The main disadvantage of these identification items is that the probability is relatively high that they can be obtained and used by others.

2. *Something user knows* A user is identified on the basis of something he knows in his mind, i.e., there is no physical access to the identification item per se. Examples of these items are: (1) personalized codes that are changed regularly (e.g., daily), and (2) catechetical sequences where the user answers a prearranged set of questions, e.g., previous address, birthplace, family member birthday, color of wife's eyes. Effectiveness of this identification item is directly related to the rate of change, i.e., the more often an item is changed (e.g., password, prearranged question), the less likely it is to be appropriated by others.

3. *User's characteristics* The user is identified on the basis of something that is a part of him and uniquely his own. These characteristics can be divided into two categories: (1) neuromuscular, such as dynamic signatures and handwriting, and (2) genetic. The genetic category covers: (1) body geometry (hand geometry identification is being used in some instances), (2) fingerprints, (3) voice response patterns, (4) facial appearance (primary use is on badges, not commercially available for computer identification), (5) eye iris and retina, (6) lip prints, and (7) brain wave patterns.

The characteristics above are special features that distinguish a person from others. However, computer technology is not commercially available for much of this kind of identification yet.

Human behavior may be more significant in slowing down or preventing the commercial application of this kind of identification than the progress of technology. People normally resist an invasion of privacy and personal self. If this kind of identification technology is viewed as a personal invasion, then no matter how reliable it may be, people will resist it. There are already "stories" circulating about the unauthorized user "kissing" a computer terminal and a clamp attaching his lips to the terminal until the security officer arrives. Or, the one about users having to stick their finger through a tiny guillotine for fingerprint identification. Unauthorized user? Goodbye finger!

4. *Location of terminals* On the basis of location, terminals can be given different classifications and level of security. For example, a terminal located in a warehouse, which is easily accessible by a variety of personnel, may be given few access privileges and permitted to perform only a few low-level tasks. The problem with this kind of identification is that if terminals have to be switched, authorization changes must be made. Consequently, it may be better to rely primarily on one or a combination of the identification methods discussed above rather than on location of terminals.

Authorization

Once a person has been identified as a valid user, the question becomes, what authority does he have? That is, what does he have the power or right to do? For instance, in the security of files in a data base, procedures must be set up to determine who has access to what files, who has the right to make additions and deletions, and who is responsible for administration of the files. The following items help to deal with the concept of authorization.

1. *Categorize authorization* This step determines specific authority of users, program, and hardware. Classes of authority can include user to documentation, user to equipment, user to program, user to file, terminal to program, program to file, program to program, and so forth. Those activities that must be designated in conjunction with classes of authority are read, write, add, change, delete, copy, create, append, display, and so forth. For example, Joe Clerk has the right to use Program 1 to read (entirely or a specific part of) File A. An example of how the categorization step can be performed is illustrated in Figure 7.1

2. *Use of codes* Codes (also called lockwords or keywords) are linked to an authority table (see Figure 7.1). The authority table is in turn

AUTHORIZED TO USER	AUTHORIZATION ACCESS FOR FILE A					
	READ ONLY	WRITE ONLY	READ WRITE	DELETE	ADD
1	X				
2		X		X	
3		X			X
.					
.					
N			X		

FIGURE 7.1.
Example of Designating Authority.

linked to an identification table. That is, the user (or terminal, etc.) is first identified as valid. Then it is determined what the valid user can do. For example, Joe Clerk may be permitted to read only parts of File A. Therefore, codes may have to be assigned not only to files but also to a category of records within files or even individual fields within records.

3. *Security program* The computer system itself must be programmed not only to identify valid users but also to make sure that proper authority is granted. To do so requires installation of a security program. Following is a general, hypothetical example of the type of instructions contained in a security program.

User/File:
DEFINE FILE (INVENTORY)
AUTHORIZE USER (JONES) FILE (INVENTORY)
FOR (READ, CHANGE)
User/Program:
AUTHORIZE USER (JONES) PROGRAM (UPDATE)
FOR (READ, CHANGE = QUANTITY-ON-HAND FIELD)

In addition, the security program should have the ability to change identification and authorization readily as well as change security requirements based on time of day, day of week, weekends, holidays, and so forth. For example, certain users would lose their authority over weekends, vacations, or holidays. Included in the program should also be a routine to report the source of any attempted violations immediately.

Authentication

Authentication procedures are required to show that something is valid or genuine. Although someone or some facility may be appropriately identified and given authority to access something or to perform some activity, the system cannot be assured that the user is valid, especially if the user is identified on the basis of "what he has" (e.g., magnetic card) or "what he knows" (e.g., code or password). Periodically, during usage of sensitive files (as well as other resources), the validity of the user should be confirmed. This confirmation may include one or all of the following authentication procedures: (1) physical observation (e.g., sending someone to the source to confirm that the user is who he claims to be), (2) periodic disconnects and call-back procedures (e.g., a terminal is disconnected and dialed back to see if the appropriate terminal responds), and (3) periodic requests for further information or reverification from the user. The following quotation testifies to the need for authentication procedures.

... Mimicking the computer they transmitted "Start Tape" signals to the district office sets, which obediently responded. The data were transmitted to the phony station, and then the district office was called. When the insurance company's computer dialed up these offices, the tape had already run out, and what the computer received instead appeared to consist of miles and miles of blank tape.

The objective here was probably sabotage, not espionage. The data losses were not discovered for some time, and reconstruction of the data, while possible, required considerable manual effort and paper work.

... The individuals who played the substitution game were eventually caught and discharged. Now, the law moves slowly, and criminal sanctions regarding computer and communications crimes are not yet fully developed.... It was therefore necessary to indict them under a law prohibiting—you guessed it—obscene telephone calls.[5]

Monitoring

Monitoring is the act of watching over, checking, or guarding something. This concept recognizes that sooner or later, either accidentally or intentionally, the aforementioned controls will be neutralized or broken. Some specific systems capabilities to support the monitoring procedure include the following.

1. *Detection of security violations*   A security system should be installed to detect any security violation as soon as it occurs. Examples of violations are mismatch of user of terminal identification code, and unauthorized request for a file.

2. *Locking of system*   If certain security violations are serious, the system should be set up to automatically lock the system from further use. For example, a terminal would be automatically locked after N unauthorized attempts, e.g., three attempts because of the learning curve effect or an authorized user inadvertently typing in a wrong number.

3. *Exception reporting*   All exceptional conditions should be reported to the internal auditor for review. Auditors should be skeptical if they receive no reports. The absence of any attempted violations may indicate that users are subverting controls.

4. *Trend reporting*   The system should collect data concerning all user access. Typical data in this report would include: (1) user, terminal, etc.; (2) type of processing (demonstration, training, testing, normal operations); (3) date; (4) time of day; and (5) items accessed (e.g., name of

---

[5]*Ibid.*, pp. 40–41.

file). These reports should be systematically reviewed by auditors and security officers.

7.5 SUMMARY

The maintenance of adequate security controls within the data processing environment is essential in order to protect valuable hardware and software as well as sensitive and potentially irreplaceable data. We have discussed many of the hazards with which data processing facilities must contend. It is interesting to note that the directors of many EDP facilities have the mistaken notion that "it can't happen here." Unfortunately a disaster must strike before proper security measures are introduced in the data center.

Physical security techniques provide guidance to prevent unauthorized access to sensitive areas, selection of optimal sites for the data processing facilities, and the protection of equipment.

Procedural security techniques are designed to assure the integrity of data as well as permit access of data by authorized individuals.

It must be remembered, that the employment of the above described security techniques will reduce the probability that unfortunate occurrences will strike the data processing center. There are no absolute guarantees implied by any of the security methods. However, the auditor must be concerned with the utilization of adequate security controls within the EDP facility. The following checklists and questionnaires will provide a guide to the auditor.

CHECKLIST FOR FIRE PROTECTION

____ 1. Non-combustible construction in computer facility.

____ 2. Non-combustible construction in record storage area.

____ 3. Physical separation of record storage area from computer room.

____ 4. Fire-resistant separation where these areas are adjacent.

____ 5. Fire-resistant computer room ceiling material.

____ 6. Fire-resistant raised flooring.

____ 7. Protection against water seepage into the computer facility from above or adjacent areas.

____ 8. Paper and other flammable supplies stored outside the computer room.

____ 9. Smoking prohibited in the computer area.

____ 10. A continuing and effective housekeeping program.

____ 11. Hand-portable fire extinguishers placed at critical points throughout the computer complex.

____ 12. Computer room and underfloor area with automatic fire suppression systems (e.g., Halon 1301, CO_2, etc.)

____ 13. Regular inspection procedures by qualified personnel for all automatic fire protection systems.

____ 14. Emergency plan of action in case of fire.

____ 15. EDP personnel assigned specific tasks for emergencies.

____ 16. Schedule periodic fire drills.

____ 17. Well-posted emergency telephone numbers.

____ 18. Regular watchman checks if EDP facilities not occupied 100% of the time.

____ 19. Air-conditioning system programmed to close dampers if fire is detected in the EDP area.

____ 20. Emergency power sources.

____ 21. A disaster contingency plan including a written agreement for use of a backup computer.

CHECKLIST FOR FIRE PROTECTION
Page 2

____ 22. A backup system at a different location.

____ 23. Backup system capable of handling current needs.

____ 24. Backup system capable of handling future needs.

____ 25. Duplicate data files stored at a separate location.

____ 26. Fully evaluated insurance coverage, including elements such as business interruption, natural disasters, etc.

____ 27. Identification of all the costs that would be incurred through loss of your EDP facility.

____ 28. An individual specifically assigned the responsibility for EDP security.

____ 29. A survey and review of all provisions for fire loss protection by a qualified fire protection engineer or safety director.[6]

FIRE EMERGENCY CHECKLIST

____ 1. Determine nature and criticalness of fire.

____ 2. Notify management and operating personnel.

____ 3. Notify fire department or other responsible organizations by telephone or fire alarm.

____ 4. If time allows, obtain checkpoint restart data of in-process computer programs.

____ 5. Turn off electrical power.

____ 6. Dismount and store all magnetic tapes, disk packs, paper cards, and documentation.

____ 7. Close all safes, vaults, and file cabinets.

____ 8. Turn off room air conditioning or heating system.

____ 9. Cover all equipment.

____ 10. Release or place all window shutters and fire curtains.

____ 11. Activate or place all fire-fighting apparatus into ready use.

____ 12. Close all doors, windows, or other room openings.

____ 13. Dispose of all exposed combustible material.

____ 14. Place backup battery lighting, generator, and water pump into ready status.

____ 15. If small fire, attempt to extinguish with portable fire extinguishers.

____ 16. Evacuate all personnel.

____ 17. Verify that all fire doors and fire dampers have been released.

SECURITY CONTROLS QUESTIONNAIRE

	ANSWER		ANSWERS BASED ON		
	Yes	No	Inquiry	Observation	Test

PHYSICAL:

1. Are sign-in/sign-out registers maintained for visitors? ___ ___ ___ ___ ___

2. Are there adequate controls over the removal of materials from the data-processing area? Are sensitive reports shredded? ___ ___ ___ ___ ___

3. Does the system make use of:
   a. guards? ___ ___ ___ ___ ___
   b. cards? ___ ___ ___ ___ ___
   c. badges? ___ ___ ___ ___ ___
   d. closed-circuit television? ___ ___ ___ ___ ___
   e. limited entry points? ___ ___ ___ ___ ___
   f. central monitoring? ___ ___ ___ ___ ___
   g. detection devices? ___ ___ ___ ___ ___
   h. alarms? ___ ___ ___ ___ ___
   i. intercom? ___ ___ ___ ___ ___
   j. man-trap doors? ___ ___ ___ ___ ___
   k. fire emergency exit-only doors? ___ ___ ___ ___ ___

4. Is the system backed-up with power, air conditioning, and redundant equipment? ___ ___ ___ ___ ___

5. Are air conditioners adequate for peak thermal loads? ___ ___ ___ ___ ___

SECURITY CONTROLS QUESTIONNAIRE
Page 2

6. Are terminals located in secure areas to prevent access to the terminals by unauthorized users?

7. Do terminals include locking devices to prevent unauthorized use?

8. Are there hardware erase or sanitizing features? That is, are memory and peripherals cleared of residue between jobs?

9. Is the computer area housed in a fire-resistive, non-combustible structure?

10. Do all the materials used in construction of the computer area (e.g., walls, doors, ceilings) have at least one-hour fire rating?

11. Are cable openings in the floor made as smooth as possible?

12. Is all the material and equipment in or near the computer area related to data-processing operations?

13. Is all the furniture in the computer area of metal construction or other material not significantly flammable?

SECURITY CONTROLS QUESTIONNAIRE
Page 3

14. Are paper supplies and other combustible materials in excess of the minimum required for efficient operations stored away from the computer area in metal files or cabinets? ____ ____ ____ ____ ____

15. Are smoke and fire detection devices installed in the computer room (also in air spaces above ceiling and below raised floor)? ____ ____ ____ ____ ____

16. Are there heat and fire detection devices inside the main computer equipment? ____ ____ ____ ____ ____

17. Does the computer area have automatic fire extinguishing equipment to protect the building, equipment, supplies, and personnel? ____ ____ ____ ____ ____

18. Does the computer area have a positive automatic drainage system to reduce water accumulation damage to the computers and wiring? ____ ____ ____ ____ ____

19. Are there hand-operated carbon dioxide extinguishers for electrical fires? ____ ____ ____ ____ ____

SECURITY CONTROLS QUESTIONNAIRE
Page 4

20. Are Class A type hand-operated extinguishers provided for ordinary files such as paper, particularly in the storage areas? ___ ___ ___   ___   ___

21. Is the space under the false floor clean? ___ ___ ___   ___   ___

22. Is the building used only for the computer system? ___ ___ ___   ___   ___

23. Are duct linings and filters noncombustible? ___ ___ ___   ___   ___

24. Are there automatic duct closures operated by the fire control system? ___ ___ ___   ___   ___

25. Are air intakes:
    a. covered with protective screening? ___ ___ ___   ___   ___
    b. located well above street level? ___ ___ ___   ___   ___
    c. located so as to prevent the intake of pollutants or debris? ___ ___ ___   ___   ___

26. Are all exterior windows (if any) near street level covered by protective metal grilles? ___ ___ ___   ___   ___

27. Is round-the-clock watchman service used? ___ ___ ___   ___   ___

28. Is the computer room hidden from the

SECURITY CONTROLS QUESTIONNAIRE
Page 5

    street, the lobby, or any other public area?

29. Are any power regulators installed that safeguard against brownouts or power surges?

30. Is the building structurally sound?

31. Is the building located away from flood, earthquake, or tornado areas?

32. Are building and equipment properly grounded for protection against electrical storms?

33. Are all electrical junction boxes under the raised flooring mounted off slab to prevent water damage?

34. Have pipe openings in walls been sealed to prevent water intrusion?

35. Are equipment protective covers available and are they used?

36. Are all modem connections and communication line junction points secured to prevent tampering?

SECURITY CONTROLS QUESTIONNAIRE
Page 6

37. Are leased lines used for communication of sensitive data?

38. Are cryptoboxes used to protect the transmission of sensitive data?

39. Is the cryptobox key changed often?

PROCEDURAL:

1. Does top management support a sound security system?

2. Are internal auditors and security officers employed?

3. Has a complete backup plan been formulated?

4. In case of emergencies, are there checklists?

5. Are employees informed about these checklists?

6. Are emergency drills conducted periodically?

7. Are identifications made by:
   a. something user has?
   b. something user knows?
   c. user's characteristics?

SECURITY CONTROLS QUESTIONNAIRE
Page 7

    d. terminal ID?
    e. by location?
    f. individual programs by name and function?
    g. files down to the field level?

8. Are accesses constrained in any or all of:
    a. classification of files (e.g., top secret, confidential)?
    b. read only, write only, add, copy, etc.?
    c. category or user?

9. Are all employees or visitors to the computer center or other sensitive areas required to have positive identification in the form of a badge with the individual's picture, name, position, and department?

10. Are procedures for issuance and retrieval of badges installed?

11. Are badge holders periodically verified?

12. Has a limit been set, generally one to three, for permitting repeated invalid attempts to access the

SECURITY CONTROLS QUESTIONNAIRE
Page 8

system (e.g., sign on a terminal)?

13. Does the security system include interrupt and call-back features?

14. Are passwords carefully guarded?

15. Are passwords (codes, lockwords, etc.) frequently changed?

16. Are terminals equipped with automatic identification generators?

17. Are keys to locks adequately protected?

18. Is a log maintained of all unsuccessful attempts to enter the computer system (e.g., via terminals)?

19. Are all attempted access violations immediately reported and followed up with corrective action?

20. Are all computer operating interventions logged and explained?

21. Does insurance cover losses by:
    a. fire?
    b. water damage?
    c. fraud?

SECURITY CONTROLS QUESTIONNAIRE
Page 9
    d. sabotage?
    e. acts of God?
    f. business interruptions?
    g. power failure?
    h. performance warranty from vendor?

REVIEW QUESTIONS

7.1 Define security controls.
7.2 List at least three undesirable situations that can occur in an insecure system. Give specific examples.
7.3 Define hazards. Give an example of a hazard that relates to computer-based information systems and another example that relates to something else.
7.4 List and define the hierarchy of hazards. Give a specific example of each.
7.5 What are the goals of security controls against hazards?
7.6 Define physical security techniques.
7.7 List the physical devices used to control access.
7.8 What relevance does physical location have to security controls?
7.9 List the physical protection devices.
7.10 Compare and contrast physical security techniques with procedural security techniques.
7.11 List and define each concept discussed under procedural security techniques.
7.12 Give an example of how the concept of isolation affects security.
7.13 List the techniques used in identification.
7.14 Define authorization. Give an example of how authority is designated.
7.15 Define authentication.
7.16 Why is monitoring important in supporting security controls?

DISCUSSION QUESTIONS

7.1 "Because our computer system is providing service to customers, maintaining the function and integrity of the system is like sitting on a powder keg."[7] Discuss this comment.
7.2 "Procedural controls can be applied either by people or computers." Do you agree? Disagree?
7.3 "Security controls are really not the concern of auditors." Do you agree? Disagree? Why?
7.4 Relate security controls to an organization's legal and social obligations.
7.5 In your opinion, what is the safest method of user identification?
7.6 "Physical provisions for restricted access can be incorporated into the site design. The concept of a 'blockhouse,' i.e., a one-story, windowless, and limited entry/exit structure, is becoming increasingly popular. Protection and 'failsafe' design of the support

---

[7]Quoted from: Edith Myers, "Computer Security: Each Case is Different," *Datamation*, April 1975, p. 108.

facilities are additional design requirements." Do you consider this statement valid? If so, why? Why not?

7.7 Develop a different hierarchy of hazards than the one in the chapter. For example, in some risk analyses, fire is shown as the most prevalent and costly hazard.

7.8 "Human errors and omission are by far the most costly hazard." Discuss the merit of this statement.

7.9 "Competitive pressures in business, politics and international affairs continually create situations where morality, privacy, and the laws all appear to give way before a compelling desire for gain. Information, for its own sake or for the price it brings, is an eagerly sought after commodity."[8] Discuss this statement. What security control techniques do you recommend under such circumstances?

7.10 An auditor should try to penetrate and actually test the information system's security as a normal point of an audit. What are the pros and cons to this argument?

7.11 "Physical security, access control, operating procedures, programming personnel, and recovery procedures must all be concerns of the auditor in his expanded role within a computer center...."[9] Do you agree? Why? Why not?

EXERCISES

7.1 Visit an organization of your choice that has a computer-based information system and, using the checklists and questionnaires at the end of the summary, go over each question with the manager of data processing, controller, or internal auditor. Make a list of "no" answers. Are they significant? Prepare a report recommending security that you feel should be implemented.

7.2 *Computerworld* reported (May 14, 1975, p. 2) the case of a police chief who was indicted by a grand jury for tampering with government records via a CRT terminal. Apparently, the chief wished to delete his own reckless driving offense from the files of a regional computer system. The alteration was uncovered during an inspection of a routine printout of transactions made at the terminal. However, there was no proof that the chief was, in fact, the individual transacting the deletion. Although an employee of the office where the terminal was located said, "He's been coming in there for months, I cannot say definitely he was there on that day," other police officers used the same terminal. Alarmed over the very real

---

[8]Douglas B. Hoyt, et al. *Computer Security Handbook* (New York: Macmillan Information, A Division of Macmillan Publishing Company, 1973), p. 56.

[9]Don Leavitt, "Auditors Should be Involved Early in Project Development Cycle," *Computerworld*, May 28, 1975, p. 13.

possibility of system abuse, the manager of the regional computer center has asked you to evaluate the security aspects of their system. Remember, an evaluation should contain both strong points and recommendations for improvement.

7.3 Miss Sally Forth, a credit approval clerk for Master Charge, was responsible for entering the credit limits for cardholders. She found that if she overspent on her own card, she could increase her personal limit the next morning, and cover the amount before the item came in. Unfortunately, Sally was prone to colds and one day, after overspending, she did not come to work. Another clerk saw that she was over her limit and drew the matter to the attention of the manager, who saw that her limit was too high for a bank clerk, and so she was caught. What kind of controls would you recommend to reduce the probability that this kind of fraud does not occur again?

7.4 A programmer in California left his place of employment at a time-sharing company and some time later accessed the data base of his old employer to steal several programs and sensitive data. What kind of controls would guard against this illegal penetration?

PROBLEMS

7.1 A bank is planning to move its computer center to another location. The board of directors want you to prepare a report that includes all the items they must consider in making this move.

7.2 Many banks are initiating Electronic Funds Transfer Systems. A portion of the system consists of keyboard terminals located at retail outlets (supermarkets, clothing stores, department stores, etc.). A customer can make a purchase at the store and have the establishment transfer money from his account to the store's account via the terminal. Some systems even allow for deposits, withdrawals, loan payments and mortgage payments to be transacted via the EFTS. Read about some of these transfer systems and then prepare a list of security considerations that should be incorporated into such a system. Consider the entire system—customers, retail outlet, terminal, bank, and any interbank bank transfers.

7.3 "The magnetic-stripe credit card, a relative newcomer on the credit card scene, shows promise for expanding the traditional role of the credit card in our society. In addition to performing all of the conventional functions of embossed, physically coded, and other forms of magnetic data storage cards, the magnetic-stripe credit card (MSCC) offers additional advantages. Prominent among these is the capability of performing online credit transactions in real time, which has led to unattended cash dispensers or online self-service banking."[10]

Research the application of the magnetic-stripe credit card and write a report on its strengths and weaknesses in the area of security controls.

7.4 Most banks are developing, or are using, a lot of data communications, either on their own computer or on a larger correspondent's computer. As the use of data communications proliferates, so do the dangers of disastrous and costly security breaches. In addition, many of the larger banks are seeking to expand their programs and their data base flexibility at a rapid rate. This expansion results in an unstable environment, one in which much emphasis is placed on getting a new product up and running, even if it does not have a proper system of controls. It seems that we are caught up in the same situation.

As an aggressive bank, we have a variety of users and consequently, we face a variety of dangers. These can be grouped as follows:

1. *Internal bank users.* We want to restrict unauthorized access to data belonging to other departments.
2. *Correspondent banks.* We want to restrict unauthorized access to files that do not belong to them and vice versa.
3. *Customers using computer facilities.* We want to restrict the customers who use our time-sharing systems from access to anything that is not their own.
4. *Past employees.* We want to guard against the dangers resulting from these people having known about certain techniques and having been granted passwords while in the employ of our company.
5. *Operators and other computer personnel.* We want to guard the computer environment from potential abuse by these people.
6. *Programmers.* These people know how to do so much, and they can be so dangerous. We want to implement controls that will reduce dangers in this area.

The statements above were actually made by an officer of a large bank. Assuming that you are the auditor of his bank, prepare a proposal for complete system of controls to help meet his concerns.

---

[10] Jerome Svigals and Herman A. Ziegler, "Magnetic-Stripe Credit Cards: Big Business in the Offing." *IEEE Spectrum*, December 1974, pp. 56–62.

CHAPTER
8

COST/EFFECTIVENESS ANALYSIS OF CONTROLS

8.1 INTRODUCTION

Auditors, and others, are all too aware of the number of articles which have appeared in the press in recent years describing such events as: the destruction of computers by militants; operator errors that resulted in the erasure of the last backup copies of master files; confiscation of preferred customer files; complex fraud schemes; or alteration of programs as part of an embezzlement plan—fiascoes that a proper system of controls might have prevented. But a system of controls costs money. The question then is, "Are the controls worth the price?" In this chapter we will present some ideas about how one might come to grips with this difficult question.

8.2 MANAGEMENT'S RESPONSIBILITY IN REGARD TO CONTROLS

If a computer-based information system is to have a proper system of controls, management, through consultation with auditors and information systems staff, must approve and support the task of developing and implementing controls. This responsibility of management involves primarily two aspects: (1) understanding the purpose of controls, and (2) optimization of controls.

Understanding the Purpose of Controls

Simply stated, if management had a general understanding of the material presented in the previous chapters of this text plus that presented in several of the references, then it would have adequate expertise on controls. But management personnel are generalists; they do not have the time to become experts in this field. They must rely on the auditor to inform them about available controls and the consequences of not installing them.

Conveying to management a synopsis of this or another similar text would be sufficient. The auditor should first find out what management's attitude is in regard to possible exposures to hazards. Then he can pursue a more specific task of investigation, review, and recommendation. For example, to get started, the auditor might use the kind of questions listed in Table 8.1. Any attempt by the auditor to analyze the control problem must begin with management. Starting with these kinds of questions gives the auditor a better overview of management's general attitude about the value and purpose of controls. If management does not believe there is any potential exposure to hazards and is, consequently, not willing to support installation of controls, then there is little the auditor can do directly. The auditor's responsibility is to give opinions, favorable or unfavorable.

Optimization of Controls

It is the fundamental responsibility of management to make decisions. Again, the auditor's responsibility is to recommend and give opinions. It is the responsibility of the systems analyst to design a system of controls and prepare cost/effectiveness figures. The auditor is involved to the extent that he helps management to make sure that the control problem is handled properly.

TABLE 8.1

Preliminary Sample Questions for Management

1. In general, I am quite concerned about such things as unauthorized access to the computer system, errors in data processing, and unauthorized changes to programs.

    Strongly Disagree 0 1 2 3 4 5 6 7 8 9 Strongly Agree

2. I am concerned about exposures to hazards and threats such as malfunctions and human error, fires, natural disasters, fraud, tapping and bugging, power and data communications failure, and sabotage and riot.

    Strongly Disagree 0 1 2 3 4 5 6 7 8 9 Strongly Agree

3. I feel that an investment of two to five percent of the total cost of the information system invested in a system of controls is generally warranted.

    Strongly Disagree 0 1 2 3 4 5 6 7 8 9 Strongly Agree

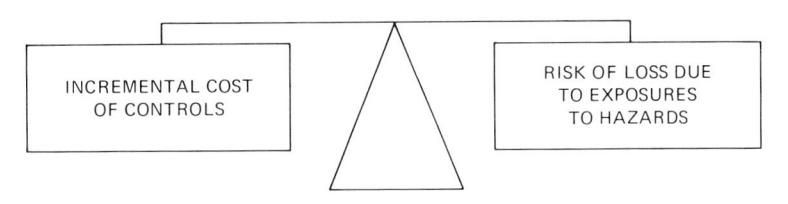

FIGURE 8.1.
An Example of How Management Must Balance Risk of Loss against the Cost of Controls to Reduce this Risk.

Therefore, with the aid of the systems analyst (in an analysis, design, implementation context) and the auditor (in a consultation, recommendation context), management must measure the information system's susceptibility to security risks, potential disaster or disruption, processing errors, loss of sensitive information, and so forth, against the cost of providing different levels of controls. Such considerations require a proper balance, as shown in Figure 8.1.

So, like most other management problems, system of controls involves a trade-off problem. Having few effective controls means low cost, but the loss due to hazards may be high. On the other hand, an increase in the number of effective controls employed will increase the cost but reduce the expected loss due to hazards. A balance must be struck between the two extremes.

8.3 SYSTEM OF CONTROLS DECISION MODEL

Coming to grips with the feasibility of a system of controls entails the consideration of three elements: (1) exposures to hazards, (2) value of the information system and its related components, and (3) available controls. These basic elements[1] are illustrated in Figure 8.2. A general methodology[2] used by the analyst in dealing with a system of controls is shown in Table 8.2. A more detailed analysis is made in the following subsections.

Exposures to Hazards and Expected Loss Analysis

Hazard and loss analysis involves the determination of how exposed the system is to various hazards and the expected loss from each hazard.

---

[1] Adapted from *Data Security and Data Processing, Vol. 3, Part 2, Study Results,* State of Illinois, 7320-1373, (White Plains, N.Y.: IBM Corporation, Technical Publications, Dept. 824, 1974).
[2] *Ibid.*

TABLE 8.2
General Methodology for the Control Decision Problem

1. What and where are the exposures to hazards	1. Categorize exposures. 2. Identify specific hazards and estimate level of probability that each will occur.
2. What is the value of all components of the system?	1. Itemize the components of the system. 2. Determine value of each component.
3. What controls are available and what are their corresponding costs?	1. Research available controls and list those appropriate with corresponding conversion and operational costs. 2. Estimate the probability of control failing.
4. What is the most cost/effective mix of controls?	1. Apply total expected cost model.

This analysis may be conducted with management and staff members of the information system using interviews and questionnaires. The questionnaires should be similar to those included in earlier chapters. In addition, management and staff should be asked questions such as: "What would you do if so and so happened? What is the probability that this hazard would occur? What would your loss be if it did occur?" In this way, a priority of exposures to hazards can be established by evaluating the probability of occurrence in conjunction with the magnitude of expected loss of each hazard.

Let us assume that the value of the information system is three million dollars. That is, in the event of a disaster causing total or near-total destruction, it is estimated that the loss would amount to three million dollars when the costs of all physical assets, recreating files, replacement of personnel, and so forth were included.

A sample of how the probability of exposures to hazards and expected losses may be quantified is shown in Table 8.3. For example, the exposure to fire hazard is determined by consulting with the fire department and/or insurance company for probability of a fire occurring at this particular site. Assume that the probability is set at 0.70 percent. In the "Probability That Hazard Will Occur" column, the 0.70 percent probability is entered. This percent represents the probability of the occurrence of a fire in a one-year period.

The next column shows the range of loss in thousands of dollars. It is estimated that if a fire occurs, the loss may range from $10,000 to total destruction, or $3,000,000. The last column represents the results of multiplying the probability of occurrence by the high and low estimated losses and then dividing by two for an approximate average expected loss. Similar estimates of probability of occurrence and ranges of loss

FIGURE 8.2.
Basic Elements in Determining Feasilibity of a System of Controls.

are made for additional exposures to hazards. Some of these estimates may be nothing more than hunches. Others, such as malfunctions and human error, may be based upon actual experience, and thus provide fairly precise results.

Even if some of the estimated figures represent hunches, the use of probabilities formalizes these hunches and intuitive judgments of management and staff. If management is going to take a "calculated risk," then some calculations ought to be involved. Moreover, this approach forces all personnel to come to grips quantitatively with what they know and what they think they know. They have to put their estimates down on paper. Also, by formalizing the measurement and decision-making process, the combined wisdom and expertise of appropriate personnel can come into play. By participating in this process, they can under-

TABLE 8.3
Hazard and Loss Analysis Table

Exposures to Hazards	Probability (%) That Hazard Will Occur (Level of Exposure)	(000) Loss Range ($)	Weighted Values ($) Low	High
Malfunctions and Human Errors:				
• Equipment	05.00	1–250	50	12,500
• Software	10.00	10–100	1,000	10,000
• Programmers	70.00	1–20	700	14,000
• Computer Operators	60.00	1–10	600	6,000
• Maintenance	90.00	1–10	900	9,000
• Users	90.00	1–15	900	13,500
• General Personnel	50.00	1–20	500	10,000
		Subtotal	4,650	75,000
		Average	39,825	
Fraud:*				
• Embezzlement	5.00	10–100	500	5,000
• Confiscation of Files	10.00	10–100	1,000	10,000
• Tapping	5.00	10–100	500	5,000
• Program Changes	20.00	5–25	1,000	5,000
		Subtotal	3,000	25,000
		Average	14,000	
Power and Communication Failures:				
• Brownouts & Failures	50.00	1–10	500	5,000
• Surges	30.00	1–50	300	15,000
• Busy	70.00	1–20	200	4,000
		Subtotal	1,000	24,000
		Average	12,500	
Fire:	0.70	10–3,000	70	21,000
		Subtotal	70	21,000
		Average	10,535	
Sabotage and Riot:				
• Internal	0.20	10–3,000	20	6,000
• External	0.40	10–3,000	40	12,000
		Subtotal	60	18,000
		Average	9,030	
Natural Disasters:				
• Earthquake	0.01	500–3,000	50	300
• Tornado	0.20	500–3,000	1,000	6,000
• Flood	0.10	500–3,000	500	3,000
• Lightning	0.01	10–1,000	1	100
		Subtotal	1,551	9,400
		Average	5,475	
General Hazards:	1.00	1–500	10	5,000
		Subtotal	10	5,000
		Average	2,505	
		Grand Total	10,341	177,400
		Average	93,870	

*Losses in this category are estimated for direct losses relative to the information system, if any, plus losses of assets that are controlled by the information system, e.g., embezzlement of funds.

stand the system better and become more aware of the purpose of controls.

In many cases, maximum losses from hazards such as fire or natural disasters receive more attention than they deserve when contrasted to losses from hazards such as malfunction and human errors, fraud, and power and communication failures. Using probabilities that hazards will occur and calculating an average expected loss give a more accurate picture of reality.

Measurement of exposures to hazards and expected losses therefrom is imprecise. Moreover, results will vary from one organization to another and even between computer systems in the same organization. Nevertheless, such an analysis provides a means of ordering the relative importance of various hazards and justifying the need for expenditures for controls to counteract the exposures to these hazards.

Of course, the main purpose of the hazard and loss analysis is to provide management with a basis for making budgetary decisions. The total weighted values in Table 8.3, include a low value of $10,341 and a high value of $177,400, or an average total of approximately $93,870 per year. This figure gives management a benchmark, i.e., management can reasonably assume that an annual outlay of $93,870 could be justified for a system of controls.

Optimum Mix of Controls

Now, as the analysis in Table 8.3 indicates, management can justify an expenditure up to approximately $93,870 for a system of controls. This money will not be spent wisely if controls are acquired indiscriminately, however. The question that must be answered is, "How can an expenditure of $93,870 (or less) be made to gain an optimum mix of controls?" In graphic terms, this question is answered in Figure 8.3.

To find this mix where the total expected cost line is at its lowest point (zero slope), the following formula is used:[3]

$TEC(K) = S(K) + L(K)$, where
$TEC(K) =$ Total expected cost (dollars/year) in using control system K
$S(K) =$ Cost (dollars/year) to install and operate controls comprising system K
$L(K) =$ Average expected loss (dollars/per year) due to exposures to hazards if control fails.

The total expected cost of a system of controls has three major components: (1) average expected loss associated with exposures to hazards (determined in Table 8.3), (2) cost of installing and operating controls that are available to combat exposures, and (3) probability that various controls fail.

[3]*Ibid.*

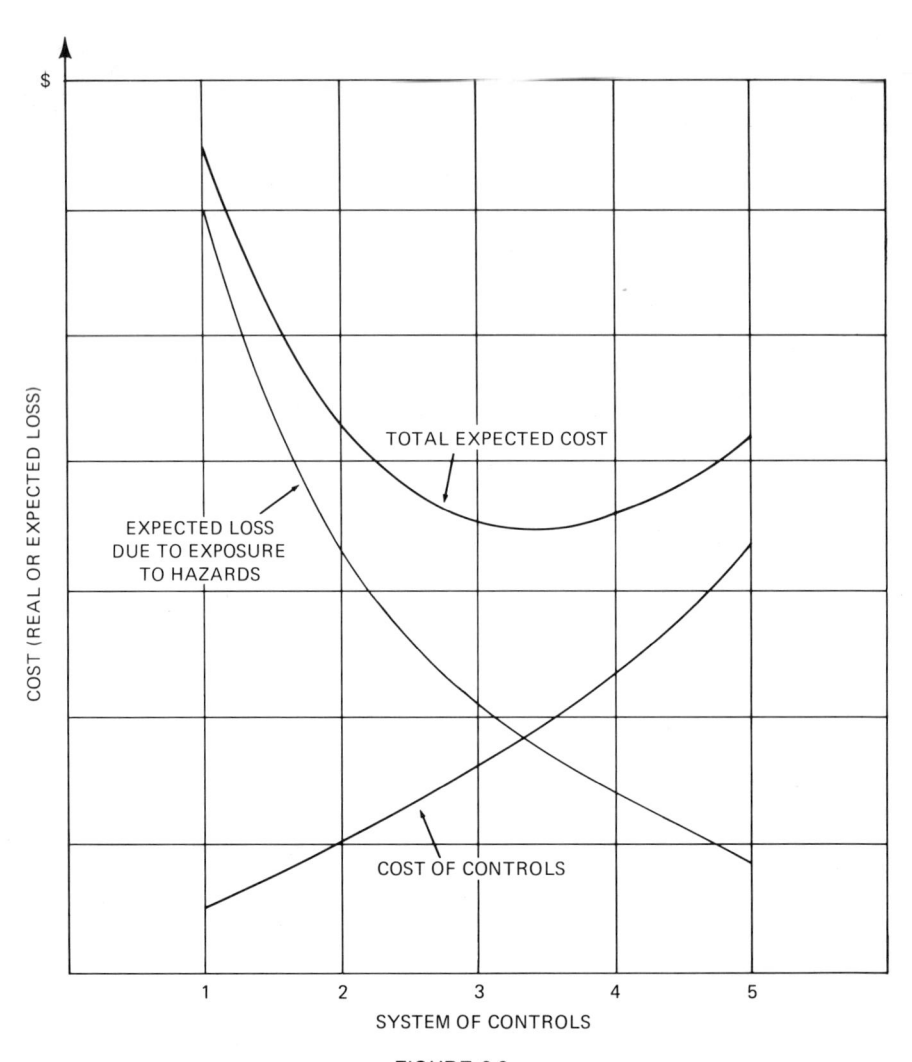

FIGURE 8.3.
Graphic Illustration of an Optimum System of Controls.

The exposures to hazards and expected losses therefrom are listed in Table 8.4. These entries represent the average losses taken from Table 8.3

In Table 8.5, the controls selected to protect exposures to hazards are shown with their probability of failure. This is an abbreviated list of controls. In practice, the table would include many more specific controls (e.g., badge system, encryption devices). However, the concept and method are the same whether the table is in detail form or not.

Each set of controls requires an expenditure of time and money. The costs to install and operate these controls are listed in Table 8.6.

TABLE 8.4
Exposures to Hazards and Expected Losses

Exposures to Hazards		Average Expected Loss Per Year ($)
E1	Malfunctions and Human Errors	39,825
E2	Fraud	14,000
E3	Power and Communications Failures	12,500
E4	Fire	10,535
E5	Sabotage and Riot	9,030
E6	Natural Disasters	5,475
E7	General Hazards	2,505
	Total Average Expected Loss	93,870

TABLE 8.5
Controls that Protect Exposures to Hazards

Controls	Exposures Protected	Description of Controls	Probability (%) Control Fails
C1	E1, E2	Administrative, Operational, Documentation	1.00
C2	E3	Backup	2.00
C3	E4	Fire Detection & Extinguishing System	3.00
C4	E5, E6, E7	Various Security Controls	1.00

TABLE 8.6
Control Costs

Controls	Cost to Implement ($)	Costs Per Year to Operate ($)
C1	10,000	3,000
C2	6,000	500
C3	2,000	1,000
C4	22,000	15,500

To determine the optimum system of controls, total expected cost for each combination of controls (system (K)) must be calculated. This cost summary is presented in Table 8.7.

Notice, in Table 8.7, that the organization will suffer an average expected loss of $93,870 without any system of controls. With the implementation of all controls C1, C2, C3, and C4 (System 15), the total expected cost of the system is $62,805. That is, without any system, the organization is out $93,870; with System 15, the organization is out

$62,805, or a cost savings of $31,065. Is this the best system of controls? No, because when the total expected cost of all combinations of controls is calculated, System 11 represents the best combination of controls with a cost saving of $93,870 less $40,614 or $53,256. Therefore, the implementation of additional controls will not always prove to be cost/effective. In other words, purchasing more controls, C4, as indicated in System 15, does not reduce expected loss from hazards enough to justify the additional cost. Sample calculations for Systems 1, 11, and 15 are presented in Table 8.8.

In conclusion, any attempt at determining the cost/effectiveness of a system of controls is imprecise at best. The methods that we have presented above allow management to: (1) select an optimum system based on financial terms, (2) objectively compose various alternatives, (3) weed out redundant alternatives, and (4) stay within budget. Conversely, this analysis ignores a long-range plan, e.g., a 5-year plan, but this could be an advantage, because the system of controls should be re-evaluated at least once a year to see if some controls could be eliminated and others added, all on a cost/effective basis. Furthermore, this analysis

TABLE 8.7

Cost Summary

Control System (K)	Control Comprising (K)	SI (K)	SO (K)	S (K)	L (K)	TEC (K)
No System	No Controls	$ 0	$ 0	$ 0	$ 93,870	93,870
1	C1	10,000	3,000	13,000	40,583	53,583
2	C2	6,000	500	6,500	81,620	88,120
3	C3	2,000	1,000	3,000	83,651	86,651
4	C4	22,000	15,500	37,500	78,561	116,061
5	C1, C2	16,000	3,500	19,500	28,333	47,833
6	C1, C3	12,000	4,000	16,000	30,364	46,364
7	C1, C4	32,000	18,500	50,500	25,274	75,774
8	C2, C3	8,000	1,500	9,500	71,401	80,901
9	C2, C4	28,000	16,000	44,000	66,311	110,311
10	C3, C4	24,000	16,500	40,500	68,342	108,842
11	C1, C2, C3	18,000	4,500	22,500	18,114	40,614
12	C1, C2, C4	38,000	19,000	57,000	13,124	70,124
13	C1, C3, C4	34,000	19,500	53,500	15,055	68,555
14	C2, C3, C4	30,000	17,000	47,000	56,092	113,092
15	C1, C2, C3, C4	40,000	20,000	60,000	2,805	62,805

EXPLANATION OF SYMBOLS:
SI (K) = Cost to implement Kth control
SO (K) = Cost to operate Kth control per year
S (K) = SI (K) + SO (K)
L (K) = The Sum of all losses from exposures to hazards and the probability that the control will fail
TEC (K) = S (K) + L (K)

ignores the time value of money and competing projects for limited funds. These two aspects could be easily added, but they are beyond the scope of this text.

8.4 SUMMARY

A system of controls is necessary in today's organizations, because computer-based information systems represent a large concentration of valuable resources in the form of personnel, equipment, buildings, and information. Moreover, dependence upon this information system for the smooth operation of the organization exposes the organization to a

TABLE 8.8
Sample Calculations for Systems 1, 11, and 15

System 1 ($):
- S (1) = 10,000 + 3,000
       = 13,000
- L (1) = 39,825 (1.00) + 14,000 (1.00) + 12,500 (100.00) + 10,535 (100.00) + 9,030 (100.00) + 5,475 (100.00) + 2,505 (100.00)
- L (1) = 398 + 140 + 12,500 + 10,535 + 9,030 + 5,475 + 2,505
       = 40,583
- TEC (1) = 13,000 + 40,583
         = 53,583

Explanation: Without controls, the probability is 100.00 percent that exposures to hazards E1 and E2 will result in an average expected loss of $39,825 and $14,000, respectively. System 1 is the application of controls C1 which protects these two exposures to hazards with a probability of failure of 1.00 percent. Average expected loss of E1 and E2 are both multiplied by this probability, reducing the average expected loss of $398 and $140, respectively. The other average expected losses, E3, E4, E5, E6, and E7, are multiplied by 100.00 percent probability because it has been determined that without controls average expected losses of $12,500; $10,535; $9,030; $5,475; and $2,505 will occur.

System 11 ($):
- S (11) = 18,000 + 4,500
        = 22,500
- L (11) = 39,825 (1.00) + 14,00 (1.00) + 12,500 (2.00) + 10,535 (3.00) + 9,030 (100.00) + 5,475 (100.00) + 2,505 (100.00)
- L (11) = 398 + 140 + 250 + 316 + 9,030 + 5,475 + 2,505
        = 18,114
- TEC (11) = 22,500 + 18,114
          = 40,614

System 15 ($):
- S (15) = 40,000 + 20,000
        = 60,000
- L (15) = 39,825 (1.00) + 14,000 (1.00) + 12,500 (2.00) + 10,535 (3.00) + 9,030 (1.00) + 5,475 (1.00) + 2,505 (1.00)
- L (15) = 398 + 140 + 250 + 316 + 903 + 548 + 250
        = 2,805
- TEC (15) = 60,000 + 2,805
          = 62,805

number of hazards. Protection from these hazards must be obtained. But protection costs money.

Management must balance exposures to hazards and potential loss from these hazards against the cost of controls to protect the organization against them, and allocate resources accordingly. Probability of occurrence of hazards and magnitude of loss therefrom must be weighed against the cost of controls plus the probability that the controls will not deter the hazards. On the basis of this analysis, the optimum mix of controls is selected. Besides making financial decisions, management must also understand and support a system of controls effort.

This chapter has presented a method for determining the best system of controls for a computer-based information system by using minimum total expected cost as the main criterion. There are other ways to reach decisions about a system of controls, some satisfactory and others unsatisfactory; however, the method presented in this chapter enables management to look at the control problem objectively, to compare various alternative controls, and to narrow the choice of alternative systems by weeding out redundant and dominant alternatives. For example, fire protection may receive more attention than it deserves in comparison with, say, protection against human errors. Moreover, this method helps management to stay within the budget.

REVIEW QUESTIONS

8.1 What is management's responsibility in developing a system of controls?

8.2 Define system of controls as a trade-off problem.

8.3 What kinds of questions would you ask management to start them thinking about the purpose of controls?

8.4 What is the auditor's responsibility relative to the development of a system of controls? If during the development and implementation of controls, the auditor took a devil's advocate role, would this in any way compromise his independence?

8.5 List and define the elements involved in determining the feasibility of a system of controls.

8.6 Explain, in your own words, the general methodology for the control decision problem.

8.7 On the basis of total expected cost, define the optimum mix of controls.

DISCUSSION QUESTIONS

8.1 Should unauthorized disclosure of information be considered a loss to the organization? Suppose you are an auditor for the Office of Vital Records for the State of New York and you have heard that in the State of Massachusetts, an employee in a similar office disclosed to a friend the adoptive parents' name and address of this friend's illegitimate child. Would this situation have any effect on your decision to install a system of controls? What if you later found out that the parents were suing for $2,500,000, and they have an almost certain chance of collecting at least $100,000, according to the best legal advice. How do you place a value on secrecy?

8.2 In a public health clinic, an administrator was asked, "What would happen if your data base was destroyed?" The response was, "If all our information is destroyed—forget it." How do you determine the expected loss in this situation? Would cost of replacement or reconstruction be an appropriate measurement of the value of the data base? If so, what is the loss relative to the inability of a physician to act or perform a medical task because of the lack of information?

8.3 "At best, the quantification of a cost/effectiveness problem is imprecise. Nevertheless, to perform meaningful analysis, all aspects should be quantified." Comment on the merits of this statement.

8.4 Discuss the comment, "A reasonable, educated approximation is better than nothing at all."

8.5 "We constantly remind our managers to be skeptical about any quantifications about the future and assume a large margin of error." Discuss this statement.

8.6 "About the worse thing that could happen to us is a fire. That's why we spend most of our protection resources on fire control devices." Comment on the merits of this statement.

EXERCISES

8.1 By using the following tables of figures, calculate the best combination of controls based on total expected cost.

Value Versus Expected Loss

Exposure Point or Route to Hazards	Value of Resource ($)	Average Number of Attempted Exposures Per Year	Expected Loss ($)
E1	100,000	.5	50,000
E2	50,000	.2	10,000
E3	20,000	1.5	30,000
E4	700,000	.1	70,000
E5	900,000	.2	180,000

Exposures to Hazards Protected by Controls

Controls	Exposure Points Protected	Description of Controls	Probability Control Fails
C1	E2, E3	Encryptoboxes	.01
C2	E1	Badge System	.02
C3	E4	Fire Control	.03
C4	E5	Emergency Doors	.01

Control Costs

Controls	Description	Cost to Implement ($)	Cost to Operate ($)
C1	Encryptoboxes	10,000	3,000
C2	Badge System	5,000	12,000
C3	Fire Control	90,000	4,000
C4	Emergency Doors	15,000	1,000

PROBLEMS

8.1 By using a typical bank or any other organization of your choice, list exposures to hazards, probability that these hazards will occur, and expected loss. From this analysis select an optimum system of controls. Use the material in this chapter as a guide.

8.2 How many more opportunities exist for crimes, accidents, and malpractices due to ineffective or insufficient data security? As each day goes by, I am constantly amazed not to read of some major bank heist pulled off by persons taking advantage of computer security weaknesses. I am equally amazed at the small amount of attention that most companies (users and manufacturers alike) are willing to devote to avoiding this.

My industry is banking; we deal in money—a readily traded commodity. We handle large amounts of this money and thus are very prone to theft and fraud by people who want to get some of our money. In addition, we carry large amounts of confidential information about customers. We should be supremely conscious of the need for computer security—but we are not. The whole matter gets swept under carpets in managerial offices and repeatedly cut from budgets. This I suspect is for two major reasons. First, good data security measures require a considerable amount of thought and decision making. Top management do not understand the EDP side of their company, and, consequently, do not understand its dangers. Second, good data security measures involve a considerable cost which renders no immediate apparent return on the investment.

There is also an implied feeling that data security should be the concern of the computer manufacturers and that, if they don't have it at reasonable cost we cannot be blamed for not implementing our own measures. This, gentlemen, is hardly true and may not stand up as an argument to your president the day someone steals $3,000,000 from your company. Neither may the argument, that you weren't given the budget. After all, when the company entrusted you with the responsibility of your job they also entrusted you with the responsibility of shouting loud enough and clearly enough (in lay language) for your management to see the need for adequate computer security.[4]

Assume that you are a consulting auditor. Prepare a report and give examples where necessary that will show how such a dilemma may be put into a proper perspective, and if not eliminated, then reduced.

BIBLIOGRAPHY

Adams, Donald L. "We Didn't Test the System But How Much Could We Lose? Would You Believe $7,500,000?" *EDPACS*, August 1974.

Alexander, Tom. "Waiting for the Great Computer Rip-Off." *Fortune*, July 1974.

Allen, Brandt. "Computer Fraud." *Financial Executive*, May 1973.

──────. "Computer Security." *Data Management*, January and February 1972.

──────. "Danger Ahead! Safeguard Your Computer." *Harvard Business Review*, November/December 1968.

American Accounting Association, Committee on Accounting Education, and AICPA Computer Education Subcommittee. "Inclusion of EDP in an Undergraduate Auditing Curriculum: Some Possible Approaches." *The Accounting Review*, October 1974.

American Institute of Certified Public Accountants. *Statement on Auditing Standards, No. 3, The Effects of EDP on the Auditor's Study and Evaluation of Internal Control.* New York: AICPA, 1974.

────── Computer Auditing Subcommittee, "Advanced EDP Systems and the Auditor's Concern." *The Journal of Accountancy*, January 1975.

──────. *The Auditor's Study and Evaluation of Internal Control in EDP Systems.* Exposure Draft. AICPA New York: American Institute of Certified Public Accountants, March 1976.

Anderson, James. "Security Threats and Penetration Techniques." *Computer Security Technology Planning Study*, United States Air Force, October 1972.

Anderson, Lane K., et al. "Self-Checking Digit Concepts." *Journal of Systems Management*, September 1974.

[4]Excerpt from a speech given by a vice-president of a large bank in western Massachusetts.

Arthur Andersen & Co. *Effective Controls for Computer Based Systems.* Chicago: Arthur Andersen & Co., 1973.

Baker, F. Terry, and Harlan D. Mills, "Chief Programmer Teams." *Datamation,* December 1973.

Bank Administration Institute. *Auditing Bank EDP Systems.* Park Ridge, Ill.: Bank Administration Institute, 1968.

_____ . *Bank Auditing.* Park Ridge, Ill.: Bank Administration Institute, 1974.

_____ . *Standards for Internal Bank Auditing in an Electronic Data Processing Environment.* Park Ridge, Ill.: Bank Administration Institute, 1972.

Bates, Robert. "Auditing the Advanced Computer Systems." *Management Accounting,* June, 1970.

Beardsley, Charles. "Is Your Computer Insecure?" *IEEE Spectrum,* January 1972.

Brandon, Dick H. *Management Standards for Data Processing.* New York: Van Nostrand Company, 1963.

Browne, Peter. "Computer Security—A Survey." *Data Base,* Fall 1972.

Burch, John G., Jr., and Felix R. Strater, Jr. *Information Systems: Theory and Practice.* Santa Barbara, Calif.: Hamilton Publishing Co., 1974.

_____ , and Nathan Hod. *Information Systems Development: A Case/Workbook Approach.* Santa Barbara, Calif.: Wiley/Hamilton, 1975.

Caffrey, J. J. "Protecting Computers." *Datamation,* October 1973.

Canning, Richard G. (Editor) "Do We Have the Right Resources?" *EDP Analyzer,* July, 1975.

Chapin, Ned, et al. "Structured Programming Simplified." *Computer Decisions,* June 1974.

"Chargeback Schemes Allow Users to Evaluate Systems." *Computerworld,* April 30, 1975.

Clark, R. Lawrence. "A Linguistic Contribution to GOTO-less Programming." *Datamation,* December 1973.

"COBOL Aid Packages." *EDP Analyzer,* May 1972.

CODASYL Data Base Task Group. April 71 Report. Washington, D.C.

CODASYL Data Description Language. U.S. Government Printing Office, June, 1973. (Catalog No. C13.6/2:113)

CODASYL Systems Committee Technical Report. *Feature Analysis of Generalized Data Base Management Systems.* New York: Association of Computing Machinery, May 1971.

Computer Controls and Audit, First edition. New York: Touche Ross & Co., 1973.

"Computer Security: Backup and Recovery Methods." *EDP Analyzer,* January 1972.

Computer Services Executive Committee. *The Auditor's Study and Evaluation of Internal Control in EDP Systems.* New York: American Institute of Certified Public Accountants, 1977.

Conway, R. W., W. L. Maxwell, and H. L. Morgan. "On the Implementation of Security Measures in Information Systems." *Communications of the ACM,* April 1972.

Corbato, F. J., H. J. Slatzer, and C. T. Clingen. "Multics: The First Seven Years." *Spring Joint Computer Conference,* Spring 1972.

Courtney, Robert H. "A Systematic Approach to Data Security." *U.S. National Bureau of Standards Symposium on Privacy and Security in Computer Systems.* March 1974.

Dean, R. N. "A Comparison of Decision Tables Against Conventional COBOL as a Programming Tool for Commercial Applications." *Software World,* Spring 1971.

Desiderio, Louis J., Dennis Sloky, Arnold Wasserman. *Measuring Computer Performance for Improvement and Savings.* C & L Reports to Management. New York: Coopers & Lybrand, 1974.

Dirks, Raymond L., and Leonard Gross. *The Great Wall Street Scandal.* New York: McGraw-Hill Book Company, 1974.

Donaldson, James R. "Structured Programming." *Datamation,* December 1973.

Dratler, Louise H. "Tenth Annual AICPA Computer Conference." *Management Adviser,* July–August 1974.

EDPACS, Automation Training Center, Reston, Virginia. A monthly newsletter which presents original articles, literature synopses and reviews, information sources, commentary, and a forum for the area of EDP auditing, security, and controls.

Ernst & Ernst Professional Development Series. *Senior Accountants Program, Internal Control and the Computer.* New York: Ernst & Ernst, 1974.

Fitzgerald, Cason, and Russell. *Systems Auditability & Control Report: Data Processing Control Practices Report.* Altamonte Springs, Florida: The Institute of Internal Auditors, Inc., 1977.

Frank, Ronald A. "Imsai Arrays Micros For Low-Cost Power." *Computerworld,* Oct. 29, 1975.

Gellerman, Harvey. "How the Computer Can be Used to Rob You Blind," *Canadian Risk Management and Business Insurance.* August/September 1971.

Gentile, E. A., and J. R. Grimes. "Maintaining Internal Integrity of On-Line Data Bases," *EDPACS,* February 1977.

Goldstein, Robert C., and Richard L. Nolan. "Personal Privacy Versus the Corporate Computer." *Harvard Business Review,* March–April 1975.

Grindley, Kit, and John Humble. *The Effective Computer, A Management by Objectives Approach.* American Management Association, 1973.

"Guidelines Set for Friday Fraud By Outside Audits." *The Wall Street Journal,* May 6, 1976.

Harper, William. *Data Processing Documentation: Standards, Procedures and Applications.* Englewood Cliffs, N.J.: Prentice-Hall, 1973.

Hebert, John P. "New York Antes Up Revamped Lottery." *Computerworld,* Sept. 27, 1976.

Hoffman, Lance. *Security and Privacy in Computer Systems.* Los Angeles: Melville Publishing Co., 1973.

Holmes, Robert W. "12 Areas to Investigate for Better MIS." *Financial Executive,* July 1970.

Hoyt, Douglas B., et al. *Computer Security Handbook.* New York: Macmillan Information, a Division of Macmillan Publishing Company, 1973.

Huemer, David. "Recovery and Restart in a Real Time System." *Data Management,* September 1973.

Hughes, Kevin, John Binns, and Arthur Cooke. "Keeping in Tune." *Data Processing,* July/August 1974.

Huhn, Gerald. "The Data Base in a Critical On-Line Business Environment." *Datamation,* September 1974.

"The Internal Auditor and the Computer," *EDP Analyzer.* March 1975.

International Business Machines Corporation. *The Considerations of Physical Security in a Computer Environment.* While Plains, N.Y.: IBM, 1972.

_____ . *Data Security and Data Processing.* White Plains, N.Y.: IBM, 1974. A six-volume work presenting the findings of an IBM study into specific aspects of data security. The study sites were MIT, the State of Illinois, TRW Systems, Inc., and the IBM Federal Systems Center.

_____ . *OS, Linkage, Editor and Loader.* Publ. No. GC28-6538-10, April 1973.

_____ . *System/360 Operating System Introduction.* Publ. No. GC28-6534-4, 1972.

_____ . *System/360 Operating System: Job Control Language Reference.* Publ. No. GC28-6704-3, April 1973.

_____ . *System/360 Operating System Supervisor Services and Macro Instructions.* Publ. No. GC28-6646-7, September 1974.

_____ . *System/370 Principles of Operation,* "Systems." Publ. No. Form GA22-7000-3, January 1973.

_____ . *Information Management System/Virtual Storage (IMS/VS), General Information Manual.* Publ. No. GH20-1260-2, April 1975.

_____ . *Introduction to IBM Data Processing Systems.* Publ. No. GC20-1684-2.

_____ . *OS System Modification Program (SMP),* Publ. No. GC28-6791-1, September 1974.

_____ . OS/VS System Modification Program (SMP), Publ. No. GC28-0673.

_____ . OS/VS System Modification Program (SMP) Logic, Publ. No. SY28-0685-1, September 1974.

_____ *PL/1 (F) Language Reference Manual.* Publ. No. GC28-8201-4, 1972.

_____ . *SMP Reference Summary.* Publ. No. GX28-0684.

Johnson, Paul D. "Mark Tick's Data Center Audit." *EDPACS,* June 1974.

Joint GUIDE-SHARE Data Base Requirements Group. *Data Base Management System Requirements,* Nov. 11, 1970.

Koehn, Hank. "Are Companies Bugged About Bugging?" *Journal of Systems Management,* January 1973.

Kuong, Javier. *Computer Security, Auditing and Control: Text and Readings.* Wellesley Hills, Mass.: Management Advisory Publications, 1974.

Lancaster, Hal. "Hit by Alarming Wave of Robbery and Fraud, Banks Take Elaborate Steps to Foil Criminals." *The Wall Street Journal,* Feb. 18, 1976.

Leavitt, Don. "Auditors Should be Involved Early in Project Development Cycle." *Computerworld,* May 28, 1975.

Leibholz, Stephen, and Louis Wilson. *User's Guide to Computer Crime: Its Commission, Detection and Prevention.* Radnor, Pa.: Chilton Book Co., 1974.

Lewis, William F. "Auditing and On-Line Computer Systems." *The Arthur Young Journal,* Winter/Spring, 1971.

Mader, Chris, and Robert Hagin. *Information Systems: Technology, Economics, Applications.* Chicago, Ill.: Science Research Associates, 1974.

Martin, James. *Security, Accuracy and Privacy in Computer Systems.* Englewood Cliffs, N.J.: Prentice-Hall, 1973.

"Mass. Gives Burroughs CJIS Equipment Contract." *Computerworld,* May 21, 1975.

McCracken, Daniel D. "Revolution in Programming: An Overview," *Datamation,* December 1973.

McGowan, Clement L., and John R. Kelly, *Top-Down Structured Programming Techniques.* New York: Petrocelli/Charter, 1975.

Meadow, Charles T. *The Analysis of Information Systems.* Second edition. Los Angeles: Melville Publishing Co., 1973.

Meigs, Walter B., E. John Larsen, and Robert F. Meigs. *Principles of Auditing.* Sixth Edition. Homewood, Ill.: Richard D. Irwin, 1977.

Miller, Edward F., Jr., and George E. Lindamood, "Structured Programming: Top-Down Approach." *Datamation,* December 1973.

$3 Million in CPUs Damaged As Fire Ravages Installation." *Computerworld,* April 19, 1976.

Mixon, S. R. *Handbook of Data Processing Administration, Operations, and Procedures.* New York: AMACOM, a division of American Management Association, 1976.

Morgan, H. L., and J. V. Soden. "Understanding MIS Failures." *Data Base,* Vol. 5, Nos. 2, 3, and 4 (Winter, 1973).

Morris, Robert. "Scatter Storage Techniques." *Communications of the ACM* (January 1968), pp. 38–44.

Murphy, John A. "Computer Facility Support Equipment & Systems, Part 1—Power Support Systems." *Modern Data*, July, 1973.

Myers, Edith. "Computer Security: Each Case is Different." *Datamation*, April 1975.

Nattaly, Stanley, Bruce Johnson, and Michael Cohen. *COBOL Support Packages–Programming and Productivity Aids.* New York: John Wiley & Sons, 1972.

Noe, Jerre D. "Acquiring and Using a Hardware Monitor." *Datamation*, April 1974.

Palme, Jacob. "Software Security." *Datamation*, January 1974.

Parker, Donn B. *Further Comment on the Equity Funding Insurance Fraud Case.* Stanford Research Institute, from *EDPACS*, January 1975.

_____, Susan Nycum, and Stephen Oura. *Computer Abuse.* Washington, D.C.: National Science Foundation, 1973. Study performed at the Stanford Research Institute which provides a general view of computer abuse; extensively documented.

Perry, William, and Donald Adams. "SMF—An Untapped Audit Resource." *EDPACS*, September, 1974.

_____ and Jerry Fitzgerald. "Designing for Auditability." *Datamation*, August 1977.

Porter, Thomas. *EDP: Controls and Auditing.* Belmont, Calif.: Wadsworth Publishing Co., 1974.

_____, and John Burton. *Auditing: A Conceptual Approach.* Belmont, Calif.: Wadsworth Publishing Co., 1971.

Price, Gerald. "The Ten Commandments of Data Base." *Data Management*, May 1972.

Reid, George, and James Demcak. "EDP Audit Implementation with General Purpose Software." *Journal of Accountancy*, July, 1971.

Report to the Congress by the Comptroller General of the United States, "Problems Found With Government Acquisition and Use of Computers From November 1965 to December 1976," FGMSD-77-14, March 15, 1977.

Robbins, Robert R. "UPS Projects and the Consulting Engineer." *Modern Data*, July, 1975.

Robinson, John, and James Graviss. *Documentation Standards Manual for Computer Systems.* Cleveland: Association for Systems Management, 1973.

Romberg, Bernard. "Eyeball Your Computer Operations Today!" *Infosystems*, December 1972.

Rotenberg, Leo. *Making Computers Keep Secrets.* Cambridge, Mass.: Massachusetts Institute of Technology, Project MAC, 1974.

Ruth, Stephen, and Paul Kreutzer. "Data Compression for Large Business Files." *Datamation*, September 1972.

Salton, Gerard. *Automatic Information Organization and Retrieval.* New York: McGraw-Hill Book Company, 1968.

Sardinas, Joseph L., Jr. "Computer Security and the Auditor's Responsibility." Doctoral dissertation, The Pennsylvania State University, November 1975.

_____, and John G. Burch, Jr. "A Systems Approach to EDP Auditing." Proceeding of the American Accounting Association Southwest Regional Meeting, San Antonio, Texas, March 18 and 19, 1976.

Sawyer, Lawrence B. *The Practice of Modern Internal Auditing.* New York: The Institute of Internal Auditors, 1973.

Schaller, Carol. "Survey of Computer Cost Allocation Techniques." *The Journal of Accountancy*, June 1974.

Schubert, Richard. Basic Concepts in Data Base Management Systems." *Datamation*, July, 1972.

_____. "Trends in Data Management, Part 2." *EDP Analyzer*, (June 1971), pp. 1–13.

Special Audit Report on the Financial and Operating Practices of the Racing and Wagering Board, Division of the Lottery. Albany, N.Y.: Office of the State Comptroller, Division of Audits and Accounts, Report No. AL-St-3576, Nov. 14, 1975.

Stone, Robert L. "Who is Responsible for Computer Fraud?" *The Journal of Accountancy*, February 1975.

Summary of Findings New York State Lottery, (Cambridge, Mass.: Arthur D. Little, Inc., Nov. 26, 1975.

Svigals, Jerome, and Jerman A. Ziegler. "Magnetic-Stripe Credit Cards: Big Business in the Offing." *IEEE Spectrum*, December 1973.

"The Advent of Structured Programming." *EDP Analyzer*, June 1974.

Thorne, Jack. "Internal Control of Real-Time Systems." *Data Management*, January 1971.

Touche Ross & Co. *Computer Controls and Audit*. New York: Touche Ross & Co., 1973.

Turn, Rein. "Privacy Transformations for Databank Systems." *National Computer Conference*, 1973.

United States General Accounting Office. *Case Studies in Computer-Based Systems Environment*. Washington, D.C.: U.S. Government Printing Office, 1971.

Ward, Patrick. "Amdahl Ends Silent Years With Unveiling of 470/V/6." *Computerworld*, November 1975.

Wasserman, Joseph. "Plugging the Leaks in Computer Security." *Harvard Business Review*, September/October 1969.

Weiss, Harold. "A Survey of Test Data Generators." *EDPACS*, April 1973.

_____. "Career Advancement for the EDP Auditor." *EDPACS*, August 1974.

_____. "Computer Security: An Overview." *Datamation*, January 1974.

_____. "The Danger of Total Corporate Amnesia." *Financial Executive*, June 1969.

Weissman, Clark. "Tradeoff Considerations in Security System Design." *Data Management*, April 1972.

Westin, Alan F. "Privacy, Security and Related Managerial Concerns." *Senior Management and the Data Processing Function*. New York: The Conference Board, 1974.

Yasoki, Edward K. "Bar Codes for Data Entry." *Datamation*, May 1975.

_____. "A New Science Emerges: Plugging the Holes in Operating Systems." *Datamation*, February 1974.

PART THREE

COMPUTER AUDIT TECHNIQUES

CHAPTER
9

GENERAL AUDIT CONSIDERATIONS

9.1 INTRODUCTION

The fundamental objective of the auditor is to express an opinion. The basis of forming an opinion is evidential matter collected by the auditor by applying audit techniques. Although these fundamental precepts of auditing remain unchanged, the environment in which the auditor performs his audit tasks has changed drastically since the advent of computers.

In Part II, we discussed the kinds of controls required to safeguard the system from a variety of hazards. In this section, we will discuss those techniques that are especially applicable to auditing a computer system. Before looking at these techniques in detail, we will present an overview and perspective on computer auditing in general.

9.2 THE AUDIT FUNCTION

As noted above, computer systems have changed the audit arena but not the professional duties of the auditor. The basic tenets and objectives of auditing remain unchanged. Organizations should still be run in accordance with sound management principles, and auditors must still exercise professional judgment.

Audit Objectives

We will not spend a great deal of time attempting to differentiate between internal and external auditors. Internal auditors serve groups within the organization, such as executive management, whereas external auditors serve external groups, such as stockholders and government agencies. Traditionally, internal auditors have been interested in operating procedures, while external auditors have been interested in rendering an opinion on the financial statements. These two areas are not mutually exclusive, because in the final analysis both audit groups are concerned with the integrity and efficiency of the computer-based information system, the output it produces (e.g., financial statements), and its effect upon the well-being of the organization it serves.

Generally, audit objectives of both audit groups should be to:

1. Insure that an adequate system of controls is implemented and used.
2. Determine whether resources are being used in a cost/effective manner.
3. Check to see that assets are properly safeguarded and not used improperly.
4. Review integrity, reliability, and efficiency of the information system and the financial reports it produces.

Attainment of Objectives

Hereafter, we will use the term auditor simply to mean anyone who is attempting to attain the objectives listed above. There is no cut-and-dried way to attain these audit objectives, because the audit function is an art rather than a science. The professional practice of auditing encompasses five elements, as shown in Figure 9.1.

At the base of the illustration above is the area of techniques. It is imperative that the auditor have in his "tool bag" a sufficient number of *techniques* and that he know how to apply them. Although some audit techniques are traditional, such as confirmation of receivables, observation of a physical count of inventory, and the examination of official papers (e.g., mortgages, insurance policies) to determine the existence of certain assets or liabilities, the computer has changed the audit environment to a degree that calls for additional audit techniques.

The auditor's professional *judgment* dictates how the techniques are applied in different audit situations. There are no precise rules to follow as to when, where, and in what combination to apply the various techniques. If there were, auditing would not be a professional endeavor but a clerical process. Moreover, after the decisions have been made about

```
┌─────────────────┐
│  INDEPENDENCE   │
├─────────────────┤
│ AGGRESSIVENESS  │
├─────────────────┤
│   CREATIVITY    │
├─────────────────┤
│    JUDGMENT     │
├─────────────────┤
│   TECHNIQUES    │
└─────────────────┘
```

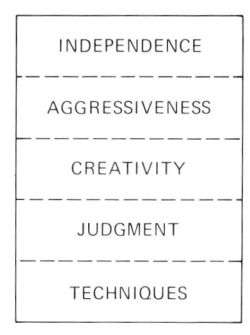

FIGURE 9.1.

Five Elements that Support the Professional Practice of Auditing.

the application of audit techniques, the auditor must evaluate the evidential information collected and form an opinion on various aspects of the system.

Creativity is an important attribute for an auditor to have. Systems and data-processing methods are constantly changing. Auditors must therefore use their imagination and creativity to develop new audit techniques or to borrow techniques from other disciplines and apply them to the field of auditing.

For too long, the auditor has played a passive role in respect to the audit of computer systems. He has avoided the computer system as much as possible. Even the more *aggressive* auditors' work has been tentative, because, quite frankly, most auditors are intimidated by the computer system and its personnel. Most of the data that the auditor reviews are provided him by some employee in the computer center (e.g., programmer). He reviews this data by recalculating totals prepared by the computer, a monumental waste of time. The computer personnel can give him anything they want to, and he will be none the wiser. The auditor may also administer a traditional internal control questionnaire that may not include many of the controls discussed in the preceding section. Worse than this, he may never test the responses to the questionnaire to see whether a particular control is in place and working as stated. The auditor must become more aggressive. He must see to it that a full system of controls is implemented. He must learn how to open up audit windows of the so-called black box and get the evidential information himself using his own audit techniques. He must view the computer as a tool that is as much his to use for his work as anyone else's.

The function of auditing has no value unless the auditor is *independent* in appearance and in fact. If the auditor gains expertise in computer control and auditing techniques, uses good judgment, breaks from outdated methods of control and auditing, and becomes more aggressive in his work, he will gain and maintain a high level of independence. Otherwise, his independence will diminish and eventually be lost, and his function will become superfluous. Without independence, the auditor has nothing.

The Audit Process

In the audit process, the auditor evaluates the system of controls, tests transactions, extracts data from the data base, and so forth to express an opinion about the reliability of financial statements and prepare recommendations for correction of irregularities. In Figure 9.2, a flowchart depicts the audit process. Each number in the flowchart points to a fuller explanation of a particular process, as follows:

1. First, the auditor must acquaint himself with the information system including personnel, hardware, software, organization, and interaction with users. Organization charts, both present and proposed, should be obtained for the organization as a whole and for the computer system. The chart for the computer system should be very detailed, showing lines of authority; position titles; number of personnel in each unit, and their names; job descriptions, duties, and responsibilities; and vacancies and incumbents. All user departments served by the computer system should be listed, together with a description of applications processed for each.

A list of inventory of computer and computer-related equipment should be made including equipment installed, planned for, and on order. From this inventory list, a computer equipment layout or configuration should be prepared for occasional review. Included in this layout would be such components as the CPU with primary storage size and other pertinent features; operating system description; terminals, data communications equipment, and auxiliary equipment. Method of acquisition should be determined, e.g., purchase, rent, or third-party lease. Processing time per day should be determined (e.g., one-shift, two-shift, split-shift, etc.), along with average monthly meter usage.

The kinds of programming languages and aids should be determined. The auditor should also see if there are published and enforced standards for working with users, systems development, programming, preparation of documentation, and operating procedures.

Much of the material discussed in Part II will help the auditor to gain an understanding of the system. For example, the master plan (discussed in administrative controls) will provide him with an understanding of systems development and processing objectives of the organization against which the system's performance can be measured.

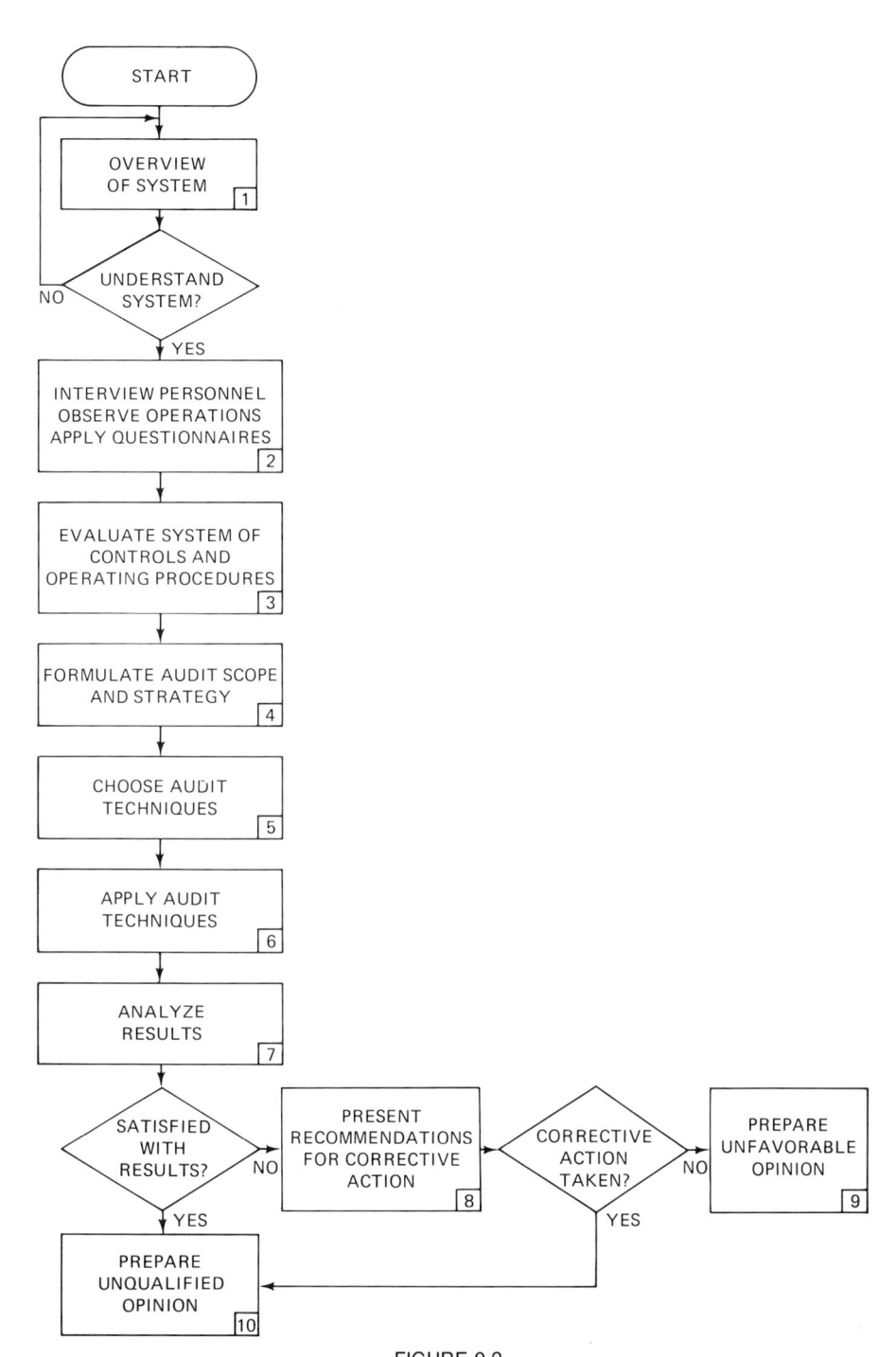

CHAPTER NINE GENERAL AUDIT CONSIDERATIONS 277

FIGURE 9.2.
A Flowchart of the Audit Process.

The documentation aids (e.g., organization charts, computer room layouts) give a clear understanding of the structure of the system plus administrative and operating procedures. Furthermore, the auditor must study the various subsystems implemented in the information system to acquire a firm understanding of the procedures, programs, data files, and controls used, because some of these items will be tested during the course of the audit engagement. A word of caution is in order. Some of the documents gathered by the auditor may be obsolete (e.g., organizational chart). If this situation occurs, creation of current documentation by the auditor is required.

2. A primary source of evidential information is questions put to information systems personnel and user personnel. For full disclosure of operating practices, personnel at all levels and across departments throughout the organization should be questioned. The users of the computer system are a prime source of evidential information for the auditor. The auditor can find out from them if the system meets commitments, produces accurate reports, practices good controls, and has a strong liaison with its users.

Many weaknesses in a system of controls are not readily apparent; otherwise management would already have taken steps to correct them. Most auditors mistakenly rely heavily on interviews with one or two key management people in the computer system. The auditor often leaves with a misguided impression based on what a manager thinks or really believes is the situation in his system. A preferred approach is for the auditor to spend more time with operating personnel and discuss their jobs as they relate to the system of controls. These personnel may not recognize the control weaknesses, but they provide the best insight into and specifics of how the task is actually performed and how it relates to other tasks. Many times there is a great variance between what management thinks is happening and what is actually happening.

Also, the auditor should do as much of his review work as possible within or close to the system itself. Many chance remarks overheard about a variety of situations can lead the auditor to discover errors, inconsistencies, or weaknesses that he might not have uncovered otherwise. On-site observation of the system under working conditions is a strong audit technique, and there is no substitute for it. Moreover, this on-site observation and interview work will enable the auditor to apply other audit techniques such as audit review of programs, test-decking, and so forth.

Many of the classical questionnaires used by the auditor are presented in Part II. Later in this part, we will present additional material about the development of questionnaires. It is important that the auditor keep the results of questionnaires in his working papers, because they provide evidential information required for expression of an opinion. If the auditòr is new on the job, it is imperative that he review prior working papers.

3. A system of controls is installed to increase the efficiency, integrity, and accuracy of data processing and to decrease the chance that assets, service, or data will be lost. To evaluate the system of controls and operating procedures, the auditor must first gain a firm understanding of good standards, operating procedures, and controls, as discussed in Part II. Second, adequate tests of compliance must be performed to establish a reasonable degree of assurance that these items are in place and operating as planned.

In Part II, control requirements and techniques used in computer-based information systems were defined. Some or all of the control techniques may be essential to a properly controlled information system. But every system will require a different set or mix of controls, because most systems have different objectives. It is up to the auditor to ascertain the adequacy of the system of controls in each case. To a great extent, the auditor relies on a system of controls to formulate an opinion. Without an adequate system of controls, the opinion, along with the auditor who expresses it, rests on sinking sand.

Many will argue that it is management's responsibility to establish and maintain a system of controls. Technically, the establishment of a system of controls and its continued supervision are the responsibility of management, but it is up to the auditor to evaluate the system of controls and point out to management any inadequacies. All recommendations made to management should be documented and maintained in the auditor's working papers. In the final analysis, it is the auditor's responsibility to judge the system of controls appropriate for each information system, to test that these controls operate as planned, and to determine any weaknesses or irregularities resulting from the absence of any specific control or the failure of a prescribed control to function as intended.

4. After the system of controls has been reviewed and studied (e.g., use of flowcharts, organization chart, general documentation) to see how it is supposed to perform, questionnaires are used and the results are evaluated. The system must then be tested to ascertain whether it does in fact operate as stated. This procedure involves compliance testing in that the auditor seeks to acquire a reasonable degree of assurance that the system of controls is in use and operating as intended and the degree to which he can rely on the system of controls for planning the substantive tests he will make.

Notice that we have mentioned two types of tests that are used in performing an audit: (1) compliance tests, and (2) substantive tests. Compliance testing is the determination that the system is operating in accordance with certain prescribed procedures. For example, an auditor may ask if the grandfather-father-son file reconstruction procedure is used. If the answer is yes, the auditor may decide to run a compliance test by taking control, sealing the current version of a master file (e.g., accounts receivable), and requesting that a current version of the same file be recreated. If the request is met, the auditor can be fairly sure that the system is operating in compliance with the grandfather-father-son file reconstruction procedure. If not, the system is not in compliance with this procedure. Substantive testing, on the other hand, is examining what a particular item consists of, i.e., the main or real part of anything. For example, an auditor reviews the same accounts receivable master file and tests a sampling of records to confirm that they are real and accurate.

A test of compliance is performed to satisfy the auditor that a particular control is in place and working as intended. *Yes* answers to items in the control questionnaires do not always represent reality. The auditor may be able to satisfy himself that a number of controls are working merely by observing operations. For example, he can observe fire suppression systems and the date and inspection tags indicating when they were last inspected. He may even take pictures of these tags for his own records for future evidence, because there have been instances where these tags were changed immediately *after* the audit. Or the auditor may observe various access control devices. He may even "try out" a particular control device to see how it works.

Satisfying himself as to the viability of various procedural controls may be tougher. For example, to determine if appropriate programming procedures are being followed may require observation, review of documents, and follow-up questions. In other cases, the only way to see if particular controls work is to set up a simulated situation and see what happens. For example, some aggressive auditors of large financial organizations such as banks and insurance companies run "disaster simulations" on a surprise basis.

To run disaster simulations, the auditor seals all current operations and online master files and tells the computer center manager the system is "down." This simulated situation requires data-processing personnel to bring the system to a current status by using cycled files (e.g., grandfather, father), backup facilities, and contingency procedures. If they fail, reasons for failure are determined and swift corrective action is taken. Also, with executive approval, the auditor "pulls the power switch" to the computer center on the night shift to test recovery procedures. Unidentified professional penetrators hired by the audit staff attempt access to the computer center using fake badges, or they see if they can gain access to the data base via remote terminals. Unexpected fire drills are performed to see if standard operating procedures are being followed. All of these simulation tests and others usually require two things: (1) complete support from the management, and (2) a warning to computer center management that certain kinds of tests will be performed in the future without specifying time and date.

The results of the compliance tests employed in the review and evaluation of the system of controls helps the auditor to formulate the audit scope and strategy and the number and level of substantive tests he will use. Obviously, an auditor who is working in an environment with a sound system of controls can place a greater degree of reliance on the data base and reports that the system produces. Therefore, he can increase or decrease the amount and kind of substantive tests accordingly. On the other hand, the review and evaluation of the system of controls can help to uncover weaknesses in data processing and guide the auditor in using specific techniques for testing those areas where he feels that a probability of error, fraud, or other mishap exists.

5. This process block in the flowchart of Figure 9.2, indicates that the auditor must choose appropriate audit techniques for performing compliance and substantive tests. Auditors have known how to handle the audit function effectively in manual systems for a long time, but the whole computer-based information system too often is a black box to many auditors. What auditors need are unbiased and reliable techniques to verify the performance in this black box, i.e., techniques that will provide "windows" where the auditor can "view" the system to determine whether it is operating satisfactorily. For example, different techniques are required to verify computer edit controls. Usually these techniques involve the use of audit test decks or test data generators. In some cases, a direct review of program logic may be required.

The requirements of auditing are to review and evaluate the system of controls, to trace and test transactions, to verify the accuracy of the data base, to form an opinion and recommendations about the reliability and integrity of the output from the system (e.g., financial statements), and properly report that opinion and recommendations. To execute these responsibilities properly, the auditor must: (1) observe and review, (2) inquire, (3) inspect, (4) test, (5) sample, (6) confirm, and (7) compare. In the following chapters of this text, we present an array of techniques that allows the auditor to perform these basic functions in a computer-based information system. None of these audit techniques alone will serve a complete audit engagement. Like a physician using a number of techniques to diagnose the condition of a patient, the auditor must choose a family of techniques to perform an effective and comprehensive audit.

6. After the auditor has chosen particular audit techniques, he must apply them using computer and/or manual means, whichever is appropriate. He applies a family of audit techniques to obtain adequate evidential information to support an audit conclusion. This evidence may

be obtained by observation and review, inquiry, inspection, testing, sampling, confirmation, and comparing one file with another. In applying a particular technique, the auditor should keep in mind that he is verifying not only the existence of a particular item (e.g., edit control, security), but also its quality.

7. Mainly, the purpose of auditing the computer system is preventive in nature, i.e., to detect trouble areas before real trouble occurs. If trouble spots are uncovered, a deeper investigation into the system is made. In any event, the results of applying a variety of audit techniques are studied by the auditor to determine whether he is satisfied with the operation of the information system as a whole.

Analysis of the evidential information enables the auditor to identify instances where the required effectiveness of specific controls was not achieved either because controls were absent or improperly applied. On the basis of the results of the audit work carried out, the auditor is able to form an opinion and prepare recommendations regarding the administration, operation, integrity, security, and accuracy of the information system.

8. On the basis of the evaluation of the system of controls and substantive tests of the data base and existence of assets, liabilities, and so forth, the auditor develops recommendations about the system of control, if necessary, and forms an opinion on the output of the system, especially the financial statements. This outcome is, of course, the primary objective of the audit function. Once the auditor has formed an opinion and developed recommendations, he is ready to make a presentation to executive management and/or the board of directors. The recommendations should present in detail the control weaknesses identified, the impact and consequences of these weaknesses, and the actions required to correct them.

The initial report of deficiencies and recommendations for improvement should be first reviewed at the preliminary stage with local management (e.g., data-processing manager) before preparing a final report. Managers at this level may be under conflicting pressures for example, to "cut costs" (e.g., which might lead to storing files on site), as well as to "improve controls" (e.g., implying off-site storage of backup files). The auditor must use common sense in working out recommendations for remedying weaknesses that local managers can live with while maintaining an adequate level of control. Differences at this level can usually be resolved to mutual satisfaction through mutual discussion. Items that cannot be resolved (often because they are beyond the control of local management) are included in the final report for executive management, the board of directors, and/or stockholders. Weaknesses in the system of controls should be categorized as serious and minor. Any abuses, inconsistencies, or weaknesses that could result in disastrous conditions should be reported on separately and immediately.

9. If sufficient corrective action has not been taken, then the auditor has no other alternative but to prepare an unfavorable opinion. There are a wide variety of reasons why the auditor may not be able to give a "clean bill of health" to the system he is auditing. For example, the system of controls may be so seriously inadequate that a satisfactory examination cannot be performed in the time it would take to correct the control deficiencies. Or it could be that management refuses to make the necessary corrections. In either case, the auditor cannot rely on the integrity of the system. In most cases, management will agree with most of the recommendations made by the auditor, and the deficiencies will be corrected. If management does not agree, something other than an unqualified opinion is in order.

From substantive tests that have been made, it may appear that the financial statements do not present fairly the client's financial position and operating results, or generally accepted accounting principles may not have been applied. Moreover, the client may place restrictions on the scope of the auditor's examination. In any of these cases, and there are many others, if the conditions are material in nature, the auditor must express an adverse or qualified opinion. If the restrictions imposed by the client are of such significance that they materially limit the auditor's compliance with generally accepted auditing standards, and the application of computer audit techniques, he will disclaim an opinion.[1]

10. Ideally, an unqualified opinion is rendered by the auditor. This kind of a report is regarded as a "clean bill of health" given by the auditor. An unqualified opinion indicates that the audit work was adequate in scope and level of testing, that the system of controls was in place and operating as intended, and that the financial statements present fairly the financial position and results of operations in conformity with generally accepted accounting principles applied on a basis consistent with that of the preceding audit period. Under these conditions, the auditor makes no exceptions and inserts no qualifications in his report.

In summary, the final outcome of the auditor's work is the expression of an opinion. The main alternatives in reporting an opinion are: (1) an unqualified opinion, (2) a qualified opinion, (3) an adverse opinion, and (4) a disclaimer of opinion.

9.3 THE COMPUTER AUDIT ENVIRONMENT

The computer audit environment presents to the auditor both a challenge and an opportunity. The precision required by a computer system

---

[1] For further discussion about auditor opinions, see, for example, Walter B. Meigs, John Larsen, and Robert F. Meigs, *Principles of Auditing*. Sixth Edition (Homewood, Ill.: Richard D. Irwin, 1977).

lends itself to a better-organized environment with clear interface and control points. With the movement toward the hiring of higher-level, professional-minded personnel in computer systems plus the increased training of accountants in computers and information systems, a better working relationship between auditors and those being audited is possible. The computer itself is a powerful, reliable tool that enables the auditor to perform more comprehensive and more meaningful audits than he could ever have performed in manual-based systems.

The Changed Environment

Computers have not changed basic accounting principles and procedures and other processing functions per se, but they have changed the logical and physical structure of files, the way by which these files can be accessed and read, and the techniques by which they are processed. In many instances, transactions can be recorded and values in the data base changed without leaving a trace.

Audit trails have changed in the sense that a flow of paper documents is no longer readily available for review by the auditor. Different forms and techniques are used, such as flowcharts, decision tables, computer record layouts, and a variety of documentation aid packages.

Probably the most significant change confronting the auditor is that all logical and physical procedures that at one time were performed by bookkeepers and clerks now reside in a library of computer programs (e.g., COBOL) that "tell" the computer how to perform these procedures. Thus many processing steps are concentrated into one self-contained system, and the traditional internal control implemented by the separation of clerical and bookkeeping duties in the recording process is eliminated.

Also, there has been a move to collect and associate traditional accounting data with operating data in a corporate data base. For example, in a manual system, the processing of a customer's order is handled through a series of separate steps, each performed by different individuals in different departments. The steps may include credit decisions, shipment scheduling, billing, reordering decisions, sales commissions, accounts receivable, and sales analysis and forecasting. By using a computer, inter-related data files, and a library of programs, all of these functions can be concentrated and performed within the computer system.

The Organized Computer System

The auditability of a computer system is dependent upon the underlying system of controls that have been built into the total system and how the

CHAPTER NINE   GENERAL AUDIT CONSIDERATIONS   285

total system is organized to effect this system of controls. Figure 9.3 presents a schematic of how a typical computer system should be organized.

The illustration in Figure 9.3 shows how a computer system should be organized to increase the effectiveness of a system of controls and thus the auditability of that system. Two areas in this illustration that require some discussion are: (1) data base administration, and (2) control group.

The data base administrator is concerned with mediation and compromising of conflicting needs among various users. The data base administrator is assumed to be a specialist working in this capacity. Technically, the data base administrator's primary functions are data definition and file creation. Other technical functions include: "... providing for restructuring the data base to accommodate new record types or new items."[2]

Specifically, the data base administrator's tasks can be divided into three categories: (1) organizing, (2) monitoring, and (3) reorganizing.

1. Organizing includes the following activities: (a) receiving data input from data users and originators where appropriate, (b) employing data structures that model the data requirements, (c) assigning names in such a manner as to assure their uniqueness, (d) selecting search techniques based on the requirements of the various users of the data base, (e) assigning privacy locks and issuing privacy keys to the users, (f) assigning areas to device media on the basis of time/space requirements, (g) loading the data base, (h) assigning names to protect the uniqueness of the names already assigned to the data base, (i) selecting and structuring the proper subset of the data base that must be available to the application programmer, and (j) where applicable, altering the privacy procedures for application programmers.

2. It is the responsibility of the data base administrator to monitor the data base for usage, response, privacy breach, and potential reorganization. He can use various logging facilities or sampling techniques to gather statistics.

3. As a result of information gathered through monitoring, or because of new information required from the users, the data base administrator may have to reorganize the data base. In this case, he may reassign areas to different devices/media, remove "dead" records, and reorganize the files.[3]

In reference to the control group in Figure 9.3, we believe the plan of organization and operating procedures for computer systems should

---

[2]CODASYL Systems Committee Technical Report, *Feature Analysis of Generalized Data Base Management Systems* (New York: Association of Computing Machinery, 1971), p. 30.
[3]*CODASYL Data Base Task Group April 1971 Report* (New York: Association of Computing Machinery, 1971), pp. 22–23.

286 PART THREE COMPUTER AUDIT TECHNIQUES

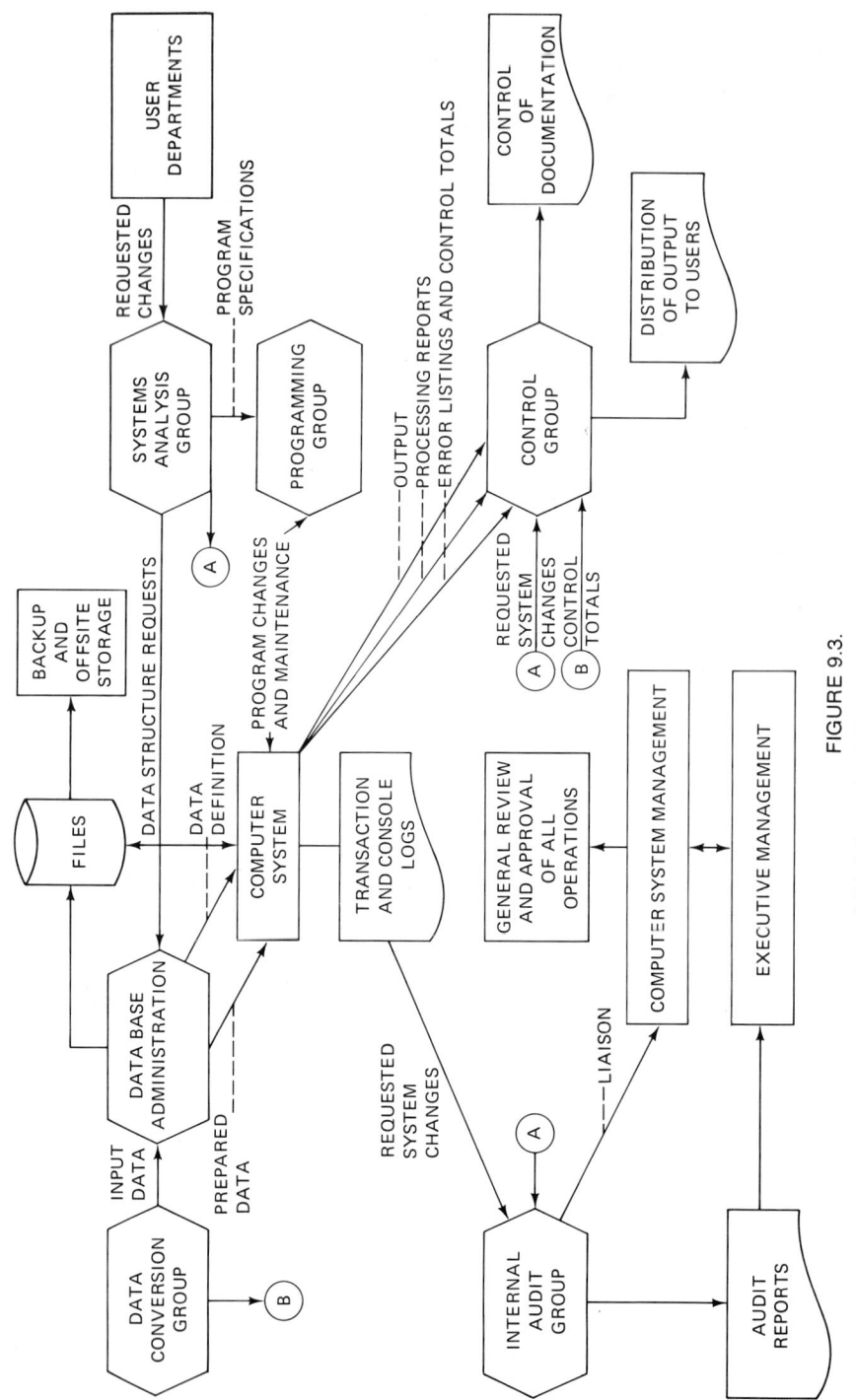

FIGURE 9.3.
A Well-Organized System for Proper Control.

provide for a control group. This control group should perform the following functions:

1. Scheduling the flow of work in the computer room.

2. Recording control totals in a control log to balance with control totals generated during computer processing.

3. Controlling errors and exception conditions occurring during processing and making sure that corrections are made.

4. Controlling the distribution of output reports to authorized users.

5. Recording and monitoring all requests for systems changes.

6. Handling of criticisms by users about output reports and providing a feedback to systems analysts, programmers, and computer system management.

The Attitudes of Personnel

People who work in manual-based systems can easily relate to the auditor, because they have similar backgrounds. For example, a bookkeeper normally has a subset of the same training program taken by auditors, i.e., they speak the same language.

Unfortunately, in many computer systems the auditor cannot relate to the systems personnel, because they have different backgrounds. The systems personnel have the necessary background and skills to operate and manage the system. The auditor should have a similar background to audit the system. Possibly, the auditor should have a more extensive background than other systems personnel, because to audit a system effectively, one must have an overall understanding of the system.

With the advent of computer systems, especially those using more integrated data bases and data communication systems, it is incumbent on the auditor to become more involved in understanding the system as well as the financial and traditional accounting activities. This involvement not only increases his technical competency as an auditor, but also enhances his ability to provide a service to the client in general and the computer system personnel specifically.

In many computer systems today the attitude of the systems personnel can be summarized by the following typical quotations: "Keep the auditors out of our hair until this system is working." "I don't want those auditors back in my computer department." "Auditors have no right in checking our security controls." "What do they know about computers anyway?" "We'll tell the auditors what information we will give them." Or, from time to time, auditors are subjected to a "snow job," computerese, or technical camouflage, and are accepted by computer systems personnel only after strong prodding from higher management.

These attitudes do not exist in all systems, but where they do exist, they must be changed. These changes will not come about by edict or management policy. They will come about only when the auditor shows the computer system personnel that he has sufficient background to conduct a comprehensive audit. He also must convey the notion that he is there to help and not to snoop around and make people look bad. To do this, the auditor must:

1. Maintain professional independence and a high level of credibility. In the long run, the auditor will gain the respect of computer system personnel. It is all right to be a "good guy," but one must do his job and maintain a professional attitude.

2. Assume that recommendations made will be helpful to computer system management, because the recommendations are intended to make the computer operations more efficient, effective, and accurate.

3. Maintain a close working relationship with computer systems personnel such as the data base administrator, control group, and internal auditor.

4. Assume that in a way these members of the information system plus the information systems manager have the same challenges as the auditor. Therefore, the techniques used to control and manage the complex computer system environment are, in many cases, the same ones needed to assure that the system of controls is working and that the data base contains accurate records.

5. Assume that computer systems auditing is an integral part of the audit effort, not the job of a specialist, unless the specialist is a member of the audit group and assist the auditor in doing his audit work. The auditor must be careful not to abdicate his responsibility to the computer specialist. All auditors who audit clients with computer-based information systems should have the ability to audit such systems.

9.4 THE USE OF THE COMPUTER AS AN AUDIT TOOL

The computer can aid the auditor in improving the quality of his work and in performing his work more efficiently. As a matter of fact, most of the audit techniques that we discuss in the following chapters require the use of a computer.

Reluctance of Some Auditors to Use the Computer

Some auditors may be reluctant to use a computer, especially the client's, in performing audit work for two basic reasons, which are: (1) lack of knowledge of how to apply computer-assisted audit techniques, and (2) reluctance to rely on the computer as an audit tool.

The first reason, lack of knowledge, can be corrected, and this text attempts to do just that. The second reason is a foolish one. This reason is reminiscent of the time when auditors did not use the client's adding and posting machines but preferred to do the arithmetic operations mentally or to use their own equipment. Auditors were also reluctant to use other equipment, such as scales for weighing of inventory items.

Today, use of various machines for auditing work is commonplace. If for any reason the auditor believes any of the equipment to be unreliable, he can test it for proper operation, e.g., standard weights can be used to test scales. The same approach can be used to test the computer if the auditor does not feel he can rely on it. Part of the audit work will include some testing of the computer system itself anyway.

Why the Computer Should be Used as an Audit Tool

The same advantages of speed, accuracy, computational power, and storage capacity that make computers a cost/effective tool for the support of information systems also make them efficient and effective tools for the auditor. The computer can be used to perform routine clerical functions, apply computer audit techniques, expand the audit scope, and reduce the overall time and cost to perform certain tests. The power of the computer provides three reasons why it should be used more extensively as an audit tool.

1. *Access to computer records*   The records in a computer system are not visible to the auditor. To perform his substantive tests, the auditor must gain access to these records. The only way to do this is via the computer.

2. *Improve audit efficiency*   The data base to be tested may be so large and complex that the use of the computer may be the most economic and efficient means available. The computer allows the auditor to reduce the manual activity involved in detailed examinations and frees him to spend his time in judgmental and creative areas, those things that humans do best. By using the computer, the auditor gains quick access to a large amount of records in the data base, applies a number of manipulative techniques, while freeing himself for analytical, creative, and judgmental activities.

3. *Increase scope and quality of the audit*   The computer audit techniques are designed to allow the auditor to increase the scope and quality of his audit by providing a practical and reliable means of examining more data, performing more complex and comprehensive calculations, and making more comparisons and cross-references of files within a limited audit budget. Manual methods usually provide tests of data only at a point in time. The computer can be used as a continuous auditing tool. Moreover, the computer can be used in an analytical context by

testing controls, displaying automatic exception conditions, and highlighting differences and trends.

How to Use the Computer as an Audit Tool

The computer can be used to assist the auditor in endless ways. Its use is limited only by the imagination of the auditor. Specifically, the computer can be used in two fundamental ways described below.

1. *Compliance testing* This type of testing examines and validates the system of controls, uncovering weaknesses and investigating possible impact on financial statements and other output. For example, the computer is used to process test data against application programs (e.g., COBOL) to determine whether these programs produce predictable results. Check of program controls can identify and list receivable accounts in excess of customer credit limits or net payroll over a reasonable limit. The auditor can also use the computer to prepare a flowchart of the logic of a particular program. The flowchart helps the auditor to evaluate the program functions more thoroughly.

2. *Substantive testing* This type of testing is directed toward verification of transaction records and the data base itself. The following list suggests only a few possible ways in which the computer can be used to perform substantive tests. These are: In the area of cash, list outstanding checks for review. Select and print confirmations. Prepare receivables aging. Prepare extensions and footings. Compare a master file in the previous period with a master file in the current period and print significant variances. In the area of inventory, select sample items for physical counts and price testing. Perform lower of cost or market analysis. Test for turnover rates and trends in inventory. Test computed interest income on investments to amounts actually received.

Normally, the auditor uses the client's computer to apply the tests listed above. However, he should not limit his use of the computer as an audit tool to the client's computer. Some accounting firms have acquired their own computer system. For some auditors, it may be more cost/effective to use timesharing services. In any case, the final results should be the same for many of the substantive tests. The client's computer must be used in performing most of the compliance tests because the system itself must be tested.

When using the client's computer, the auditor should assume as much control over the system as possible. For complete control, the auditor shuts down all other processing activities and executes all audit procedures without interference from other processing activities and systems personnel. Although this approach has the advantage of giving better control to the auditor of the computer system, it would normally not be cost/effective for the client. An alternative approach is to execute the computer-assisted procedures along with regular client programs. When this approach is used, it is strongly recommended that the auditor personally supervise the execution of his audit procedures.

9.5 SUMMARY

The basic objective of auditing is to express an opinion. To attain sufficient evidential matter for the expression of an opinion, the auditor is required to use an optimum mix of computer audit techniques and to exercise sound judgment and creativity. Although judgment and creativity cannot be taught per se, the aspiring auditor can be given an audit process to follow and an explanation of a host of computer audit techniques and how to apply them.

Some auditors look upon computer systems as a threat to the audit function. However, because there is normally more precision, reliability, and structure in computer systems, the results of computer auditing are potentially more reliable. In manual systems, the basic clerical and bookkeeping procedures are scattered throughout different departments, in a situation characterized by duplication, errors, and poor control. In a computer system, the processing procedures reside in a centralized and self-contained system. This situation has changed not only the flow of processing tasks and the general arena in which the auditor performs his activities, but also the working relationship with systems personnel. His interaction is now with people with different skills, attitudes, and jargon than those of accounting clerks and bookkeepers. To build a better rapport and working relationship with these people, the auditor must make major changes in his attitudes. Also, to gain the respect of these people and to perform high-quality audits, the auditor will have to learn more about the computer and start using it as a full-fledged assistant in his audit work.

REVIEW QUESTIONS

9.1 What is the basic objective of the auditor? How does he attain his objective?

9.2 What are the five elements that support the practice of auditing?

9.3 Review and explain each step in the audit process.

9.4 List and explain the kinds of opinions that can be rendered by an auditor.

9.5 Have computer systems changed basic accounting principles and procedures? If so, how?

9.6 Define the functions of the data base administrator and control group.
9.7 List the points that will help change the auditor's attitude and his relationship with personnel in the computer system.
9.8 Why are some auditors reluctant to use the computer as an audit tool?
9.9 List the reasons why the computer should be used as an audit tool.
9.10 How should the computer be used as an audit tool?
9.11 Compare and contrast compliance tests with substantive tests.

DISCUSSION QUESTIONS

9.1 What are the basic differences between external and internal auditors? What should the relationship be between these two kinds of auditors?
9.2 Why do we make reference to the "practice of auditing?"
9.3 Explain what is meant by providing "windows to the black box."
9.4 Why does the computer environment as opposed to the traditional manual environment present both a challenge and an opportunity to the auditor?
9.5 Discuss the following comment: "A computer is nothing more than a lot of transistorized clerks and bookkeepers housed in a black box."
9.6 Discuss the attitude of some computer systems personnel toward auditors. Are these attitudes justified?
9.7 Discuss the following comment: "I can audit a computer system just as well using manual techniques as someone else can using computer-assisted audit techniques."
9.8 The control of input and output to and from the computer system should be performed by an independent control group. Do you agree? Disagree?
9.9 Discuss the following comment: "Computers crank, people think."
9.10 Many auditors feel insecure in a computer system environment. Do you agree? Disagree? Why?

EXERCISES

9.1 Punched cards are converted to magnetic tape. Presumably, edit controls are required to screen out bad data. List at least four controls you would test for.
9.2 Exception reporting is an activity that can easily be performed by the computer. For example, an exception report is prepared daily by detecting exception transactions that result from the accounts

receivable update run. Some exceptions appearing on the report may include orders from new customers, orders received from customers with delinquent accounts, orders received over credit limit, and so forth. List at least three other exception conditions that could be programmed and automatically processed by the computer. If you have a sufficient computer programming background, write the specific instructions required to handle these exception transactions.

9.3 All master files are stored on magnetic tapes in the tape library. Control totals (e.g., for the accounts receivable file) are maintained in the general ledger in the accounting department. How should these control totals be reconciled with the master files?

PROBLEMS

9.1 Describe how computer audit techniques could be used in performing audit procedures for: (a) cash, (b) accounts receivable, (c) inventories, (d) investments, (e) accounts payable, (f) liabilities, (g) fixed assets, and (h) payroll.

9.2 Described below are examples of some of the data fields one would find in a typical accounts receivable file. List at least three compliance and substantive tests that you would perform. Make any necessary assumptions.

Field Name	Positions Required
Customer Number	8
Customer Name	20
Customer Address	20
Credit Limit Code	1
Type of Customer Code	1
Number of Transactions this Month	2
This Month's Charges	7
This Month's Payments	7
This Month's Credits	7
Balance Due	7

CHAPTER
10

BASIC COMPUTER AUDIT TECHNIQUES

10.1 INTRODUCTION

During the years when computers were first used in business organizations, auditors attempted to audit these systems the same way that they audited manual systems. When it was realized that such an approach would not be sufficient, auditors had to become a little more involved in the computer system. We will discuss these basic and classical techniques of auditing the computer system under four major headings: (1) questionnaires, (2) around the computer, (3) through the computer, and (4) test deck. The audit review of application programs is also included in this chapter as a basic computer audit technique.

10.2 QUESTIONNAIRES

Questionnaires were used by auditors long before computers came on the scene, and they are still being used today. Typical questions still being asked for general review of traditional accounting internal control are: "Is the accounts payable department clearly designated as the group responsible for verification and approval of invoices for payment?" "Are the daily totals of cash registers or other mechanical devices verified by an employee not having access to cash?"

In Part II, we presented a fairly comprehensive and standard list of questionnaires used for review of a system of controls without discussing the questionnaire itself very much. In this section, we will discuss general aspects of questionnaires, different questionnaire formats, and their use as an audit technique.

The Questionnaire in Perspective

In the audit engagement, especially in the review of the system of controls, the questionnaire is a classical technique. The questionnaire is used to gather evidential matter and study facts as to the nature of the system and the manner in which it is operating. The auditor evaluates the probable strengths and weaknesses of the system and then makes compliance and substantive tests in appropriate areas. Although most accounting firms have developed their own questionnaires, they are fairly standard throughout the auditing community.

Questionnaires have some shortcomings, just like any other technique viewed in isolation. Moreover, like other techniques, they have been misused, in some cases. Some improper uses and shortcomings of using questionnaires are listed below.

1. Copying answers from the preceding period's questionnaire onto the current one.

2. Automatic giving of "yes" or "no" answers by the respondent without understanding the question.

3. Because questions are phrased so that a "no" answer indicates a weakness in the system of controls, some respondents have a strong propensity to give "yes" answers to *all* questions.

4. Some auditors who administer computer control questionnaires do not understand the questions that they are asking. The respondent can easily detect this lack of understanding and, as a result, may lose confidence in the auditor. A loss of credibility is a severe blow to any professional, especially an auditor.

One must remember, however, that the questionnaire is only one tool in the auditor's tool bag. Other tools that he should use along with the questionnaire to gather evidential matter and study facts are decision tables, flowcharts, organization charts, computer room layouts (all discussed in Part II), and direct interviews.

The major use of the questionnaire is for the general review of the system. It is designed to help the auditor analyze the overall system of controls and operating practices within and around the computer system, and to guide him in determining the extent to which further review should be made and where compliance and substantive tests are to be used. The questionnaire flags trouble areas and weaknesses and gives a sound basis for further audit work. The less indication there is of good control, the more extensive and intensive the tests should be.

A Tutorial on Preparation of Questionnaires

The auditor will not always use a standardized questionnaire. Because of changing situations and needs, he will, from time to time, have to prepare additional questions to: (1) gather additional study facts, (2) obtain a consensus, (3) verify other responses, (4) gather statistical data, and (5) gain a sense of direction.

Below are some general guidelines for preparing questions. Following these guidelines are several formats that can be used to prepare questions for a questionnaire. It should be noted that the content of these example questions are only illustrative; they may have little to do with a specific audit engagement. The guidelines are:

1. Explain the purpose, use, security, and disposition of the responses.

2. Give detailed instructions as to how to complete the questions.

3. If the questionnaire is not directly administered by the auditor, give a time limit for returning the questionnaire.

4. Ask positive and precise questions.

5. Questions should be formulated with consideration as to the method by which they will be tabulated, mechanically or manually.

6. Sufficient space should be provided for complete responses and comments. Lack of sufficient space can be both a physical and psychological constraint.

7. Questions should be phrased clearly.

8. Questions should be phrased in such a way that they do not elicit predictable responses. For example, the question, "Have you taken the proper precautions against fire and smoke hazards?" directed to an EDP manager is almost always going to be answered affirmatively. First, he doesn't want to be put in a bad light, so he automatically answers "Yes." Second, he may, rightly or wrongly, think that he has the necessary fire and smoke controls. To determine if adequate controls actually exist, several specific questions may have to be put to the EDP manager. For example, "Are smoke and heat detectors installed in the computer center?" "Are fire drills performed quarterly?"

9. If there are aspects of a question that cannot be responded to objectively (e.g., yes or no), an opportunity should be available for the respondent to add a specific comment, give a weight, provide an observation, or make a choice between several alternatives.

10. Be brief and precise, but include appropriate explanation.

11. Include in each questionnaire form documentary material such as title, name, job description, department, and date. If possible, have the respondent sign or initial the questionnaire. Remember, the auditor should retain the questionnaire in his working papers, so each question-

naire may also require an indexing and coding structure to facilitate quick retrieval.

Following are several formats that can be used to prepare questions for a questionnaire.

Check-off question These kinds of questions are structured to enable the respondent merely to check an appropriate response(s). Examples are as follows:

1. Which vendor is the supplier of your CPU?

    ___ Burroughs   ___ DEC   ___ IBM
    ___ CDC   ___ Honeywell ___ UNIVAC
    Other _____

2. What access does the application programmer have to the computer center? (check one)

___ unrestricted access
___ unrestricted access (e.g., by password, magnetic card)
___ controlled access by permission of data-processing manager
___ other _____

3. The data base system can best be described as (check one*):

___ an integrated directory system
___ a tree structure
___ an inverted list
___ a distributed directory system

*You may phrase a similar question and specify in parentheses "check all that apply."

In addition to the formats above, a simple checklist format can also be used as follows:

FIRE PROTECTION CHECKLIST
(PARTIAL)

___ 1. Smoke and heat detectors are placed at strategic locations.
___ 2. Excess combustible materials are removed on a regular basis from the data-processing center.
___ 3. Portable fire extinguishers are placed at points for ready access.
___ 4. All emergency telephone numbers are posted for ready access.
___ 5. Emergency exit doors are checked daily for obstructions.
___ 6. Fire drills are conducted monthly.

Yes/No questions This kind of question format is a standard in auditing and is used extensively.

	ANSWER		ANSWERS BASED ON		
	Yes	No	Inquiry	Observation	Test
1. Are all out-of-balance or error conditions brought to the attention of the accountant?	___	___	___	___	___
2. Is the EDP department independent of all department managers for which it processes data?	___	___	___	___	___

A simple yes/no question with explanation is illustrated as follows:

	Yes	No	Not Applicable
1. We use 24 hours service on our communications equipment?	___	___	___

If not applicable, explain _____

_____

All yes/no questions should be phrased in such a way that responses run in predetermined directions. For example:

	Yes	No
1. Do you prepare telephone budgets?	x	___
2. Do you pay toll bills without verification?	x	___

There are two "yes" responses. If the preparer of these questions meant that a preponderance of "yes" answers would indicate good accounting controls, then he has failed, because the answer to the second question is also "yes." Of course, the disadvantage of this format is that responses run in one direction, i.e., all "yes" answers indicate good control. This situation may lead to automatic responses.

	Yes	No
2. Do you verify bills before payment?	___	x

In this case, a "no" answer "flags" inadequate accounting controls.

Opinion or choice questions These questions are phrased to allow the respondent to give an opinion or make a choice in a very specific area.

1. For each of the following situations, choose one of the three listed responses:
   a. Responsibility rests with accounting department.
   b. Responsibility rests with systems department.
   c. Responsibility rests with data-processing manager.
   (1) ___ preparation of telephone operating budget
   (2) ___ control of telephone maintenance
   (3) ___ tabulation of toll calls
   (4) ___ monitoring of after-hour calls
   (5) ___ installation of new equipment

2. If your operating system is modified, note the relative importance of each of the following goals in your design process. (Scale of 1 through 10 where 1 is least important and 10 is most important.)
   ___ improve throughput or service level
   ___ maximize number of concurrent processes
   ___ interface to special equipment
   ___ protect operating system from user processes
   ___ increase reliability
   ___ provide special accounting or billing
   ___ protect system files
   ___ protect user files
   ___ simplify command language
   ___ simplify file access or sharing

3. You are currently receiving enough information to help control the toll calls made from your department? (circle one)

   Strongly   Strongly
   Disagree   1 2 3 4 5 6 7 8 9 10   Agree

4. Rate on a scale of 1–10, the control-consciousness of the control of the cost of fuel usage. (circle one)

   Not   Very
   Concerned   1 2 3 4 5 6 7 8 9 10   Concerned

5. Circle one of the five numbers to indicate your disagreement or agreement with the following statement.

   1 = strongly disagree
   2 = disagree
   3 = neutral
   4 = agree
   5 = strongly agree

Departments about which records are maintained on the tabulation of toll calls, maintenance expense allocation, and equipment costs should have the following rights:

1 2 3 4 5 to be informed of the existence of such records
1 2 3 4 5 to review on demand by department managers the contents of records concerning them
1 2 3 4 5 to be furnished monthly reports of budgeted toll calls and expenses as compared to actual expenses incurred for that month

Quantitative evaluation of responses Some auditors may want to prepare some questions that can be quantitatively evaluated to produce a score. Following is an example of how this can be done.

General Example of Question Conducive to Scoring	Possible Rating Value Responses
How would you rate the effectiveness of the fire control system?	Outstanding = 5 points Above Average = 4 points Average = 3 points Below Average = 2 points Poor = 1 point Inadequate = 0 point

Scoring of these kinds of questions is illustrated as follows:

Responses from Questions	Rating Values	Weighted Values (100%)	Score
Question 1 = Below Average	2 points	40%	80
Question 2 = Average	3 points	25%	75
Question 3 = Outstanding	5 points	20%	100
Question 4 = Inadequate	0 points	15%	0
		Total Score	255

Interpretation of Score

450–500 = Excellent
350–449 = Very Good
250–349 = Good
150–249 = Acceptable Under Specific Conditions
 50–149 = Generally Unacceptable
  0– 49 = Totally Unacceptable

A Final Comment on Questionnaires

To perform his audit function properly, the auditor needs to ask questions that may or may not directly relate to the computer system. Traditional accounting controls are just as important and relevant today as they ever were, no matter what data-processing method is used. No amount of computer technology and processing procedures should ever be allowed to obscure this basic fact. Moreover, the auditor should still obtain third-party sources of evidential information (e.g., confirmations, discussed later) where possible. The auditor should observe the physical count of inventory and other physical assets as well as examine official papers such as title papers, mortgages, insurance policies, securities, and so forth to determine the existence of assets or liabilities and restrictions or liens, if any, placed upon them.

Auditors have traditionally used various forms of internal control questionnaires to help insure that all necessary accounting controls were in place and operating as intended. In different systems, the auditor may have to make some modifications in the control questionnaire to fit a particular situation. However, the general use of these questionnaires will continue to be relevant. Examples of the kinds of questions to be implemented in the control questionnaire are listed below.

1. Are there procedures for a periodic review of inventory for obsolete, surplus, or slow-moving items?

2. Can computer-prepared book inventory be readily reconciled with actual physical inventory?

3. Are credits for returns and allowances approved by an employee who has no access to cash receipts or other funds?

4. Is every shipment promptly and accurately billed?

5. Is every invoice supported by proper evidence of shipment?

6. Is every customer payment currently recorded, promptly deposited, and properly credited?

7. Are all past due accounts receivable identified as to amount and number of days past due?

8. Can all payments to vendors be supported by approved requisitions and purchase orders, legible receiving documents, and accurate invoices?

Computers represent changes in technique, environment, capacity, and data-processing power, but they do not change the logic of information processing or the need for sound business controls. A variety of questionnaires will always be used (and new ones developed) by auditors to help them obtain an overall view of the system and help them determine whether good, sound controls are being used.

10.3 AUDITING AROUND THE COMPUTER

Many functions in the audit process are performed independently of the computer system, such as verification of physical inventories and petty cash. The major focus of this text, however, is on those areas that pertain to the audit of the computer system. The three categories that are used to discuss the audit of computer systems are: (1) auditing around the computer, (2) auditing through the computer, and (3) auditing with the computer.

Many will argue that auditing through the computer and auditing with the computer are the same. Technically, this is true, but since the auditing of computer systems began, auditing through the computer has generally meant the use of a test deck and little more. Auditing with the computer, as it is used in this text, has a broader scope; it means the full exploitation of the computer to apply a multiple array of computer-assisted audit techniques. In this chapter, we will present auditing around and through the computer and then devote the remainder of Part III to the full use of the computer as an audit tool.

Definition of Auditing around the Computer

The practice of auditing around the computer began in the early days of computer usage, when the typical auditor was unfamiliar with computer technology, programming, and controls used in computer-based systems. At that time, the audit approach was to view the computer system and programs as a black box and to review input and output documents only. The controls and procedures used in processing the data were considered unimportant by the auditor so long as the output generated by the computer could be traced back to the input, and the input was deemed valid. The auditor selected input and tested them against appropriate output and vice versa. If they matched and proved to be accurate and valid, then it was assumed that the system of controls was in operation and that it was operating properly.

How Auditing around the Computer Works

In Figure 10.1 is an illustration of the auditing around the computer approach. The audit is performed by selecting a sample of actual transactions that have already been processed. These transactions are traced from their point of origin as source documents to the output records or records produced. For example, the auditor selects source documents to be tested, such as employee time cards, traces them through computer printouts, such as payroll register and paychecks. Both the validity and accuracy of the selected payroll transactions are verified. The rationale behind this approach is that if the source documents are properly reflected in the master files, the master files in turn are supported by source documents, and the output produced therefrom is correct, then the processing functions of the computer system (e.g., the black box) must be performing correctly. The manner in which the processing functions were performed is deemed of little consequence.

Advantages and Disadvantages of Auditing around the Computer

Many auditors continue to debate the relative merits of auditing around the computer and other approaches, namely, auditing through the computer and auditing with the computer. In earlier times, the around the computer approach worked well, because systems used the batch processing method exclusively. Transactions were recorded manually and the audit trail was characterized by extensive printouts. However, as computer systems become more advanced, this auditing method becomes more cumbersome and more costly, but less effective.

In more advanced systems with multiprogramming, integrated files, automatic input, extensive use of data communications, and so forth, this method is inadequate. Where computer systems are still being used in a batch processing mode, auditing around the computer has some relevancy. In such situations, it can still be considered a viable audit technique. Its advantages and disadvantages are listed below.

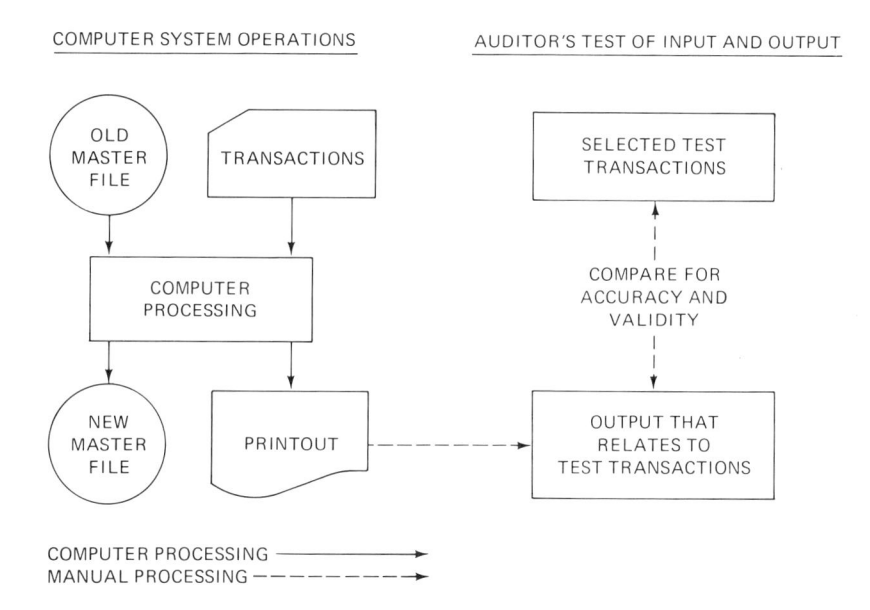

FIGURE 10.1.
Example of Test of Input Transactions with Output using Around-the-Computer Audit Technique.

The advantages are:
1. There is no risk of tampering with live data.
2. Little technical training of the auditor is required.
3. It is simple, straightforward, and easily understood by everyone.
4. Cost of audit resources is generally low.

The disadvantages are:
1. Many computer systems data bases are too voluminous for manual testing.
2. No means are provided by which auditors can get involved and gain a firm understanding of computer systems.
3. It ignores the system of controls and thereby fails to recognize potential errors or weaknesses within the system.
4. It represents after-the-fact rather than preventive auditing.
5. It makes no use of the most powerful and valuable audit tool, the computer.
6. For all intents and purposes it does not achieve the auditor's goals.

10.4 AUDITING THROUGH THE COMPUTER

As the limitations of auditing around the computer technique became more significant, as newer and more sophisticated systems procedures were implemented, and as auditors became more knowledgeable in computer operations, auditing techniques also began to change. Selected test transactions began to be tested *through* the computer.

Definition of Auditing through the Computer

The auditing through the computer technique places a greater emphasis on testing the computer system that produces the output rather than testing the output itself. The auditor tests and verifies (1) the effectiveness of control procedures over computer operations and computer programs, and (2) the correctness of internal processing. This audit technique requires two basic tasks, which are: (1) the review and verification of source transactions, and (2) the actual testing of the computer program logic and program controls.

How Auditing through the Computer Works

Auditing through the computer is illustrated in Figure 10.2. With this approach, the auditor assumes that the computer itself is an accurate tool and that, when properly programmed, it will provide reliable out-

```
         TEST              COMPUTER            PROCESSING
     TRANSACTIONS          PROGRAMS             RESULTS

                                              AUDITOR'S COMPARISON
                                                  OF RESULTS

       MASTER                                   WORKSHEET OF
       RECORDS  ------------------------------- PREDETERMINED
                                                   RESULTS

        WHAT         PROCESSED MANUALLY       DETERMINE
         IS      --> BY THE AUDITOR TO    --> WHAT SHOULD BE
```

COMPUTER PROCESSING ─────────►
MANUAL PROCESSING ─ ─ ─ ─ ─ ─►

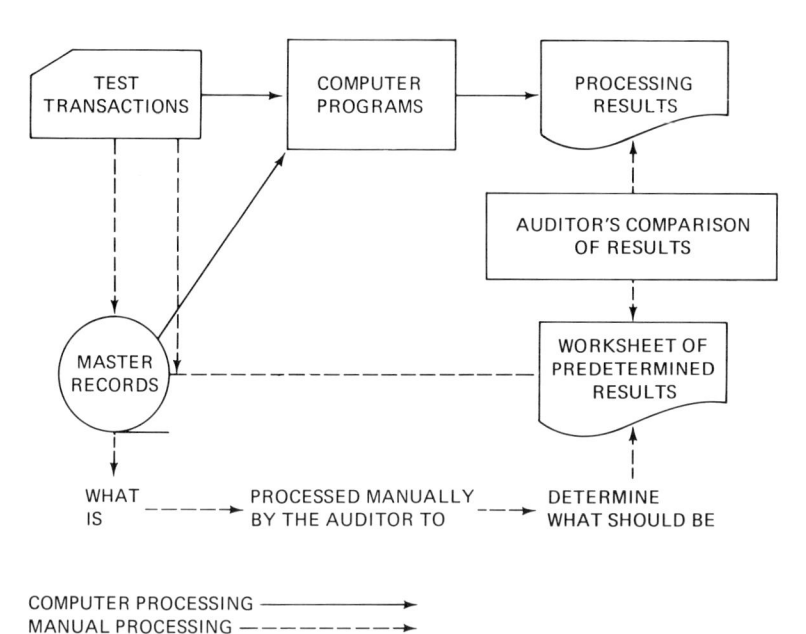

FIGURE 10.2.

Example of Testing the Internal Processing of the System using Through-the-Computer Audit Technique.

put. Therefore, the audit tests should be thought of as testing the program logic rather than as testing computer accuracy.

One of the key tools in applying this audit technique is the preparation of a series of test transactions, normally referred to as a test deck (discussed in the next section). The test deck is run on the computer system using the same programs that were used to operate the particular application that is being tested. The test is designed to assess the effectiveness of the controls and accuracy and generality of the programs. For example, three conditions can exist in regard to FICA in a payroll program: no FICA withholding, full FICA withholding, and limited FICA withholding based on year to date earnings. The computer program should be able to account for and handle all three alternatives. Simulated transactions in the test deck test to determine whether all three conditions can be handled by the program.

Examples of other conditions that can be tested are:
1. out-of-sequence conditions;
2. processing with wrong files;
3. out-of-limit conditions;
4. invalid unit of measure;
5. invalid dates, account codes, and field relationships;
6. numeric data where alphabetic data should be or vice versa;
7. loss of negative sign where a number is in fact negative, etc.

Advantages and Disadvantages of Auditing through the Computer

The advantages of auditing through the computer technique are:

1. It helps the auditor to become more involved in the system, thereby increasing his knowledge and ability to perform more complex audits in the future.
2. It works as an aid in making compliance tests and in the evaluation of programmed controls.
3. It increases service to clients because controls and operations are checked or at least observed by the auditor.
4. The test results are readily identifiable and can be used as measures of internal processing reliability.
5. It utilizes the computer as a tool for performing auditing functions.

The disadvantages of this audit technique are:

1. It requires computer time.
2. It requires more technical knowledge and more skilled audit personnel.
3. It represents after-the-fact testing rather than preventive testing.
4. It represents only a limited test of the system.

10.5 TEST DECK

Test data are simulated or dummy transactions that ideally include every possible type of condition, including those that the system, because of lack of proper controls, is incapable of handling. That is, the list of simulated transactions should test for both valid and invalid conditions. The simulated data, usually in card form for computer input, are processed with the regular computer system's programs.

Purpose of the Test Deck

The auditor cannot physically see the operations and controls within the black box, but he can see an output listing of the results of the test where, for example, some transactions that were supposed to be rejected were not, or where overflow conditions caused errors, or where out-of-limit transactions were processed as if they were correct (e.g., customer transactions exceeded credit limit). The auditor can also determine whether the black box is properly processing valid transactions. Use of the tesk deck opens up windows in the black box, because the simulated transactions are processed through the computer system and generate results that are compared by the auditor with results he has already prepared by hand. That is, before executing the test deck, the auditor calculates what the results of using the test deck should be and then compares these results with the results obtained during the test. The New York State Lottery could have benefited from the test deck approach.

> ... the Tax Department's EDP Bureau implemented a procedure whereby a programmer would "lock out" the computer file that generates ticket numbers so as to prevent unauthorized use of the file after the lottery tickets have been completely prepared for distribution. However, between the time the Racing and Wagering Board took over the responsibility for the Lottery EDP operation (January, 1975) and September 11, 1975, the "lock out" program was discontinued. As part of a routine monthly audit of lottery ticket stock, an auditor from the Department of Audit and Control tested the security "lock out" program on October 8, 1975 and was able to print ticket numbers on blank paper for a drawing which had already been held. The absence of the security "lock out" program was immediately reported to the Director of the Lottery and to the Directors of EDP at the Racing and Wagering Board and the Department of Taxation and Finance. They indicated that the lock program would be reinstituted immediately to prevent the printing of tickets after they have been distributed to banks. Audit and Control personnel tested the "lock out" program again on October 21, 1975. They were not able to print tickets for the October 16, 1975 drawing but they were able to print ticket numbers on blank paper for the October 23, 1975 drawing. Thus, it was apparent that the EDP Section of the Racing and Wagering Board had not fully implemented the security lock program as of October 21 because tickets could be printed for a drawing for which the tickets had been distributed to sales agents. This flaw was called to the attention of the Director of the Lottery. He communicated this to the Director of EDP for the Racing and Wagering Board and the situation was corrected.[1]

How to Prepare a Test Deck

Generally, the test deck is applied as follows:[2]
  1. The entire system of controls must be reviewed.
  2. On the basis of this review, transactions are designed to test selected aspects of the system or the entire system.
  3. The test data are transcribed to the particular system's input forms.

[1]*Special Audit Report on the Financial and Operating Practices of the Racing and Wagering Board, Division of the Lottery* (Albany, N.Y.: Office of the State Comptroller, Division of Audits and Accounts, Report No. AL-St-35-76, Nov. 14, 1975), pp. 13–14.
[2]Study Group on Computer Control and Audit Guidelines, *Computer Audit Guidelines* (Toronto: The Canadian Institute of Chartered Accountants, 1975), p. 252.

4. The test data are converted to machine-sensible form. The conversion should be verified by the auditor either through a balancing routine or through a check of a printout of the resulting punched card or magnetic tape files. The verified data should be controlled by the auditor until it is processed. This control can be achieved by using the balancing routine or by sealing or retaining the files.

5. The test data are processed using the regular production programs and operating systems. The auditor must insure that the regular production programs are being used. The auditor should be present during the processing of the test data to insure that: (1) no additional information is introduced; (2) standard machine operating procedures are used; (3) nothing irregular takes place which can affect the test; and (4) all hard copy produced by the computer is retained by the auditor.

6. The results from Item 5 should be compared with the predetermined results.

Audit Controls over Computer Programs that are Being Tested

The major objective of using the test deck is to test the client's operational computer programs to see if they are operating as intended. The auditor must make sure that the program being tested is the one that is used in actual production. There is no absolutely sure way to guarantee this situation, but there are a few things that the auditor can do to make himself feel more confident that the program being tested is the "real" program.

First, those controls discussed in Part II such as procedures for changing programs and the use of librarian packages, provide good audit control over programs. A number of librarian packages are available from a variety of vendors that can be used to provide very effective control over libraries of source code. Combined with sound operating standards and controls, as discussed in Part II, these librarian packages furnish a high degree of program integrity. Unauthorized changes in application programs can also be detected by having the system loader pass control to a security program after loading, but prior to passing control to the loaded application program. The security program then computes a check-sum of the bytes or words comprising the loaded application program. This check-sum is compared to a security table of valid check-sums of all application programs. The check-sum table is accessible only by the security program. If the check-sum comparison fails, the program is aborted, and the control group and/or the internal auditor is notified. In addition, the auditor should periodically obtain an official report of all program changes.

Second, the program that is to be tested should be requested on a surprise basis and duplicated on a computer-readable medium such as magnetic tape or disk. The auditor should also get a computer printout of the source code of the program so that he can compare it with his previous copy to note any changes. With this approach, the auditor has a copy that he can test at his convenience, and to increase his confidence that it is the real operational program, he can request on a surprise basis that his copy be used for production. If this request is denied by the computer operations personnel, he should determine why. If he is told that there have been changes since his copy was generated, he should get a listing of the current program and compare it with his copy, noting all changes.

Third, the auditor can request on a surprise basis that the production program be left in the CPU immediately after completing a production run. The auditor can then take control of operations and perform his test on this current version of the program.

Applications of the Test Deck

The auditor must have a transaction record layout to prepare his test transactions. This layout should contain the program name of each field, the size of the field, and the type of characters used (alphabetic, numeric, or alphanumeric). For example, a simple transaction record layout for sales from inventory is depicted in Figure 10.3. To a great extent, the auditor merely inserts his own data into the appropriate fields to produce predetermined results. If the test results do not agree with these predetermined results, further investigation is made to ascertain the reason for the variances.

FIGURE 10.3.
Simple Illustration of a Transaction Record Layout.

Character Position	Program Name	Type of Character*
1– 8	ITEM-NUM	N (8 9's)
9–30	ITEM-DESC	AN (22 X's)
31–32	WAREHOUSE-LOC	N (99)
33–37	ITEM-COST	N (999V99)
38–42	ITEM-PRICE	N (999V99)
43–47	QTY-PURCHASED	N (99999)

*N = Numeric specified by 9's in the PICTURE clause of COBOL with V representing an assumed decimal point.
AN = Alphanumeric specified by X's in the PICTURE clause of COBOL.

Following are some of the items that would normally be included in the application of the test deck.

1. Check to see if control totals are prepared and reported back to the control group. For example, if 100 test records are processed, the number of transactions processed should read 100.

2. Try to process a sensitive transaction without proper authorization (e.g., change of customer's credit limit) and see if the system rejects it.

3. Make numeric, alphabetic, and special character checks. If all characters in a customer number are supposed to be numeric, input an alphabetic character in this field. A proper numeric check will detect this mistake before processing is performed. The same can be done for alphabetic fields. And so forth.

4. Input a field with a negative sign and see if it is handled as a negative sign. In some systems, without proper control, the negative sign is converted to a positive sign.

5. Make validity checks. For example, input an invalid code or try to process one department number as another department number.

6. Make limit and reasonableness checks. If no employee can work more than 60 hours per week, process a time card with more than 60 hours worked. For another example, if the clients of a bank cannot make a withdrawal of more than $2,500 without proper authorization, test to see if management policy is being followed.

7. Where transactions are supposed to be in sequence, reverse the order of several test transactions so they are out of sequence.

8. Include an account number with a predetermined self-checking digit and see if it is properly processed by the computer system.

9. Use different units of measure, e.g., feet for pounds.

10. Input several fields with incomplete or missing data.

11. Insert characters in fields that cause an overflow condition.

12. Try to read or write a wrong file.

The following test deck case represents the kinds of abuses and errors that can be uncovered in some systems. Notice that the simulated test transactions required to test this system were simple but quite effective.

In one large railroad company, the auditors decided that it would be a good idea to have the computer reject inaccurate records—after the EDP system involving freight car records had been in effect for some time. The auditors worked up an audit test deck. Essential data was deliberately omitted. Incorrect data was deliberately added. For example, the test deck showed cars interchanged with the L & N when the railroad had no interchange at all with the L & N. The test deck showed interchanges with nonexistent railroads, with nonexistent car numbers, and in one instance a car interchanged on May 53. Any self-respecting computer program with appropriate edit routines would have screamed TILT when the test deck was introduced. But this program happily processed and printed out all the invalid (among valid) transactions, including 22 days extra per diem for the car interchanged on May 53.

The same auditors examined the computer application for the payroll. Employee pay was being machine-calculated by matching the clock numbers that were listed on the current time sheets with a purportedly "active" employee file. The auditors discovered to their horror that many of the employees on the "active" file had left the company as long as three years before. So if the number of the terminated employee appeared (or was placed) on the time report, there was nothing to prevent the preparation of a paycheck.[3]

Test data development guidelines are summarized in Table 10.1. Files that are to be tested should be copied on special work files (scratch files) to allow the auditor to perform a variety of tests. Some tests result in changing fields in records, adding or deleting records, or performing updates that are invalid. Obviously, the auditor does not perform these tests on the operating data base, but a copy of it, or part of it.

Advantages and Disadvantages of the Test Deck

The advantages of using the test deck are:

1. The auditor does not have to have a great deal of technical knowledge.
2. It has good application where the possible variety and combinations of transactions are limited.
3. It gives an objective evaluation and verification of program controls and other operations in which the same appraisal would be impracticable or impossible to accomplish by other means.
4. Test decks can be applied on a surprise basis to discourage the unauthorized modification of programs and to increase the overall effectiveness of other tests performed.

The disadvantages are:

1. A lot of time and effort are required to prepare a representative test deck and maintain it. Any change in the system, record layouts, and programs normally requires that the test deck be altered.
2. In some instances, the auditor may not be testing the real systems production program.
3. In a complex system with a large variety of transactions, it is difficult to anticipate all significant conditions and variables that should be tested.

---

[3]From Lawrence B. Sawyer, *The Practice of Modern Internal Auditing* (Orlando, Fla.: The Institute of Internal Auditors, 1973), p. 222.

TABLE 10.1

Test Data Development Suggestions

For master files:
1. Duplicate master records.
2. Process out-of-sequence records.
3. Mount and attempt to process wrong files.

For new records:
1. Set up a new record before the first record now on the master file (low-sequence test).
2. Set up a new record after the last record on the master file (high-sequence test).
3. Set up three or four new records with consecutive record keys with no existing records in between.
4. Set up a record for non-existent division, plant, department, inventory item, vendor, employee, customer, and so on.
5. Set up two or more new header records, one immediately after the other.
6. Set up a new record with record keys of zeros.
7. Set up a new record with record keys of nines.
8. Set up a new, but incomplete, record (e.g., only one or two fields of a possible ten).

For transactions:
1. Post transactions to the first record in the file.
2. Post transactions to the last record in the file.
3. Post transactions to records other than the first and last records in the file.
4. Post transactions to a new record set up on the same run (if allowed).
5. Post transactions to several consecutive records.
6. Post various combinations of transactions to one record.
7. Attempt to post transactions to non-existent records that would be lower in sequence than the first existing record, higher in sequence than the last existing record, and between existing records, as well as to several consecutive non-existent records.
8. Post transactions to a record to make balances or totals (e.g., inventory, deposits) go negative. Verify the effect on other fields in the record.
9. Post several large amounts or quantities to a record to create an arithmetic overflow in total or balance fields. Examine results.
10. If a header record followed by detail records is being used, create detail records for the first record in the file, the last record in the file, two consecutive records, one existing record, and several non-existent records.
11. Check for results of transactions with mispunched data in significant fields, such as salary and hours worked.

For inactive and deleted records:
1. Drop the first record from each file.
2. Drop the last record from each file.
3. Drop three or four consecutive records from each file.
4. Attempt to drop a non-existent record.
5. Code a record as "inactive" and attempt to post data to that record in the same run.
6. Attempt to post data to a record that was coded "inactive" in a previous run.
7. Reclassify an "inactive" record as "active," and post transactions in the same run.

For dates:
1. Insure that all date fields on records are being updated properly. Check data records, control records, and header identification records.
2. Input a date with 00 and 13 month, 00 and 32 day, and invalid year.
3. Where appropriate, enter a date that exceeds the maximum interval between posting runs. Try a date more than seven days old, for example, and another date more than seven days in the future in a weekly update system.
4. Make two posting runs using the same date.

For logic and processing tests:
1. Check all calculations that produce averages or percents with small, average, and large numbers (e.g., 0, 1, 500, 9999).
2. Create a condition for all division routines with a zero divisor.
3. Create data for *all* exceptions and errors.
4. Create test data for the minimum and maximum values for each field, such as minimum hourly rate and maximum salary.
5. Enter data that are below the minimum value and above the maximum value for each field.
6. Create data that include multiple exceptions and errors in the same transaction. Enter several combinations.

For edit programs, test data for an alphabetic field will include:
1. Completely full field.
2. Blank field.
3. First position in the field only.
4. First position in the field blank.
5. Mixed alphabetic and numeric characters.

Test data for each field for a quantity or amount will include:
1. Field of nines.
2. Field of zeros.
3. Field of blanks.
4. Exact lower limit of field, if any.
5. Exact upper limit of field, if any.
6. Typical quantity or amount, between any limit.
7. Value above limit, if any (not all nines).
8. Value below limit, if any (not all zeros).
9. Value with wrong sign (plus or minus).
10. Alphabetic data in each field.

For update programs:
1. Create data to set up several complete master file records.
2. Develop change data for a non-existent master file record.
3. Create data to set up a new record when a record with the same key is already in the master file.
4. Create data with a record key of zeros.
5. Create data with a record key of nines.
6. Create one or two items to establish a new but incomplete master file record.
7. Create data to set up a new record, and post changes in the same run.

For process programs:
1. Enter data that produce calculation results of low, average, and high values.
2. Enter data that will create a condition for multiplication and/or division by zero.
3. Enter data that will cause an out-of-balance condition on the file control record. Examine results.
4. Make several illogical accounting entries (e.g., debit accounts receivable and credit depreciation expense).
5. Enter data that will cause an arithmetic overflow.
6. Enter data that will cause an out-of-balance crossfoot condition.

For report programs:
1. Include test data with minus values to insure that minus signs are printed for each field, on each type of detail, and on total lines.
2. Create test data with all nines in the fields to see if all digits are printed and not being overlaid by other data.
3. Enter test data with all zeros in the fields to check zero suppression.
4. Check all sum and calculation results.[4]

[4]Entries in this table adapted from S. R. Mixon, *Handbook of Data Processing Administration, Operations, and Procedures*, (New York: AMACOM, a division of American Management Association, 1976), pp. 262–266.

4. The auditor must be fairly familiar with the program logic he is testing.

5. The test itself does not test all errors, i.e., many potential errors can still exist after the test has been applied. In complex programs, there may be tens of thousands of different possible paths through the program. It is neither practicable nor possible to trace through all the different paths during testing.

6. There is a high probability that the test deck will not detect improper manipulation of a specific account and/or amount.

10.6 AUDIT REVIEW OF APPLICATION PROGRAMS

If one agrees that the application program is the most vulnerable point of the system, then it is obvious that the auditor of a computer-based system should make a detailed analysis of source code of the production programs. Some may argue that audit of computer programs represents an advanced technique, but the technique can be as advanced as the auditor wants to make it. Any serious auditor should make a review of some of the programs if only to see that they are reading labels correctly.

An incomplete review of a computer program can have disastrous consequences.

> A Brevard County official on the way to his father's funeral was shot and killed . . . recently by a Florida state trooper who mistook his car for a stolen vehicle after checking with the state's crime computer. The victim's auto bore a license number identical to another issued for the year 1971 which was still in the state's active stolen vehicle data base. . . . Any police officer knows . . . that it takes two criteria—the plate number and year issued—to correctly identify a vehicle . . . [however] a police inquiry into the state criminal justice information system can indicate a 'hit' without that second identification criteria. . . . Had both the year and the tag number been required to access the file, [the victim] . . . probably would be alive today because [the] query would have found no record in the stolen vehicles file.[5]

General Analysis of Audit Review of Programs

With the use of a test deck, the black box remains largely black, as far as the general logic of programs is concerned. With the actual review of programs, the auditor is looking directly at the program itself and thus opening windows to the black box. The auditor reviews the program for

[5] Nancy French, "Man Killed After DP Crime Check," *Computerworld*, Dec. 10, 1975, pp. 1 and 4.

controls, program completeness, and proper processing logic. Typical input data should be manually traced (in contrast to the running of a test deck via the computer) through the program processing paths to identify possible errors. In a way, the auditor attempts to play the role of the computer.

> . . . To confirm that the explanation was indeed correct, we took the original program, repeated the program steps reported to have been taken, and then ran the program. The results were replicated. We have confirmed and can document that the cause was indeed a human (programmer) error. The machine did exactly as it was instructed to do; it simply received erroneous instructions.[6]

In some instances, the programmer may be meeting all user requirements and have a sound system of controls built into the program, but he may also have built into the program "trap doors" or devious little routines that perform unauthorized operations. Or there may be simple, honest errors of logic or technique. The audit review of the program source code helps to detect these things.

For example, below are three types of programs that can all exist in a system, abide by basic edit controls, and produce output that appears to be meeting users' needs.

1. *Sneaky Pete Program*   Sneaky Pete, in addition to having the program perform properly, writes in special routines that do illegal things. For example, a master file is properly processed and updated, but while it is being processed, the program is reading and writing selected information for Sneaky Pete's personal gain. This kind of program includes what some people refer to as "trap doors" and "Trojan horses." Sneaky Pete can build a trap door in the logic that allows unauthorized access to files and programming changes.

The procedure is to insert code into a program in such a way that when a particular sequence of instructions or a particular event happens, the trap door is flung open. Through this trap door, Sneaky Pete can gather sensitive data, or credit and debit accounts illegally. Like the trap door, the Trojan horse involves the illegal insertion of instructions into a production program. Sneaky Pete writes a program and adds extra instructions in the middle that are triggered by the series of events or by a special code or account number. The probability of detecting these trap doors and Trojan horses by the application of a test deck is very low. But with a rigorous review of the program itself, combined with the application of a comprehensive test deck, the probability is very high that any trap doors and Trojan horses will be detected. As a matter of fact, audit review of the program itself is the only technique

---

[6]*Summary of Findings New York State Lottery* (Cambridge, Mass.: Arthur D. Little, Inc., Nov. 26, 1975), p. 3.

that gives the auditor a fairly strong assurance that Sneaky Pete programs (and the other two kinds listed below) will be uncovered.

2. *Crash Craddock Program* Crash is as honest as the day is long, but he is a lousy programmer and fails to follow a good system of controls. Although his program produces proper output under normal conditions, a number of items in the program may cause trouble. For example, Crash has not followed program standards, labels are not created, improper blocking factors are used, and so forth.

3. *Coo Coo Pacioli Programs* These programs are basically sound and well structured, and they contain proper controls, but they also include improper accounting procedures. For example, Coo Coo may be using unacceptable inventory valuing procedures. This situation is understandable, since Coo Coo failed to follow in the steps of his ancestor, Luca Pacioli, the father of double-entry bookkeeping.

In theory, the audit review of source program code is one of the strongest audit techniques. One of the major advantages of a computer-based system in comparison with a manual system is the computer's consistency and predictability. Humans may do the same thing in different ways from one day to the next, but, given the same program and the same data, a computer will always run the job in exactly the same way and will produce identical outputs.

If the auditor has reviewed the program, understands how it works, and has verified the correctness of its processing, then he is in a position to place a great deal of reliance on the output it produces. Further, as long as that program remains unchanged, the auditor has good reason to continue relying upon the correctness of its processing.

The major drawback to using this technique is that it is very time-consuming. The auditor must also have a strong understanding of the programming language used, especially if the language is something other than COBOL or PL/1, the two easiest languages to read, in comparison with BASIC, FORTRAN, APL, and so forth. No matter what the language, if the programmer has not used good programming practice (e.g., structured programming) and standard data names, the auditor will have a difficult time understanding someone else's program. Further, as is true of the test deck technique, the auditor cannot guarantee that the program he is reviewing is the same as the production program. Still, with these drawbacks, this technique is potentially one of the most powerful in the auditor's tool bag, and in any audit some level of audit review of several of the sensitive application programs should be performed, even if it's very basic.

Reasons for Audit Review of Programs

There are numerous reasons why auditors might want to review program code. These are:

1. To detect or discourage programmed fraud.

2. To establish conformity to legal and regulatory requirements. Further, the auditor can check to see if administrative controls are being followed. For example, this area would include the use of structured programming, standard data names, and meaningful paragraph names instead of those of the programmer's girlfriend.

3. To see if generally accepted accounting principles are being followed and to uncover honest errors or surreptitious practices. For example, in a conversion to a new inventory system, the method of valuing inventory was changed without authorization. A public accounting firm learned that a credit manager had set up a private method of coding the real collectibility of accounts receivable. Needless to say, the reserve for doubtful accounts was increased once the system was decoded.

4. To evaluate the efficiency of programming. Such practices as the use of inefficient and prohibited commands and techniques might be found. For example, an analysis could be made to determine if optimum blocking factors are being used or if there is redundant programming (e.g., duplicated data descriptions).

5. To establish how the computer is generating information in areas otherwise difficult to determine, e.g., work-in-process inventory.

6. To determine if program documentation is current. For example, the review may turn up legitimate transaction codes that are not in the documentation.

7. To facilitate the review of subsequent program modifications. Once a sensitive program or application has received a review, it is easier for auditors to follow subsequent changes. Revisions can be subjected to selective test checks.

8. To provide an educational exercise for an auditor who has had a programming course, say, in COBOL, but lacks real experience with the language. By reviewing a professional programmer's code, the auditor could acquire a feel for real-life programming.

9. To allow the auditor to become more involved in the system and to increase his confidence. It also helps him gain the respect of computer personnel. With the increased emphasis on computer fraud, reviews of sensitive program applications may be politically useful to auditing. It is one of several strong audit techniques for detecting and deterring fraud.

An Organized Approach to Audit Review of Programs

As a starting point in the review of programs, the following should be done:

1. Review the programming and documentation standards that have been established within the installation. Unfortunately, many in-

stallations do not have such standards, although they should. These standards set the framework for the preparation and documentation of programs. They provide the auditor with a feel for what to expect when digging into a program. As such, they provide a very useful frame of reference. The auditor can get by without them, but, if there are standards, the auditor's job will be somewhat simplified.

2. Select a particular program or system for review. Obviously, the auditor would opt for the most sensitive system for his first choice. However, if this is the initial foray into program code review, it would be a good idea to start with a relatively modest or simple system, one in compiler language. It is always wise to learn to walk before trying to run. A few small triumphs make a much better start than would a single, complex failure. If the auditor is reviewing a system made up of a number of programs and one programmer wrote several of them, start the review with the simplest one; this will allow the auditor to develop a feeling for the particular programmer's style. Programming is very much an art form rather than a scientific discipline. Once an appreciation of a particular person's style has been developed, it is much easier to understand more complex logic evolved by the same mind.

3. Obtain a copy of the program's source code listing. The easiest approach would be to ask the programmer for a copy. Chances are that that worthy individual has a number of copies of the listing on hand. Unfortunately, none of them is likely to be the most current version. The best approach is to have a listing printed out from the system's source library. This listing probably would be current.

If the auditor has any doubts about the listing, they can be dispelled. Ask the EDP operations people if the listing is current. If the answer is "no," ask them to supply a current listing. If the answer is "yes," ask them to prove their conviction by compiling the source code and using the resulting object code in the next production cycle. Should the operations people balk at this request, the auditor should have grave doubts about the value of the source code listing. If the request does not induce a state of shock and is complied with, the auditor can be sure that the review will be based upon solid ground. The source listing then reflects the current version of the program.

4. Obtain a copy of the program documentation. In many cases the auditor will be able to complete this step quite quickly. There will be no documentation, so there won't be anything to request. Down deep inside, sometimes very deep, the EDP people know that they should have documentation. They are likely to be a little defensive on the subject. The auditor's request was a reasonable one. If there is no documentation, the review will be very difficult and considerably more time-consuming.

Sit down with the EDP people, develop agreed-upon minimum documentation requirements, and ask that it be prepared before proceeding any further. There is no need to make a difficult job even more difficult if it can be avoided. If the installation does have documentation, the auditor should ask that it be brought up-to-date before the code review begins. Documentation gets stale very quickly, so it is always wise to do everything possible to insure that the review is based on the current facts.

5. Determine what input and output files are being used and how they are used. Without input/output, a program cannot do very much; hence a good grasp of the files employed is an essential part of any review.

Review the SELECT clauses in the ENVIRONMENT DIVISION. Each file must be related to a specific hardware device or to a class of devices. This relationship is established by the SELECT clauses. As a result, if the auditor can account for all the files mentioned in SELECT clauses, the file review will cover all the files employed.

Now look at the DATA DIVISION and the detailed definition of each file. Compare that definition to the related documentation. Be particularly alert for fields that are defined in the program but are not documented. Either the documentation is out-of-date, or the program has been the subject of unauthorized modification. The auditor should be especially careful when researching the reason for a difference between the definition of a file and its documentation. This difference may be an early indicator of a very serious problem. One easily implemented type of unauthorized manipulation is based on the use of a special field or fields as the key to initiate some kind of unauthorized processing.

Within a COBOL program, a REDEFINES clause can be used to assign a different layout to an area or file that has been previously defined. This is a very useful capability and one quite often utilized. For example, two different record types with different layouts may be recorded on one file. Typically, one record format will be defined within the COBOL program. The alternate record will be described by REDEFINEing the first record. In this way the program will be able to handle two different record formats from one input file. Unfortunately, this same approach could be used to provide an unauthorized alternate definition that contains key fields required to trigger fraudulent processing. The auditor should be alert to the use of REDEFINES and should review them carefully to determine that they are valid.

6. Confirm the understanding of the files and records that you have gained. Obtain a two- or three-page printed dump of each file. Be sure they are "display" dumps. A hexadecimal or binary dump is very difficult to read, and there is no reason to make the review more complex then absolutely necessary. Compare the contents of the dumps to the related file layouts on a record-by-record and field-by-field basis. Investigate any differences, and, if they cannot be reconciled, ask questions. Do not be bashful. This is a sensitive area, and the auditor is entitled to a full explanation of any anomalies. If the story does not seem to make

sense, keep asking questions. In this part of the review, the auditor must not allow himself to be put off by impressive but evasive explanations.

7. Review the program and make note of OPEN and CLOSE commands. There should be one of each for each file. If there is more than one, ask why. There are valid reasons why this might happen, particularly in regard to disk files. When a file is being both created and updated within the same program, it may be OPENed and CLOSEed twice. Along these same lines, if three different report formats are being produced from one program, there might be three sets of OPEN and CLOSE statements for the printer file. On the other hand, multiple sets of these verbs might be present for fraudulent purposes. The second set might be used to make the file available for unauthorized processing. In any event, if there is more than one set of OPEN/CLOSE statements for a file, the auditor should be sure to understand why more than one is required.

8. Now that the files are nailed down, start to take a look at the logic of the program. In any program the most important parts of the code are those that involve making logical decisions. Within a COBOL program, decisions are made by statements that contain IF verbs. Scan the program and locate all statements that contain an IF. There may be a lot of them, but do not get discouraged. This is a very important element in the program review. If the installation does not provide program standards to guide the programmers, the IF statements may be hard to follow. Again, do not be afraid to ask questions. Ask for an explanation of all IF's that do not appear to be logical or that are confusing. There should be a valid reason for each one. Do not leave any loose ends in this regard. The one IF you let slide by might be the vital one. Basically, there are no unimportant IF statements. In the event someone wants to fiddle with a program, about 99 times out of 100 it will involve the use of an IF.

9. Next in importance are the GO TO statements. The IF's control logic and the GO TO's direct the processing flow. Incidentally, with use of structured programming the use of the GO TO should decline, a trend the auditor should be grateful for. The auditor should scan the program, make a list of all GO TO's, and then determine what they do in regard to the transfer of control and why. Most GO TO's will be related to or a part of an IF statement, so you should have a head start in this portion of the review. Once again, do not leave any loose ends. Account for and verify every GO TO statement.

10. Now you are in the homestretch. By this time you should have a good basic understanding of the program's files, logic, and flow of control. There is still one more thing to check. The program you are looking at may be using the services of another program or module to perform some of its processing. Review the code and look for verbs ACCEPT,

CALL, ENTER, FILL, RETURN, and ZIP. They all indicate that some external influence is being applied to the program under review. Check these out carefully and make sure you understand them. Review of these external programs or modules is also required.

11. Put the computer to work to help in the program review. Use program aids such as flowcharters, cross-reference listings, test data generators, and so forth where possible. Without the use of such aids, audit of programs can be a tedious task.[7]

10.7 SUMMARY

There are four basic, classical audit techniques that have been used a great deal by auditors since the advent of the computer. These are: (1) computer control questionnaire, (2) auditing around the computer, (3) auditing through the computer, and (4) use of the test deck. Actually, auditing through the computer assumes the use of the test deck, but the two have been separated in this chapter for a clearer analysis.

Traditionally, many auditors have audited around the computer by performing tests using control ledgers and hard copy printouts of control totals in much the same way that they audited manual systems. In recent years, it appears that auditing around the computer is insufficient. Auditors will be more effective if they approach their work by auditing through the computer and using the computer to apply a family of audit techniques.

The basic tool used in auditing through the computer is the test deck, which is nothing more than a series of simulated transactions that test the processing logic of computer programs and various data controls. Both valid and invalid conditions should be included in the test deck. In order to develop a test deck, the auditor must have the record layout, a knowledge of the system, and the processing objectives of the program being tested. While applying the test deck, the auditor should attempt to insure himself that the program being tested is the one that is actually used in production. This can be done by entering test data at the end of a processing run on a surprise basis or taking control of a program copy and reentering it on a surprise basis into the system as a substitute for the production program. Moreover, all changes to programs should be monitored and tightly controlled.

Since the computer programs of a system represent the instructions for processing the data the auditor must perform some direct review of these programs. This technique appears to be basic for meaningful au-

---

[7]The section above adapted from Donald L. Adams, "Audit Review of Program Code-I," *EDPACS*, August 1975, pp. 1–5, and Harold Weiss, "Audit Review of Program Code-II," *EDPACS*, August 1975, pp. 6–7.

dits of computer systems. The auditor can start with simple programs first and build to more complex ones on a step-by-step basis. Furthermore, the auditor can combine the use of the test deck technique with the review of programs to perform a rigorous examination of the logic of the system.

REVIEW QUESTIONS

10.1 What are the four basic and classical audit techniques that have been used since the advent of computer systems? Briefly describe each and their relationship with one another.
10.2 Explain the similarity (if any) of these techniques to those used in the audit of manual systems.
10.3 Is the computer system of controls questionnaire any more important than traditional internal control questionnaires? Explain.
10.4 What are the potential misuses and shortcomings of questionnaires?
10.5 List the guidelines for preparation of questionnaires.
10.6 Differentiate between auditing through the computer and auditing with the computer.
10.7 List the advantages and disadvantages of auditing around and through the computer.
10.8 Define a test deck. What is its purpose?
10.9 List as many items as you can that can be tested using a test deck.
10.10 How does the auditor help insure that the program he is testing is the same one used in production?
10.11 Briefly list why the auditor should perform an audit review of computer programs.
10.12 Briefly list the steps used in performing an audit review of computer programs.

DISCUSSION QUESTIONS

10.1 Discuss the role of questionnaires in computer auditing.
10.2 Why is it poor audit practice for an auditor to administer a system of controls questionnaire when he does not understand the controls he is asking about? Discuss the various ramifications of such a situation.
10.3 Are there situations that require question formats to be prepared by the auditor that require something other than a yes/no response? Explain.
10.4 Why should the results of the questionnaire be well documented and kept in the auditor's working papers.

10.5 "Auditing through the computer is more effective than auditing around the computer." Discuss this comment.

10.6 "All I care about as an auditor is what goes into the black box and what comes out. I don't care what goes on in between; therefore, I see no purpose in using a test deck." Comment on the merits of this statement.

10.7 "OK, this is the way I see it. In the system of controls questionnaires, the respondent may have said that a particular control exists. With the use of a test deck, I'm satisfying myself that this particular control does in fact exist and is working as intended. This then is a compliance test." Explain and discuss this comment.

EXERCISES

10.1 List the kinds of test transactions that would be appropriate to a payroll system.

10.2 In an election system in one of the country's major cities, it was stated that the system was "so full of holes that one could drive a truck through." It was further stated that an absence of edit controls was one of the system's major failures, e.g., the system would accept any number of voter cards that were exactly alike and would even accept blank cards. Needless to say, the citizens lost confidence in the system. Auditors were brought in to examine the system. The investigation consisted of a test deck of 2,000 cards of every type error imaginable.[8]

Write a short report about the kinds of controls that should have been implemented into the system and list at least ten types of simulated test cards you would have prepared to test the system. Make any assumptions you deem necessary.

10.3 In another welfare debacle, a programming error resulted, in one day's operation, in an overpayment to welfare recipients of $10.5 million. Overpayments are expected to be well over a billion dollars before a final determination is made, all because a series of program instructions handled recipients as if they had been underpaid for a year.[9]

Write a short report contrasting and comparing the necessary controls for a manual and a computer system to handle these welfare payments. Also, include in your report the kind of test deck you would have prepared to test the program. Also, explain

---

[8] Adapted from Nancy French, "Court Orders Recount in El Paso Election," *Computerworld*, Aug. 6, 1975, p. 2.
[9] Adapted from Edith Holmes, "Flaw Causes $10 Million Welfare Error," *Computerworld*, Sept. 3, 1975, pp. 1 and 3.

how an audit review of this program would have helped to uncover inappropriate instructions.

PROBLEMS

10.1 Following is a listing of a simple COBOL program that is supposed to read a customer master file, extract those customers with a poor pay performance, and generate a report for the credit manager. Review the program and see what you think it's doing and how. (*Hint:* Mailing lists represent valuable assets, and the goal of auditing is to help safeguard assets.) You do not have to be an expert in COBOL to gain a pretty good idea of what is going on. However, it is emphasized that in a real application, a typical program would be more lengthy and more complex, and not quite so obvious. Go to next page.

10.2 Following is an abbreviated audit case performed in a bank. It is used here to help summarize some of the points we have discussed. Review it and see if there are any additional steps you would take as an auditor on the basis of the stated objectives.

AUDIT OBJECTIVES:
1. To determine the quality of the data-processing system.
2. To determine what operating policies insuring the continuing protection of generated data remain effective.
3. To determine that the department is being adequately managed and that operations are efficient.

AUDIT STEPS TO BE COMPLETED:
1. Determine that proper computer programs are being used. (One or more of the following may be required. This step may be waived if application audits have already established the propriety of the programs.)
   a. Computer comparison of operating program with controlled copy (to be used if program has been defined as mature and audit copy created).
   b. Computer audit model of production program with exception analysis.
   c. Test decks of dummy transactions applied against dummy master records to establish proper processing.
2. Determine what systems, programming, and documentation standards remain effective.
   a. Review selected program files to determine that they contain proper documentation of the program logic (flowcharts, narrative, halt listing, description of inputs and outputs, and source language program listings).
   b. Check flowcharts for standard subroutines and standard library routines.

PROBLEM 10.1

IDENTIFICATION DIVISION.
PROGRAM-ID. PRINTOUT POOR PERFORMANCE CUSTOMERS.
AUTHOR.   SNEAKY PETE.
REMARKS.   INPUT MASTER TAPE USED TO PREPARE POOR PERFORMANCE
            REPORT OF CUSTOMER FOR CREDIT MANAGER.
ENVIRONMENT DIVISION.
CONFIGURATION SECTION.
SOURCE-COMPUTER.   BIG NUMBER CRUNCHER
OBJECT-COMPUTER.   BIG NUMBER CRUNCHER.
FILE-CONTROL.
        SELECT NAME-ADDRESS-FILE ASSIGN TO TAPE-DRIVE-ONE
        SELECT PRINT-FILE ASSIGN TO PRINTER-ONE.
        SELECT PREFERRED-LIST-FILE ASSIGN TO TAPE-DRIVE-TWO.
DATA DIVISION.
FILE SECTION.
FD   NAME-ADDRESS-FILE
     RECORD CONTAINS 119 CHARACTERS
     LABEL RECORDS ARE OMITTED
     DATA RECORD IS NAME-ADDRESS-RECORD.
01   NAME-ADDRESS-RECORD.
     02   NAME-IN   PICTURE X(30).
     02   ADDRESS-IN   PICTURE X(35).
     02   CITY-IN   PICTURE X(25).
     02   CREDIT-LIMIT   PICTURE 9(4)V99.
     02   AMOUNT-OWED   PICTURE 9(4)V99.
     02   JOB-TITLE   PICTURE X(20).
     02   PAY-PERFORMANCE-CODE   PICTURE 9.
          88   EXCELLENT   VALUE 1.
          88   GOOD   VALUE 2.
          88   POOR   VALUE 3.
     02   SEX-CODE   PICTURE 9.

```
            88  MALE                              VALUE 1.
            88  FEMALE                            VALUE 2.
        02  MARITAL-STATUS            PICTURE 9.
            88  MARRIED                           VALUE 1.
            88  SINGLE                            VALUE 2.
FD  PRINT-FILE
    RECORD CONTAINS 132 CHARACTERS
    LABEL RECORDS ARE OMITTED
    DATA RECORD IS PRINT-RECORD.
01  PRINT-RECORD.
    02  FILLER                        PICTURE X(5).
    02  NAME-OUT                      PICTURE X(30).
    02  FILLER                        PICTURE X(5).
    02  ADDRESS-OUT                   PICTURE X(35).
    02  FILLER                        PICTURE X(3).
    02  CITY-OUT                      PICTURE X(25).
    02  FILLER                        PICTURE X(5).
    02  AMOUNT-OWED-OUT               PICTURE 9(4)V99.
    02  FILLER                        PICTURE X(24).
FD  PREFERRED-LIST-FILE
    RECORD CONTAINS 129 CHARACTERS
    LABEL RECORD IS PREFERRED-LIST-RECORD.
01  PREFERRED-LIST-RECORD.
    02  P-NAME                        PICTURE X(30).
    02  P-ADDRESS                     PICTURE X(35).
    02  P-CITY                        PICTURE X(25).
    02  P-CREDIT-LIMIT                PICTURE 9(4)V99.
    02  P-JOB-TITLE                   PICTURE X(20).
    02  P-SEX                         PICTURE X(6).
    02  P-MARITAL-STATUS              PICTURE X(7).
PROCEDURE DIVISION.
```

CHAPTER TEN BASIC COMPUTER AUDIT TECHNIQUES

```
BEGIN-JOB.
    OPEN INPUT NAME-ADDRESS-FILE, OUTPUT PRINT-FILE, PREFERRED-
        LIST-FILE.
READ-A-RECORD.
    READ NAME-ADDRESS-FILE AT END GO TO EOJ.
    MOVE SPACES TO PRINT-RECORD.
    IF EXCELLENT GO TO WRITE-PREFERRED ELSE NEXT SENTENCE.
ROUTINE-PROCESS.
    IF    POOR
          MOVE NAME-IN TO NAME-OUT.
          MOVE ADDRESS-IN TO ADDRESS-OUT.
          MOVE CITY-IN TO CITY-OUT.
          MOVE AMOUNT-OWED TO AMOUNT-OWED-OUT.
          WRITE PRINT-RECORD AFTER ADVANCING 3 LINES.
          GO TO READ-A-RECORD.
WRITE-PREFERRED.
    MOVE NAME-IN TO P-NAME.
    MOVE ADDRESS-IN TO P-ADDRESS.
    MOVE CITY-IN TO P-CITY.
    MOVE CREDIT-LIMIT TO P-CREDIT-LIMIT.
    MOVE JOB-TITLE TO P-JOB-TITLE.
    IF MALE, MOVE 'MALE' TO P-SEX ELSE MOVE 'FEMALE' TO P-SEX.
    IF MARRIED MOVE 'MARRIED' TO P-MARITAL-STATUS ELSE MOVE
        'SINGLE' TO P-MARITAL STATUS.
    WRITE PREFERRED-LIST-RECORD.
    GO TO READ-A-RECORD.
EOJ.
    CLOSE NAME-ADDRESS-FILE, PRINT-FILE, PREFERRED-LIST-FILE.
    STOP RUN.
```

c. Check program source listing for use of standard subroutines and standard labels (names of procedures and storage areas).
   d. Check record layouts for use of standard layout techniques and conventions.
3. Determine that standard procedures are used to protect data generated.
   a. Computer operators account for all files used during processing runs.
   b. Trace a sample of newly created files to library.
   c. Trace a sample of printed data creation through control section to delivery to external group (bank department or customer).
4. Determine that library procedures provide for backup files or for the capability of recreation of the files.
   a. Check conformance to grandfather-father-son concept for magnetic tape files.
   b. Check file copy procedures for direct access magnetic files.
   c. Confirm that magnetic transactions files are retained through a complete file copy cycle to permit master file recreation.
   d. Inspect some master tape files for proper removal of the tape ring.
5. Determine that computer operators use standard processing methods.
   a. Inspect console-run book to determine that it is being kept current and, on a test basis, that instructions are complete.
   b. Determine by random observations that operators follow the instructions.
   c. Determine by observation that operators handle card decks and magnetic tapes and disks properly.
   d. Determine by interview that the operator is familiar with the procedures to be followed when an unprogrammed halt occurs.
6. Determine administrative adequacy.
   a. Determine by observation that work is well organized and is processed on schedule.
   b. Review department overtime payments for a period of time to determine adequacy and proper utilization of personnel.
   c. Determine by observation that work area is kept neat and clean with supplies stored in an orderly manner.
   d. Interview personnel to establish knowledge of procedures to be used in case of a fire or other emergency.

e. Determine by interview that programmers must obtain permission from a representative of department to run their own programs.[10]

10.3 A complete COBOL program for the GO 'n SPEND supermarkets is presented for your inspection. The program is to print out the list of products carried by the markets and the unit profit on each item. Examine the program. Identify by program line number those aspects of the program that you, as an auditor, would consider to be in need of improvement. In addition, compile a list of questionable programming practices that this program exhibits. Go to page 330.

10.4 The important segments of the monthly interest calculation and update program for Yukon-Bank-On, Inc. are illustrated below. According to the specifications found in the program documentation book, the program processes depositor records (Type 80). If the balance is above the minimum set by the bank ($10.00), interest is calculated for the account, added to the account balance and used to increase the control totals being accumulated in the Type 90 control record. When a depositor does not have the minimum balance, the interest calculated is considered to be unpaid. This figure is accumulated in both the depositor record and the control record.

Examine the program and determine:
1. if the program is accomplishing its designated tasks.
2. if the program is executing any operations that run counter to the proper calculation and updating of monthly interest.

Using the methods employed in this program as a starting point, establish a list of rules that could be used in examining any COBOL program to assist an examiner in uncovering devious programming. Go to page 332.

10.5 Formulate a test deck to be used in examining a clothing manufacturer's commission payment system. The layout for transactions required to pay regular commissions (transaction type "04") is provided below. A decision table for these commission rates is also illustrated.

In formulating the test deck, transactions should be constructed which test valid, out-of-sequence, invalid character, out-of-limit, and overflow conditions. Be sure to include both valid and invalid transactions. Indicate the nature of the error(s) you would expect the commission payment system to locate for each transaction. Go to page 336.

---

[10]From: *Auditing Bank EDP Systems* (Park Ridge, Ill.: Bank Administration Institute, 1968), pp. 91–93.

PROBLEM 10.3

```
01      IDENTIFICATION DIVISION.
02      PROGRAM-ID. SUPER-LIST.
03      ENVIRONMENT DIVISION.
04      CONFIGURATION SECTION.
05      SOURCE-COMPUTER. WIZ-O-CRUNCH-O.
06      OBJECT-COMPUTER. WIZ-O-CRUNCH-O.
07      INPUT-OUTPUT SECTION.
08      FILE-CONTROL.
09          SELECT INPUT-FILE ASSIGN TO TAPE01.
10          SELECT SQUASH ASSIGN TO DISK01.
11          SELECT GARBAGE ASSIGN TO PRINTER.
12      DATA DIVISION.
13      FILE-SECTION.
14      FD  SQUASH LABEL RECORDS ARE OMITTED.
15      01  SQUASH-DETAIL
16          05 UPC                      PICTURE 99999.
17              10 PRODR                PICTURE 9(5).
18              10 PROD                 PICTURE X(25).
19          05 DESC                     PICTURE 9(6).
20          05 Q                        PICTURE 9(4)V99.
21          05 P                        PICTURE 9(4)V99.
22          05 C
23      FD  INPUT-FILE LABEL RECORDS ARE OMITTED.
24      01  INPUT-DETAIL                PICTURE X(50).
25      FD  GARBAGE LABEL RECORDS ARE OMITTED.
26      01  GARBAGE-DETAIL
27          05 FILLERA                  PICTURE XXXXX.
28          05 UPC                      PICTURE 9(10).
29          05 FILLERB                  PICTURE XXXXX.
30          05 DESC                     PICTURE X(25).
31          05 FILLERC                  PICTURE X(5).
```

CHAPTER TEN   BASIC COMPUTER AUDIT TECHNIQUES

```
32          05  Q                      PICTURE 999999.
33          05  FILLERD                PICTURE X(5).
34          05  PR                     PICTURE 9(4).99.
35          05  FILLERE                PICTURE XXXXX.
36          05  CST                    PICTURE 9(4).99.
37      WORKING-STORAGE SECTION.
38      77  EOJ                        PICTURE 9(10) VALUE 9999999999.
39      77  BUCKET                     PICTURE 9(5)V99.
40      77  BUCKET-1                   PICTURE 99999.
41      77  BUCKET-2                   PICTURE 9(5)V99.
42      PROCEDURE DIVISION.
43      GO. OPEN INPUT SQUASH OUTPUT GARBAGE.
44      HERE.
45          READ SQUASH AT END GO TO WHAMO.
46          IF UPC EQUALS EOJ GO TO ENDO.
47          IF PRODR EQUALS 38000 GO TO HERE.
48      KETCHUP.
49          ADD 1 to BUCKET-1.
50          MOVE CORRESPONDING SQUASH-DETAIL TO GARBAGE-DETAIL.
51          MULTIPLY C BY Q GIVING BUCKET.
52          MOVE SPACES TO FILLERA, FILLERB, FILLERC, FILLERD, FILLERE.
53          MULTIPLY P BY Q GIVING BUCKET-2.
54          SUBTRACT BUCKET-2 FROM BUCKET GIVING PR.
55          WRITE GARBAGE-DETAIL.
56          GO TO HERE.
57      WHAMO. DISPLAY "TOTAL" BUCKET-1.
58      ENDO.
59          DISPLAY "TOTAL" BUCKET-1.
60          CLOSE SQUASH GARBAGE.
61          STOP RUN.
```

PROBLEM 10.4

IDENTIFICATION DIVISION.
PROGRAM-ID. MONTHLY-INTEREST-CALC-UPDATE
INSTALLATION. YUKON-BANK-ON INC.
        ⋮
ENVIRONMENT DIVISION.
INPUT-OUTPUT SECTION.
FILE-CONTROL.
    SELECT OLD-SAVING-ACCT-FILE ASSIGN TO TAPE 01.
    SELECT NEW-SAVING-ACCT-FILE ASSIGN TO TAPE 02.
DATA DIVISION.
FILE SECTION.
FD OLD-SAVINGS-ACCT-FILE
        ⋮
    DATA RECORD IS OLD-DEPOSITOR-RECORD.
01 OLD-DEPOSITOR-RECORD.
    05 RECORD-TYPE   PICTURE 99.
    05 ACCOUNT-NUMBER   PICTURE 9(7).
    05 FILLER   PICTURE X(50).
    05 ACCT-BALANCE   PICTURE 9(7)V99.
    05 MONTHLY-EARNED-INTEREST   PICTURE 9(5)V99.
        ⋮
    05 LAST-TRANSACTION-DATE   PICTURE 9(5).
        ⋮

CHAPTER TEN BASIC COMPUTER AUDIT TECHNIQUES

```
FD  NEW-SAVINGS-ACCT-FILE
        DATA RECORD IS NEW-DEPOSITOR-RECORD.
01  NEW-DEPOSITOR-RECORD.
    05  RECORD-OUT                      PICTURE X(150).
WORKING-STORAGE SECTION.
77  RECORD-COUNT                        PICTURE 9(7). VALUE ZEROES.
77  MONTHLY-INTEREST-RATE               PICTURE 99V999 VALUE 00425.
77  MISS-BAL                            PICTURE 999V99 VALUE 01000.
77  DATE-CHECK                          PICTURE 9(5). VALUE ZEROES.
77  ONE-YEAR-AGO                        PICTURE 9(5). VALUE ZEROES.
01  DEPOSITOR-RECORD.
    05  RECORD-TYPE                     PICTURE 99.
        88  DEPOSITOR-RECORD            VALUE IS 80.
    05  ACCOUNT-NUMBER                  PICTURE 9(7).
    05  FILLER                          PICTURE X(50).
    05  ACCT-BALANCE                    PICTURE 9(7)V99.
    05  NON-EARNED-INTEREST             PICTURE 9(5)V99.
    .
    .
    .
    05  LAST-TRANSACTION-DATE           PICTURE 9(5).
    05  YTD-UNPAID-INTEREST             PICTURE 9(5)V99.
    .
    .
    .
01  CONTROL-RECORD.
    05  RECORD-TYPE                     PICTURE 99.
        88  CONTROL-RECD                VALUE IS 90.
```

PROBLEM 10.4 (continued)

```
    05  RECARD-COUNT                   PICTURE 99V99999.
    05  FILLER                         PICTURE X(50).
    05  OUTPUT-RECORDS                 PICTURE 9(9).
    05  MONTHLY-INTEREST-PAID-TOTAL    PICTURE 9(6)V99.
    .
    .
    .
    05  UNPAID-MONTHLY-INT-TOTAL       PICTURE 9(5).
01  INTEREST CALCULATION.
    05  MONTHLY-EARNED-INTEREST        PICTURE 9(5)V99999.
    05  MO-EARNED-INT REDEFINES MONTHLY-EARNED-INTEREST.
        10  MO-EARNED-INT              PICTURE 9(5)V99.
        10  ONE                        PICTURE PP999.
PROCEDURE DIVISION.
HOUSEKEEPING.
    .
    .
    .
    ACCEPT DATE-CHECK FROM DAY.
    SUBTRACT 365 FROM DATE-CHECK GIVING ONE-YEAR-AGO.
READ-RECORD.
    READ OLD-SAVINGS-ACCT-FILE.
    IF RECORD-TYPE OF OLD-DEPOSITOR-RECORD EQUALS 81 GO TO END-OF-PROGRAM
    MOVE OLD-DEPOSITOR RECORD TO DEPOSITOR-RECORD.
    .
    .
    .
CALC-MONTHLY-INTEREST.
    MULTIPLY ACCT-BALANCE OF DEPOSITOR-RECORD BY MONTHLY-INTEREST-RATE GIVING
        MONTHLY-EARNED-INTEREST ROUNDED.
CMI.
IF  ACCT-BALANCE OF DEPOSITOR-RECORD IS GREATER THAN MIN-BAL, ADD MO-
    EARNED-INT TO MONTHLY-INTEREST-PAID-TOTAL, ADD MO-EARNED-INT TO
    MONTHLY-INTEREST-PAID-TOTAL, ADD MO-EARNED-INT TO ACCT-BALANCE OF
```

CHAPTER TEN BASIC COMPUTER AUDIT TECHNIQUES 335

```
        DEPOSITOR-RECORD, ADD MO-EARNED-INT TO MON-EARNED-INTEREST OF
        DEPOSITOR-RECORD.
        OTHERWISE ADD MO-EARNED-INT TO UNPAID-MONTHLY-INT-TOTAL, MOVE MO-
        EARNED-INT TO YTD-UNPAID-INT.
    CMIE.
        PERFORM WRITE-A-RECARD.
    NEXT-PARAGRAPH.
        .
        .
    WRITE-A-RECARD.
        ADD ONE TO RECARD-COUNT.
        IF LAST-TRANSACTION-DATE OF DEPOSITOR-RECARD IS NOT GREATER THAN ONE-
        YEAR-AGO ADD YTD-UNPAID-INTEREST TO RECARD-COUNT, SUBTRACT MO-
        EARNED-INT FROM UNPAID-MONTHLY-INT-TOTAL.
        PERFORM WRITE-A-RECORD.
        .
        .
    WRITE-A-RECORD.
        WRITE NEW-DEPOSITOR-RECORD FROM DEPOSITOR-RECORD.
        ADD 1 TO RECARD-COUNT.
        .
        .
    END-OF-PROGRAM.
        MOVE RECARD-COUNT TO MO-EARNED-INT.
        PERFORM CMI THRU CMIE.
        MOVE RECORD-COUNT TO RECARD-COUNT.
        WRITE NEW-DEPOSITOR-RECARD FROM CONTROL-RECARD.
        .
        .
        STOP RUN.
```

Field Name	Length	Type	Explanation/Comments
Input ID:			assigned during input microfilming
Year	2	numeric	
Date	3	numeric	Julian Date—cannot be greater than the current date
Batch number	3	numeric	
Batch Sequence	2	numeric	no sequential edits needed
Salesman number	5	numeric	valid range 10000 to 67000
Salesman location	3	numeric	current valid values 001 to 263
Check digit	1	numeric	arithmetic progression, modules 11 method used on the combined salesmen number/location field*
Transaction type	2	numeric	must = 04
Date of transaction	6	numeric	in YY-MM-DD format, reasonability edit performed
Customer number	6	numeric	assigned range of 000001 to 800000
Product ID:			
Market code	1	numeric	1 = children 2 = teenage boys 3 = teenage girls 4 = women 5 = men 6 = governmental
Product line	2	numeric	01 to 53 valid
Major product	2	numeric	all numbers valid
Sales amount	8	numeric	no editing symbols
Authorization code	3	alpha	needed on sales greater than $5,000, current code=AKL, otherwise, blanks

*For example,
Salesman Number 15432
Salesmen Location 78

```
  1   5   4   3   2   7   8
  x   x   x   x   x   x   x
  8   7   6   5   4   3   2
  ─────────────────────────
  8 + 35 + 24 + 15 + 8 + 21 + 16 = 127
```
Sum of arithmetic progression less the closest multiple of 11-check digit
Check digit = 127 − 11(11) = 127 − 121 = 6

Commission Payment Transaction Record Layout

			1	2	3	4
IF	Sale greater than $2,500		x		x	
	Sale less than $2,500			x		x
	Division code = 1 or 5				x	x
Commission rate =						
		6%	x			
		8%		x		
		11%			x	
		13%				x

Commission Payments Decision Table

10.6 During an examination of M. Growit, Inc., you have been assigned to scrutinize one program within the payroll system. The essential segments of the COBOL program where payroll deductions are calculated and the payroll records are updated to reflect these calculations are presented below.

Review the program to determine if it is acqually performing the calculations required.

Specifications

Payroll deductions and payroll detail update.

FICA—5.85% of the first $12,000 earned each year.

State Income Tax—3.75% of gross pay if the STATE CODE is equal to 05, 17, or 26.

Update—FICA and State Income Tax calculated on the weekly runs of the system are to be accumulated in the appropriate year-to-date fields on the payroll records.

```
1    IDENTIFICATION DIVISION
         .
         .
         .
2    ENVIRONMENT DIVISION
         .
         .
         .
3    DATA DIVISION.
4    FILE SECTION.
         .
5    01   PAYROLL-DETAIL
6         05
         .
7         05  YEAR-TO-DATE-EARNINGS        PICTURE 9(6)V99.
8         05  THIS-WEEKS-GROSS-PAY         PICTURE 9(4)V99.
9         05  STATE-CODE                   PICTURE 99.
10        05  YEAR-TO-DATE-FICA            PICTURE 9(4)V99.
11        05  YEAR-TO-DATE-STATE-TAX       PICTURE 9(4)V99.
         .
12   WORKING STORAGE SECTION.
13   77   FICA                             PICTURE 99V999 VALUE 05.850
14   77   STATE-TAX-RATE                   PICTURE 99V999 VALUE 03.750
         .
```

```
15  01  UPDATED-PAYROLL-DETAIL.
16      05
17          05  YEAR-TO-DATE-EARNINGS        PICTURE 9(6)V99.
18          05  THIS-WEEKS-GROSS-PAY         PICTURE 9(4)V99.
19          05  STATE-CODE                   PICTURE 99.
20          05  THIS-WEEKS-FICA              PICTURE 9(4)V99.
21          05  THIS-WEEKS-STATE-TAX         PICTURE 9(4)V99.
22          05  YEAR-TO-DATE-FICA            PICTURE 9(4)V99.
23          05  YEAR-TO-DATE-STATE-TAX       PICTURE 9(4)V99.
24  PROCEDURE DIVISION.
         . . . .
25  FICA-CHECK.
26      IF YEAR-TO-DATE-EARNINGS OF PAYROLL-DETAIL IS LESS THAN 01200000
27          PERFORM FICA-CALCULATION THRU FICA-CALCULATION-EXIT
28          ELSE MOVE ZEROS TO THIS-WEEKS-FICA OF UPDATED-PAYROLL-DETAIL.
29      MOVE THIS-WEEKS-FICA TO YEAR-TO-DATE-FICA OF UPDATED-PAYROLL-DETAIL.
30  STATE-TAX-CHECK.
31      IF STATE-CODE OF PAYROLL-DETAIL EQUALS 05 AND 17 OR 26
32          THEN MULTIPLY STATE-TAX-RATE BY THIS-WEEKS-GROSS-PAY OF PAYROLL-DETAIL
33              GIVING-THIS-WEEKS-STATE-TAX
34          ELSE MOVE ZEROS TO THIS-WEEKS-STATE-TAX.
35      ADD THIS-WEEKS-STATE-TAX TO YEAR-TO-DATE-STATE-TAX.
```

```
36  UPDATE-RECORD.
37      MOVE CORRESPONDING PAYROLL-DETAIL TO UPDATED-PAYROLL-DETAIL.
            . . .
38  FICA-CALCULATION.
39      MULTIPLY THIS-WEEKS-GROSS-PAY OF PAYROLL-DETAIL BY FICA GIVING THIS-WEEKS-FICA.
40      ADD THIS-WEEKS-FICA TO YEAR-TO-DATE-FICA OF UPDATED-PAYROLL-DETAIL.
41  FICA-CALCULATION-EXIT.
42      EXIT.
```

CHAPTER
11

COMPUTER-ASSISTED AUDIT TECHNIQUES

11.1 INTRODUCTION

As stated earlier, to perform meaningful and comprehensive audits, the auditor must rely on a family of audit techniques rather than one technique alone. Most of these techniques require the use of the computer to support their application. In the previous chapter, we noted that to make compliance tests of programmed controls, test decks are prepared and run via the computer. Application of this technique represents a classic use of the computer as a powerful audit tool. Further tests (e.g., substantive tests) must also be performed by the auditor, inasmuch as the audit strategy entails verification of the accuracy and existence of records in the data base and various audit information that can be obtained therefrom. The material in this chapter addresses itself to computer-assisted audit techniques that are applicable to this area of auditing.

11.2 USING THE COMPUTER AS AN AUDIT TOOL

The auditing process involves three steps: (1) review of the system of controls, (2) evaluation and testing of the system of controls, and (3) verification of record contents and generation of evidential information from the data base. Whereas test decks and audit review of programs are used to evaluate the quality of controls, procedures, and instructions, other techniques are needed to determine the quality of information produced by the system.

Computer-assisted audit techniques make it possible to expand the scope of the third step above and to do so more efficiently. The auditor can gain a greater level of assurance in the reliability of financial statements and other outputs of the system by extending the scope of his examination and increasing the number of items tested. The speed and predictability of the computer permits the auditor to gather more accurate audit information economically and practically without any of the restrictions imposed by clerical procedures.

Specific Uses of the Computer as an Audit Tool

In Figures 11.1, 11.2, 11.3, 11.4, and 11.5 are complete examples of using the computer as an audit tool. Below are some additional, more specific examples of how the computer can be used to provide evidential information to the auditor.[1]

1. List all employees who worked more than a predetermined number of hours in a given week.
2. Prepare footings and subtotals of any master file.
3. List all accounts over ninety days old.
4. Calculate rebate due for all loans by control group.
5. Prepare trial balances of all loans by control group.
6. Calculate the cost-to-retail ratio on individual items in inventory.
7. Use dollar estimation sampling procedures to value the warehouse inventories at each warehouse by stratifying the client's warehouse inventory file and selecting random samples of items within selected dollar-value strata. Then price and quantity test each selected item.
8. Estimate the effect of the difference between pricing inventory at "last invoice price" and pricing at FIFO.
9. Compare last year's inventory balances with current balances, listing for manual review all items that: (a) are present this year but not last year, (b) were present last year but not this year, (c) increased or decreased in quantity or price in relation to last year by 20 percent, and (d) have had little or no movement during the year.
10. Calculate a number of ratios in order to highlight relationships and trends. Examples are: (a) capital to liabilities, (b) current assets to current liabilities, (c) working capital to current liabilities, (d) sales to inventory, (e) cost of goods sold to average inventory, (f) sales to receivables, and (g) net income to invested capital.
11. Check prices charged for inventory items against an official master table of prices.
12. Verify extensions and summarization of inventory amounts.
13. Select by random sample items for physical count and price testing.

[1] Examples adapted from: *The Computer as an Audit Tool*, A Computer Impact Series Report Prepared by the Committee on Electronic Data Processing Palo Alto, Calif.: California Society of Certified Public Accountants.

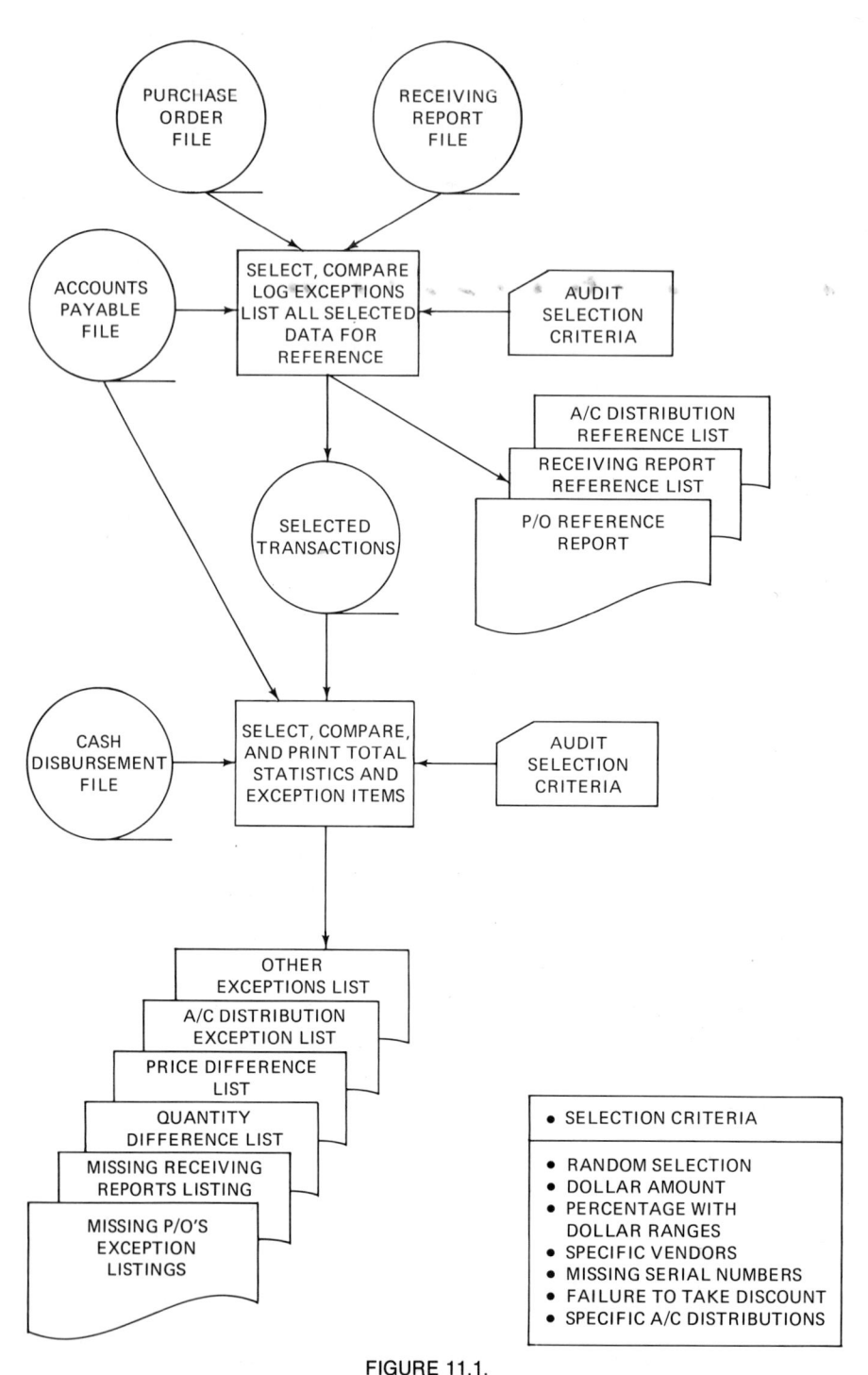

FIGURE 11.1.
Tests of Accounts Payable and Cash Disbursements Case.

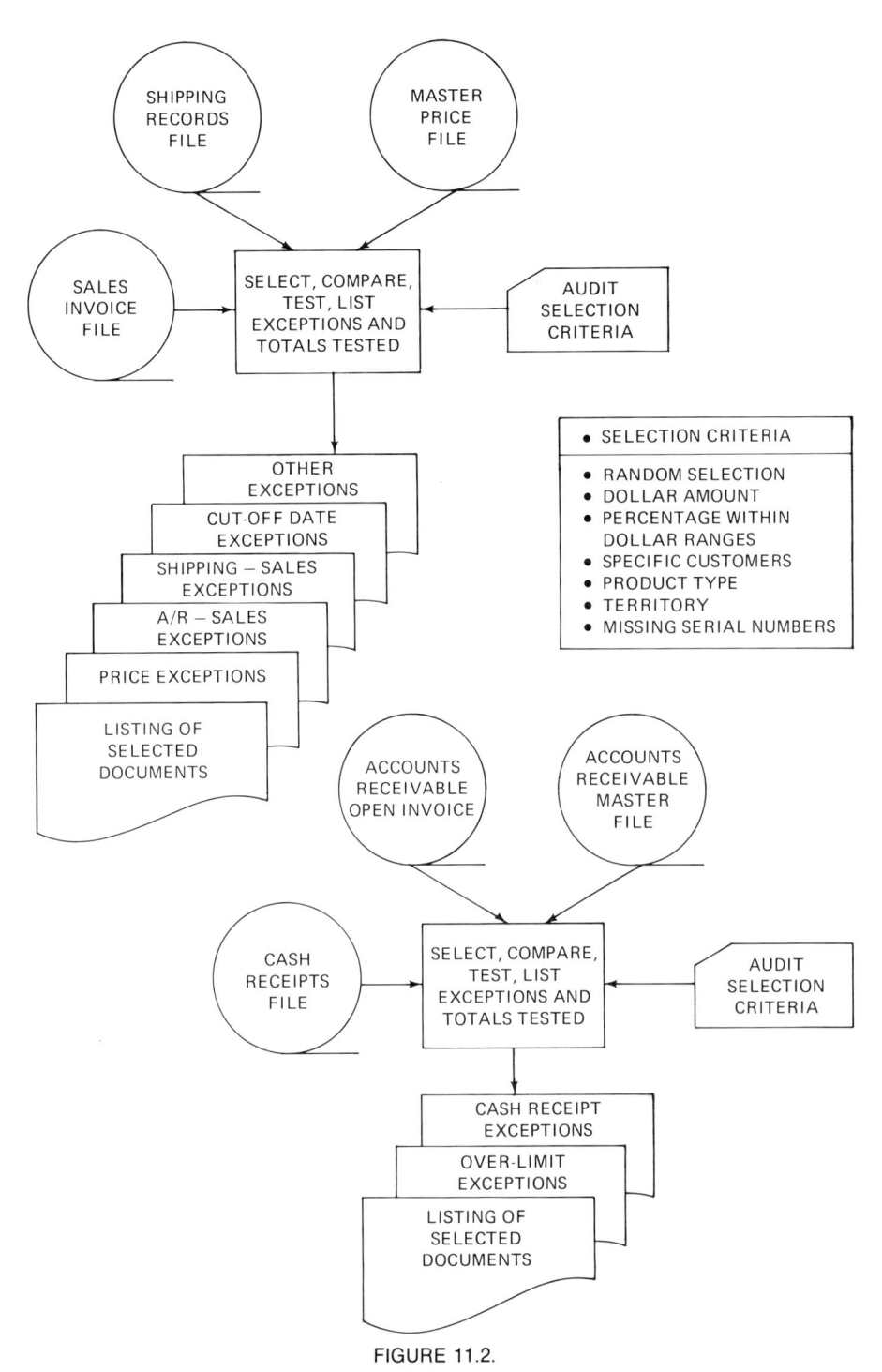

CHAPTER ELEVEN   COMPUTER-ASSISTED AUDIT TECHNIQUES   343

FIGURE 11.2.
Tests of Sales, Accounts Receivable, and Cash Receipts Case.

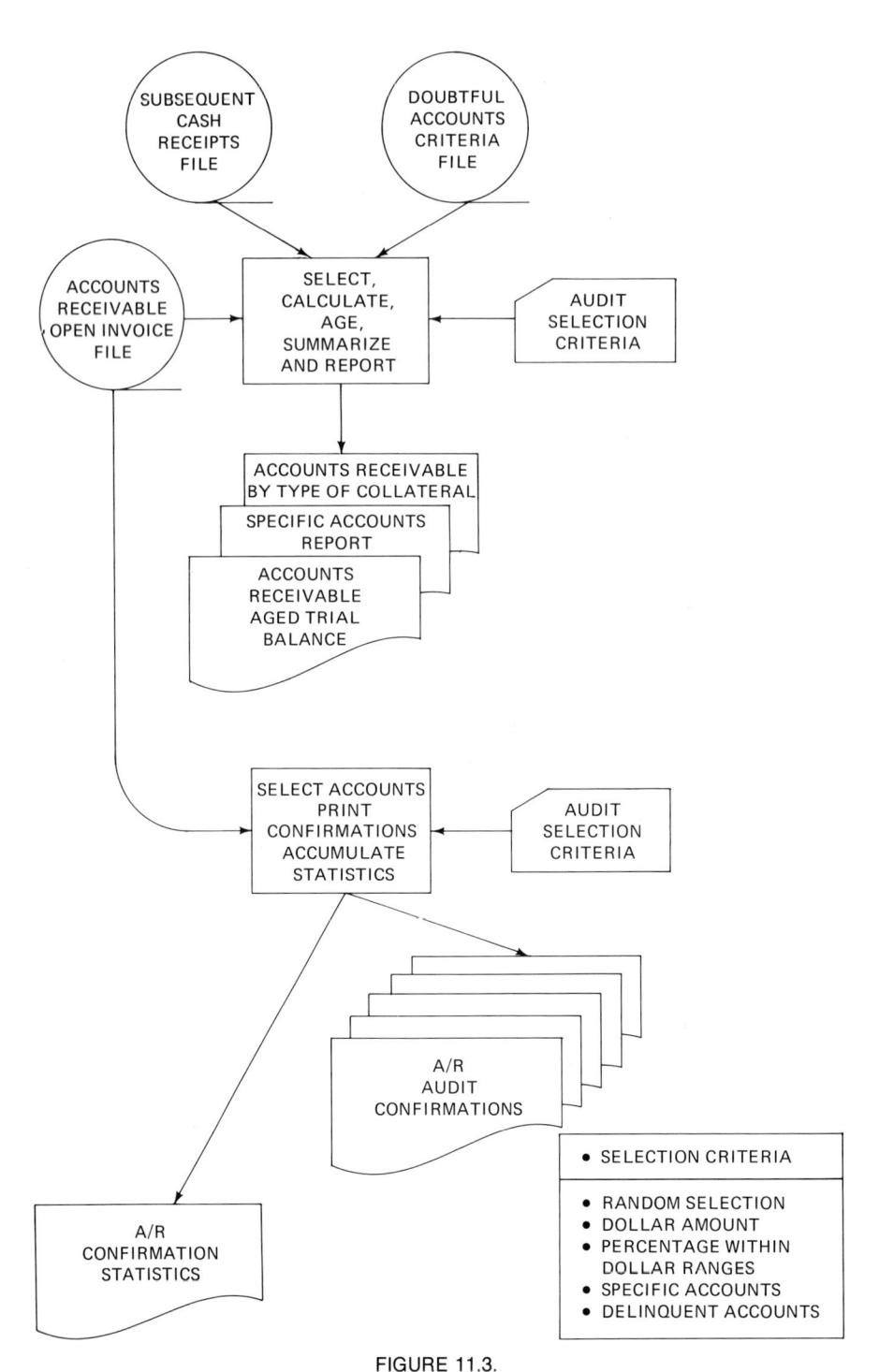

FIGURE 11.3.
Verification and Evaluation of Accounts Receivable Case.

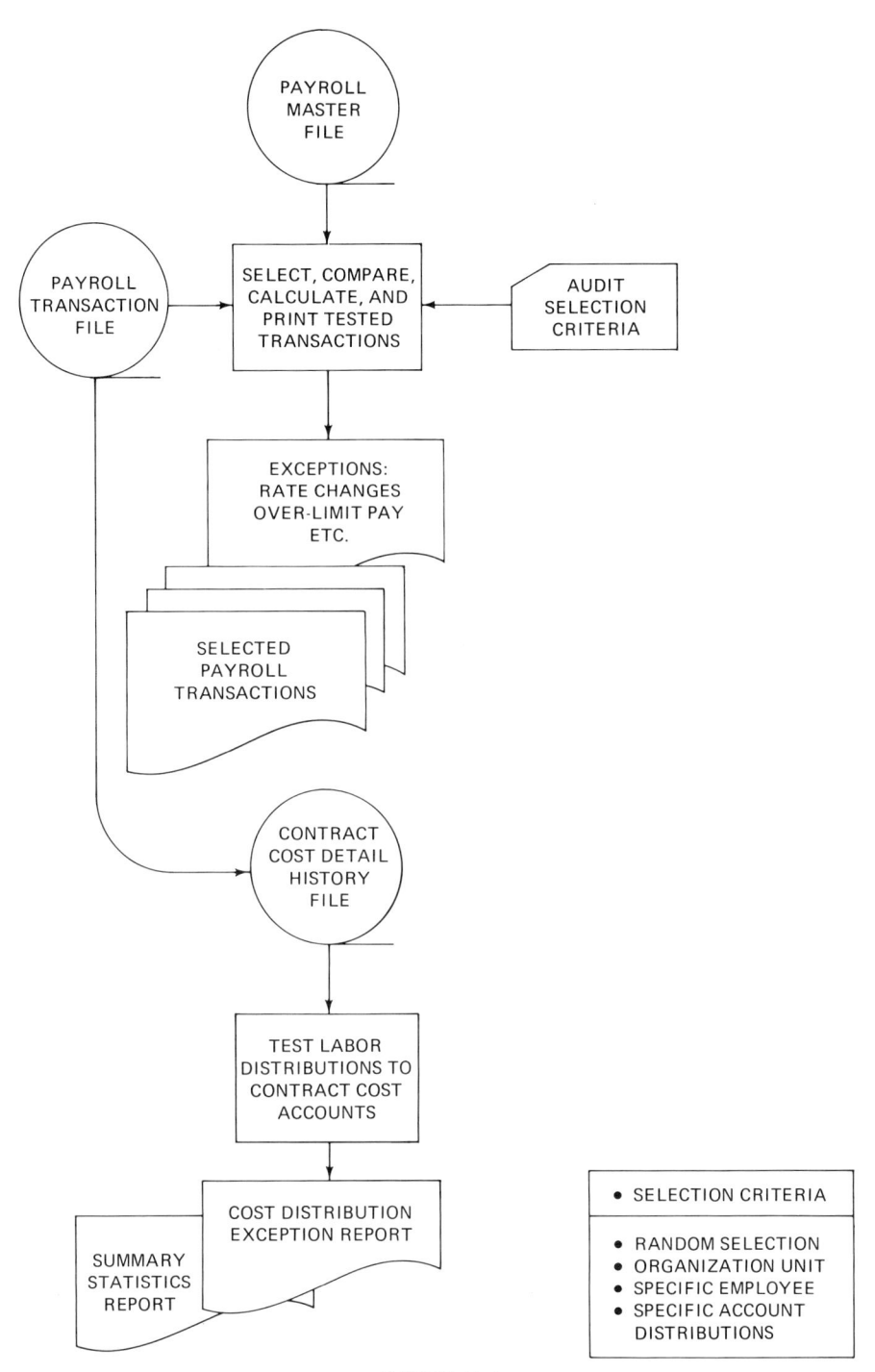

CHAPTER ELEVEN   COMPUTER-ASSISTED AUDIT TECHNIQUES   345

FIGURE 11.4.
Tests of Payroll and Labor Costs Distribution Case.

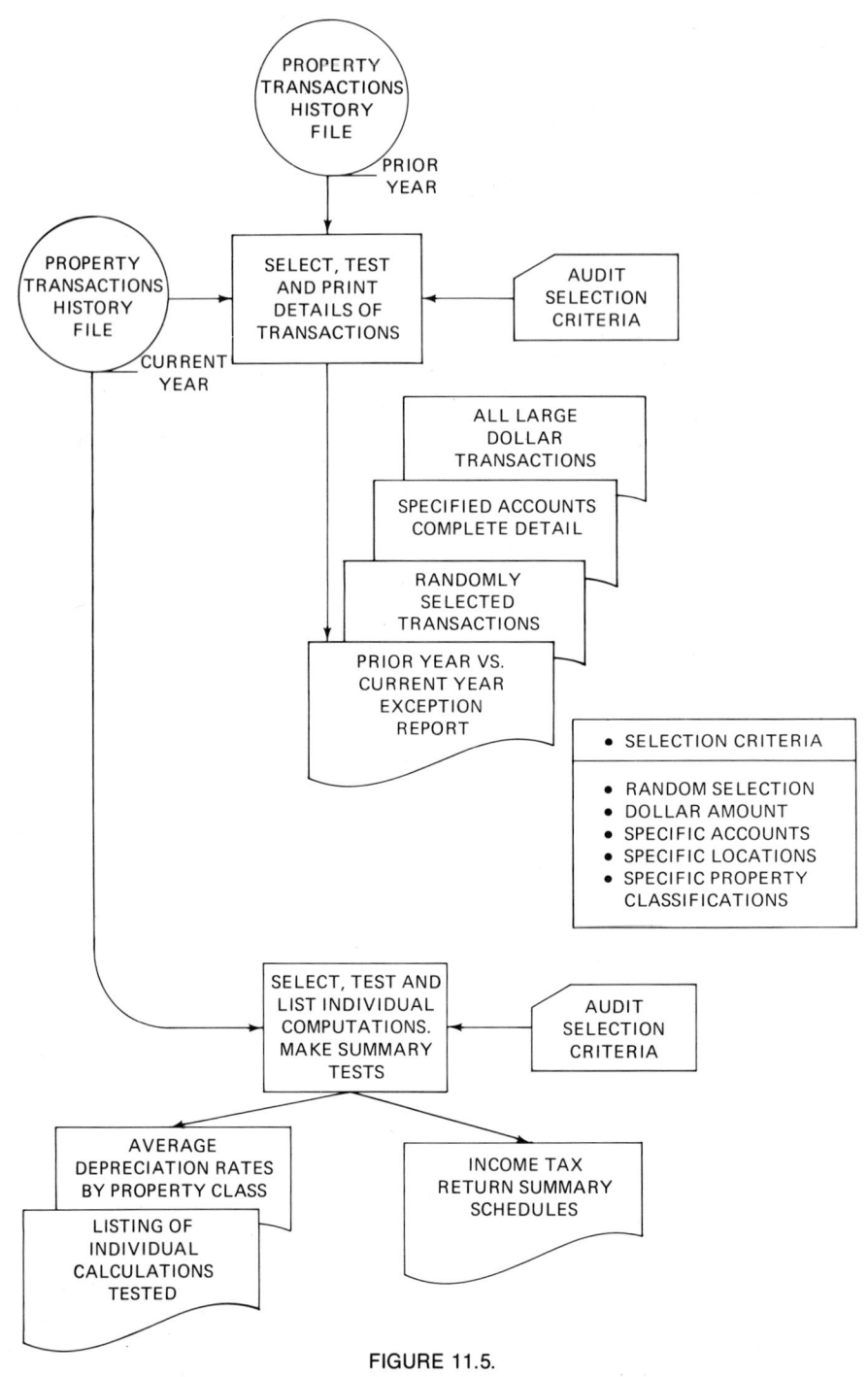

FIGURE 11.5.
Tests of Property, Plant, and Equipment Accounts Case.

14. Stratify data elements by: (a) age—report all checking accounts on which there has been no activity for nine months, (b) type—report all consumer loans in particular classifications, (c) status—report all savings accounts on which special interest calculation codes are in effect, and (d) amount—report all investments that exceed legal or policy limits.

15. Perform random-sample systematic sampling (e.g., every nth one), or stop-or-go sampling on a file of accounts for further review, confirmation, physical count, price testing, and so forth.

16. Perform lower of cost or market analysis.

17. List outstanding checks for review.

18. Prepare aging of accounts receivable report and highlight all customers who have accounts over N days old for review.

19. Identify and list accounts receivable in excess of customer credit limits as recorded on the master file.

20. Select and list suppliers' invoices over a stated dollar limit for vouching.

21. Identify and list for follow-up any numbered source documents that are missing from the transaction files.

22. Search out and list all large and exceptional items, such as: (a) loan balances over $5,000, (b) overdraft deposit balances, (c) dormant accounts, (d) past due loans, (e) all installment loan balances that do not equal total payments remaining, (f) mortgage loan balances that exceed limits based on appraisal, (g) duplicate account numbers in the file, and (h) all account numbers outside of an established range of account numbers.

23. Select accounts receivable for confirmation. Designate all past due accounts for positive confirmation. Prepare confirmation forms using master address files.

Treatment of Confirmations

One popular fallacy that is floating around today holds that some of the old fraudulent schemes will not work anymore because of the computer. Nothing could be further from the truth. Age-old fraud schemes work just as well today as they did before the advent of computers. Without a sound system of controls and employment of aggressive auditing practices, the old schemes may work even better, because computers are reliable and predictable, and the wrongdoer does not have to worry about some bookkeeping clerk accidentally fouling up his scheme.

The best way to perpetrate a fraudulent or embezzlement scheme is through the creation of fictitious entities or items, such as companies, people, accounts, and goods and services. Some examples are: (1) company pays for goods and services it did not receive; (2) payments are made to a non-existent company, person, or account; (3) goods are shipped to customers without sending invoice and vice versa; (4) one item is shipped but the customer is invoiced for something else; and (5) non-existent pensioners or personnel are maintained on files and processed as real people.

The purpose of a confirmation is to verify the existence or accuracy of companies, people, accounts, and goods and services. The auditor performs this verification by one or a combination of the following procedures.

1. *Use of a positive confirmation* The confirmation form containing the status and amount of the confirmation object (e.g., accounts receivable) is addressed and mailed to the appropriate respondent (e.g., customer), asking him to confirm directly to the auditor the accuracy of the confirmation report (e.g., balance owed). The essential characteristic of the positive confirmation is that it calls for a reply in every case.

2. *Use of a negative confirmation* The overall approach to preparing a negative confirmation is the same as with a positive confirmation, except the respondent is requested to advise the auditor only if the confirmation form is in error.

3. *Use of physical confirmation* This approach is used when the auditor actually goes to the object of confirmation and observes its existence. For example, an auditor may go to Detroit to see for himself if a particular warehouse exists. Or he may go to a railroad yard in Pennsylvania to see that, in fact, 200 boxcars are being repaired.

4. *Use of third-party confirmation* This approach is used when the auditor relies on an official third source for the existence of the confirmation object. For example, the auditor may confirm that Company ABC is in fact a real company, because it is listed in Dun and Bradstreet or Moody's. Valid companies can be coded in a security table in the computer; then, every time a transaction occurs concerning some company, it is compared against the security table of valid companies. Failure to match a valid company number causes the system to automatically notify the control group and/or the internal auditor.

The computer can be used to extract certain accounts for confirmation and automatically prepare positive and negative confirmation forms, as illustrated in Figure 11.6. The audit program can be written to print out confirmation forms for mailing, and at the same time, a confirmation log can be generated on a magnetic file such as magnetic tape or disk. As the auditor receives confirmation replies from the client's customers, the results are stored on a computer-readable file. Another computer program can be created, compare the confirmations received with the confirmation log, and produce an exception report for the auditor of all confirmation replies received that do not agree with the master file records, as well as all confirmations not received by a specified time. For

```
┌─────────────────┐     ┌──────────────────────────┐     ┌──────────────────┐
│ AUDIT PROGRAM   │───▶ │ 1. PROGRAM SELECTS       │───▶ │ NEGATIVE CONFIR- │
└─────────────────┘     │    ACCOUNTS ACCORDING    │     │ MATIONS TO BE    │
                        │    TO CRITERIA.          │     │ MAILED BY AUDITOR│
┌─────────────────┐     │ 2. PRINTS NEGATIVE       │     └──────────────────┘
│ AUDITOR PREPARES│     │    CONFIRMATIONS.        │
│ SELECTION CRI-  │───▶ │ 3. PRINTS POSITIVE       │
│ TERIA.          │     │    CONFIRMATIONS.        │     ┌──────────────────┐
└─────────────────┘     │ 4. STORES POSITIVE       │───▶ │ POSITIVE CONFIR- │
                        │    CONFIRMATIONS ON      │     │ MATIONS TO BE    │
┌─────────────────┐     │    CONFIRMATION LOG FOR  │     │ MAILED BY AUDITOR│
│ ACCOUNTS RECEIV-│───▶ │    FUTURE REFERENCE AND  │     └──────────────────┘
│ ABLE MASTER FILE│     │    ANALYSIS.             │
└─────────────────┘     └──────────────────────────┘
                                   │
                                   ▼
                            ┌─────────────┐
                            │ CONFIRMATION│
                            │    LOG      │
                            └─────────────┘
```

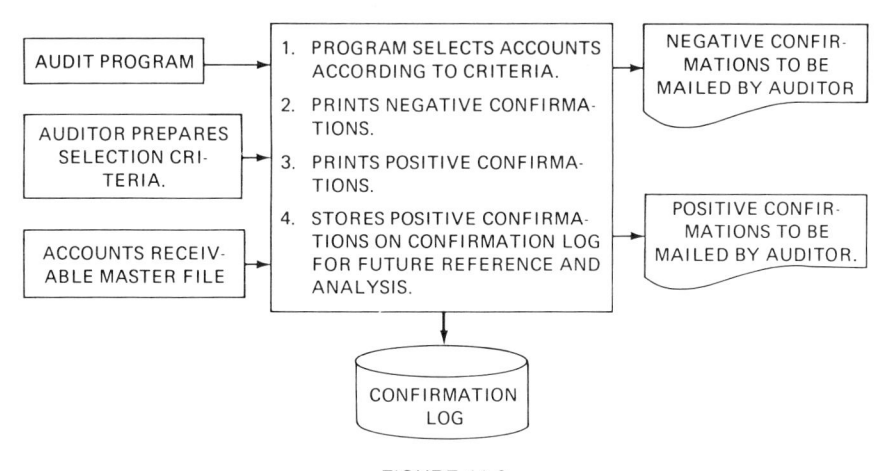

FIGURE 11.6.

Example of how the Computer, along with Appropriate Audit Programs, can be used to Prepare Confirmations for Accounts Receivable.

customers who have not responded, the program can also automatically prepare a second mailing.

Since confirmation is one of the most powerful audit techniques in verifying the existence and accuracy of records in the data base, the following guidelines are included in this section. These guidelines represent a fairly comprehensive list of what the auditor should do in performing a confirmation, whether it is for banks or any other organization.[2] These guidelines also show that the auditor has a lot of work to do on his own, even with the aid of a computer.

1. *Preparation*   The preparation phase of applying the confirmation techniques should be handled as follows:

   a. Setting the date. Decide on a specific date for the job, allowing sufficient time to assemble the required stationery and equipment and to plan personnel assignments.

   b. Frequency of confirmation. A confirmation program may cover all accounts each calendar year. But complete coverage generally is neither practical nor necessary. Test confirmations using samples varying from 10% to 33% of the accounts are considered more effective than complete verifications at longer intervals. The Comptroller of the Currency requires that national banks confirm 20% of their loan and deposit accounts annually. When statistical sampling techniques are used, it is possible for acceptable results to be achieved with smaller sample sizes, depending on population size and precision requirements. The use of a statistical sample permits objective determination of the sample size and objective appraisal of the sample results.

[2] Adapted and abridged from The Bank Administration Institute, Park Ridge, Illinois.

c. Element of surprise. To be effective, the verification must be made without advance notice to any person having the responsibility for keeping records, securities, or accounts to be verified. If outside accountants are engaged to perform the verification job, care should be taken to assure surprise. Some banks authorize their outside accountants to select a date and undertake the work without prior notice to any director, officer, or other employee of the bank. If surprise is not complete, the verification may lose its value.

d. Separate post office box. If the auditor does not have a separate post office box under his sole control, arrangements should be made to obtain one. It is absolutely essential that all verification replies be returned directly to the auditor. Any possibility of interception by unauthorized personnel should be eliminated.

e. Notice to customers. Some banks inform their customers at the time of opening accounts that verification forms requesting confirmation will be sent to them periodically. Whether this notification is done or not, the verification form should be simple to understand and should meet all requirements of courtesy to the customer. Before a confirmation program is begun, it is advisable to explain the procedure to the bank staff, but this explanation should apply only to the program, not to the dates on which verifications will be made. The explanation, in addition to obtaining the cooperation of bank personnel, will help to deter fraud.

f. Determining the scope. Determine the approximate number of each type of account to be verified. Where test verification is to be made, the number of accounts to be verified may be estimated by applying the percent of coverage desired to the total number of each type of account on the books.

g. Selection of accounts. In the selection of accounts for test verification, preference may be given to those not responding to a previous request, past due or slow accounts, and accounts with minimum activity. The test should also include a representative sampling from all ledgers and asset accounts having large balances. For commercial deposits and collection items, adequate test verification should also be made of open accounts temporarily showing no balances. Dormant commercial and savings accounts should be verified once a year. Random sampling techniques may be used in lieu of specific selection methods.

h. Positive form. The positive form is recommended for verifying loans, collateral, and other accounts having voluminous detail. It is the more effective and satisfactory form for verifying collection items, particularly if the accounts have not been verified previously. It should always be used for verification of accounts for which statements or passbooks are forwarded to special addresses, held at the customer's request until called for, or delivered to customers by members of the official or clerical staffs, and for accounts having foreign addresses.

i. Negative form. Where volume is high and the system of internal control is good, the negative form provides reasonably good protection. If monthly statements are mailed to all checking account customers, and if internal rotation and segregation of duties are observed, a certain degree of direct verification is achieved.

j. Ordering supplies. It is advisable to place forms and stationery orders well in advance of the start of the verification job.

k. Job plan. If performance of the verification job is to require the services of several persons for one or more days, it will be helpful to prepare in advance a written plan covering all phases of the work.

2. *Performance* The performance phase of applying the confirmation technique should be handled as follows:

a. Control of records. All records pertaining to the accounts to be verified must be placed under control of the auditing group. These accounts must be controlled until proving has been completed, and information entered on the verification forms. Postings in process, required for the recording of transactions completed prior to the verification date, should be permitted.

b. Proof of related accounts. All accounts related to those being verified should be proved and reviewed to be sure they are not being used for temporary concealment. Suspense and cash items are examples of related accounts.

c. Record of request sent. In some instances, a copy of negative forms need not be prepared. In fact, many banks simply use stickers attached to statements as negative forms.

d. Proving and checking amounts. Prove the records and check the amounts entered on the forms. When this has been done, control over the records can be released. Ledger records subject to verification must be proved and balanced to the general ledger before the mailing of verification forms.

e. Address checks. In addition to checking amounts, the auditor should make a test check of the addresses appearing on the forms. Telephone and city directories are commonly used in making this test check. If practical, addresses of officers and employees should be checked against the forms. For example, when the address of an employee appears on an account other than his own, the case should be thoroughly investigated.

f. Dating forms. It is very important to date the forms and to call the date of verification to the customer's attention. Since a period of time always elapses before the customer receives the verification form, the balances could well be different, and lack of a date could cause many apparent exceptions.

g. Special mailing instructions. All special mailing instructions issued by the customer, such as requests for mailing a duplicate to a second party (address other than that shown on ledger sheet) or requests for the statement to be held, must be followed to avoid customer complaints. These verification forms should be withheld and referred to an officer for mailing instructions. If verification with the customer is considered unwise, the auditor should list the accounts in his report, noting the reason for non-verification. In addition, the auditor should make sufficient audit of these accounts to satisfy himself of the validity of the transactions and balance.

    h. *Mailing.* Verification forms should be delivered to a U.S. Post Office or deposited in a government mailbox by members of the auditing group.

    i. *Improper addresses.* Particular attention should be given to requests returned to the post office because of improper address. A search of the files and discussions with officers or others who know the customers will frequently disclose correct addresses. If a correct address cannot be found, the debit entries to these accounts should be examined by the auditor to determine their regularity. Names of customers, balances, and other details of accounts with improper addresses should be listed, and these accounts should be carefully reviewed during the next verification.

    3. *Follow-up* The follow-up phase of applying the confirmation technique should be handled as follows:

    a. *Review replies.* All replies must be reviewed promptly. Those incorrectly completed by customers or those reporting exceptions should be segregated for immediate investigation and response. Some exceptions may represent errors in the preparation of verification forms. In these cases, letters of apology should be sent to customers over the auditor's signature. Exceptions representing items in transit or transactions in process at the date of the verification should be covered by explanatory letters from the auditor.

    b. *Verifying signatures.* The genuineness of signatures on all forms returned by customers should be verified. A check should be made against the signature file by members of the auditing group or by employees who do not have access to the accounts or records. For greatest convenience, allow replies to accumulate for several days before undertaking signature verification. In very large verification programs, it may be desirable to check signatures on a test basis.

    c. *Improper signatures.* Confirmation forms bearing no signature or improper signatures should be returned to customers accompanied by a letter from the auditor. A suggested form follows:

> Thank you for returning the enclosed confirmation sent to you in connection with one of our periodic audits. We notice that the form does not bear your signature (or that the signature does not agree with the signature on file with us).
>
> While we regret troubling you further, it would be appreciated if

you have an authorized signature added to the confirmation and return it to me in the enclosed envelope.

d. Follow-up letters. When positive verification forms are not returned by customers within a reasonable time—usually two weeks for domestic and one or two months for foreign addresses—a second request should be mailed. The words "Second Request" should appear in a prominent position on the form. Maintain a record of second requests by stamping the words "Second Request," followed by the date sent, on the duplicate copies of original requests or on the auditor's list of requests sent. If a similar record has been kept of replies received, the auditor's records will bear notations "Confirmed—date" or "Second Request—date" as a continuous record of the status of the verification job.

While many banks send only one follow-up letter, poor response or excessive time lapse since last correspondence with the customer may warrant the mailing of a third or even fourth request. A personal request for response over the signature of an officer known to the customer is frequently effective. Some banks have adopted the practice of sending third requests by certified mail.

e. Accounts not responding. Prepare a list showing names, addresses, and balances of accounts not responding to requests for signed verification. Further action can be taken, such as telephoning, writing special letters to the customers, or personal visits. The auditor should examine the accounts and relative correspondence files. Review the list with senior officers or others known to the customers. Where circumstances warrant, audits should be made of entries to the account. The auditor should keep in mind that the chance of fraud exists in the accounts that are not verified and he should strive for 100% response, although it is not always practical or possible.

f. Reporting results. Reports of results of verification involving domestic accounts can be prepared five or six weeks after the start of the job. Where numerous foreign accounts are involved, several months may be required for receipt of responses. In these cases, one or more preliminary reports can be issued to show the progress of the job. The final report should include the number and dollar amount of the total for each group being checked and of verifications sent, as well as the number and dollar amount of verifications received, together with a notation of any serious exceptions.

A Final Comment on Using the Computer as an Audit Tool

The computer can be used to access and manipulate data elements as required by the auditor. The computer can be used to generate reports of exception conditions, summarize massive volumes of data, identify discrepancies within and between files, calculate trends and significant ratios, and produce a wealth of analytical information. The computer can be used to select a statistical sample of accounts for confirmation, print the confirmation forms, and perform follow-up processing.

Use of the computer provides a wealth of analytical and trend information that is useful not only to the auditor but to management as well. This kind of information allows the auditor to move from historical or after-the-fact auditing to current-status auditing. With trend information readily available, the auditor has the opportunity to move to a preventive philosophy in his auditing approach, i.e., an approach to auditing that prevents abuses from occurring rather than uncovering and reporting on them after they happen.

If the computer is so beneficial to the auditor, one may wonder why it's not used more extensively. The catch is that the auditor cannot simply press a button and wait for the computer to do the rest. The computer by itself is a dumb animal; it can perform only in obedience to the instructions it receives from a program written by a human, somewhat like the direction an animal receives from an animal trainer. Therefore, the only way that the computer can be used by the auditor as an audit tool is through the execution of some computer program.

There are four sources for these computer audit programs: (1) programs written by a programmer who works for the organization that is being audited, (2) programs written by or under the supervision of the auditor, (3) generalized audit programs developed by accounting firms and software companies, and (4) utility programs and special purpose packages supplied by computer vendors. The remainder of this chapter will be devoted to presenting these four sources.

11.3 PROGRAMS WRITTEN BY CLIENT'S PROGRAMMER

If generalized audit or vendor utility programs are not available, or if the auditor, for whatever reasons, cannot write his own audit programs, the auditor might work with the client's programmer to develop or make available programs that serve his purpose. Management may be quite willing to support this alternative because, as stated earlier, much of the evidential information needed by the auditor is also beneficial to management for planning, controlling, and decision-making. The advantage to the auditor in having the client's programmer write his programs is that it saves time and other resources for program development. The major disadvantage is that the auditor must rely on computer systems personnel to do much of the critical work for him. In doing so, he compromises his independence and may lose the respect of client personnel. Moreover, the computer system remains a black box to him.

Types of Programs Available

Audit programs furnished by the client generally fall into the following categories[3]:

1. A program designed purely to satisfy a specific audit requirement, such as a simple sampling program for selection of transactions, determination of exception conditions, or trends and ratio analysis.

2. A program designed to satisfy an audit requirement, but also useful to management on a continuing basis, such as a program to age accounts receivable or analyze inventory turnover and obsolescence.

3. Modification of an existing program to accomplish an audit task simultaneously with normal processing operations, such as printing of selected accounts receivable confirmations at the same time that the accounts receivable statements are being prepared.

4. Existing programs and data processed under controlled conditions, such as accumulation, pricing, and extension of inventory.

Control over Programs

If the auditor is to be able to rely on programs written by client personnel, the system must include controls such as programming standards, librarians, and documentation. Moreover, if the program is written for the auditor by personnel from the organization being audited, the auditor will need to test (e.g., test deck) the program before he can use it. The extent of testing will depend upon the reliance he can place on the programmer, in particular, and on the installation's control over programs and operations, in general.

Again, the classic problem is to make sure that the program is executed in accordance with audit objectives, and that the program being run is the same as that being reviewed and tested by the auditor. The auditor's copy of the program should be under his continuous control and he should closely supervise the running of the program. When supervising the running of these audit programs, the auditor should be particularly observant of unnecessary operator intervention and the risk of program substitution, particularly in a multiprogramming environment.

If an installation's system of program maintenance and security over files contains weaknesses, the auditor may wish to establish additional controls over the use of programs he has had developed. The same degree of control should be exercised over programs that are existing

---

[3]Adapted from Study Group on Computer Control and Audit Guidelines, *Computer Audit Guidelines*, (Toronto: The Canadian Institute of Chartered Accountants, 1975), p. 251.

programs or modifications of them, as would be exercised over the writing of an entirely new program.[4]

11.4 PROGRAMS WRITTEN BY THE AUDITOR

The underlying principle of auditing is auditor independence. With the installation of more and more computer systems, many auditors have watched their independence dwindle because of their increasing reliance on computer personnel to act as intermediaries between them and the computer system they are auditing. To be effective, the auditor must re-establish his independence. One of the best ways to do this is for the auditor to write his own audit program; thus he relies solely upon himself and the computer to provide him with evidential information.

Overview of this Audit Technique

The most direct way for the auditor to gain access to the data base is to write the audit program himself or to have an aide do it under his close supervision. To do so, the auditor must possess a firm knowledge of the computer system and competency in a programming language that can be executed by the computer system.

Some of the higher-level languages available to the auditor are COBOL, PL/1, FORTRAN, and BASIC. It is relatively easy to gain a moderate level of competency in any of these programming languages. Most of these languages are fairly universal. If the auditor learns how to write in COBOL, for example, he can feel confident that this language will be compatible with a large number of systems. However, it must be emphasized that a number of systems may not be compatible with a particular language that the auditor can write in. Probably the language used most widely throughout the commercial community is COBOL. Therefore, if the auditor is to learn one language, it is recommended that he choose COBOL.

In determining whether or not to write his own program or to use any of the other techniques, the auditor must understand the processing factors and balance them against what he would have to do without the use of a particular audit technique, such as writing his own computer audit program. These processing factors are: (1) the *volume* of data elements involved, (2) the *complexity* of the required data-processing operations, (3) processing *time* constraints, and (4) *computational* demands.

If the auditor is to select the proper audit technique, he must understand the four elements that impact upon his objectives. In many sys-

[4]*Ibid.*

tems one element is so dominant that the other three may not be carefully defined or considered. For example, the review of a payroll file that contains 5,000 employee records alone might justify the development of a program to make this review because of the volume. Or the job of computing the earned interest of only 500 accounts might also justify this technique on computational demands alone. In most systems all of these elements work together to make it quite difficult for auditors to use manual techniques. In summary, as the volume of data increases, as complexity increases, as time constraints become more severe, and as computational demands become more sophisticated, an increased use of audit programs written by the auditor, as well as from other sources, will be warranted.

How to Use this Audit Technique

The first program written by the auditor should be fairly simple, yet effective. A simple program gets him into the system, gives him experience with the system and the programming language, and gives him confidence. At the same time, he should obtain some good results to win respect of computer systems personnel and to show higher management what can be done.

The auditor might begin with a check of all employees who worked more than 55 hours for the current week. The master payroll file contains 5,000 records that are stored on magnetic tape. Even if these records were in human-readable form, it would take a long time for the auditor to perform this simple review. So the auditor writes a program to do this task for him, as illustrated in Figure 11.7. Note that each payroll record contains 200 characters, but the only fields in the record that the auditor is interested in are EMPLOYEE-NUM, EMPLOYEE-NAME, and HOURS-WORKED. The size and position of these fields in the master payroll record would be included in the record layout in the payroll documentation manual. If not, then the auditor would have to rely on someone to give him this information.

Once some degree of success has been achieved, the auditor can move to bigger things. He can do all of those things listed earlier in this chapter such as printing out exceptional conditions, preparing financial ratios, highlighting trends, preparing confirmations, and generating analytical information. For example, it would not be too difficult to make an analysis by geographic regions of accounts receivable 90 or more days overdue. This analysis would highlight locations where more investigation would be useful. It might also indicate that collection procedures should be improved. This analysis might even uncover poor controls and fraud.

IDENTIFICATION DIVISION.
PROGRAM-ID.   SIMPLE AUDIT PROGRAM.
AUTHOR.   JIM SMART.
REMARKS.   THIS PROGRAM PRINTS OUT THE EMPLOYEE NUMBER, NAME, AND
           NUMBER OF HOURS OF ALL EMPLOYEES WHO WORKED MORE THAN 55
           HOURS.
ENVIRONMENT DIVISION.
CONFIGURATION SECTION.
SOURCE-COMPUTER.   BIG NUMBER CRUNCHER.
OBJECT-COMPUTER.   BIG NUMBER CRUNCHER.
INPUT-OUTPUT SECTION.
FILE CONTROL.
    SELECT PAYROLL-MASTER ASSIGN TO TAPE-UNIT-ONE.
    SELECT AUDIT-REPORT ASSIGN TO PRINTER-ONE.
DATA DIVISION.
FILE SECTION.
FD PAYROLL-MASTER RECORD CONTAINS 200 CHARACTERS LABEL RECORDS ARE
    STANDARD VALUE OF ID IS 'PAYROLL-MASTER' DATA RECORD IS PAYROLL-
    RECORD.
01 PAYROLL-RECORD.
    02 EMPLOYEE-NUM   PICTURE X(5).
    02 EMPLOYEE-NAME   PICTURE X(30).
    02 FILLER   PICTURE X(50).
    02 HOURS-WORKED   PICTURE 99V99.
    02 FILLER   PICTURE X(111).
FD AUDIT-REPORT RECORD CONTAINS 133 CHARACTERS LABEL RECORDS ARE
    OMITTED DATA RECORD IS AUDIT-RECORD.
01 AUDIT-RECORD.
    02 FILLER   PICTURE X(10).
    02 EMP-NUM-OUT   PICTURE X(5).
    02 FILLER   PICTURE X(5).

```
02    EMP-NAME-OUT              PICTURE X(30).
02    FILLER                    PICTURE X(5).
02    HOURS-WK-OUT              PICTURE 99.99.
02    FILLER                    PICTURE X(73).
PROCEDURE DIVISION.
OPEN-FILES.
    OPEN INPUT PAYROLL-MASTER, OUTPUT AUDIT-REPORT.
BEGIN-WORK.
    READ PAYROLL-MASTER AT END GO TO END-OF-JOB.
    MOVE SPACES TO AUDIT-RECORD.
    IF HOURS-WORKED IS GREATER THAN 55.00 MOVE EMPLOYEE-NUM TO
        EMP-NUM-OUT MOVE EMPLOYEE-NAME TO EMP-NAME-OUT MOVE
        HOURS-WORKED TO HOURS-WK-OUT WRITE AUDIT-RECORD AFTER
        ADVANCING 3 LINES ELSE GO TO BEGIN-WORK.
END-OF-JOB.
    CLOSE PAYROLL-MASTER, AUDIT-REPORT.
    STOP RUN.
```

FIGURE 11.7.
Simple Example of an Audit Program that Prints Out All Employees Who Worked More than 55 Hours.

Advantages and Disadvantages of this Audit Technique

As with any audit technique, there are good points and bad points to this one. The probable advantages of the auditor writing his own audit programs are as follows:

1. Increases the auditor's independence from computer systems personnel.
2. Enhances the respect toward the auditor of computer systems personnel and management.
3. Increases the auditor's expertise and confidence about computer systems in general by becoming more involved in the system.
4. Improves auditor's flexibility by allowing him to set or formulate any selection criteria he wants.
5. Gives the auditor the ability to audit any system so long as the language is compatible with the computer. This point is important because some generalized audit programs are compatible on ABC computer but not XYZ. Therefore, having a knowledge of programming improves overall audit capability and flexibility.
6. Gives the auditor a strong tool to deal with volume, complexity, timing, and computational requirements.

The probable disadvantages are:

1. The set-up costs may not be justified. The time and money invested in the effort to write a computer program must be justified on the basis of limited audit resources and the benefit to be gained in future periods.
2. Some of the programs may be good for a one-shot engagement, but they may not be general enough for repeated use.
3. In some instances, the auditor may need a long lead time to prepare the audit programs.
4. The programs, once developed, normally require maintenance to meet changing conditions. Without maintenance, the programs can quickly become obsolete.

Use of Programmer under Direct Supervision of the Auditor

Because the auditor may feel that his time can be better spent performing other tasks, he may hire a programmer to do the coding and maintenance of the audit programs. The programmer should work under direct supervision of the auditor. The auditor should still formulate the selection criteria and objectives of the audit. He should also be involved in the testing and implementation of the program. Using a programmer in no way reduces the need for the auditor to gain an understanding of the computer system and ability to write a program. His computer and programming expertise should be just as great when he uses a programmer to write audit programs as when he develops his own, perhaps greater.

If the auditor would like to use a programmer on an experimental basis at first, he can contract with some outside service such as a software company or a service bureau for a programmer. This approach will allow the auditor to get started and help him get a feel for using audit programs. This approach represents a good interim step but should not be used for more than a year.

Another approach is simply to hire a programmer for the audit staff on a full-time basis. The duties of the audit programmer would be: (1) work with members of the audit staff to develop specifications and objectives of audit programs; (2) review client's documentation and define record layouts; (3) design logic, code, test, and implement program under direct supervision; (4) prepare complete documentation of all audit programs; (5) develop, catalog, and maintain an audit program library; (6) maintain and change programs as necessary to meet changing computer systems and conditions; (7) in technical areas, serve as a liaison between computer systems personnel and auditors; (8) supervise the development, implementation, and operation of other computer auditing techniques, such as integrated test facilities (discussed later) and utility programs supplied by vendors; (9) act as a technical consultant to the audit staff; and (10) keep current with changing computer and programming technology.

11.5 GENERALIZED AUDIT PROGRAMS

In far too many cases, there is a wide gap between the auditor and the computer. The advent of generalized audit programs represents a significant development that has helped auditors to keep pace with computer systems and narrow this gap. Basically, these programs have been designed to make it easier for the auditor to use the computer in his audit work. These programs also help the auditor to independently select computerized data for evaluation and interpretation. These programs reduce the auditor's reliance on computer systems personnel and thus increase his independence. In short, generalized audit programs facilitate audit analysis of computerized data, improve audit performance, and provide management and the auditor with a wider variety of information.

Definition of Generalized Audit Programs

A generalized audit program is a prewritten computer program or group of modules logically linked together which is designed to perform a variety of audit tasks specified by the auditor. Some programs are written in a high-level language such as COBOL. Others are written in a combination of assembler and high-level language. They are available for lease or purchase from software companies and public accounting firms. A general schematic of a typical generalized audit program application is shown in Figure 11.8.

Note that the auditor does not write the programs to perform the audit tasks, but he has to give the audit program well-defined instructions to describe the record fields and the processing operations to be performed. These instructions, called file description and parameter cards, are fed into the computer along with the audit program and files that are being audited. The generalized audit program can be used on a variety of computer systems. The only variation necessary is the preparation of new parameter cards for each new audit application.

The extraction capability of the generalized audit program allows the auditor to select those records that meet predetermined parameters.

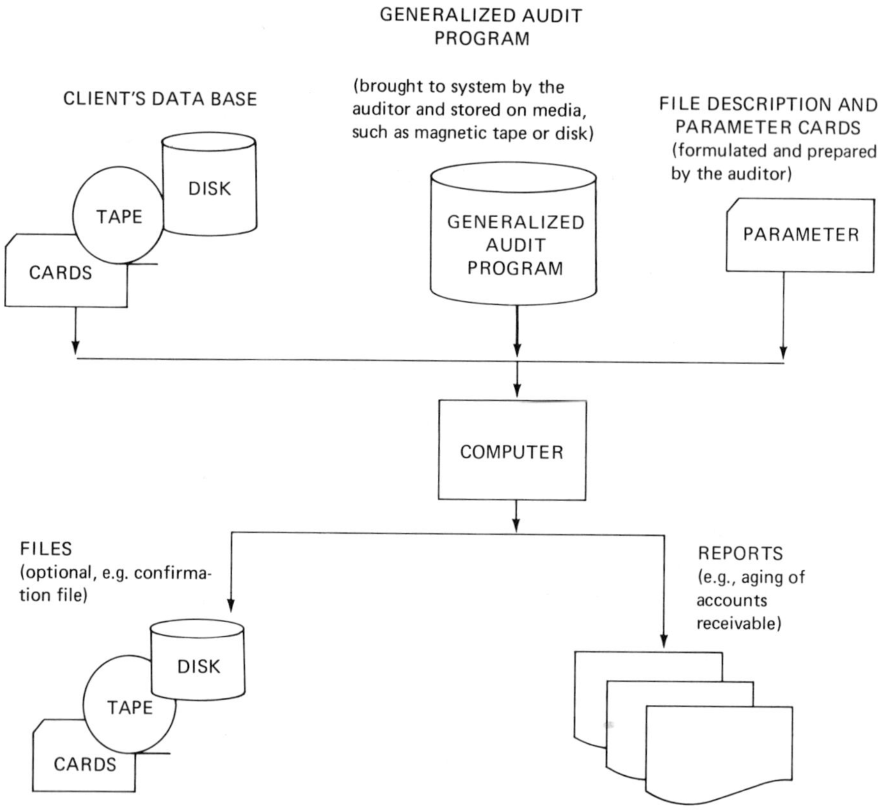

FIGURE 11.8.
Simple Schematic of how a Typical Generalized Audit Program works with the Computer.

Specification of these parameters is handled by parameter control cards that can be changed from one application to the next, depending upon the particular needs of the auditor. These parameter cards permit the selection of records on the basis of inclusion in or exclusion from a range of values or on the basis of a match. They also express various manipulations and other functions that are discussed later.

Objectives of Generalized Audit Programs

The objectives of the generalized audit program are:
1. To apply the concept of generality, thus the term *generalized* audit program, wherein the auditor can use it anywhere without regard to the application or computer system.
2. To provide the auditor with a high level of independence, especially from computer systems personnel.
3. To improve ready access to large volumes of computerized data and convert them into human-readable form.
4. To increase the number of audit techniques available to the auditor.
5. To minimize the need for the auditor to have an extensive background in computer and programming technology. In the long run, this objective may work against the auditor if he relies too much on this technique.

Functions and Applications of Generalized Audit Programs

The basic processing operations required to perform audit tests of the data base vary little from one audit engagement to another or from one computer system to another. The specifics and scope of the audit may change, but generally the overall objectives are the same. For example, the auditor will set parameters to select certain items from a file; or perform calculations on a variety of data items; or sort, merge, and compare files; and so forth. Therefore, to meet this generalized status, all audit programs must perform certain basic operations, such as mathematics, extracting, sorting, comparing, merging, summarizing, reporting, and so forth. Following is a list of the functions that generalized audit programs should perform to meet the concept of generality. Presented along with these functions are examples of practical audit results.
1. *Search and retrieve* The auditor can have the program scan large files and retrieve specified items that have audit significance. For example, it can search depositors' accounts for unusual charges or it can identify dormant accounts.

2. *Select samples* The program can select a sample of records from a file population. Stratified sampling can be specified on the basis of upper and/or lower limits. Systematic sampling can be performed where every nth record is selected for further review or confirmation. Or simple random sampling can be specified with automatic generation of random numbers whereby records are selected on a random basis. Some programs can calculate and select a sample necessary to meet desired statistical confidence levels. Further, the program can calculate the arithmetic mean, standard deviation, and variance of the population. Inferences can be made from these statistics, such as estimation of total inventory from a sample.

3. *Perform basic calculations* The generalized audit program performs addition, subtraction, multiplication, and division. It also performs less than, greater than, or equal to logic operations to compare items. Much of the work done by the auditor requires a great deal of calculation, such as multiplying unit cost times quantity of items in inventory, deriving ratios, cross footing and balancing, verifying extensions, recomputation of interest and service charges, aging of accounts receivable, calculation of markup percentages, flagging inventory items with turnover less than a specified number, testing of payroll calculations, and determining amounts that are less than or greater than certain limits.

4. *Prepare subtotals* Totaling functions enable the auditor to print out subtotals and item counts. For example, in payroll auditing, the program can give levels of subtotals, such as by department, by plant, by state, by region, and so forth. It can also give end-of-file totals, such as number of records in the file, and total debits and credits.

5. *Compare, sort, and merge* Data, either alphabetic or numeric, can be sorted or merged in ascending or descending order. For example, this function allows the auditor to sort sales by salesman, customer, and region; sort inventory by department, item number, and price; sort cost variances by material and direct labor; or sort and merge geographically separate perpetual inventory files. The auditor can also match files on a given sequence and compare the data in one file with that in another. For example, a confirmation reply file can be compared with the confirmation log file and then print out for a second mailing those accounts not responding within a specified time. Or the auditor can compare payroll files for different periods based on employee number and department to see if there has been any significant change in pay rates, salaries, etc. from the last period.

6. *Copy data* This function simply copies records or fields from one file onto another. It can produce a tape file of all accounts to receive positive confirmation. The auditor may have the program create for him a work file of items that are of special interest, such as selling prices, item costs, payroll rates, and commission rates.

7. *User exits* To increase even further the generality and power of a generalized audit program, user exits are provided to permit the auditor to insert his own computer audit program. This capability enables the auditor to meet certain very specific audit requirements that cannot be handled by the general program.

8. *Summarize* Large-volume computer files can be quickly summarized to lessen the burden of making detailed reviews. This function creates desired totals and subtotals for a group of related records in a file.

9. *Printout* This function allows the auditor to specify the audit results in almost any format desired with descriptive major and minor headings over columns of data. Moreover, a great deal of flexibility is provided to the auditor for spacing, paging, and ordering of the output. This function enhances the organization and readability of the audit information.

Some practical results of applying generalized audit programs are listed below.

1. *Purchasing* In an automatic reordering system, the auditor discovered that certain parts were still being ordered, although the company was no longer manufacturing this particular unit. The auditor made his discovery by extracting all inventory items that had not had any activity for three months. The system was programmed to automatically order $190,000 of this particular part.

2. *Banking* The auditors recomputed monthly service charges and discovered that the bank was undercharging its clients by $48,000 per month.

3. *Inventory* The auditors discovered that 23 percent of the items carried in file were no longer manufactured. The company was able to reduce the size of its files by purging them of these items.

4. *Department store billing* The auditors extracted all accounts more than 150 days old and sorted them into date order. It was discovered that 80 percent were suspense accounts that were uncollectible and, therefore, that accounts receivable were being overstated. Further analysis detected numerous cases of fraud, loose credit practices, and inadequate procedures for error correction.

5. *Telephone billing* The auditors received a magnetic tape of the toll billing from the telephone company. The toll calls were sorted by terminating number. The auditors then extracted toll messages on the basis of predetermined dollar values, volume of calls made to a particular number, and calls made after normal working hours. The results of their finding indicated that 13 percent of the calls were non-business and that 1 percent were made by unauthorized personnel.

6. *Government agency* It was found through audit tests that more than 50 percent of spare parts requisitions were for amounts less than $25. Since the cost of processing each requisition was in excess of this

amount, losses were incurred on each transaction. New methods of handling spare parts requisitions resulted in significant cost savings.[5]

7. *Accounts receivable*   The receivables file was on magnetic tape. The file was footed and aged. High-value and credit items were selected for further verification. Review of the system had indicated there might be problems in the application of cash receipts to open receivable balances. The software package was used to foot and age unmatched cash items. It turned out that unapplied collections were equal to about 50 percent of the open receivable items. Of this, 12 percent were related to items more than five months old. Remedial systems changes were suggested.

8. *Obsolete inventory*   The finished parts inventory was on a disk file. The software package was used to foot the file and also to select high-value, negative balance, and items not physically counted for further investigation. Year-end provisions for obsolete and slow-moving stock were calculated by a computer program the client had developed. Audit software was used to simulate the client's processing and to provide a further check by comparing the calculated provision to records of past usage. The client's provision for obsolete or slow-moving inventory was found to be adequate.

9. *Insurance claims*   At year end, an insurance company had to provide a contingent liability for claims that had not been filed and claims for which the amount was uncertain. The computer audit software package was used to prepare statistical tables based upon activity over the past five years. On the basis of these tables, it was possible to develop a reasonable estimate of the contingent liability for the current period.

10. *Test of programmed controls*   Beyond its ability to test the contents of a data file, an audit software package can sometimes be used to verify the implementation and effectiveness of programmed controls. For example, a system that identifies or otherwise reports unbilled items might be tested by using the computer audit software to produce a list of unbilled accounts and then comparing that list to the one produced by the system. This would be another implementation of a simulation technique.[6]

11. *Interest overpayments*   The internal audit department at a major bank in Providence, Rhode Island, recently acquired a computer audit software package. They used it to check the interest computations on savings accounts. They discovered that the bank had been overpaying interest ever since it had computerized its savings accounts. There was a bug in the interest program. While individual overpayments involved

---

[5]Applications 1 through 6 are from Joe Wasserman, "Selecting a Computer Audit Package," *The Journal of Accountancy*, April 1974, p. 34.

[6]Applications 7 through 10 are from Robert S. Lynn, "Computer Auditing, A Broader Perspective," *The Chartered Accountant in Australia*, February 1975, pp. 15–18. Quoted from the Abstracts and Commentaries section of *EDPACS*, August 1975, pp. 14–15.

only a penny or two per customer per month, the total overpayment was more than $100,000. This is one case where the computer audit software paid for itself very quickly. Its very first application struck pay dirt.[7]

Advantages and Disadvantages

A generalized audit program offers the auditor many advantages. Most of these advantages stem from the fact that the program uses the computer as an audit tool. These advantages are:

1. The auditor can do more in less time. For example, the manual selection and examination of a large number of accounts receivable or preparation of a number of subtotals would be a fairly time-consuming process. With application of a generalized audit program, these kinds of tasks can be performed quickly and accurately. The morale of the audit staff may remain higher when tedious clerical tasks are relegated to the computer.

2. When there are severe problems related to volume, complexity, computation, and timing, application of a generalized audit program will most certainly result in a significant cost savings.

3. Greater reliance can be placed on the audit results. For example, rather than relying on test footing of the client's receivables trial balance, the auditor can use the generalized audit program to foot the complete file.

4. Only a few weeks of training and a minimal knowledge of computer technology are required. In the long run, however, this brief training may be a disadvantage, because the auditor should learn as much about computer programming and systems technology as he can.

5. The generalized audit program is under the control of the auditor. Therefore, he remains basically independent of computer systems personnel.

6. The program can perform a variety of audit tasks in many different systems. Therefore, special audit programs are not required for each job or each type of audit.

The disadvantages are:

1. Diversity of programming languages, computers, systems designs, and different data structures found in data base management systems may make the generalized audit programs incompatible and inoperative in a number of situations.

2. Some auditors, probably without justification, say that it requires too much time in training and that one must gain a lot of experience to use the program effectively.

---

[7]Donald L. Adams, "Score One for Audit Software and Consumers," *EDPACS*, February 1975, p. 7.

Selection Criteria

No one generalized audit program is the best for all situations. Many questions must be asked by the auditor before a decision can be made to select the appropriate program for his purposes. Cost is certainly a direct consideration, but the least expensive audit program may require much more computer time to run each audit; therefore, over a period of time the cost of additional computer time will more than offset the cost of the package. Other areas that should be considered in evaluating the purchase or lease of an audit program are:[8]

1. Does the package operate directly on your files, or do the files have to be converted or reconditioned? (File conversion increases running time.)
2. Does the package operate in your operating environment (e.g., core size, operating system, partitioned storage, etc.)?
3. Is the package efficient in terms of the auditor preparation time and computer time needed to process large files?
4. Are the editing routines comprehensive enough to insure complete and accurate processing?
5. If more than one computer center is to be audited, is the system portable?
6. Is the package largely self-documenting? (By retaining the original instructions, do you have a clear record of what was processed?)
7. Is there a user's group to provide for the sharing of audit information?
8. Does the vendor provide package maintenance? For what period of time?
9. What is the quality of the vendor's documentation?
10. Will the vendor provide a list of all its users? What is the vendor's reputation?
11. What is the quality of the training and installation program provided by the vendor?

Additional questions include:[9]

1. What data media must be processed? The particular client data to be processed must be evaluated in terms of the media used to record data. If the records are on a disk pack. the package selected must be able to handle disk.
2. Can the program handle different data structures? For example, some programs can process only the fixed portion of variable length records. This limitation could create an audit problem.
3. Can the program be run in a multiprogramming environment or used to extract specific records from an integrated data base?

---

[8] Wasserman, *op. cit.*, p. 32.
[9] Adapted from Gary F. Clark, "Software to Audit Computer Records," *Journal of Systems Management*, December 1974, pp. 26–30. For further information, see Gary F. Clark, "A Survey of Audit Retrieval Packages," *EDPACS*, October 1973.

4. Can the auditor add his own audit programs to the generalized audit program?

5. What computer systems is it compatible with? It's difficult to find programs written for computers other than IBM.

6. What media can be used as output? For example, some programs will not produce a card file.

7. What is the level of installation support? The extent and quality of installation and conversion support can be of vital importance. If a purchaser is paying a substantial amount for a package, say more than $10,000, he should expect a reasonable amount of initial onsite installation support. The extent of the onsite support included in the purchase price should be clearly spelled out, and any charges for additional services should be identified in advance.

11.6 UTILITY PROGRAMS SUPPLIED BY COMPUTER VENDORS

Most leading computer vendors have a large number of general-purpose utility programs in their libraries. Most of these programs are not viewed as audit programs per se. However, because audit functions require extracting data from computer file media, sorting, copying, analyzing, testing, and monitoring processes, and many of these programs perform these same functions, they can readily be included in the auditor's tool bag as effective audit techniques.

The availability of these programs to the auditor may not be obvious, because they have not been generally employed in a traditional auditing context. The auditor may have to make inquiries to vendors, stressing the need for utility programs that can be used to perform audit tasks.[10] The obvious advantages of these programs to the auditor are: (1) they provide meaningful audit information that may be difficult to obtain by other techniques, (2) they give the auditor assurance of operation, because they have already been tested and debugged and performance is guaranteed, (3) they provide a high level of integrity because they are developed by an independent third party, (4) they are usually supported by good documentation, and (5) they are useful in performing a one-time audit task that does not justify the development of a special audit program.

11.7 SUMMARY

All of the audit techniques presented in this chapter require use of the computer. There is an almost unlimited number of tasks that the com-

---

[10] IBM has published a catalog listing 124 programs that may be helpful to computer auditors. This publication is *Auditability Information Catalog,* Pub. No. GB21-9883, (White Plains, N.Y.: IBM, Data Processing Division).

puter can perform for the auditor quickly and accurately. The only way auditors can get at computerized data, analyze them for audit information, and perform many of the tasks they want performed is by means of some kind of audit program.

Four sources of these audit programs are: (1) programs written by a programmer who works for the organization that is being audited, (2) audit programs written by or under the supervision of the auditor, (3) generalized audit programs developed by accounting firms and software companies, and (4) utility programs and special packages supplied by computer vendors that can be used to perform additional auditing tasks. All of these audit programs have an important role to play in the practice of auditing.

Not all audit tasks require the use of the computer, even in a highly computerized system. Many manual and judgmental tasks will always have to be performed directly by the auditor without the aid of the computer, and just because an audit task can be computerized does not necessarily mean that it should be. In most instances, however, computer-assisted audit techniques provide many advantages. Accordingly, auditors should become familiar with these techniques and make intelligent application of them. In the past, many auditors have tried to go around the computer or find an easy way to auditing. Application of these audit programs is not as easy as it may sound, and the auditor will need more than a superficial knowledge to use these techniques properly. The auditor who is unprepared risks not only disenchantment with computer-assisted audit techniques but also the risk of generating inaccurate or meaningless results.

REVIEW QUESTIONS

11.1 Why should the auditor use computer-assisted audit techniques?
11.2 List and describe at least ten uses of the computer as an audit tool.
11.3 What is the purpose of a confirmation? What role can the computer play in the confirmation process? Are there tasks that the computer cannot perform? Explain.
11.4 List and give a brief description of the four sources of computer-assisted programs.
11.5 List the advantages and disadvantages of the auditor writing his own audit programs.
11.6 List the duties of a full-time programmer on the audit staff.
11.7 List and explain the functions of a generalized audit program.
11.8 List and explain the main issues in selecting a generalized audit program.

DISCUSSION QUESTIONS

11.1 "Old fraudulent schemes will not work on new computer systems." Discuss the merits of this statement.

11.2 Explain how to perpetrate fraud or embezzlement through the use of fictitious accounts.

11.3 Compare the merits of an auditor writing his own audit program and the merits of other alternatives.

11.4 Discuss the concept of generality as it applies to computer audit programs.

11.5 "The functions of a generalized audit program are really not any different from the functions in any audit program." Explain what is meant by this statement.

11.6 "Programs are programs; it doesn't matter what you call them." Discuss.

11.7 List and discuss at least four audit applications of vendor-supplied programs.

EXERCISES

11.1 Develop a receivables confirmation plan, listing and explaining each step you would follow. What use would you make of the computer in your confirmation process?

11.2 A CPA's client, Boos & Baumkirchner, Inc., is a medium-sized manufacturer of products for the leisure-time activities market (camping equipment, scuba gear, bows and arrows, etc.). During the past year, a computer system was installed, and inventory records of finished goods and parts were converted to computer processing. The inventory master file is maintained on a disc. Each record of the file contains the following information:

> Item or part number
> Description
> Size
> Unit of measure code
> Quantity on hand
> Cost per unit
> Total value of inventory on hand at cost
> Date of last sale or usage
> Quantity used or sold this year
> Economic order quantity
> Code number of major vendor
> Code number of secondary vendor

In preparation for year-end inventory, the client has two identical sets of preprinted inventory count cards. One set is for the client's inventory counts and the other is for the CPA's use to make audit test counts. The following information has been keypunched into the cards and interpreted on their face:

- Item or part number
- Description
- Size
- Unit of measure code

In taking the year-end inventory, the client's personnel will write the actual counted quantity on the face of each card. When all counts are complete, the counted quantity will be keypunched into the cards. The cards will be processed against the disc file, and quantity-on-hand figures will be adjusted to reflect the actual count. A computer listing will be prepared to show any missing inventory count cards and all quantity adjustments of more than $100 in value. These items will be investigated by client personnel, and all required adjustments will be made. When adjustments have been completed, the final year-end balances will be computed and posted to the general ledger.

The CPA has available a general-purpose computer audit software package that will run on the client's computer and can process both card and disk files.

Required:
- **a.** In general, and without regard to the facts above, discuss the nature of general-purpose computer audit software packages and list the various types and uses of such packages.
- **b.** List and describe at least five ways a general-purpose computer audit software package can be used to assist in all aspects of the audit of the inventory of Boos & Baumkirchner, Inc. (For example, the package can be used to read the disk inventory master file and list items and parts with a high unit cost or total value. Such items can be included in the test counts to increase the dollar coverage of the audit verification.) AICPA adapted.

11.3 Explain what the following COBOL audit program does.

11.4 A payroll master file typically contains records of full-time, part-time, and inactive employees for the past year. Some employees are salaried, others are paid at an hourly rate. Employee records are coded to designate home office or field office employees. Also a code designates department worked in. Given a typical payroll master file stored on magnetic tape, describe how you would go about auditing it and what kind of evidential information you

PROBLEM 11.3

IDENTIFICATION DIVISION.
PROGRAM-ID.   AUDIT-PAYROLL.
AUTHOR.   MARK TICK.
ENVIRONMENT DIVISION.
CONFIGURATION SECTION.
SOURCE-COMPUTER.   BIG NUMBER CRUNCHER.
OBJECT-COMPUTER.   BIG NUMBER CRUNCHER.
INPUT-OUTPUT SECTION.
FILE CONTROL.
    SELECT TIME-CARDS ASSIGN TO CARD-READER.
    SELECT AUDIT-REPORT ASSIGN TO PRINTER.
DATA DIVISION.
FILE SECTION.
FD TIME-CARDS LABEL RECORDS ARE OMITTED
    RECORD CONTAINS 80 CHARACTERS
    DATA RECORD IS RECORD-IN.
01 RECORD-IN.
    02 EMPLOYEE-NO-IN   PICTURE X(4).
    02 NAME-IN   PICTURE X(20).
    02 HOURS-IN   PICTURE 99V9.
    02 RATE-IN   PICTURE 99V99.
    02 FILLER   PICTURE X(49).
FD AUDIT-REPORT LABEL RECORDS ARE OMITTED
    RECORD CONTAINS 132 CHARACTERS
    DATA RECORD IS AUDIT-RECORD.
01 AUDIT-RECORD.
    02 FILLER   PICTURE X(20).
    02 NAME-OUT   PICTURE X(20).
    02 FILLER   PICTURE X(5).
    02 GROSS-PAY-OUT   PICTURE 999.99.
    02 FILLER   PICTURE X(81).

```
WORKING-STORAGE SECTION.
77    GROSS-PAY                        PICTURE 999V99.
PROCEDURE DIVISION.
OPEN-FILES.
    OPEN INPUT TIME-CARDS, OUTPUT AUDIT-REPORT.
BEGIN-AUDIT.
    READ TIME-CARDS AT END GO TO END-OF-JOB.
    MOVE SPACES TO AUDIT-RECORD.
    MULTIPLY RATE-IN BY HOURS-IN GIVING GROSS-PAY.
    IF GROSS-PAY IS GREATER THAN 600.00
        MOVE NAME-IN TO NAME-OUT
        MOVE GROSS-PAY TO GROSS-PAY-OUT
        WRITE AUDIT-RECORD
    ELSE GO TO BEGIN-AUDIT.
END-OF-JOB.
    CLOSE TIME-CARDS, AUDIT-REPORT.
    STOP RUN.
```

would extract from it. Make any assumptions you deem necessary.

PROBLEMS

11.1   In a squat concrete building on the outskirts of town, a bank of IBM 370 computers receives, stores, updates, and distributes credit information on about 50 million Americans.

If the past is any guide, those 50 million Americans include at least a few phantoms, undetected by the computers. Despite tight security measures, con men and fraud rings have devised schemes to feed phony credit histories and identities into the computer files. And they have been able to doctor credit references of actual people to turn poor loan prospects into A-1 credit risks.

This particular data bank, called TRW Credit Data, is operated by a unit of Cleveland's TRW Inc. It is the biggest service providing information to subscriber businesses granting consumer credit—banks, finance companies, oil companies and large merchants.

As such, it has become a juicy target for con artists who are giving a new technological twist to the credit-fraud game. But TRW Credit Data isn't alone. Many credit-reporting services, including other large data banks, are being victimized with a frequency that suggests a growing crime wave.

Taking advantage of this, enterprising crooks are subverting the data banks in a number of ways. Some set up fictitious businesses that subscribe to the data services with the sole purpose of then pumping into the computer bogus transactions that establish bogus credit records in the data bank. Others use crooked employees at legitimate subscriber businesses to do the same thing. And some have been able to use employees at the data banks themselves, inducing them to file bogus information directly into the computers. The crooks then tap the artificially created credit themselves or peddle clean credit records to others.[11]

What audit techniques would you suggest to help detect such fraud? Explain how you would implement and perform them. Also indicate controls that may be helpful in combating this fraud.

11.2   Write an audit program in the computer language of your choice. If you cannot write in computer language, write the program in English. The following represents the input record layout.

EMPLOYEE NUMBER	EMPLOYEE NAME	HOURS WORKED	PAY RATE	GROSS PAY
PICTURE X(4)	PICTURE X(20)	PICTURE 99V99	PICTURE 99V99	PICTURE 999V99

[11]G. Christian Hill, "Large Loan Swindles Spread with Reliance on Central Data Banks." *The Wall Street Journal,* March 12, 1976, p. 1.

Have your program recalculate all employees' GROSS-PAY. Print out any variances. Also, print out all employees who worked more than 40 hours, who made more than $950, and who had a PAY-RATE greater than $12.50. Compute the total GROSS-PAY for a control total.

11.3 Following is a portion of the MASTER-SALES-FILE.

SALESMAN NUMBER	SALESMAN NAME	CURRENT SALES	PREVIOUS YTD SALES	SALES RETURNS
PICTURE X(5)	PICTURE X(15)	PICTURE 9(6)V99	PICTURE 9(6)V99	PICTURE 9(4)V99

Write a computer audit program to print out every SALESMAN-NUMBER and SALESMAN-NAME that meets the following conditions:

1. CURRENT-SALES over $5,000.
2. YTD-SALES equal to or greater than three times CURRENT-SALES.
3. SALES-RETURNS over $750.
4. SALES-RETURNS greater than 2 percent of CURRENT-SALES.

CHAPTER
12

MOVEMENT TOWARD EVENT PROCESSING SYSTEMS

12.1 INTRODUCTION

More advanced computer-based information systems are being developed at a rapid rate. The major purpose of these advanced systems is to capture the event when and where it takes place, so that it can make its impact on the system immediately.

These event processing systems have combined computer data processing technology with data communications technology whereby remote input/output terminals can gain ready access to the data base that is stored on direct access storage devices. The auditor must become more aware of these systems and their impact on auditing.

The purpose of this chapter is to discuss: (1) periodic versus event processing systems, (2) computer technology that supports event processing systems, (3) advanced information systems concepts, and (4) controls that are especially applicable to event processing systems. All the computer audit techniques that we have discussed so far are applicable to this kind of system. The next chapter will include those audit techniques that have special significance for event processing systems. Before discussing these control and audit techniques, a strong in-depth review should be made of this kind of system.

12.2 PERIODIC VERSUS EVENT PROCESSING SYSTEMS

There are basically two methods of processing data via computer systems: periodic and event processing systems. Other terms are used to describe these two methods. For example, periodic processing is also known as batch, sequential, serial, and offline processing, while event processing is often called online, inline, random access, time-sharing, or online real time systems. Although even experts disagree on the usage of such terms, in this text, periodic processing systems are those that process data and react to changes in the system on a periodic or cycle basis, and event systems process events as they occur and react immediately to changes. Following are the characteristics, advantages, and disadvantages of both processing systems.

Periodic Processing System Characteristics

With periodic processing (see Figure 12.1), source document forms are prepared that represent transactions or events, e.g., sales transaction, patient checking into a hospital, collection of cash. These forms are then keypunched and verified. The resulting punched cards are sorted in accordance with a key number and validated to determine whether there are any inaccuracies or omissions. Any forms that do not pass the validation process are rerouted for correction. Validated batches of these transactions are sorted and merged into a transaction file in the same order as the old master file stored in the file library. Both files are mounted and processed by matching a transaction key in the transaction file with a key of a record in the old master file. In this way, the record is updated and written on a new master file in sequence. Also, any reports needed can also be printed out at the same time. The new master file is returned to the library until the next process, when it becomes the old master file. Summary characteristics of periodic processing systems are as follows.

1. *Job shop-oriented* Each application is viewed as individual jobs or batches, each of which receives varying degrees of attention. For example, all jobs may be discontinued on Friday morning of every week to process payroll.

2. *File availability* As soon as they are updated, files are returned to the library. They are not available for processing until the next update cycle.

3. *Timing* The rationale for periodic processing is that transactions should be grouped into batches and processed periodically according to a planned schedule. The new master file is created during the current update cycle (e.g., payroll) by posting transactions that have accumulated during the period (e.g., time cards).

4. *Updating* The master file is updated by writing on a new file and the old master file is kept intact. For example, with magnetic tape processing, the old master file is mounted on a tape unit separate from

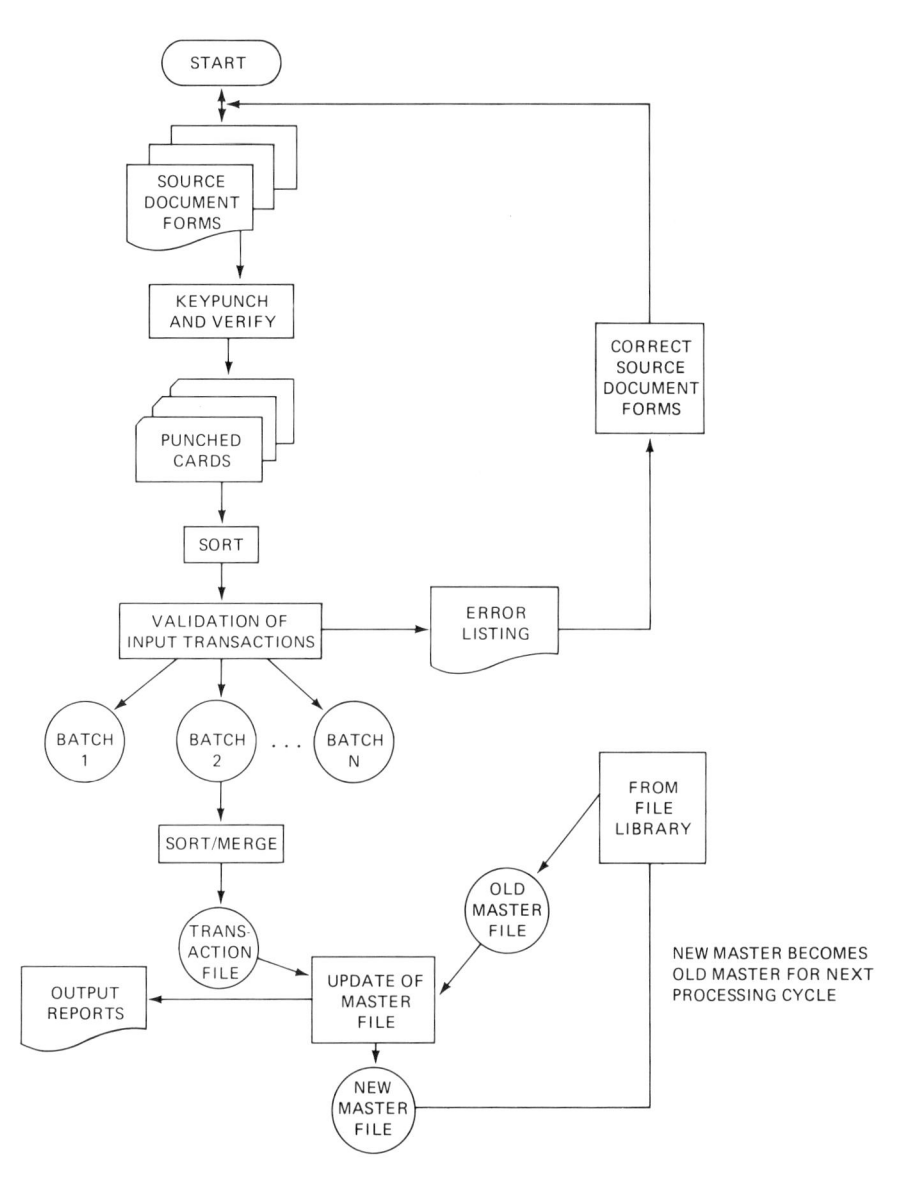

FIGURE 12.1.
The Sequence of Operations of a Typical Periodic Processing System.

the tape that will record the new master file. When the updating is completed, both the master file and the new master file exist, and the difference between the two is reflected in the transaction file.

5. *Organization of records* Records are stored and processed in a predetermined sequential order, usually in ascending order based on a

key such as account number. Before processing, both the transaction file and the master file must be sorted in the same sequence. Processing begins at the first record in both files, and they are related to each other by the appropriate number. When there is a match, the transaction record is posted to the master record and the results written on the new file. Processing ends when both files have been completely read from the first record to an end-of-file condition. Any file media can be used for sequential data organization, e.g., punched cards, magnetic tape, or disk.

6. *Interrelationship of processing functions* Similar activities of the organization may be handled in different ways and at different times. For example, a customer of a bank may have a savings account, a demand deposit account, and a loan, and all three files may be processed differently, so that, in effect, the customer is treated as three different customers.

Event Processing System Characteristics

With an event processing system (see Figure 12.2), transactions are input to master files as they occur on a random basis without presorting into batches. Each event location that captures the transaction as it occurs has a terminal device connected to the central computer and data base. The data base files are stored on direct access storage devices that are available at all times to add, delete, or change a record. Many of the terminals are input/output devices (e.g., CRT) that can also be used for interrogation purposes, i.e., a user can receive a specific response based on a specific inquiry. Typical applications include airline reservation systems; motel/hotel reservation and accounting systems; law enforcement systems; and savings, loan, and demand deposit accounting. It is important to realize that an event processing system is more than just an online system. Event processing implies real time, that is, the response from the computer has an impact upon the external environment. An example of such an impact is the production of an airline ticket via computer terminal. Summary characteristics of event processing systems are as follows:

1. *Process-oriented* Data are processed on a continuous basis, in contrast to the processing of jobs on a periodic basis. The computer system acts as an integral part of the total operations of the organization.

2. *File availability* Files are online and available to the system at all times for updating and inquiry purposes.

3. *Timing* The event processing system eliminates the time interval between the point an event takes place and the time the results of that event are entered into the system. Thus the data always reflect current conditions.

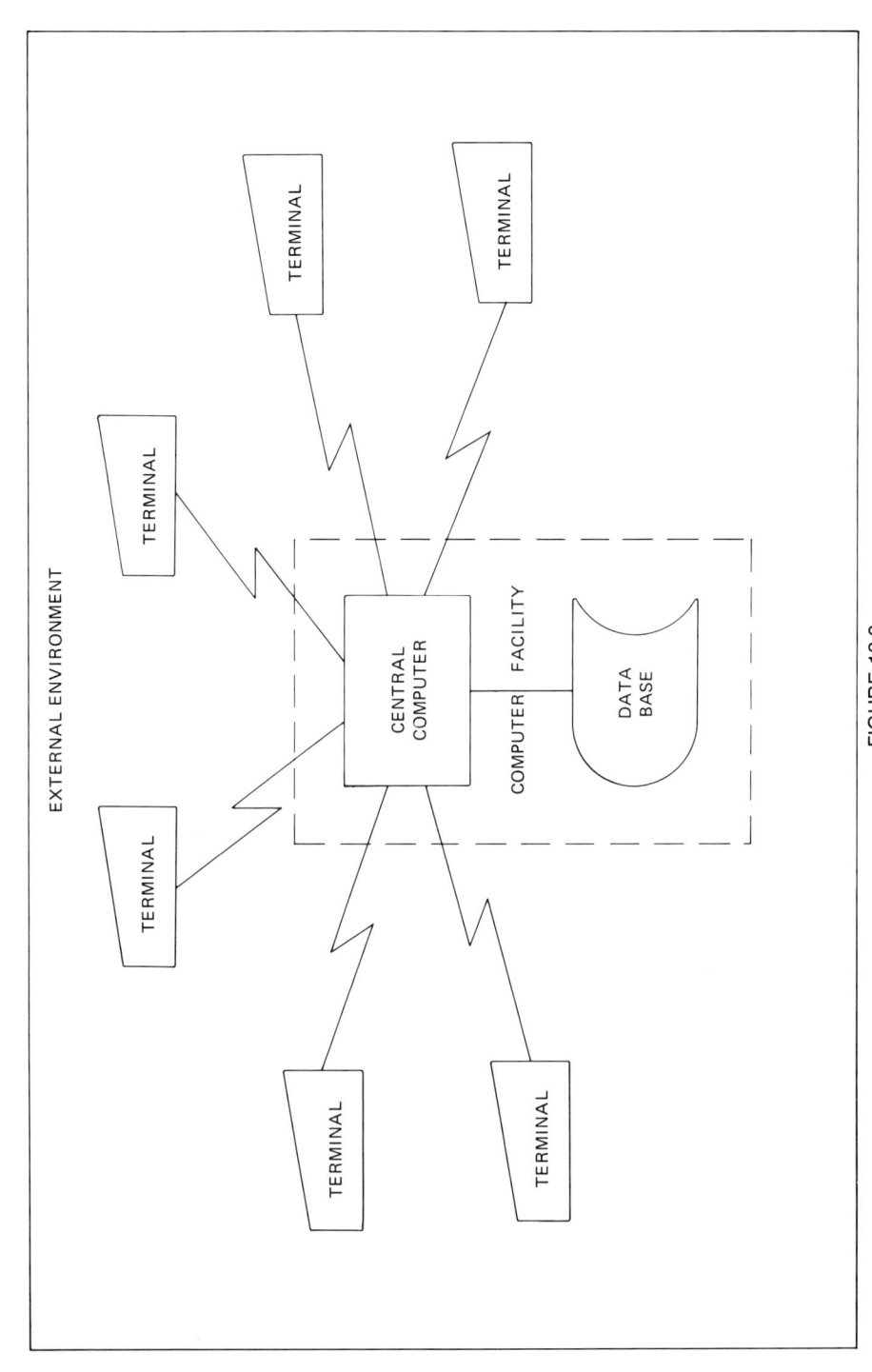

FIGURE 12.2.
Event Processing System.

4. *Updating* When an event occurs that requires a change in the master files, a record is accessed from a file into the central processing unit, updated, and written back to its original physical location. The original value of the record is lost or destroyed unless the updates are recorded on a transaction log in another file. This method of updating is called destructive or overlay updating, and it requires the use of direct access storage devices such as magnetic disk.

5. *Organization of records* Records are stored and processed in an indexed-sequential or direct manner. To access a certain record, the read-write mechanism of the direct access storage device need only position itself at the physical location of the record in question.

With indexed-sequential, data records are physically arranged in some predetermined sequence, as in sequential organization. However, in addition to this sequence, a table of addresses is established which equates to selected keys in the data records. The actual addresses are assigned to the records and inserted in the table as the file is created. The computer operating system has control over the location of the individual records. When a user needs to access a record, the desired record key is matched against the index table. Such an arrangement enables the user to locate a particular record without reading all preceding records. This approach is similar to using a card index to locate a book in the library.

To use direct organization, an access key in the record converts to a physical address by the use of a transformation technique, e.g., prime number division method. For example, the key of a record is 55; when it is divided by the prime number 13, a remainder of 23 is used to store this record in track 3 of cylinder 2. When the record is accessed, the same transformation algorithm is used to move the read/write mechanism to cylinder 2 and track 3. Using this method requires no predetermined sequence of records. They are, in fact, processed on a random basis.

6. *Interrelationship of processing functions* All similar activities of the organization are interrelated. For example, a sales transaction updates all pertinent files simultaneously, e.g., inventory, accounts receivable, sales, shipping.

Advantages and Disadvantages

The advantages and disadvantages of both processing systems are summarized below.

ADVANTAGES OF PERIODIC PROCESSING SYSTEMS

1. Ideally suited to applications where sequential ordered files make processing easier and where the nature of the application relates to a definite cycle, e.g., payroll.

2. Ideally suited to applications where a large portion of records are processed each time the file is accessed or during each processing cycle. For example, if there are 5,000 records in a payroll file and 4,500 of them had activity for the week, the activity ratio is 45/50 or 90%. This means that 4,500 records are changed in some way, and the other 500 are merely read from the old master file and written on the new master file unless some are deleted. As this activity ratio drops, it becomes less and less efficient to use the periodic approach.

3. Requires less expensive equipment and personnel.

4. Easier for many people to understand and work with because it is less integrated and complex.

5. Relates well to traditional accounting because all jobs and applications represent beginning and ending periods.

DISADVANTAGES OF PERIODIC PROCESSING SYSTEMS

1. Sequential organization of records increases searching time for a particular record and therefore is a poor application where output must be produced instantaneously.

2. Portions of the data base do not represent the current status of the organization, i.e., the system is constantly out of sync with the conditions in the organization. For example, an inventory file may show that there are 300 wrenches in stock, but because 100 have been sold since the last update cycle, the system has overstated by 100 the number of wrenches on hand. Such out-of-date information can obviously cause a number of operational problems.

3. Poor application where the activity ratio is low. For example, if during the day sales transactions represent only 10 percent of the file, the entire file would still have to be processed to update the 10 percent, and the 90 percent would be written unchanged on the new file. This situation wastes a lot of valuable processing time.

4. At times, reports that are available on a periodic basis may be irrelevant for decision-making. Any inquiry about the status of something may have to go unanswered until the processing cycle is completed.

5. As indicated earlier, periodic processing requires that both transaction and master files be sorted in sequential order. A lot of time and money are spent in sorting these records.

ADVANTAGES OF EVENT PROCESSING SYSTEMS

1. Ideally suited where timeliness of response is imperative.

2. Ideally suited where the master files are volatile, i.e., where records must be randomly accessed for information, or new records have to be added or deleted, or items in records must be changed in a spasmodic manner rather than in a periodic, routine manner.

3. By updating the files as pertinent events occur, the data base reflects the current status of the organization.

4. By logically relating and integrating files, the organization is viewed as a total system, rather than as an aggregation of disjointed departments working on their own. A single transaction can call into execution a number of programs and can simultaneously affect a number of master files; thus it can illustrate the interdependency of functioning within the organization.

5. Direct access storage devices provide for the read/write access mechanism to point to any record location without going through a sequential search.

6. Less offline data conversion and human intervention are required. For example, in periodic processing, the transaction may have to go through several stages before it can be read by the computer. With event processing, the transaction is captured and input directly into the system.

7. If sequential ordering of files is appropriate in some situations, direct access storage devices, particularly portable disk packs, can be efficiently used as sequential processors. This capability obviously provides additional flexibility, because sequential files such as magnetic tape cannot be used to support indexed-sequential or direct organization.

8. Input/output terminals can be located at the source of events, which are normally remote from the central processing unit. For example, many retail stores use online point-of-sale terminals to capture and record sales as they occur.

DISADVANTAGES OF EVENT PROCESSING SYSTEMS

1. It can be expensive and complex, requiring highly skilled personnel.

2. It represents a poor application where the activity ratio is high on all applications and where timeliness of information is not too important.

3. This approach, because of its high level of integration, requires stringent control procedures, especially in the area of backup and access security controls.

Hybrid Processing System

Although there is a strong movement toward event processing systems, many organizations continue to use both periodic and event processing systems to exploit each system's advantages. What they end up with is a hybrid system that encompasses both approaches.

Certainly, no organization has to use one approach or the other exclusively. For example, in many organizations, if not most, a hybrid system can be set up in one of two ways: (1) processing activities can be performed at different times, such as online activities during the business day and all of the accumulated transactions at night; or (2) both processing activities can be executed concurrently. In the latter case, what is required is multiprogramming that gives event transactions priority over periodic transactions. In this way, the computer system is used more efficiently, because it does not sit idle, waiting for the next online inquiry or periodic update to be processed.

A typical hybrid system is illustrated by the following characteristics of a banking operation:

1. *Response time* Response to a loan or demand deposit account status request by a teller must occur within a few seconds. The response time for other information requests, e.g., trust accounts may not be as critical.

2. *Mixed transactions* An online savings system may incorporate the processing of savings transactions, Christmas club payments, savings certificates, and mortgage payments in the transaction stream. However, probably only the savings transactions are posted immediately. All others are accumulated for periodic processing performed at night.

3. *Transaction queuing* Bank transactions tend to peak during relatively short periods of the day, e.g., 9:30–11:30 A.M. and 1:30–3:30 P.M. The event processing system receives more dedicated support during these peak times.

4. *Data communications network* A large bank with its many branches requires a network of data communications and many terminals.

5. *Complex operating system* The operating system that controls and supervises all the operations must have the ability to set background, foreground, priorities, interrupt procedures, and paging. These operations are discussed in more detail later in this chapter.

6. *Systems dependability and integrity* Since the lifeblood of a banking operation is the flow of data, it is imperative that the information system have a high degree of integrity and dependability. Any breakdown of the system, say, for more than a day, would be catastrophic.

12.3 COMPUTER TECHNOLOGY THAT SUPPORTS EVENT PROCESSING SYSTEMS

The development of sophisticated computer technology in recent years has made the ideas and concepts of event processing systems a reality. The key components of a computer configuration required to support these system concepts are: (1) advanced central processing units, (2) large-capacity direct access storage devices, (3) terminals, (4) communication channels, (5) modems, (6) multiplexers and concentrators, and (7) programmable communications processors. Some of the more significant aspects of these components are discussed below.

Overview of the Central Processing Unit

The heart of any computer configuration is the central processing unit, or CPU. First, the CPU is defined, and then a few methods are presented that help to increase its processing power.

The CPU is really the "computer" in a computer configuration, and all computer configurations perform five basic functions, which are:

1. *Input* The data to be operated upon and the instructions as to the method of operations are made available to the central processing unit in a form it can utilize via input media.

2. *Primary Storage* From the input media, data and instructions are entered into the main storage section of the central processor. Other storage media (e.g., magnetic tape, magnetic disk) are considered auxiliary to primary storage.

3. *Arithmetic-Logic* The processor manipulates the data in accordance with the algorithm of instructions. These manipulations are performed in the arithmetic-logic section, one operation at a time, and

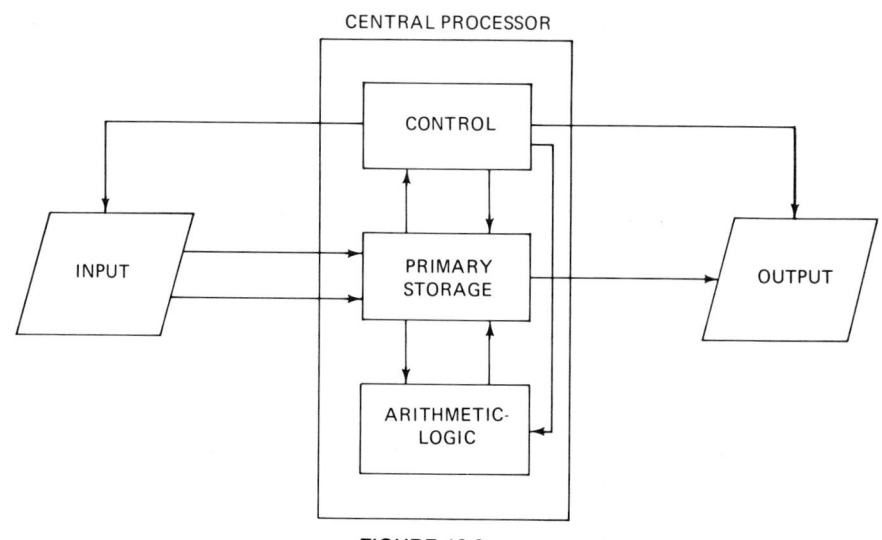

FIGURE 12.3.
General Diagram of a Central Processor.

intermediate results are placed back in primary storage. The arithmetic-logic section performs addition, subtraction, multiplication, division, and certain logical operations, such as comparing the magnitude of two numbers.

4. *Controls* Controls are required inside a computer system to: (1) tell the input media what data to enter into primary storage and when to enter it; (2) tell the primary storage section where to place these data; (3) tell the arithmetic-logic section what operations to perform, where the data are to be found, and where to place the results; (4) tell what file devices to access and what data to access; and (5) tell what output media the final results are written on.

5. *Output* This function refers to the output of the results of the data processed within the central processor. This final result is written on any one or a combination of the various output media.

A schematic of a computer system, emphasizing the central processor, is illustrated in Figure 12.3. All digital computers, regardless of size, speed, and details of operation, follow this same basic logical structure.

Operating Systems

Operating systems are also known as supervisor systems, control systems, and system control software. An operating system, or these other terms, is defined as an integrated system of programs which supervises the operations of the CPU, controls the input/output functions of the computer system, translates programming languages into machine languages, and provides various support services. It acts as an interface package between the users (e.g., application programmer) of the computer hardware and the hardware itself. These series of vendor-supplied software packages, which are stored both in the CPU and on auxiliary storage devices, are designed to increase the efficiency of operator requirements and computer usage with a minimal amount of human intervention. Operating systems have become indispensible for event processing systems to handle overlapped processing and multiprogramming requirements.

MULTIPROGRAMMING TECHNIQUE

Multiprogramming requires the allocation of portions of primary storage among various jobs and job segments. The operating system subdivides primary storage into several fixed or variable partitions. As shown in Figure 12.4, primary storage is subdivided into three partitions: one for the operating system, a foreground partition for high-priority programs, and a background partition for low-priority programs. For example, an event processing system such as inventory con-

```
        PRIMARY STORAGE
    ┌─────────────────────────┐
    │    OPERATING SYSTEM     │
    ├─ ─ ─ ─ ─ ─ ─ ─ ─ ─ ─ ─ ─┤
    │   FOREGROUND PROGRAM    │
    │  (Inventory control and │
    │   order entry processing)│
    ├─ ─ ─ ─ ─ ─ ─ ─ ─ ─ ─ ─ ─┤
    │   BACKGROUND PROGRAM    │
    │   (Payroll processing)  │
    └─────────────────────────┘
```

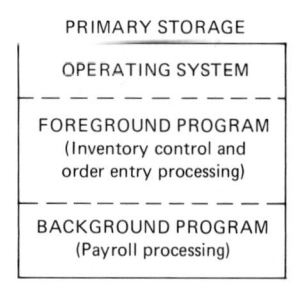

FIGURE 12.4.

Typical Example of a Multiprogramming System with Partitions.

trol and order entry connected to a number of remote terminals would use the foreground partition, while a periodic system such as payroll would use the background partition.

The foreground program(s) has priority over other background programs in the CPU. When data are not being processed by the foreground program, an interrupt occurs and a background program is executed. To handle the interruption and switching back and forth between programs, a supervisor program of the operating system remains in residence throughout processing. The CPU executes the instructions of one of the programs while a channel performs input/output operations. With the use of multiprogramming, periodic programs are processed by the same computer system that is available at all times for event processing programs.

VIRTUAL STORAGE TECHNIQUE

The basic idea behind virtual storage is the dynamic linking of primary storage of the processor and auxiliary storage so that to each user (several may be using the system concurrently) it appears that he or she has at his or her disposal a very large primary storage, usually measured in megabytes. Parts of a program or data associated with it may be broken up and scattered both in primary storage and magnetic disk or drum, thus giving the "virtual" effect of a much larger primary storage to the programmer. This technique is illustrated in Figure 12.5.

Normally only the instructions and data necessary for immediate processing are located in primary storage in the form of "pages" which are transferred between primary storage and slower auxiliary (DASD) storage automatically. With this approach, jobs are loaded into partitions or regions of a very large auxiliary storage space. During processing, small blocks or pages of instructions and data are transferred between auxiliary storage and processor storage according to the momentary needs of each job.

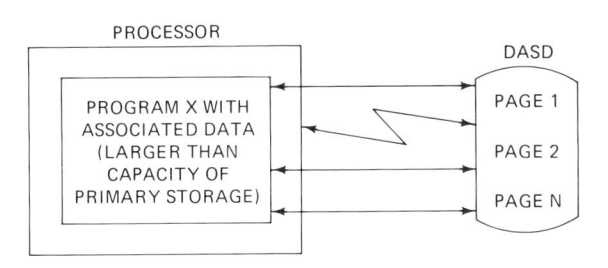

CHAPTER TWELVE   MOVEMENT TOWARD EVENT PROCESSING SYSTEMS   389

FIGURE 12.5.
Illustration of Virtual Storage.

With virtual storage, extremely large programs can be processed easily, since programs do not have to reside entirely in primary storage, and subdividing large programs into segments is no longer necessary. Only those pages of a program containing the specific instructions and data actually being processed are required in primary storage at one time.

The versatility of the virtual storage technique can be illustrated in the following summary points.

1. The limited amount of available primary storage space has been a barrier to applications. From a programmer's viewpoint, virtual storage allows him or her to write a much larger program without worrying about whether it will fit into the confines of primary storage. In many applications, it is not unusual for a program to run over 200K. Many conventional processors were unable to hold a program of this size; consequently, a great deal of time and cost was spent segmenting the program so it could be used in multiple-job steps. In the past, as high as 20% or more of programming productivity went into trying to get programs to fit primary storage.

2. Virtual storage will have a noticeable effect on the flexibility provided systems analysts and programmers in the design of new applications. The availability of such a large address space creates an entirely new environment in which to plan program modules and job runs. There are no basic changes in the approach to the actual programming or operations as such. Although addresses in virtual code may specify locations far outside the limits of primary storage, all such virtual addresses will be referenced automatically by means of dynamic address translation handled by the computer's operating system. Since the task of managing primary storage and of transferring pages between primary storage and auxiliary storage is performed by the operating system, all of these functions are said to be "transparent" to the programmer, i.e., he or she need not be concerned with them.

3. An online teleprocessing application that faces a varying message volume will not need a large dedicated space in processor storage. Such

a terminal-oriented, event-driven application may be supported for longer hours, perhaps into the second shift, since background jobs will use almost all resources when the top-priority application does not need them.

4. A data base application, which would otherwise be handled on a once-a-day batch basis because of its extensive storage requirements, may be put online to terminals for at least a few hours a day.

5. A high-priority job can usually be started immediately without disrupting any long-running jobs with extensive storage space. In many cases, a significant improvement in turnaround time may result for urgent jobs. For example, in a configuration, at one time, there could be a resident writer, resident teleprocessing program, a region reserved for "hot" jobs, and two or more batch regions large enough for the running of large jobs.

Terminals

Terminals are devices that are used to get the data into the system and the information out of the system. Terminals are fundamental to an online system. Terminal hardware varies with the needs of the different users throughout the organization. Terminals vary from simple teletypewriters to card readers, high-speed printers, CRT's, magnetic tape units, and so on. The distance of the terminal from the central processor has no effect on its function. Move a magnetic tape unit to a plant 500 miles from the central processor, add a communication data control unit, connect it to a communication channel, and it becomes a remote job entry (RJE) terminal. Hook up a CRT to the data base and one has an interrogative terminal, and so on.

In this section, the discussion involves primarily three types of terminals: (1) telephone terminals, (2) intelligent terminals, and (3) point-of-sale (POS) terminals.

TELEPHONE TERMINAL

The Touch-Tone (sometimes used with the Picturephone)* is an example of a low-speed terminal in the sense that it can handle effectively only low volumes of data. This telephone can be used for voice or data communications. It can be used to update files, retrieve response information either by voice answer-back or printout or visual display on other devices. Two examples of the use of telephone terminals are given below.

*Touch-Tone and Picturephone are registered trademarks of the Bell System.

(1) Such a system can help to maintain up-to-the-minute status on a multiplicity of inventory items during their transit through the logistics system. For example, a dispatcher from a plant transmits shipping information such as load location, size, content, and shipping priority by a simple numeric code to the organization's warehouse. The warehouseman who receives this information via a teletypewriter can then prepare available space and coordinate loading and unloading facilities with maximum efficiency.

(2) Such a system can provide credit status on credit card customers. Clerks type in an access code to the central processor, the customer's account number, and the amount of the purchase. By voice answerback, heard only by the clerk, the central processor either approves the transaction or instructs the clerk to call the credit department for further instructions. The computer has a 64-word recorded "vocabulary" which makes possible as many as 48 different types of responses, depending upon the transaction. Sixty Touch-Tone telephones in a system can handle as many as 720 inquiries per hour. A similar system could be used as an order entry system in conjunction with reporting inventory availability to incoming calls from customers and/or salesmen.

INTELLIGENT TERMINAL

An intelligent terminal incorporates a processing capability, usually in the form of a minicomputer. This minicomputer has the capability to perform operations on the data it handles in addition to transmitting it to a central processor.

Minicomputers have three basic characteristics. They are: (1) physically small; (2) relatively inexpensive; and (3) stored program with at least 4K words of primary storage where word lengths vary from 8 to 24 bits, the most common being 12 and 16 bits.

A minicomputer has three basic uses: (1) as a data communications control device, (2) as a general-purpose computer system with a variety of peripheral devices and software wherein it functions as a full-capacity computer system in its own right, and (3) as an intelligent terminal.

Intelligent terminals are used to: (1) extend the power of the central computer, and (2) accept data at its origin and perform some level of processing. Many of the intelligent terminals include minicomputers which can be used for different purposes depending on how they are configured and programmed. For instance, by using one set of peripherals and programs, a remote job entry (RJE) system is developed, and by using a different set of peripherals and programs, a data entry system such as a remote key-to-disk system is created.

With the advent of lower costs and greater availability of computers and data communication systems, the use of RJE systems has become cost/effective for small users who cannot economically justify their own data-processing systems. Also, this RJE technique is applicable to the distributed information systems approach with a large organization wherein different plants or divisions have their own subsystems which, in turn, are connected to other subsystems or to a central processor.

Also, intelligent terminals are used to provide a form of backup for the central computer. If non-intelligent terminals are connected to the main processor, and this processor breaks down, the terminals are disabled, and for all practicable purposes, the entire system is down. Transactions cannot be entered and processed. At most, transactions might be captured on paper tape or magnetic tape for later transmission to the computer. With an intelligent terminal, it is feasible for the terminal to accept transactions and perform some of the processing when the main computer is down or the data communications system is disrupted. This capability is one of the main reasons why banks and retail stores have selected intelligent terminals. Sales transactions in a store or savings transactions in a financial institution can be recorded at the terminal for processing and later transmitted if necessary, even though the central computer is down.

Another reason for using the intelligent terminal is that it can relieve the central processor of some of the processing workload. This situation helps to reduce an overload on the central processor and enables the system to get along with a smaller central processor than would otherwise be the case.

POINT-OF-SALE (POS)

Point-of-sale systems provide a method by which vital data are captured at the point-of-sale, for example, in department stores, supermarkets, and large discount stores. However, the same technique is applicable to other user categories where it is important to capture data at the time of an event or transaction. For example, in a production control system, a POS system can capture data and report production information in the time frame where it is still valid.

This technique uses either hand-held "wand" readers or stationary sensors which capture price, stock, and other data from merchandise tags or tickets that contain either optical or magnetic characters (e.g., bar codes). All of these readers in the organization are linked either to a central processor or to an intelligent terminal. The main advantages are:

1. It provides large-scale data collection and online capabilities.
2. A large department store sells thousands of items at many different locations. There must be quick identification of such items as credit status and trends in sales of high-fashion merchandise.

3. The method of reading optically or magnetically encoded characters on tickets and product items speeds up the sales transaction to the mutual benefit of the buyer and seller.

The magnetic-stripe credit card (MSCC) is a relatively new type of card that works quite well in a POS environment. It makes the idea of a cashless society more feasible by transferring money from the bank account of the buyer who is the holder of the MSCC to the bank account of the seller. The entire payment transaction is handled through a terminal connected to the bank's computer. No money passes hands, i.e., the payment is made electronically.

The terminal, such as a hand-held wand or slot reader, reads the customer's account number of the MSCC, and the clerk keys in the amount of purchase and any other data needed in the system. The CPU in the bank immediately makes a number of control checks, such as checking to see if the account number is on the hot list file, frequency of use, and acceptability of purchase with respect to credit limit. If the credit purchase is acceptable, an authorization number is automatically displayed on a CRT at the POS terminal (audio response or hardcopy printers can also be used to provide the authorization number). This operation closes the transaction. Such a system requires little human intervention as only a small number of referral clerks are needed at the bank to handle exceptions.

Communication Channels

Communication channels are comprised of one or a combination of the following: (1) telegraph lines, (2) telephone lines, (3) radio links, (4) coaxial cable, (5) microwave, (6) satellite, and (7) experimental laser beam and helical waveguides. Depending on the terminal equipment and the application required, the channels can be arranged for operation in one or more of the three basic transmission modes:

1. *Simplex*   Transmission is made in one direction only.
2. *Half-duplex*   Transmission can be in both directions, but not at the same time.
3. *Full-duplex*   Transmission can be made in both directions at the same time.

Channels are graded on speed of transmission, which is directly proportional to bandwidth. For example, telegraph lines are narrow-band, telephone lines are voice-band, and coaxial cable or microwave are broad-band. The bandwidth of a channel is measured by a unit called a Hertz (Hz), which means cycles per second. Empirical studies have shown that the bandwidth of a channel should be approximately twice the number of bits to be transmitted per second. For example, if one is to transmit data at 1,200 bits per second (bps), then a channel with a bandwidth of 2,400 Hz is required. However, it is simplest to classify communication channels as: (1) low-speed, (2) medium-speed, and (3) high-speed.

LOW-SPEED CHANNELS

This grade is narrow-band and was originally developed for use with teletypewriters (TTYs). It transmits data in the range of 45, 75, 110, 150, and 300 bits per second. AT & T developed the TWX (Teletypewriter Exchange Service), which consisted of a network of channels and teletypewriters that covered the United States and Canada. This service has been sold to Western Union but will continue over the Bell System network for the next several years. This system will eventually be integrated with Western Union's TELEX system.

With the TWX system, each customer is assigned a TWX number which is listed in a nationwide TWX directory. Any user can transmit data to another user by dialing the central operator, who makes the connection. This method is called a "switched" service, which means that a connection is made by dialing and is disconnected at the end of transmission. A "dedicated" line, on the other hand, is a line that remains connected between its terminal points for the duration of the lease.

A usage charge is based on the airline distance between two stations and the connect time between the two stations for switched lines. For dedicated lines, a charge is made monthly.

MEDIUM-SPEED CHANNELS

This grade is voice-band and is provided by the Bell System and the independent telephone companies. These voice-band channels are used interchangeably for voice and data communications. Their typical transmission rate is 300–9600 bits per second. Three types of service are available: (1) private line, (2) the dial-up network, and (3) WATS.

1. *Private Lines* The major differences between this system and a dial-up system is that the channel remains connected for the duration of the lease, the routing can be chosen, and the line can be electrically conditioned so that the transmission rate can be increased. Private lines are leased on a monthly basis with unlimited usage. The rate is a function of airline miles from point to point.

Conditioning refers to the process by which the telephone company maintains the quality of a specific, privately leased line so that it conforms to a certain standard of permissible error rate. Such conditioning adjusts the frequency and phase response characteristics of the channel to meet closer tolerance specifications.

An additional type of private line service of interest to the systems analyst is the foreign exchange line (FX line). This service in effect connects a user to an exchange other than his or her own; thus allowing toll-free calling to telephones served by that exchange. However, channel conditioning is not available.

2. *Dial-up or Public Switched Network* The dial-up or public switched network is currently the most commonly used method of transmitting data. The channel is available as long as the connection is made, and payment varies according to mileage, time of day or night, and duration of connect time. The rate approximates the rate for a normal voice telephone call. The average speed of transmission is generally from 2000 to 2400 bits per second.

Since each dial-up connection may involve a unique combination of channels, the telephone company does not guarantee the characteristics of the dial-up channels. Consequently, to achieve high transmission rates (2000–2400 bps) on a dial-up network, the required conditioning must be performed within the modem. Such a modem rapidly determines the channel characteristics and compensates for them at the start of the connection and then continuously adapts to any changes during connect time.

3. *Wide Area Telephone Service (WATS)* WATS is a pricing arrangement for users of large-volume data (and voice) transmission over long distances. WATS offers two billing plans: (1) a full-period service, and (2) a measured time service. Under full-period service, the subscriber may use the channel as much as he or she wishes in the geographical area for which he or she subscribes at a flat monthly rate. Under measured time service, the basic monthly rate covers the first ten hours of use per month for calls to Data-Phones (or telephones) within the subscribed service area. An additional charge per hour of actual use is levied beyond the first ten hours; however, the tariff that governs this service is extremely complicated, and full explanation of it is beyond the scope of this text.

HIGH-SPEED CHANNELS

Where data are to be transmitted at high speeds and very high volumes, a broadband service should be used. Both the Bell System and Western Union offer leased broadband services. These broadband lines comprise a group of channels of voice grade. Each channel when properly arranged can carry voice, computer data, or facsimile signals. Two classes of services (formerly called **TELPAK**) are offered.

1. *Type 5700 Line* Has a base capacity of 60 voice grade channels and a maximum equivalent bandwidth of 240 kHz (Kilo-hertz).

2. *Type 5800 Line* Has a capacity of 240 voice grade channels and a maximum equivalent bandwidth of 1,000 kHz.

This service is quite flexible because it can be used as a single broadband channel for fast and voluminous data transmission or as several individual lower-speed channels. In certain cases, two user groups with similar needs may share a line, whereas they could not afford such a service on an individual basis. A flat monthly rate is charged for this service, regardless of the volume of data transmitted. This rate is based on the number of channels, total capacity, and distance between transmission points.

Some companies have found it more economical and efficient to develop and use their own private-line microwave systems. Oil companies, in particular, have made use of microwave communication. Other broadband transmission services with capacity up to 230,000 bps (bits per second) are available only to United States government agencies.

In the future, it is projected, the user will connect the computer to a satellite transmission system in the same way that a dial-up user now connects to a telephone system. These systems will use several differing technologies including cables, microwave, and time-division multiplexing. The carrier that provides satellite channels will have to provide the user with the same transparency that he or she currently receives with other data communication systems, which means that software and hardware will remain basically the same. It is also projected that users will turn to satellite transmission in the future for two reasons: (1) the greater bandwidth available and the superior quality of the circuits will make them much more desirable than present telephone facilities, and (2) it will provide inexpensive digital transmission facilities.

Modems

Modem is an acronym for *mo*dular-*dem*odulator and is known as a data set. Modems are used to handle the data stream from a peripheral device to the central processor or vice versa through the common carrier network. The modem can operate in simplex, half-duplex, or full-duplex mode.

Telephone channels were developed for voice transmission, which is analog. In communication applications involving digital data, the modular portion of a modem converts digital dc pulse, representing binary 1's and 0's, by the computer or peripheral equipment, to an analog, wavelike signal acceptable for transmission over analog telephone channels. The demodulator reverses this process, converting the analog telephone signal back into a pulse train acceptable to the peripheral or computer at the other end. For example, see Figure 12.6. If a modem was not used to convert/reconvert data signals, and the computer or peripheral was directly connected to the telephone channel, the signal would be degraded and the data made unintelligble by the electrical characteristics of the channel.

Modems can be categorized into two broad types: (1) those handling asynchronous data, and (2) those handling synchronous data. Asynchronous modems are usually associated with keyboard entry terminal devices such as CRTs and TTYs. Synchronous modems are used with continuous data sources such as punched paper tape readers, magnetic tape, and magnetic disk.

Multiplexers and Concentrators

The basic aim of using multiplexers or concentrators is to permit connection of more peripherals to the central processor using fewer channels. Their use, therefore, is not a technological decision but an economical one.

MULTIPLEXERS

When a number of low-speed and/or low-activity remote terminals are connected online to the central processor, it is desirable to provide some method of allowing access for each of the flow or infrequently used terminals to the central processor. A voice-band grade channel capacity ranges from 300 to 9600 bits per second according to type of service and line conditioning. However, many of the most widely used remote terminals operate at speeds between 45 and 300 bits per second, with 100–150 bits per second being typical. Where there are a number of such terminals in one or more areas outside the toll-free zone of the central processor, the common carrier tariff structure makes it economically attractive to operate a group of such terminals through one voice-band grade channel instead of connecting them separately to the central processor via a number of narrow-band grade channels. In most situations of this type, multiplexing will reduce the cost of the communication

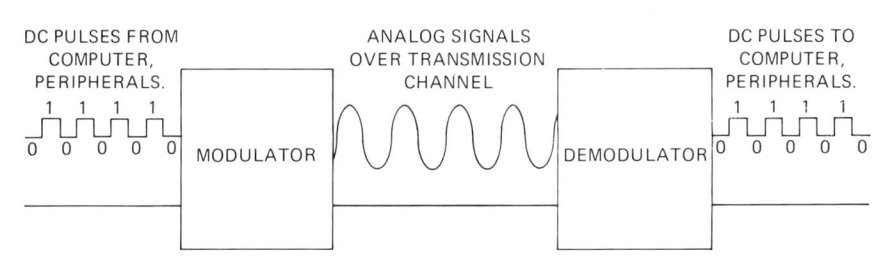

FIGURE 12.6.
Illustration of modulation-demodulation.

network by allowing one voice-band grade channel to substitute for many sub-voice (slow-speed, telegraph) channels that might otherwise be poorly utilized. Figure 12.7 illustrates a communication system before and after multiplexing.

As shown in the example below, the multiplexer accepts inputs from several terminal sources, combines these inputs, and then transmits the combined input over one channel, and at the other end (not shown) a similar unit again separates the discrete data inputs for further processing.

CONCENTRATOR

A concentrator differs from a multiplexer because it allows contention in the system. For example, a concentrator accommodates X number of terminals but allows only a portion of them to transmit their data over the available lines. There may be twelve terminals but only six channels. All terminals must contend for the channels, and those that do not make connection are "busied out." With a multiplexer, all terminals can be accommodated because the basic assumption is that all terminals are used 100% of the time.

The concentrator works as a normal switching device that polls one terminal at a time. Whenever a channel is idle, the first terminal ready to send or receive gets control of one of the channels and retains it for the duration of its transaction. The concentrator then continues to poll the

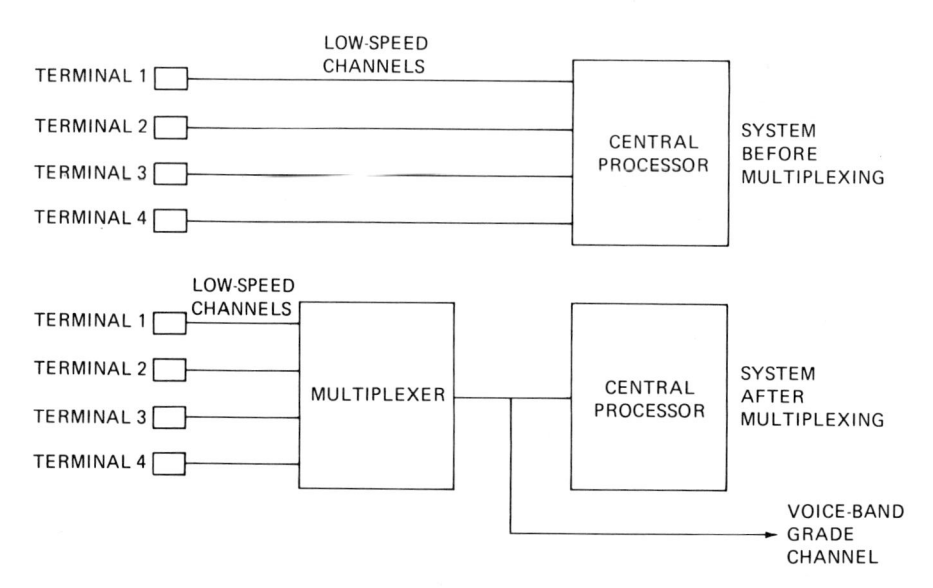

FIGURE 12.7.
Communication System before and after Multiplexing.

other channels in sequence until another terminal is ready to transmit. Each terminal has a code address by which it identifies itself when it requests transmission and to which it responds when addressed by the central processor. Whenever any terminal is engaged in a transaction with the central processor, the voice-band grade channel is unavailable to the other terminals for sending or receiving, i.e., the other terminals are "busied out" by the active ones. If several transactions occur simultaneously, each terminal must wait its turn on a FIFO (first-in, first-out) basis.

The cost savings in using a multiplexer are based on combining the data, and the cost savings in using a concentrator are based on the amount of data traffic in the system. In effect, the use of a concentrator is based on the assumption that all of the terminals will not be in contention for the available facilities at any one time.

Programmable Communications Processors

As long as the total number of peripherals, local and remote, and the amount of data transmitted are maintained at a certain level, the computer operating system (in residence) can execute the interrupts, move the data into and out of storage, and perform the necessary housekeeping without significant throughput penalty. However, if the number of terminals and volume of data increase to a point, computer throughput is significantly reduced. At this point, it may be more economical to move these functions out of the computer mainframe and into a communications processor. These processors perform some, if not all, of the following functions:

1. Housekeeping—the handling of message queues and priorities, processing of addresses, data requests, message blocks, file management, and updating the executive on peripheral activity.

2. Error checking and retransmission requests to prevent incomplete messages from reaching the host processor.

3. Code translation into the "native" code of the host CPU.

4. Preprocessing and editing.

5. Communications analysis processing—error analysis, the gathering of traffic statistics, and so forth.

6. Establishing and acknowledging the required channel connections including automatic dialing, if this is a feature of the system.

7. Verifying successful completion of the message, or detecting line breaks and either calling for or executing remedial action.

8. Disconnecting after a completed message, to permit polling to resume.

9. Assembling the serial bit stream into a bit-parallel buffered message.

10. Routing messages to and from required memory locations and notifying the software as required.

The major advantage of moving these functions from the central processor (host computer) to a communications processor is economic. With a large number of terminals or communications lines, as much as half the processing time of the host computer (even a large one) can be spent in input-output processing and line control. A separate, specialized computer can perform the same functions with fewer steps and simpler software, reducing direct processor time costs, programming costs, and debugging time. The lease or purchase price of the communications processor is often one or two orders of magnitude lower than that of the main computer; if it can assume work that formerly occupied half the main computer's time, it can obviously be justified economically.

The increased use of programmable communications processors can be directly attributed to the current proliferation of low-cost flexible minicomputers, and also to the developments in integrated circuit technology that have made it possible to manufacture digital computers at greatly reduced costs. The application of programmable communications processors are described below.

MESSAGE-SWITCHING

In message-switching, the communications processor acts principally as a data traffic director. It normally does not perform any data-processing activities (there are exceptions) beyond handling the message itself. In most systems a terminal transmits (or "talks") only to the host computer, but with a message-switching system, a terminal can talk directly to another terminal by going through the message-switching processor. This processor, then, becomes the central exchange in a fully interconnected communications network.

The message-switching computer itself can perform many of the functions of a front-end processor (discussed next), including error checking and correcting, code conversion, preprocessing and editing, and other functions previously listed in this section. In addition, it constantly monitors data traffic on the channels, directing messages through the most efficient and least costly route. It can compensate for channels going down and reroute data traffic accordingly.

FRONT-END

The front-end processor takes over most, if not all, of communications functions from the host CPU. Channels from various terminals and remote concentrators end at the front-end processor, and this processor in

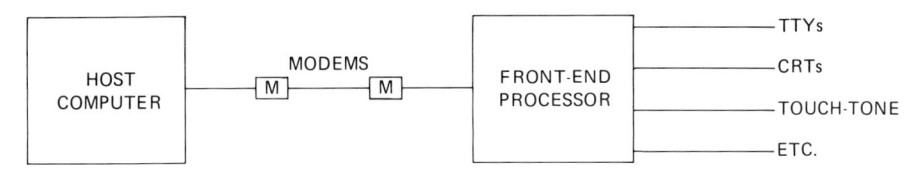

FIGURE 12.8.
Typical Front-End Processor Communications System.

turn transmits "clean" data to the host computer. It performs all of the functions listed at the beginning of this section. A typical front-end processor communications system is illustrated in Figure 12.8.

REASONS FOR USING PROGRAMMABLE COMMUNICATIONS PROCESSORS

Programmable communications processors are enjoying increased popularity in various parts of data communications systems because they are demonstrating themselves to be more cost/effective. General factors that contribute to this cost/effective edge include the following:

1. A large host processor is designed to work optimally when it can function continuously, executing a full set of program instructions on one application before branching to another. Interruptions and delays in handling data communications traffic consume large amounts of primary storage, which, in turn, reduces productivity and throughput.

2. The communications processor presents a standard I/O interface so that programmers do not have to constantly adapt software to terminals.

3. Its capability to adapt to changing requirements adds flexibility to the total system. For example, it can easily accommodate, without major modification, new terminals, more channels, and new devices with different characteristics.

4. A group of processors can very readily support a distributed system. They can be programmed to perform varying amounts of productive processing and can share portions of the overall processing load with other processors in the system, including the central processor.

5. When programmable communications processors are not involved in their principal data communication tasks, they can often be used as stand alone data-processing systems. Simple media conversion tasks, such as card-to-tape and tape-to-print, can be valuable by-products from these otherwise communications-oriented processors. They can also act as a backup to the host computer, and thus increase system reliability.[1]

---

[1]This section adapted from John G. Burch, Jr., and Felix R. Strater, Jr., *Information Systems: Theory and Practice* (Santa Barbara, Calif.: Hamilton Publishing Company, 1974), Appendix B.

12.4 INFORMATION SYSTEM CONCEPTS THAT REQUIRE EVENT PROCESSING SYSTEMS

Information system concepts are not new. Much of the current thought in this area has carried over directly from the design concepts of earlier data-processing systems, both manual and computer-based. In recent years, some of the concepts have been implemented. The current state of the art in the area of information systems bodes well for further development of more sophisticated information systems.

GOAL OF THE INFORMATION SYSTEM

Apparently, many chief executives have a clear idea as to what kind of system is required to produce information. Witness, for example, the following definition, which received a 95 percent acceptance among 600 responding executives surveyed by the Financial Executives Institute:

> ... A system designed to provide selected decision-oriented information needed by management to plan, control and evaluate the activities of the corporation. It is designed within a framework that emphasizes profit planning, performance planning and control at all levels. It contemplates the ultimate integration of required business information subsystems, both financial and nonfinancial, within the company. To be effective, it requires interrelated coding, processing, storage and reporting. It involves a systematic approach toward providing information that is timely, meaningful, and readily accessible. The subsystems will satisfy both the routine and special reporting needs of management efficiently and effectively, to plan and control the acquisition, use and disposition of corporate resources.[2]

Analysis of Information Systems

To attain the goal of management outlined above, the information system will have to be developed in accordance with the simplistic model depicted in Figure 12.9. This model is similar to any conversion process whereby raw materials, in this case data, are converted into a finished product, information. Information produced by the processes becomes a valuable resource used by managements and constituents of organizations to increase knowledge and make effective decisions. The key concepts of the information system are explained below. These are: systems concept, procedures and models, and the data base.

[2]Richard L. Nolan (Editor), *Managing the Data Resource Function* (Boston: West Publishing Co., 1974).

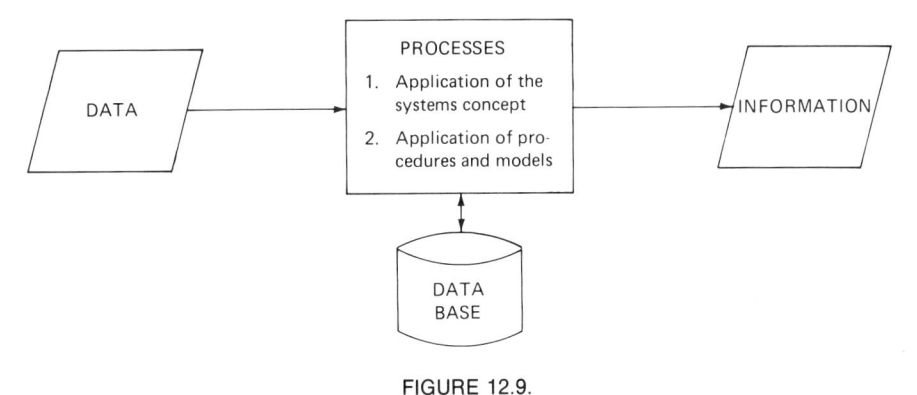

FIGURE 12.9.
Simple Model of an Information System.

SYSTEMS CONCEPT

The systems concept represents a philosophy of how information systems should be developed. The organization is viewed as a system of interrelated subsystems, each affected by the other, and the information system is developed in the same manner. With the ability of computer technology to capture transactions at the source at the time they happen, to distribute processing and inquiry capabilities throughout the organization, and to manipulate voluminous amounts of interrelated data elements at incredible speeds, it is possible today to apply the systems concept philosophy to the development of information systems.

How the systems concept can be applied to information systems development is illustrated in a typical manufacturing organization. This hypothetical organization manufactures compressors, each made up of a number of subassemblies and components. All data elements pertinent to the organization are stored in direct access storage devices, which are connected online to terminals. The data elements are logically interrelated within and between physical files.

When an event takes place, the resulting transaction is captured, input into the information system, and cascades throughout the system, updating all files simultaneously and keeping all aspects of the organization synchronized. For example, assume that a salesman takes an order for an XYZ compressor on credit. The sales transaction is keyed into the system by a salesman via a remote, portable terminal. The transaction passes through a control and edit screen to check the order for validity, reasonableness, accuracy, and so forth. A credit check is made and, assuming that credit can be granted, the compressor requested is either determined to be in stock or placed on special order. If the compressor is in stock and the order successfully passes through edit and other controls, the order entry system is updated, and a variety of technical documents (e.g., shipping papers) are prepared. Also, all appropriate files are updated. This sales transaction also brings into the CPU other programs to update the sales forecast, reassess budgets, analyze cash flow, and schedule production.

If the compressor is out of stock, then engineering files are accessed and the system automatically prepares an explosion list of subassemblies and components needed to produce it. This explosion list is compared to process parts inventory to see if the needed items are available. If not, the system can schedule orders and, in addition, reschedule other resource requirements for production. Moreover, the information system can combine a multiplicity of other factors, both financial and operations, and thus provide relevant and timely information to all managers at all levels and across functions.

PROCEDURES AND MODELS

A variety of procedures and models make the system more responsive to users. Procedures include filtering, interrogating, monitoring, and external data gathering. Filtering is a process of screening or extracting irrelevant data from a report before it is distributed to different users. A report can be filtered through summarizing and classifying operations that give only the detail necessary for a given level of decision-making. Interrogating allows a man-machine interface where the user formulates ad hoc inquiries, inputs them in the system without aid from others, and receives specific responses. Monitoring is another procedure that improves the effectiveness of information systems as it performs functions that humans do not perform very well. Implementation of this procedure allows the information system itself to monitor events and provide informational outputs on an automatic basis.

There are three ways to apply this procedure: (1) exception reporting, (2) programmed decision-making (e.g., credit checking or automatic reordering of inventory), and (3) automatic notification (e.g., rescheduling maintenance crews when a particular task has been completed). The high-level or strategic user is in dire need of information that comes from sources outside of the organization. Consequently, a great deal of relevant information can be generated by using the external procedure, i.e., gathering demographic data, competitive data, financial data (e.g., from Interactive Data Corporation), customer data, and so forth, and converting it into information that can be used to set organization objectives and long-range plans.

Models are structures that manipulate data in a logicomathematical manner to convert it into information. These models include, for example, the basic accounting equation, statistical methods, and management science models such as PERT and linear programming. The use of models to transform data into information is becoming increasingly important as a means of providing needed information to a variety of decision makers throughout the organization. The major advantages to using models are that they: (1) provide action-oriented information; (2) provide future-oriented information; (3) present alternative courses of action to be evaluated before implementation; (4) provide a formal, structured description of a complex problem situation; and (5) provide a scientific approach to replace intuition and speculation.

THE DATA BASE

The actual foundation of and key ingredient in the information system is the data base. Traditionally, data files were designed to accommodate individual applications such as bill of materials, payroll, accounts receivable, accounts payable, inventory, and so forth. With this appli-

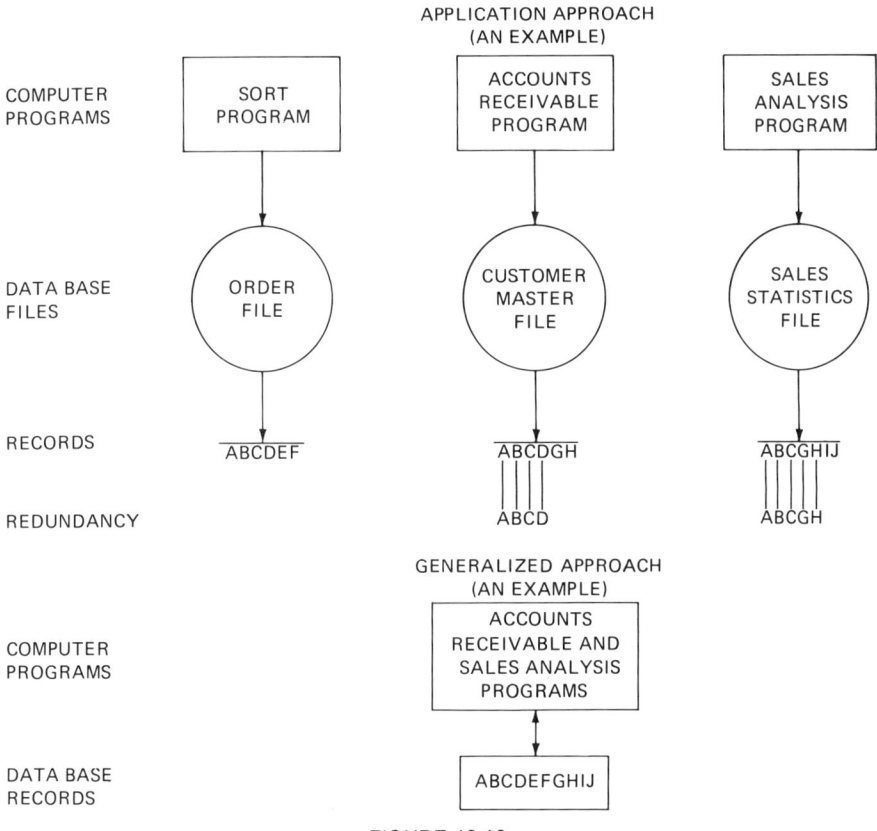

APPLICATION APPROACH
(AN EXAMPLE)

COMPUTER PROGRAMS	SORT PROGRAM	ACCOUNTS RECEIVABLE PROGRAM	SALES ANALYSIS PROGRAM
DATA BASE FILES	ORDER FILE	CUSTOMER MASTER FILE	SALES STATISTICS FILE
RECORDS	ABCDEF	ABCDGH	ABCGHIJ
REDUNDANCY		ABCD	ABCGH

GENERALIZED APPROACH
(AN EXAMPLE)

COMPUTER PROGRAMS	ACCOUNTS RECEIVABLE AND SALES ANALYSIS PROGRAMS
DATA BASE RECORDS	ABCDEFGHIJ

FIGURE 12.10.
A Schematic Showing an Example of the Difference between the Application and Generalized Approaches in Structuring a Data Base. In the Top Example, Records ABC are Present in each of the Three Files. In the Bottom Example, all Records are Present only once within the Data Base, and all Data Elements are Interrelated.

cation approach, there was little logical relationship between the files, each being processed at different times as a separate job. This application approach is contrasted with the data base concept, which provides for a generalized data base system. The difference is illustrated in Figure 12.10.

A key technique used to logically relate data elements in the data base is referred to as a chain and pointer system. Chains are used logically, not physically, to link records together on the basis of commonalities and functional interrelationships of data elements in the data base. A pointer represents the address of a particular data element. The chaining operation is achieved by using pointers, which may or may not be embedded in the records themselves. Regardless of whether or not a chain has embedded or non-embedded pointers, the essential aspect of a chaining operation is that there are pointers directly or indirectly associating one record in the chain to the next record in the chain.

An example of a popular method of using a chain and pointer system with pointers embedded in the records is called a circular list (also called a ring structure). It is illustrated in Figure 12.11. This simple example shows a logical chain associating all records that represent suppliers with a rating of 30. The number at the left represents the address of the record. The number at the right represents the pointer that points to the next record in the logical chain that meets the condition of a supplier rating of 30. This method accesses only those records that meet certain conditions without having to read every record. A variety of selection criteria can be met by formulating different combinations of chain and pointer systems.

An example of a chain and pointer system that does not use embedded pointers is shown in Figure 12.12. It is called an inverted list. In this example, the inquiry is: Who is the programmer in the Atlanta office who has a B.S. degree? This inquiry points only to D. Pesnell, located at

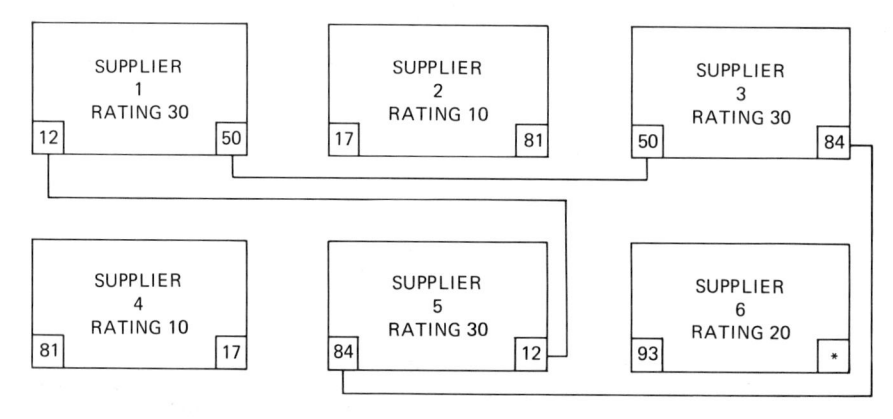

SUPPLIER 1 RATING 30 12 — 50	SUPPLIER 2 RATING 10 17 — 81	SUPPLIER 3 RATING 30 50 — 84
SUPPLIER 4 RATING 10 81 — 17	SUPPLIER 5 RATING 30 84 — 12	SUPPLIER 6 RATING 20 93 — *

FIGURE 12.11.
Simple Circular Chain List that uses Embedded Pointers.

address 27, because he is the only one in the personnel file who meets the inquiry specifications.

The advantages of the data base concept are:

1. Data can be organized in a manner that is suitable and appropriate to the interrelated functions of the organization.

2. Users can be provided with a direct interface with the data base.

3. Data elements may be associated more logically so that the organization can be perceived as a system rather than a group of isolated departments. Thus a broader, more coordinated, and more relevant information service is provided to users throughout the organization.

4. Faster response to user needs is possible.

5. Changes in management can be accommodated without major revision. If the data base is organized on the basis of functional relationships, thus modeling the operations and flow of activities, then a major change in users of the system should not create a need for significant changes in the general data base design. Theoretically, Manager B might replace Manager A, make many more requests than A, and have a higher (or lower) threshold for detail, and still be accommodated by the data base without major changes.

The disadvantages of the data base concept are:

1. The design and implementation of the data base concept require highly skilled personnel.

2. The initial investment is extremely high.

3. Any major "crash" in the system could be significantly detrimental to the organization as a whole.

4. A high level of security safeguards and backup is required.

5. A number of errors might develop throughout the data base because of errors in a single transaction.

INTEGRATED AND DISTRIBUTED SYSTEMS

Basically, there are two ways in which information systems can be organized: (1) the integrated system, and (2) the distributed system. Both are developed using the systems concept.

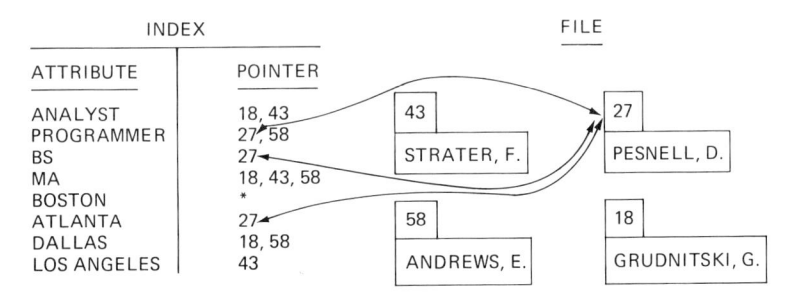

FIGURE 12.12.
A Chain and Pointer System using an Inverted List.

The integrated information systems approach attempts to channel all data of an organization into a common data base and service all data-processing and information functions for the entire organization. This kind of system can provide many benefits. It can also present some problems if management is not ready to make the commitment necessary to install such a system. Since an integrated system is somewhat monolithic in concept, anything less than a total commitment may result in chaos. The development of this kind of system requires: a total commitment from management at all levels based on a long-range master plan, the employment of highly skilled personnel, and the acquisition of sufficient computer technology.

The alternative to an integrated systems approach is a distributed systems approach. Whereas the integrated system is monolithic in nature, the distributed system is modular. The integrated system uses a central data-processing facility with a common data base. The distributed system, on the other hand, employs a group of interrelated information systems arranged in a network of subsystems.

The basic aim of the distributed systems approach is to establish relatively independent information subsystems which are tied together in the organization via data communication interfaces. Subsystems are located at, and customized to, areas of need. In such a system of subsystems, three basic conditions exist: (1) some of the subsystems will need to interact with other subsystems, (2) some will need to share files with others and even share data-processing facilities, and (3) some subsystems will require very little interaction with other subsystems and, for all intents and purposes, will be fairly isolated and self-sufficient.

The problem is to decide whether one should lean toward a more distributed system with a minimum of integration or toward a highly integrated system. The makeup of the particular organization that the information system serves has a lot to do with how it should be structured. The general rule is that the more homogeneous the operations of the organization, the more integrated the information system should be and vice versa.

Commercial airlines, banks, and insurance companies are all examples of organizations that have fairly homogeneous and unified operations. For example, in a typical airline company, all operations such as general administration, scheduling, and maintenance revolve around the reservation system. Therefore, it appears from the interdependencies among these areas that a highly integrated information system is appropriate.

In a large manufacturing organization with a number of divisions manufacturing different items, management, budget cycles, production, and marketing are diverse activities. The manufacturing organization with its divisions is looked upon as an economic and operational entity, but owing to the diversity and different needs of the divisions, a distributed system is appropriate.

12.5 CONTROLS REVISITED

Event processing systems are subject to the same threats and abuses as other systems; however, because of the interdependency of functions and the ability of a variety of remote users to access the system, a stringent system of controls is a must. Controlled access to event processing systems is now most important. If, for example, dynamic signature readers or encryption devices seemed farfetched in Part II, they now seem more feasible, especially where any person has access to a terminal in a store that in turn is connected to a bank's computer, and through this terminal funds may be withdrawn or transferred from one account to another. Without proper controls, such a system is wide open to a number of abuses.

In earlier systems, nearly all the devices that had access to the computer system were housed together within the same physical facility. Now, with remote terminals, often miles from the CPU, it is extremely difficult for the auditor to rely on the integrity of the system in any way. Therefore, strong, reliable control techniques must be employed to identify and authorize appropriate users and terminals and to control their access to the computer, programs, and data base. Although all aspects of a system of controls were discussed in Part II, this section reiterates, in summary form, problems and appropriate controls with specific application to event processing systems.

Critical Controls Required at Transaction Point

When an event takes place and causes a transaction to be input into the system, there is normally little intervention in the transaction's impact upon the system. Certainly it does not pass through the hands of a number of bookkeepers and accounting clerks, because their functions are now performed by computer programs. Therefore, a single transaction executes a number of programs, changes the contents in a number of files, and generally cascades throughout the system.

By definition, event processing systems capture and input a transaction as soon as an event occurs. At the point where the transaction is input into the system there must be sufficient controls to help insure that: (1) the user is authorized to input a transaction, (2) the transaction itself passes edit controls, and (3) all transactions are accounted for. Access controls, programmed edit controls, and transaction logs effect these objectives.

ACCESS CONTROL

The major requirements in providing access control are to: identify, authorize, authenticate, and monitor those things (e.g., people and terminals) that have the potential of accessing the system. Access to the information system should be restricted to specified terminals and users.

Identification is made by passwords, magnetic-stripe cards, handprints, voice recognition devices, dynamic signatures, and so forth. Each terminal can also be identified by its location and by a hardware identification code that is matched to an entry in the software's internal tables. By means of this code, each terminal's transmission over a common line can be identified and processed further. The same thing happens for the password or user code. Also, restricted time periods can be established for designated terminals.

Identification of the user and terminal does not mean that the transaction or inquiry made will be valid or correct; it simply verifies the right of access to the system. Once a connection to the system is achieved, the problem becomes one of authorization. For example, each combination of user and terminal according to rank, responsibility, function, or some other criterion is given authority to retrieve and update or read only specified fields of data within specified files. For example, the terminal and/or user code is matched to the software's internal authorization table that is used to restrict access to: (1) system applications such as payroll, premium collection, billing, inventory control, and so forth; (2) functions within a system application such as entering update transactions, check preparation, inquiry only, and so forth; and (3) transactions within a function such as recording hours worked. See, for example, Figure 12.13.

In the example above, location of a specified terminal with proper programming would prevent P1250 and P1251 from updating customer data. For example, a terminal located in the production department would not recognize these two codes even though these codes are authorized to update customer files, i.e., only specified terminals in specified locations using these codes can update. In effect, this approach is analogous to classical internal control, where only certain people, depending on who they are and where they are, can do certain things. Moreover, in many systems some terminals, because of cost constraints, do not have the same level of physical security controls. Consequently, some terminals in remote locations that do not have the same level of physical security as other terminals may be able to perform only a limited number of operations.

The system should be organized to require frequent authentication or confirmation that valid users and terminals are accessing the system. In the update example in Figure 12.13, an unauthorized person who gets

CHAPTER TWELVE MOVEMENT TOWARD EVENT PROCESSING SYSTEMS 411

USER NUMBERS	ASSIGNED AUTHORITY							
	TIMESHARE ONLY FOR ANALYTICAL PROCESSING (8K)		TIMESHARE ONLY FOR ANALYTICAL PROCESSING (UNLIMITED STORAGE)		INQUIRE ONLY: QUANTITY ON HAND INVENTORY FILE		UPDATE: CUSTOMER MASTER FILE	
	TERMINAL LOCATION		TERMINAL LOCATION		TERMINAL LOCATION		TERMINAL LOCATION	
	CREDIT DEPT	PRODUCTION DEPT	CREDIT DEPT	PRODUCTION DEPT	CREDIT DEPT	PRODUCTION DEPT	CREDIT DEPT	PRODUCTION DEPT
R NUMBERS		X						
S NUMBERS	X	X	X	X	X	X		
P 1250 AND 1251 ONLY							X	

FIGURE 12.13.
Simple Example of Authorization Table.

access to P1250 can perform anything that the code allows. To insure that valid codes are being used, a procedure should be employed to issue new codes frequently and delete the old ones from the authorization file. Another way to authenticate the user is to use automatic call-back whereby the computer interrupts the connection with the terminal and requires the user to make an appropriate response.

Monitoring access to the system requires that all invalid attempts to access the system and exceptional conditions be accounted for and reported to the appropriate control group. Also, a procedure should be established to automatically terminate a terminal hookup that has indicated no activity for a specified period of time. This procedure guards against an authorized user leaving the terminal unattended after a connection has been made or failing to sign off properly after a job has been completed. Otherwise, the terminal is available for access to anyone who chooses to use it.

If unauthorized access attempts are made, the system should immediately lock the keyboard of the terminal and make no response to the transaction or inquiry. An officer from the control group should investigate the situation immediately. For review purposes, the monitoring system should also maintain a log of all unauthorized attempts at access. Also, the time of attempted access, the location of the terminal, and the files being accessed should be accounted for to provide a pattern of trouble areas. If there are particularly sensitive files, it may be a good idea to maintain a log of all *authorized* accesses and to audit this log to determine who is accessing it, their frequency of access, what operations they are performing on it, and any accesses made after working hours.

PROGRAMMED EDIT CONTROLS

The immediate use of a transaction makes programmed edit controls a must. In a periodic processing system, transactions normally pass through several hands before finding their way into the system. Thus, there is always a chance that errors or invalid conditions can be detected before they make an impact on the system. With event processing systems, transactions receive little if any manual review before entering the system.

There are a number of programmed edit controls that can be implemented in the system. These are: character checks, sign checks, validity checks, limit and reasonableness checks, sequence checks, self-checking digit checks, overflow checks, and logical relationship checks. For a detailed discussion of these controls, review Part II.

TRANSACTION LOG

A basic control of event processing systems is the preservation of an adequate transaction trail, normally referred to as a transaction log. A transaction log is usually maintained on a magnetic tape, as shown in Figure 12.14. The transactions are written on the log in order of occurrence and control all data necessary for reprocessing of transactions in the event of loss of data or other malfunction. The transaction log is also maintained for audit review because it provides a wealth of audit information if computer audit techniques are used. All transactions can be sorted by point of origin and summarized by type of transaction, by user, by dollar amount, and so forth. Exception conditions can be printed out and cross references made. Again, with a transaction log, the auditor has the opportunity to perform strong examinations in a relatively short period of time.

In addition to the detail data of the transaction itself, each logged transaction should also contain a serial number, time, and date for the transaction which can be automatically generated and assigned by the computer. These serial numbers, like serial numbers for any controlled items (e.g., paychecks, passbooks, tickets), provide a method of keeping track of all transactions entering into the system. Any transactions automatically generated by the system (e.g., automatic reorder of inventory) are also assigned the same identifying information. In addition, the log should contain the status of the record in the master file before the update, assuming that it is not an inquiry transaction, and the status of the master record after the update.

Backup

In a periodic processing system, backup is desirable. In an event processing system, backup is imperative. In most cases, the justification for an event processing system is based upon the ability to provide processing support to run the organization's operations on a continuous

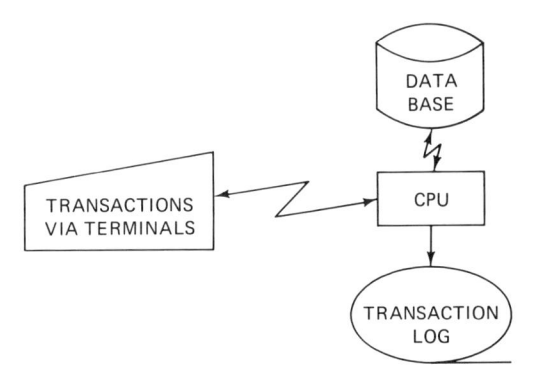

FIGURE 12.14.
Illustration of how a Transaction Log is Created for Event Processing Systems.

basis without disruptions. For example, if an airline reservation or an electronic teller system stopped operating for even a few hours, chaos would result. This level of dependence on event processing systems makes it absolutely necessary that backup be provided in the event of a systems failure.

The ideal situation is to backup everything as many times as possible. For example, if the probability of failure of one CPU is $P=.01$, then the probability of failure of two CPU's is $P=(.01)^2$, or $P=.0001$. Three CPU's would be even better, but most commercial systems cannot afford such luxury. Normally, cost/effective controls call for duplication of critical online files, programs, and, possible, a second CPU.

The data base demands the most extensive fallback, recovery, and restart procedures. The recovery and restart procedures for event processing must provide for continued operation in spite of the loss of data at any time during processing. The recovery procedures must further provide a way to quickly return to the status of the files just prior to failure or loss of data. The primary ingredients (see Figure 12.15) of data base backup are: (1) transaction log, (2) duplicate files for critical files, and (3) periodic dump of files for less critical files. The transaction log was discussed in the previous section. The duplicate file is basically just that. When transactions occur, the main file and the duplicate file are updated simultaneously. The recovery procedure would be initiated simply by having the computer shift to the second online file. With the periodic file dump procedure, certain files in the data base are copied on backup files such as magnetic tape one or more times a day. If data loss or malfunction occurs, the system is stopped and the backup file is

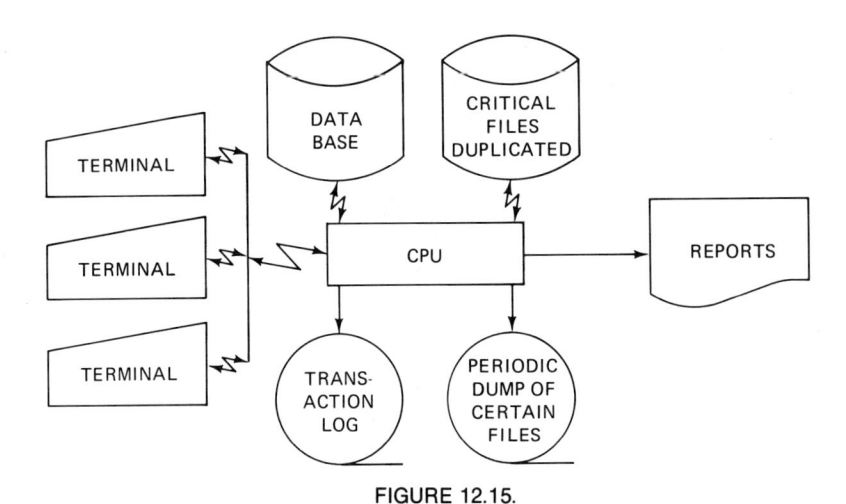

FIGURE 12.15.
Backup for Data Base to Recovery from Data Loss or Other Malfunction.

brought up to date by posting from the transaction file all transactions that have occurred since the last dump.

With the duplicate file procedure, minimum time is required to recover from a failure, but it is expensive to implement. The alternate procedure of periodically dumping data files onto another physical file on a scheduled basis seems to be the one most often used. This procedure is less expensive than the duplicate file procedure, but considerably more recovery time is required. To minimize this recovery time, the dumping operation can be performed more frequently. If errors are input into the system, both the main file and the duplicate file contain these errors. An advantage of the dumping procedure over the duplicate procedure is that each time the files are dumped, additional edit checks can be applied to catch any errors that somehow got through earlier edit controls. Auditing techniques can also be applied at this time without unduly disrupting the system. Moreover, a by-product of the dumping operation can be the execution of file maintenance procedures such as restructuring indexed-sequential files, reducing wasted space, and deleting inactive records.

12.6 SUMMARY

Advanced computer-based systems are developed and organized to capture and process an event when it occurs. The advantage of this kind of processing is that it synchronizes the actual events taking place with the operations of the organization. Not all operations of the organization demand instantaneous response. Therefore, many advanced systems combine both periodic and event processing to exploit the advantages of both.

The basic computer components required to support an event processing system are: (1) sophisticated central processing units with advanced operating systems, (2) large-capacity direct access storage devices, (3) a variety of terminals, and (4) advanced data communication systems. Information system concepts that support event processing include: (1) the system concept that views the organization as a synergistic whole, rather than an aggregate of isolated, disjointed departments; and (2) application of procedures, models, and quantitative methods to make the system more responsive to users' informational and decision-making needs.

A system of controls was discussed in detail in Part II, and some major controls that have special meaning and application to event processing systems were reiterated in this chapter. These controls are: (1) access controls, (2) programmed edit controls, (3) transaction log, and (4) backup.

REVIEW QUESTIONS

12.1 Differentiate between event and periodic processing systems.
12.2 List the characteristics of an event processing system.
12.3 What is meant by destructive or overlay processing?
12.4 Compare advantages and disadvantages of event processing systems and periodic processing systems, respectively.
12.5 List and define the computer components required to support an event processing system.
12.6 Define multiprogramming and virtual storage.
12.7 List those controls that have special significance and applicability to event processing systems. Explain why.
12.8 What makes a magnetic disk a direct access storage device? Fully explain.

DISCUSSION QUESTIONS

12.1 Discuss the impact of destructive or overlay updating on the control and auditing of an event processing system.
12.2 Why is it important to synchronize the events that impact upon an organization with the operations of that organization? Give an example.
12.3 Why should hybrid systems be used? Discuss a typical application.
12.4 Discuss those information systems concepts that support event processing systems.
12.5 Discuss the impact of the data base concept on auditing and control.
12.6 Differentiate between the integrated and distributed approaches to organizing information systems.
12.7 Why does the transaction log provide a wealth of audit information? Give at least three examples.

EXERCISES

12.1 Give a complete example of a periodic processing system and a list of major controls applicable to it. Do the same for an event processing system. What controls seem to be especially applicable to event processing systems?

PROBLEMS

12.1 A court information system as shown in Figure 12.16, maintains all data concerning criminal cases and the defendants involved.

CHAPTER TWELVE   MOVEMENT TOWARD EVENT PROCESSING SYSTEMS   417

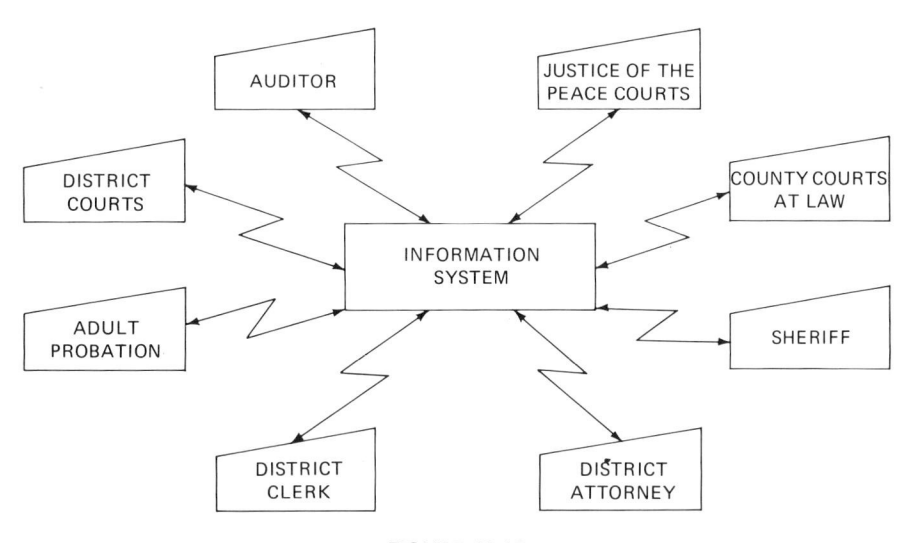

FIGURE 12.16.
Schematic of Court Information System.

All information is available, via printed reports and remote terminals, to the District Clerk, District Attorney, Sheriff, Probation Officer, and to the various courts. As a litigant progresses from one step in the judicial process to the next, information regarding this progress is recorded in the information system. Any authorized inquiries will therefore always receive current status information concerning any litigant.

As the system monitors the progress of each case, it periodically prepares action reports. These action reports include lists of persons being held for no apparent reason, cases that are ready for trial but have not been calendared, and persons whose probation periods have elapsed but have not been officially terminated. The system also provides numerous written reports which assist the criminal justice officials in preparing a case for trial, scheduling each event of the trial, and preparing local and state statistical reports. The data are in a data base consisting of direct-access storage files that are online, via data communication systems, to online terminals. Other files are set up for periodic processing.

Prepare a schematic of what you think the total computer configuration looks like. Write a report recommending a proper system of controls with appropriate justification. Indicate how and what computer audit techniques should be used to audit this kind of system adequately. Be specific and make any assumptions you deem necessary.

CHAPTER
13

EVENT AUDITING FOR EVENT PROCESSING SYSTEMS

13.1 INTRODUCTION

Auditing objectives are not changed by the introduction of event processing systems. The auditor's responsibility remains one of expressing an opinion on output produced by the system and making recommendations on correcting variances from management standards and a sound system of controls. There is no change that requires the auditor to ferret out sufficient evidential matter to base an opinion. The major change brought about by the installation of event processing systems as compared to periodic processing systems lies in the audit techniques that are employed to collect that proper evidential information.

Although objectives of auditing have not changed, the philosophy must. A preventive auditing philosophy must replace after-the-fact auditing, i.e., event auditing techniques must be applied to event processing systems. Audit modules must be designed into the system to provide current evidential information. The computer itself must be looked upon as *the* audit tool. Auditors must have ready access to the system at any time via terminals. Event processing systems require tough standards and control. Therefore, auditors should have authority to make sure that proper controls and audit modules are designed into the system as it is being developed. These changes also require a strong rapport, coordination, and working relationship between internal and external auditors.

13.2 EVENT PROCESSING REVISITED

In the previous chapter, we described the handling of transactions in an event processing system. Following is a practical illustration of an event processing system that helps to emphasize auditing implications of such a system. Note that transactions in this example are not subject to manual review by several individuals, as is the case in more traditional systems. Manual review tends to detect many obvious errors and inconsistencies. Also note that the transaction cycle is almost instantaneous, impacting upon the entire system. Longer transaction cycles in periodic systems allow time to review and correct unusual occurrences.

Assume that a customer places an order that passes a credit check. An order entry clerk, by means of an online terminal, enters the customer number, the purchase order number, the transaction number, the inventory item number, and the quantity to be shipped. As a result of this one transaction, the system: (1) notifies the shipping department to ship the order, (2) automatically prepares invoices and shipping papers, (3) credits inventory and checks the reorder points for items that are shipped, automatically selects appropriate vendors, and prepares the necessary purchase order papers to replenish any items falling below their reorder point, (4) makes a debit entry to the accounts receivable control account and the customer's own account, (5) makes a debit entry to cost of goods sold, and (6) a credit entry to sales.

One of the major points that concerns the auditor is the fact that these manipulations and changes in the files are made by a program in a computer rather than by a cadre of bookkeeping clerks. The accounts receivable control account and individual customer accounts are updated simultaneously and housed within the same system. All traditional general ledger accounts such as accounts receivable, sales, inventories, purchases, cost of goods sold, and so forth, are updated together on an item-by-item basis. Perpetual inventory is no longer maintained on card systems but is integrated into the data base. The system automatically makes programmed decisions such as credit checking, pricing, and purchasing. The system, therefore, generates transactions itself with limited human review. Traditional control totals are no longer present. For example, an independent group who had no cash or accounts receivable posting responsibilities would generate a control total of the individual accounts in accounts receivable. This control total had to match the control total prepared by those people who posted to cash and accounts receivable. These kinds of controls are obviously missing from event processing systems and their absence is the reason why a strong system of controls and the application of new approaches to auditing are so important.

The auditor must open windows to the black box to make sure that it is not Pandora's box. The auditor must insist upon strong access controls and surrounding physical security controls. He should make sure that all transactions are subjected to comprehensive edit controls and accounted for. Once the auditor has satisfied himself as to the adequacy of these and other controls, he must address himself to the programs of the system to make absolutely sure that they are properly developed and maintained, and that they are performing all the integrated manipulations properly.

Event processing systems, such as the one described above, are already being applied in many organizations, and they are indicative of the type of all systems for the future. Obviously, this situation presents a number of significant auditing implications for both internal and external auditors.

Some people, both practicing auditors and educators, have indicated their unconcern with system changes. They feel that it is feasible and proper to supplement audit of computer systems with a so-called computer audit specialist. This kind of reasoning will eventually spell doom for those who abide by it. In integrated systems with generalized data bases, the computer system is in fact the accounting system, and vice versa. Without the proper application of appropriate audit techniques, the *accounting system itself will become a black box to the auditor.* Such a situation is unthinkable.

Some technical support is necessary in any profession, but it makes little sense to expect a specialist to do all the work. If one carries this thinking too far, the specialist who was supposed to *supplement* the traditional auditor will *replace* him. As stated earlier, it is difficult, if not impossible, to separate accounting from the computer in an event processing system, because they are one and the same, inextricably tied together. So to review and test the integrity, reliability, and control of the accounting system and to attest to the financial reports it produces, the auditor must review and test the computer system. To determine that assets are properly safeguarded and not used improperly, the auditor must review and test the computer system. To see to it that operations adhere to prescribed management policy, the auditor must review and test the computer system. To audit the accounting system is to audit the computer system. To rely too heavily on the computer audit specialist, would be to abdicate most, if not all, of the auditor's responsibility.

To discharge the responsibility of the auditor properly, additional audit techniques must be applied. The audit techniques discussed in previous chapters are still effective in the audit of event processing systems, but in some instances they perform after-the-fact auditing. Instantaneous and remote processing of transactions require that the system be subject to constant monitoring audit techniques. These audit techniques support the preventive audit philosophy, and, at the same time, provide the auditor with a wealth of evidential information upon which he can make sound decisions.

The combination of audit techniques described in the remainder of this chapter gives the auditor the ability to evaluate an event processing system independently and thoroughly. All of these techniques support the preventive auditing philosophy in the sense that some will catch errors and inconsistencies before they happen, while others will at least catch them while they are happening and help prevent additional errors. These audit techniques are feasible and viable, but the decision to use them must be made early in the design and development of an application system. It is also imperative that support for their use be received from top management.

13.3 TRANSACTION TRAIL

In manual and periodic computer processing systems, the so-called audit trail includes source documents that support entries to journals, the chronological journals used in posting to ledger accounts, and the ledgers. In these systems, the audit trail is used in tracing accounting transactions from the accounting statements to the source documents, or tracing accounting transactions through to the statements. Auditors are accustomed to a visible paper trail of these transactions.

We prefer to call the tracing of these transactions a transaction trail rather than an audit trail, because, as we have already seen, the auditor is concerned with more than the tracing of transactions, and the term audit trail implies an all-inclusive auditing strategy. Whatever one calls the tracing and control of transactions, some people believe that the advent of event processing systems has meant the disappearance of the transaction trail. Nothing could be further from the truth. There is nothing whatever to prevent the development of more complete and comprehensive transaction trails than any that could be found in manual systems. In fact, an event processing system is tailor-made for providing transaction trails. Moreover, to develop any event processing system without a transaction trail is to court disaster.

The availability of a comprehensive transaction trail depends upon how effective management and the auditor are during the design and development of systems. The auditor must insist that techniques to provide the transaction trail be designed into the programming logic *before* implementation. Once the system has been implemented, changes in program and computer design are difficult and time-consuming.

Two techniques can be used to provide a transaction trail. One is the transaction log discussed in the previous chapter. The other technique is what most auditors refer to as tagging and tracing, whereby certain transactions are printed out at critical points as they are processed through the system. It is emphasized that one technique is not a substitute for the other; both should be used in the system to provide a comprehensive transaction trail for the auditor.

Transaction Log

To insure that an event processing system is effective and secure, all transactions should be logged on magnetic tape or disk. In the previous chapter, the use of transaction logs for backup and recovery was emphasized. For audit purposes, the transaction log should include information about where, when, and from what terminal transactions originated plus the user number. For example, in an insurance company, the transaction log supports all entries to the general ledger accounts. An entry into the general ledger for the day or week debits accounts receivable and credits written premiums, is simultaneously recorded in the transaction log, and contains the following detail support: initiator, terminal, and user identification numbers; time of day; day of week; policy number, premium; and other identifying data. At any time, the auditor can have the system produce for him a hardcopy listing of the transaction log for manual review.

In a system with a transaction log, transactions can be traced from the original source, to the point of entry to the computer system, and finally to a printout (if desired) of transactions processed by the computer. Moving in a reverse direction, the current status of any master record updated by transactions can be reconstructed. A common example of doing this is to provide for a "date of last transaction" on the status printout and a "date of last transaction" on each entry on the transaction log.

Any transactions that fail to pass the edit controls should be entered on a transaction error listing. These transactions should be corrected and re-entered for processing. Control of errors is concerned with the quality of the procedure for recognizing, identifying, and recording errors in the system. A proper system of controls insures that edit checks are designed into the system to recognize error conditions. When errors happen, they should be properly identified with error codes and documented in an error listing. Once an error is identified, it should be corrected promptly.

Normally, one person is given the responsibility for controlling the error listings. When a correcting transaction is prepared, a notation is made on the error listing indicating date of correction, person making correction, transaction number of the correction, and so forth. The individual responsible for error control reviews the listing on a regular basis to insure that all errors have been corrected. Another control over the correction of errors involves establishing an interim data file (e.g., on magnetic tape) of errors with diary dates for correction. The file is read daily and reminders displayed for errors that are late for correction. All correcting transactions are processed against the error file where they either delete the error or indicate correction information on it.

All logs should be available to the auditor at any time for extraction and examination. With the application of audit techniques such as those discussed earlier (e.g., generalized audit programs), the auditor will have the transactions in a form that can be subjected to unlimited examination and analysis. The auditor should also review the error listings periodically to make sure that errors are being properly corrected and re-entered into the system.

Transaction logs should be recorded and maintained in a secure location with controlled access. No access should be granted to systems analysts, programmers, computer operators, and so forth. Moreover, none of these people should have access to terminals that can originate transactions. Periodically, all transactions should be balanced against independent records of transactions maintained in user departments.

An ideal situation would be one in which the internal auditor has a separate terminal in his department under his control. He could select certain transactions for testing and follow-up, just as selected items are tested in a quality control system.

The transaction log, however, is not only for the use of the auditor. The results of transactions draw a large number of inquiries from other sources such as customers, employees, vendors, and government officials. There must, therefore, be a means by which the initiation and authorization of the transaction and its effect upon accounts can be traced. Furthermore, the Internal Revenue Service specifically requires that taxpayers with computer-based information systems be able to answer such inquiries.

The IRS regulation, which has become a generally accepted standard, applies equally to non-profit organizations. Following are excerpts from Internal Revenue Procedure 64-12.

1. "The audit trail should be designed so that details underlying the summary accounting data, such as invoices and vouchers, may be identified and made available to the Internal Revenue Service upon request."

2. "The records must provide the opportunity to trace any transaction back to original source and forward to a final total. If printouts are not made of transactions at the time they are processed, then the system must have the ability to reconstruct those transactions."

In event processing systems, transactions are usually initiated without any document support via a data entry device such as a CRT or POS terminal. In any case, when the event is accepted by the system, it should be posted to the transaction log and impact on the data base simultaneously. Along with the transaction number, date, time of day, description, and other identifying data, the identification of the operator and the terminal must be entered in the transaction log. This additional identification, make it possible to trace any exceptional items back to the terminal operator. In many instances, only the terminal operator can reconstruct the transaction through documents or verbal authorization. Then, documents, if any, and the person making the authorization can be investigated before final disposition of the item.

Tagging and Tracing

Some people say that hardcopy of transactions and related data in various intermediate stages of processing is less easily available with event processing systems than it is with more traditional systems. With application of tagging and tracing routines in the programming logic, all transactions and related data can be traced through the system. As each processing step is performed, the interaction of the selected transaction with other data and related tests is displayed. Control and selection of tagged transactions can be controlled by the auditor using a terminal in his office. Printouts of the resulting transaction trails are in turn displayed on his terminal.

HOW TAGGING AND TRACING WORKS

The tagging and tracing audit technique flags selected transactions by some special notation or code. These transactions are processed as normal transactions by the programming logic and SNAPSHOTS[1] are taken of the status of these transactions as they flow through the system. This technique, if installed into the programming logic while the programs are being developed, requires relatively little extra time and cost, and provides a powerful technique to obtain a comprehensive transaction trail.

After tracing a transaction through the system, the auditor can feel fairly confident as to how the files are being processed. He may find that transactions are being processed properly or he may find some unusual results. For example: "On the subject of tagging and tracing, an interesting war story is presented. A company had a large number of vari-

---

[1] See William E. Perry, "SNAPSHOT—A Technique for Tagging and Tracing Transactions," *EDPACS*, April 1974, pp. 1–7.

ations between perpetual inventory records and physical counts. After a great deal of checking, they found that an inventory price change caused the perpetual on-hand quantity to be set to a zero value. Tagging would have uncovered this problem very early in the life of the system."[2]

The tagging and tracing technique has three characteristics: (1) some identifier must be used to tag the selected transactions, (2) program instructions must be written into the application programs to recognize the tagged transactions, and (3) write routines must be prepared to print out the results of the tagged transactions and related data at key points in the system.

A transaction can be tagged in two different ways. One way is to provide a designated position in the transaction record to signify that a particular transaction has been marked for tracing through the system. For example, the first position of all transaction records is set aside for tagging purposes. Whenever the auditor wishes to trace certain transactions through the system, he inserts a code letter or number, say, a "T," in this position. From that point on, the system takes over and traces the designated transactions through the system.

The second method obviously produces a transaction trail, too, but rather than setting aside a special position for the tag to be inserted, a character in one of the working fields (e.g., account number) of the transaction itself is used for tagging. Following, in Figure 13.1, is a partial, simplified version of a payroll program written in COBOL. Highlighted in this program are three SNAPSHOTS of tagged transactions and related master file data. The fourth character of the employee number in the time card records is used for a tag.

The most difficult and time-consuming part of implementing the tagging and tracing technique is the determination of the SNAPSHOT points and what data are to be printed out for those points. In a complex computer system there might be a hundred or more SNAPSHOT points. Each one must be selected by the auditor. Some typical SNAPSHOT points are:

1. The place where the transaction enters the computer system.
2. The points at which the transaction enters each program (module).
3. The place where the transaction exits from each program (module).
4. The interface points between each transaction and a secondary record in the system.
5. Major logic points where data are materially changed. The SNAPSHOT should show the transaction both before and after the change.[3]

[2]Stephen W. Leibholz and Louis D. Wilson, *Users' Guide to Computer Crime* (Radnor, Pa.: Chilton Book Company, 1974). Quoted from Book Previews section of *EDPACS*, August 1975, p. 11, prepared by F. Andrew Best.
[3]Perry, *op. cit.*, p. 4.

```
IDENTIFICATION DIVISION.
PROGRAM-ID.  PAYROLL SYSTEM.
AUTHOR.  JOHNNY TRACER  .
       .      .             .
ENVIRONMENT DIVISION.
       .
FILE-CONTROL.
       SELECT TIME-CARDS ASSIGN TO CARD-READER.
       SELECT PAYROLL-FILE ASSIGN TO DISK-ONE.
       .        .                  .
DATA DIVISION.
FILE SECTION.
FD   TIME-CARDS
01   TIME-RECORD
     02  EMP-NUM                       PICTURE 9(4).
         03  TAG-1                     PICTURE 9.
         03  TAG-2                     PICTURE 9.
         03  TAB-3                     PICTURE 9.
         04  TAG-4                     PICTURE 9.
         (These tags allow the auditor to use one character, in our
          example, TAG-4, to flag particular transactions.)
     02  EMP-NAME-IN                   PICTURE X(20).
     02  DEPT-NUM                      PICTURE 9(3).
     02  HOURS-WORKED                  PICTURE 99V99.
```

CHAPTER THIRTEEN   EVENT AUDITING FOR EVENT PROCESSING SYSTEMS   427

```
FD  PAYROLL-FILE
        .
        .
01  PAYROLL-RECORD.
    02  EMP-MASTER-NUM          PICTURE 9(4).
    02  EMP-NAME                PICTURE X(20).
    02  EMP-DEPT-NUM            PICTURE 9(3).
    02  PAY-RATE                PICTURE 99V99.
02  YEAR-TO-DATE-PAY            PICTURE 9(6)V99.

FD  TRANSACTION TRAIL
        .
        .
01  TRANSACTION-TRAIL-RECORD.
    02  FILLER                  PICTURE X.
    02  EMP-NUM-TRACE           PICTURE 9(4).
    02  FILLER                  PICTURE XX.
    02  EMP-NAME-TRACE          PICTURE X(20).
    02  FILLER                  PICTURE XX.
    02  EMP-DEPT-NUM-TRACE      PICTURE 9(3).
    02  FILLER                  PICTURE XX.
    02  HOURS-WORKED-TRACE      PICTURE 99.99.
    02  FILLER                  PICTURE XX.
    02  PAY-RATE-TRACE          PICTURE $ZZ.99.
    02  FILLER                  PICTURE XX.
    02  GROSS-PAY-TRACE         PICTURE $ZZZ,ZZZ.99.
    02  FILLER                  PICTURE XX.
    02  YEAR-TO-DATE-PAY-TRACE  PICTURE $ZZ,ZZZ.99.
```

WORKING-STORAGE SECTION.
77   GROSS-PAY   PICTURE 9(6)V99.
77   TAG-VALUE   PICTURE 9.

(This is the value input by the auditor. If he inputs a 3, all transactions with a value of 3 in Position 4 of EMP-NUM will be tagged and traced.)

PROCEDURE DIVISION.
OPEN-FILES.
    OPEN INPUT TIME-CARDS.
    OPEN I-O PAYROLL-FILE AND TRANSACTION-TRAIL.
DESIGNATE-TAG.
    ACCEPT TAG-VALUE FROM AUDIT-TERMINAL
        (The auditor inputs any value from 0 through 9.)
READ-TIME-CARDS.
    READ TIME-CARDS AT END GO TO EOJ.
    IF TAG-4 = TAG-VALUE PERFORM WRITE-TRANSACTION-TRAIL-ONE.

    (All transactions designated by the auditor are printed out for the auditor as soon as they are read into the computer system.)

READ-AND-PROCESS.
    READ PAYROLL-FILE.
    IF EMP-MASTER-NUM = EMP-NUM GO TO PAYROLL-PROCESS.

PAYROLL-PROCESS.
    IF TAG-4 = TAG-VALUE PERFORM WRITE-TRANSACTION-TRAIL-TWO.

    (Values of the tagged transactions and their matching master
    records are printed out for the auditor just *before* they are
    processed.)

    COMPUTE GROSS-PAY = HOURS-WORKED * PAY-RATE.
    ADD GROSS-PAY TO YEAR-TO-DATE-PAY.
      .
      .
    WRITE PAYROLL-RECORD.
    IF TAG-4 = TAG-VALUE PERFORM WRITE-TRANSACTION-TRAIL-THREE.

    (Values of the tagged transactions and their matching master
    records are printed out for the auditor *after* they are processed.)
      .
      .
WRITE-TRANSACTION-TRAIL-ONE.
    (After this routine prints out the values of the tagged trans-
    actions before they are matched against the payroll records,
    control is automatically returned to READ-AND-PROCESS.)
    MOVE SPACES TO TRANSACTION-TRAIL-RECORD.
    MOVE EMP-NUM TO EMP-NUM-TRACE.
    MOVE EMP-NAME-IN TO EMP-NAME-TRACE.
    MOVE DEPT-NUM TO EMP-DEPT-NUM-TRACE.
    MOVE HOURS-WORKED TO HOURS-WORKED-TRACE.
    WRITE TRANSACTION-TRAIL-RECORD.

430   PART THREE   COMPUTER AUDIT TECHNIQUES

WRITE-TRANSACTION-TRAIL-TWO.
    (This routine prints out the values of tagged TIME-RECORD and matching PAYROLL-RECORD *before* any values are changed. Control is then returned to the second instruction in PAYROLL-PROCESS.)

    MOVE SPACES TO TRANSACTION-TRAIL-RECORD.
    MOVE EMP-NUM TO EMP-NUM-TRACE.
    MOVE EMP-NAME-IN TO EMP-NAME-TRACE.
    MOVE DEPT-NUM TO EMP-DEPT-NUM-TRACE.
    MOVE HOURS-WORKED TO HOURS-WORKED-TRACE.
    MOVE PAY-RATE TO PAY-RATE-TRACE.
    MOVE YEAR-TO-DATE-PAY TO YEAR-TO-DATE-PAY-TRACE.
    WRITE TRANSACTION-TRAIL-RECORD.

WRITE-TRANSACTION-TRAIL-THREE.

    (This routine gives the auditor a snapshot of the designated PAYROLL-RECORD *after* it has been processed. Two critical values are GROSS-PAY-TRACE and YEAR-TO-DATE-PAY-TRACE. Also, other values such as PAY-RATE-TRACE are printed out to allow the auditor to see if there have been any improper changes. Control is automatically passed to other instructions in PAYROLL-PROCESS for additional processing.)

    MOVE SPACES TO TRANSACTION-TRAIL-RECORD.
    MOVE EMP-NUM TO EMP-NUM-TRACE.
    MOVE PAY-RATE TO PAY-RATE-TRACE.
    MOVE GROSS-PAY TO GROSS-PAY-TRACE.
    MOVE YEAR-TO-DATE-PAY TO YEAR-TO-DATE-PAY-TRACE.
    WRITE TRANSACTION-TRAIL-RECORD.

FIGURE 13.1.
Example of How Tagging and Tracing Routines are Implemented in the Program Logic.

TAGGING AND TRACING CONSIDERATIONS

The following points should be considered in the implementation of the tagging and tracing technique.

1. SNAPSHOT requires preplanning on the part of the systems developer and the user. It cannot be as easily implemented on an after-the-fact basis. The auditor must develop his specifications at a very early point in the design cycle.

2. Data-processing personnel must be heavily involved in the implementation of the SNAPSHOT technique. Because the present state of the art requires in-line coding to implement this approach, data-processing personnel know what the auditor is trying to accomplish. They could easily circumvent the technique, so it cannot be used as a primary means of detecting embezzlement or fraud. Rather, it shows an audit trail through the logic of the system.

3. Because the technique is embedded within the computer system, it must undergo maintenance as the system changes. The addition of new programs (modules), the elimination of records, the addition of records, the shortening or lengthening of records, or other types of record modification could and probably would create a need for maintenance to be performed on the SNAPSHOT segment of the system. Someone must be responsible for overseeing the SNAPSHOT portion of the computer system.

4. The trail of transactions through a computer system can be drastically altered at points within the system where data are summarized. For example, the transaction being traced might be summarized along with several other transactions into one summary record which is then processed. The auditor needs to determine if the tracing should stop at that point or if it should include the summarized record. He must also provide for the case where two or more tagged records are included in the same summary record.

5. A case similar to the one above occurs when a transaction being tagged and traced is split into two or more records that follow different paths. The auditor must decide whether to stop tracing at this point or whether to trace all or some of the subsequent records.

6. The auditor must decide whether to limit tracing to one computer system (application) or whether to pass the tagging from system to system.[4]

13.4 INTEGRATED TEST FACILITY (ITF)

One of the most critical problems facing the auditor who audits event processing systems is to obtain assurance that proper controls and de-

[4]*Ibid.*, p. 6.

cision rules are actually in place and operating correctly. As noted before, in event processing systems, personnel are removed from direct interaction with events and transactions as the computer system replaces many of the traditional manual functions. This transition from clerks and bookkeepers to the computer can create many control gaps that result in costly errors. With the use of traditional audit techniques, these errors may go undetected for a long period of time and cause irreparable damage to the organization.

In an event processing system's environment, the auditor must restructure his audit approach to correspond with the characteristics and nature of the system itself. The integrated test facility (ITF) audit technique (sometimes referred to as the minicompany audit technique) enables the auditor to break through the black box barrier and obtain a clear mirror image of the total operations of the computer system and its interaction with the entire organization. Use of the ITF allows the auditor to input selected transactions into the system simultaneously with normal, live transactions. The flow of ITF transactions is traced through the various functions of the system.

The object of this audit technique is to permit auditors to: (1) enter a computer system under normal operating conditions, (2) test transactions for which the results have been predetermined, and (3) compare the results actually produced with the predetermined results.[5] ITF gives the auditor another strong computer audit technique for auditing event processing systems in that it tests the system concurrently, i.e., it tests the system as it is operating rather than after the fact.

Definition of the ITF

The ITF involves the establishment of a fictitious entity (e.g., customer, department, division, employee) in the data base of the system against which test transactions, unbeknown to the systems personnel, can be processed as if they are regular, live transactions (see Figure 13.2). This approach integrates permanent test data into the system and permits the auditor to continuously monitor the performance of the system. The ITF requires that the auditor establish a system himself for recording and processing the test transactions to provide predetermined results to check against the results of the computer system.

Some aspects of the ITF audit technique are similar to those of the test deck technique, and some are similar to tagging and tracing. With the test deck approach, the auditor prepares a set of dummy transactions

---

[5] See Joe R. Fritzmeyer and D. R. Carmichael, "ITF—A Promising Computer Audit Technique," *The Journal of Accountancy*, February 1973; William E. Perry, "Try ITF, You'll Like ITF," *EDPACS*, December 1973, pp. 1–6.

and requests a special computer run to process them. The results of this run are checked against predetermined results to verify program edit controls, among other things. The test deck is an effective audit technique and one that should be included in the auditor's tool bag. As pointed out in an earlier chapter, however, it has some limitations, especially when applied in an event processing systems environment. These limitations are stated below:

1. The test deck requires special set-up and computer time.

2. The test deck approach is more amenable to periodic processing than to event processing systems.

3. The auditor usually must rely on someone else (e.g., a computer operator) to run the test deck. Also, a number of people in the system know when the test deck is being run. Both of these aspects reduce the auditor's independence.

4. The test deck limits the number and combinations of things that the auditor can check.

5. Maintenance of the test deck is costly and time-consuming because of frequent changes in programs.

6. The auditor is not sure that the program(s) he is testing is the

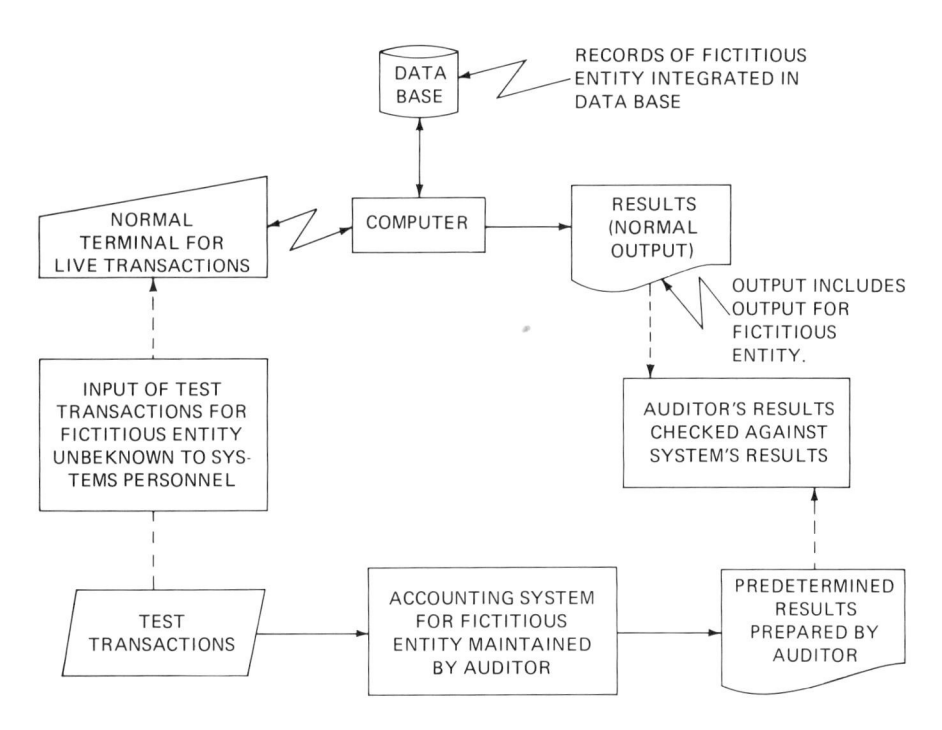

FIGURE 13.2.
Schematic of an Integrated Test Facility (ITF).

production program(s). With live transactions, this weakness is eliminated because with the application of ITF, test transactions are mixed with normal company transactions and processed together.

7. There are peripheral operations that the auditor cannot check with the test deck, e.g., he cannot observe how customer orders are handled.

The ITF should not be looked upon as a substitute for the tagging and tracing technique. The tagging and tracing audit technique is employed for the express purpose of providing a visible trail of the results of transactions and related data as they flow through the system. With ITF, the purpose is to see what impact transactions have on the organization and how they are handled by the computer system and various interface functions. With tagging and tracing, modules are embedded in the normal programming logic. The operation of the ITF is separate from the system and under the control of the auditor. The integration aspect of the ITF stems from the fact that: (1) the fictitious entity account is in the normal data base, and (2) test transactions are integrated into the flow of normal transactions.

Implementation of the ITF

Auditors who apply the ITF normally use one of the following subsystems: order entry, accounts receivable, purchasing, and payroll. Since these subsystems are well defined and familiar to the average auditor, it is suggested that the auditor choose one of them for a first-time application of the ITF.

If the accounts receivable function represents a large and significant part of the system, the auditor could set up a fictitious customer account in the normal manner with as few people as possible aware of the purpose of the account. The identity of this account and all test transactions should be kept secret, and reality of operations should be maintained at both the initial introduction of the account into the data base and where subsequent test transactions are input and processed against it.

The auditor should use an outside address. Products would be ordered and shipped to the ITF customer, and invoices would be processed as always. The product could be expended, used in company operations, returned to stock, or the shipment could even be stopped in the shipping area, depending on its nature. During this process, the auditor can make a number of tests. For example, bills can be paid, overpaid or underpaid, or not paid at all. Items can be returned for credit, complaints processed, credit terms violated, or any other test of operations can be made. The auditor is limited only by his imagination.[6] Playing the role

---

[6]Fritzmeyer and Carmichael, *op. cit.*, p. 76.

of a customer tests not only the data-processing system but also many peripheral functions. The feedback from such tests can be eye-opening.

Auditing, which is normally a very passive, after-the-fact function, can become an active one when the ITF is employed. Moreover, the reason that this powerful audit technique is not employed more often is that auditors are concerned lest they severely disrupt business operations or, even worse, blow up the computer system. Certainly, there is a risk in using the ITF, because it can cause errors in the financial statements if not properly controlled.

In any event, it is essential that top management support be obtained by the auditor before employing the ITF. This support should be sought as soon as the auditor has researched the problem sufficiently and has decided that he wants to use the ITF audit technique. The auditor should try to convince management that the risk of using a technique such as the ITF is less than the risk of not using it. Most managements can readily understand use of the ITF in auditing computer systems because it parallels quality control in manufacturing. The three groups of management who need to be convinced of viability of an ITF approach are: (1) audit management, (2) data-processing management, and (3) financial management.[7]

In summary, the following steps are normally followed in order to implement the ITF audit technique:

1. The capability of entering test transactions under ITF requires the establishment of a fictitious, unique entity into which the data can be processed. For example, this entity may be a fictitious division, store, dealer, department, employee, plant subsidiary, account, or any other basis of accumulation of accounting information. It is a rarity when the auditor cannot find some vehicle for accumulation of accounting data which can be used for his test entity.

2. Once the entity has been established, the auditor should arrange to have the auditing department control a master record(s) in the system corresponding to the entity. The same steps should be followed that any legitimate unit of that type would go through to become a recognized user of the system. If, for example, you were setting up an ITF facility in the payroll system and the audit department wanted to establish employee records for test purposes, they should go through the normal entry procedures and forms completion required for any newly hired employee.

3. The auditing department needs to determine what tests to make in exercising the data-processing system. This is the most difficult part of using the ITF concept, since the auditor must have a detailed appreciation of the system's scope in order to develop effective test criteria. In a billing system the auditor can, for example, test quantity discount pric-

[7]Perry, *op. cit.*, pp. 3, 5.

ing, calculation of sales tax, and the pricing of special order type items. If the auditor wants to include a test of the accounts receivable function, he can test delinquency of payments, the taking of cash discounts after the discount period, the overpayment of accounts, and duplicate payments to an account.

4. The auditing department needs to maintain its own set of books and accounts so that it can properly record the transactions processed. Depending on the type of entity (e.g., outside dealer), an outside address might be used rather than addressing correspondence to the entity in care of the internal auditing department.

5. A determination must be made as to which type of implementation process the auditing department wants to employ: whether to modify the computer programs or to adjust the effects on the books of the test transactions by adjusting journal entries. If program modification is selected, the auditing department must work with data processing in order to specify and implement the changes. If adjusting journal entries is selected, the auditing department must work with the accounting department to determine the frequency, timing, and methods of making the adjusting journal entries.

6. The auditor can now start processing test transactions.

7. Regular follow-up reports (initially issued on a frequent basis) should be directed to management. The reports should detail the type of audit findings, good or bad, that have been obtained by using the ITF technique.[8]

As pointed out above, the two methods used to implement the ITF are: (1) program modification that filters out ITF transactions, and (2) the use of reversing entries. The first method requires a great deal of program modification, which data-processing management is normally opposed to. Moreover, if this approach is used, then test transactions are filtered out prior to their inclusion in any meaningful report or operation. Because this approach effectively eliminates many of the objectives of the ITF, it is not recommended.

The second method allows the inclusion of test transactions throughout the entire system, including the financial processing cycle. The test transactions flow through the system and eventually work their way to the general ledger, at which point manual journal entries are prepared to reverse the effects of the test transactions. Financial management may be opposed to this method because of the adjusting journal entries, but it is by far more powerful and meaningful to the auditor and therefore is recommended.

The concept of an ITF poses certain problems to the auditor attempting to develop a workable sample of test transactions. Some operations may be extremely difficult or cumbersome to test if the auditor tries to enter data directly via a fictitious entity. To overcome this difficulty, and

[8]*Ibid.*, pp. 3 and 4.

still permit the auditor complete freedom in developing his tests, different methods of input are required.

There are two general methods of entering transactions into the ITF facility:

1. Utilization of live simulated transactions. This method involves submitting actual work for processing through the fictitious entity. The auditor will select the type of transactions that fulfill his needs for a particular test. These transactions will be entered into the normal business cycle of the organization as part of the input stream. As an example, if the test is of a billing-receivables system, the auditor would either complete an order form or order products by telephone.

2. Submission of dead transactions into some intermediate point within the data-processing system. A dead transaction is one requiring no product movement or consumption of service. An example of this method would be to prepare input cards representing the transaction. In the case illustrated in No. 1 above, the auditor would have prepared the necessary order forms or telephone call and submitted the test transaction just as would any outside user of the system. However, in the dead transaction concept, the auditor might prepare the transaction records like the shipping department, indicating that the product has been shipped and should be billed. These cards would be placed in the job stream at the proper point within the system.

Each of these methods of data entry has certain advantages. The use of live transactions affords the following benefits:

1. It tests the entire scope of the system (e.g., order entry to cash receipts).

2. It allows the system to be tested on a surprise basis.

3. It provides a technique to verify work status at all appropriate locations within the organization. For example, if a company has six warehouses, and the auditor is testing the order entry system, transactions could be made up affecting all six warehouses.

Entering dead transactions into the ITF facility offers the following advantages:

1. It provides an unlimited range of products and services to be tested because under this concept it is not necessary to actually use the items involved in the test.

2. It allows testing of other controls and error reporting by insertion of faulty data. It may be difficult under the live transaction concept to simulate various error conditions, because such errors may be caught at an early point (perhaps manually). Errors that are caught early would not test the logic within the entire data-processing system.

3. It simplifies ITF record-keeping by eliminating the need to handle cash and product movement.

In addition to considerations as to the form of input, other major operating requirements are:

1. The need to enter input data that cannot be identified by the system as a test.
2. The development of a procedure by which to report deficiencies uncovered by the use of the ITF in many parts of the organization.
3. The need to eliminate the effect of the test transactions on financial records.
4. Consideration of using the ITF concept in conjunction with normal audits. For example, a non-computer audit engagement concerned with the handling of material charges could incorporate ITF test results into the usual audit program.[9]

An ITF Case

Following is a real ITF payroll case involving a major manufacturing organization.

After several meetings with Systems and Procedures management of our regional service centers and the public accountants, it was recognized that a different method of auditing payroll was needed to insure, on a continuing basis, that our company's wage payrolls are processed properly. The decision was made to develop an integrated test facility covering our Uniform Wage Payroll System.

Rather than adding test data into real payrolls, we elected to establish a separate payroll cycle for ITF. This enabled us to conduct the systems test on an independent basis; it was tailored to our specific input, output, and timing requirements (paralleling regular payroll cycles) but excluded any possibility of live payroll, statistics, or government reports being affected.

The Audit Division accepted responsibility for overall coordination of the project, for determining test conditions to be included in the ITF, and for designating any special audit requirements. Systems and Procedures agreed to prepare the necessary operating system documentation and to arrange for the installation. The certified public accountants were directly involved during the planning and design stages in order to be satisfied that their audit objectives would be accomplished.

From our regular payroll audits, we knew that actual working conditions were often much more dramatic than any fictitious data we could dream of. Recognizing this and the work involved in formulating fictitious conditions, we decided that data from a current live payroll processing could be used as a starting point in developing U.S. Steel's ITF. Having established a workable test facility, we could add more tests at a later time. For this purpose, we established a multiplant ITF so that, if we desired, some data could be held static in future reprocessing,

[9]*Ibid.*, p. 4.

whereas new or revised conditions could be entered without disturbing our ability to readily reconcile new test results to original test results.

For the initial ITF, data were mechanically extracted from four master files and sixteen detail files of a real steel plant payroll that covered 2,000 employees. Data for 800 of these employees were converted into three ITF plants, so that the multiple-plant processing now used for normal purposes could be simulated with our ITF with some reduction in the volume of data.

However, prior to processing this ITF payroll on a production basis, the premium specified in the union agreement for work performed on Sundays increased from one-quarter to one-half. Except for the control adjustments necessitated by this contract and program change, the ITF and the live payroll used the same answers as a starting point. This also gave us an opportunity to verify that the recent contract change had been properly implemented.

To be certain there had been no program changes during our processing and that ITF was using the same programs as current wage payrolls, system messages were reviewed and program catalogs examined. To determine that essential ITF tapes were mechanically cataloged and would be retained, microfiche copies of data-file catalogs were examined. As backup, duplicate copies of all ITF input tapes were made and sent to Archives.

We now had installed a modified ITF patterned after regular payrolls and had processed the ITF on a production basis. Our ITF had the same type of documentation and clerical controls as live payrolls. The output of our processing had been reconciled to the live payroll from which we had mechanically extracted input data. Next, we had to analyze what we had in ITF and to determine what would be done in the future.

This ITF includes examples of the usual employees who work five regular eight-hour days on afternoon or night shifts. Also, approximately 115 special conditions were tested at least once, including nonstandard shifts, call-out time, daily and weekly overtime, Sunday and holiday work, employees' reporting late or leaving early, incentive work, multiple positions worked, etc. In many instances, several overlapping conditions were tested for the same fictitious employee.

Using the company's administration manuals, which we checked for consistency with the union agreement, we found that, in our ITF, we had tested 92% of the conditions under which an employee could work. We also found that most of the conditions not included in our test facility covered situations that had to be determined administratively. In the future, we planned to add the few conditions that had not yet been tested.

Of course, the Uniform Wage Payroll System may still be tested on a manual basis. In some instances this approach may be a more economical method of assuring ourselves that any required changes are properly made in the mechanical system. Inasmuch as this method is much more time-consuming, however, it could not be used frequently; moreover, the results would be limited by the volume that could be reviewed manually. We feel that significant reductions in audit costs have materialized through the use of the corporate-wide ITF.

A final word of caution: While we believe ITF is a necessity for auditing our payroll function, there is an initial development expense in both manpower and money that must be considered. More than one man-year of audit time was required. Also, we used auditors who had had many years of experience, particularly in EDP and payroll auditing.[10]

Advantages and Disadvantages of the ITF

The ITF has the following advantages:

1. The ITF has the ability to test the flow of data from system to system, and the ability to verify for the test account the accumulation of statistics for a week, month, or year. If the test account is accumulated correctly, the auditor has some assurance that all the required data files were included in the update runs, and that the accumulation routines were operating correctly.[11]

2. The auditor can test the actual operation of a system and the test transactions concurrently. This approach identifies problems and inconsistencies quicker, thus allowing the auditor to practice a preventive audit philosophy. In many cases, it is difficult to tell the cause of a problem. An error or problem may show up in the computer system, but the cause of it may be a procedural problem outside the computer system (e.g., receiving clerk filled out a form incorrectly). ITF helps the auditor to differentiate between procedural and processing problems.

3. The auditor has a high level of assurance that the actual production programs are being tested and that the test transactions are being processed as normal transactions.

4. Use of the ITF provides additional audit information that would be difficult, if not impossible, to obtain using other techniques (e.g., how return of goods is handled).

5. The ITF technique provides a means by which auditors without extensive knowledge of computer technology can effectively use the computer as an audit tool.

6. The auditor's independence and effectiveness are improved be-

---

[10] Abridged from B. L. Thurman, Jr., and Regis C. Cunningham, Jr., "Using An Integrated Test Facility in Audits of Multiplant Payrolls," *The Internal Auditor*, November/December 1974, pp. 50–56.

[11] Perry, *op. cit.*, p. 76.

cause he does not have to request special computer time since the test transactions are processed simultaneously with live transactions.

The ITF has the following disadvantages:

1. The auditor must reverse the effects of the ITF technique and remove all traces of the test transactions. Incorrect data and mishandling of assets or services might cause problems if not controlled and corrected in time.

2. There is a possibility of erasing other real data. The probability of this happening is extremely low.

13.5 PARALLEL TEST FACILITY (PTF)

The major difference between an integrated test facility (ITF) and a parallel test facility (PTF) is that the PTF does not affect the actual data base because the test transactions do not flow through the system. There are two ways to employ a PTF: (1) parallel processing, and (2) parallel simulation.

Parallel Processing

The parallel processing approach permits the testing of an entire application system without requiring access to the actual data base by copying the production programs (and in some instances the operating system), extracting a representative part of the data base and dumping it on separate file media, and processing representative transactions via another computer. The purpose, as with other audit techniques, is to determine that the operating system and application programs meet established requirements and that they are functioning as designed. By creating and maintaining a close but small representation of the data base and test transactions, it is possible to process a wide variety of test transactions and generate all types of output results for evaluation (see Figure 13.3). Note that the two major differences between this approach and the ITF are that: (1) the live data base is not affected, and (2) the auditor can test an unlimited number of transactions across all subsystems.

Parallel Simulation

Parallel simulation is similar in concept to auditing around the computer. This technique is based on the idea that one should be able to take the input transactions, master files, and logic that produced a computer output and reproduce the result. For an illustration, see Figure 13.4. Parallel simulation consists of the preparation of separate computer programs that simulate the same functions as those used for daily application processing. The simulation programs accept the same transactions as the application programs, use the same records in the data base (these records would have to be copied on a direct access storage device (DASD) because of destructive updating), and attempt to simulate the appropriate results.[12]

Parallel simulation can duplicate all kinds of program processing routines, but it is more suitable for some types than others. The simple logic of update and file maintenance can be readily simulated, but the traditional methods of external confirmation, physical inventory, or comparison with a similar independently maintained file are often easier and just as effective. More productive areas for simulation are the processing of edits and control totals and the simulation of conditions

---

[12] William C. Mair, "Parallel Simulation—A Technique for Effective Verification of Computer Programs," *EDPACS*, April 1975, pp. 1–6. *Computer Controls and Audit.* First edition (New York: Touche Ross & Co., September 1973), pp. 5–13—5–15.

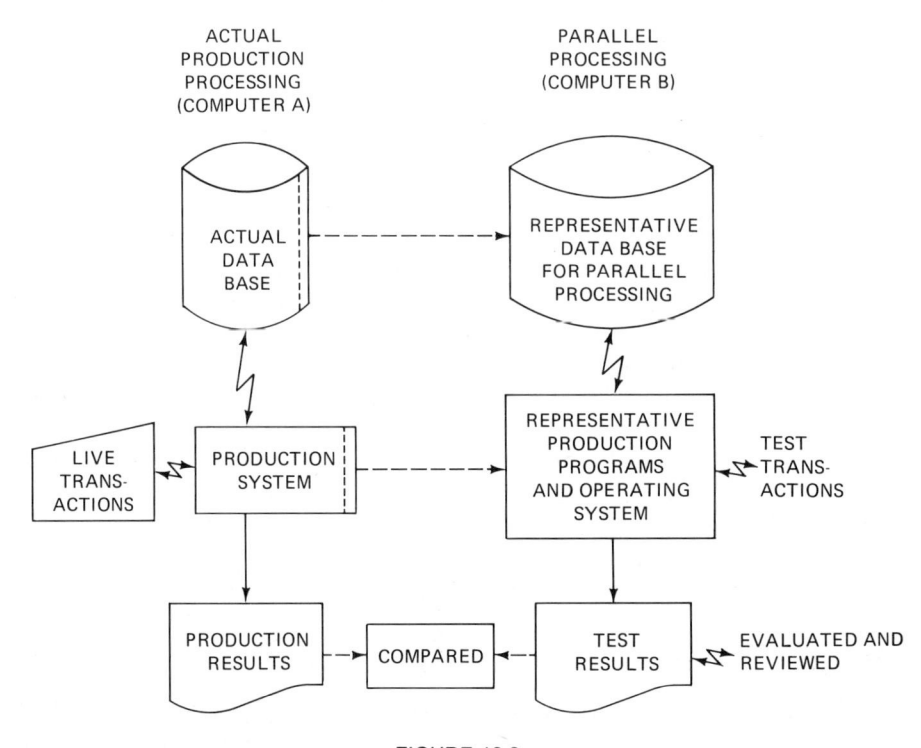

FIGURE 13.3.
Schematic of a Parallel Processing System.

that cause transactions to be internally generated within the computer. The internally generated transaction, more often than any other type, defies external verification since the external techniques used to accomplish it rely upon some kind of documented transaction trail. Common examples of internally generated transactions are: (1) recognition of interest on deposits, (2) recognition of interest on loans, (3) reorder of out-of-stock inventory items, (4) automatic write-off of uncollectible receivables, (5) authorization of payment on accounts payable, and (6) calculation of earned premium income.[13]

To implement parallel simulation:

1. The auditor must gain a general understanding of the business application system under examination before he can make an informed decision about which application areas he wishes to verify.

2. The auditor must gain an understanding of the program logic that applies to the areas of his direct concern. He should omit from his parallel simulation any complex logic that applies only to rare situations. He can manually resolve any differences caused by this omission. The detailed understanding must include: (a) accurate descriptions of records and transactions, (b) meaning of codes used in the computer files, (c) specific formulas or decision criteria used in the "live" application, and (d) the number of decimal places to which calculations are carried.

[13]Mair, *op. cit.*, p. 2.

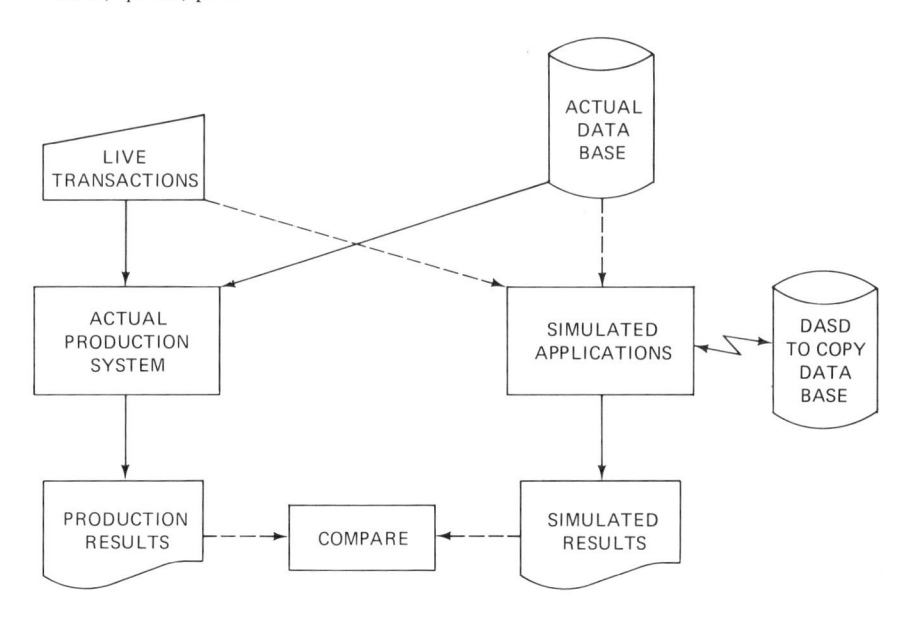

FIGURE 13.4.
Schematic of a Parallel Simulation System.

3. The auditor must acquire representative master files and transactions. Obviously, a large set of transactions and master file records can be obtained from the live system. Care must be taken, however, to assure that the selected data include all the conditions that the auditor wishes to test. This determination can be made in most situations by a review of processing control reports that list the quantity of transactions according to type.

If the files used for testing do not include certain transaction types, the auditor has two alternatives. He may add his additional transactions to the "live" files; this process would represent a combination of parallel simulation and test decking. As an alternative, he may accept the available files as being representative of the actual transactions.

Verification of certain rare situations may not be necessary, since errors associated with them would not be significant. A decision to ignore rare situations must be made consciously and carefully, but it is proper to weight audit tests toward those situations that represent the greatest potential for error or abuse.

4. Once the auditor has obtained his data and understands the logic of the application being audited, he is ready to prepare the computer program logic needed to simulate the processing of the original system. Although any computer programming language may be used to create this logic, the auditor will find it most efficient to use a generalized audit software language.

Generalized audit software is available from many major public accounting firms and a number of commercial software organizations. A variety of systems exist, all of them suitable for the parallel simulation technique. The only audit software capability that is of particular interest in using parallel simulation is the extent of arithmetic and logical operations that can be performed. Systems that limit the quantity of arithmetic and/or comparison operations may restrict the scope of the application systems the auditor will be able to verify. The kinds of data and files that can be read and the nature of the reports that can be produced are also of concern.

5. The auditor processes the simulation programs and analyzes the results.[14]

It should be added that the idea of exception reporting could be easily designed into the parallel simulation audit technique. Editing for reasonableness is particularly beneficial in that it automatically reports any transactions that exceed defined limits.

Moreover, time-sharing facilities and canned programs can be used in simulating operations. However, the use of timesharing is not applicable only to parallel simulation, because it is a strong audit technique

[14]*Ibid.*, p. 3.

in its own right. Canned programs are available from most CPA firms, along with other companies (e.g., General Electric Timesharing) and universities. These packages provide: what-if analysis, relationships, trends, and inconsistencies; earnings per share; depreciation schedules; mortgage schedules, present value; imputed interest, ratios; regression analysis; and so forth. Timesharing insures ready access, because wherever there is a telephone, the auditor can connect his terminal to the computer.

13.6 MONITORING SYSTEMS

Earlier in Part III, we presented a number of vendor utility programs that appear to be useful to the auditor. Additional packages discussed in this section can be put to good use by the auditor to provide computer usage, control, and performance information. This information is collected as a by-product of the normal operations without requiring extensive programming or special work by the auditor. The packages presented in this section are: (1) systems management facilities, (2) software monitors, and (3) hardware monitors.

System Management Facilities (SMF)

IBM's System Management Facilities (SMF) can be used by auditors to obtain large amounts of useful audit information about a computer system's operating environment. SMF is a feature of IBM's System/360-370 operating systems (OS and VS only), although most other computer manufacturers have similar systems.

The SMF package handles two broad types of processes: (1) data collection, and (2) user exits. Data-collection routines cause records to be written to an SMF file on magnetic tape or disk. These records provide information to the auditor to analyze the handling of data while application programs are being executed, accounting information about computer operations, and additional information that can be used to evaluate operational efficiency. User exits provide for the integration and execution of audit programs written by the auditor to provide additional audit information to be written into the SMF file. The SMF file thus contains a wealth of audit information that can be processed and printed out by a report writer program.

Six general categories of information are furnished by the SMF system. These are as follows:

1. *Accounting records* This category consists of records that show who used the system and how long they used it. The information con-

tained in these records includes: (a) identification of job or job step, user, hardware features; (b) job priority; (c) date and time of job initiation; (d) date and time of job termination; (e) type of job termination (for abnormal terminations, the reason for the ABEND is indicated); and (f) amount of main storage in bytes used to execute the job. These records provide an audit trail of the system resources utilized and the jobs and/or personnel responsible for the use of these resources. These records are often used as the basis for charging users for their utilization of the computer facility. Information contained in these records is used by the accounting department as the basis for developing EDP cost allocation and charging users accordingly.

This billing of users represents a strong control, because the thing data-processing people are most likely to steal is computer time. If there is no method of charging users for computer time, then it requires little effort on the perpetrator's part to use the computer improperly.

Other things that the auditor can look for are: (a) job steps with a significant variation in CPU time for execution on different occasions; (b) job steps run at unusual times, e.g., daily jobs being run six times a week instead of five or extra runs of a weekly job; (c) insertion of an extra job step, i.e., one included only occasionally in a standard daily run; (d) unusual number of ABEND codes to identify error-prone programs.

2. *Data set activity records*   These records provide information about which data files were used to perform a computer job or job step (a subunit within a job) and who requested the use of the data sets (files). They furnish an audit trail of data usage. This trail is one of the principal benefits the auditor will find within SMF. These records also supply considerable information about the characteristics of the data sets.

There are four basic records that describe data sets: input files, output files, scratched files (data erased from files), and renamed files.

The information produced for input and output files is almost the same and encompasses: (a) data set name, (b) data set organization (e.g., sequential, random, indexed-sequential), (c) record format and length, (d) number of disk packs or tapes required, and (e) serial numbers of file media.

It is useful to sort the records created for each file opened by the job identification and compare this information with production work orders (PWO) to insure that all the data sets used by a job are authorized to be used by it. It is helpful to re-sort these records by data set name and send a report to the proprietor of the data set so that he can see if it is being accessed by unauthorized or unknown jobs.

If a data set is scratched, the following information is recorded: (a) file name, (b) number of magnetic tapes or disks, and (c) serial number of magnetic tapes or disks. When a data set is renamed, the following information is recorded: (a) the old name, (b) the new name, (c) the number of magnetic tapes or disks, and (d) their serial numbers. Each time the operating system reads or writes a data set, an SMF record can be produced. This recording can be used to provide positive control over file usage and activity.

3. *Volume utilization records* These records indicate the amount of available space on direct access devices and give basic error statistics for tape files. They also record the number of records contained in each data set. These records are used by the data-processing department in its efforts to obtain better utilization of space within direct access storage devices. In the case of tape files, the error statistics are helpful in assessing the quality of a particular reel of tape. For example, when the number of errors on a tape reaches a certain level, the tape should be either cleaned or discarded. The information in the volume utilization records has little meaning for auditors. They might want to review this data in an attempt to determine whether or not the data-processing department is making effective use of this information. The auditor would not usually have any reason to look at these records unless there are problem symptoms at the installation that might be clarified by such review.

4. *System usage records* This category contains records that show the portion of the hardware configuration being utilized by each job and job step, such as the number of disk accesses. These records can be used to develop some appreciation of the effectiveness with which the resources of the system are being applied. Within this category, approximately twenty different records are produced. It includes some information the auditor can use in controlling SMF. System use records indicate which SMF options are in effect or have been in effect since the last time the system was subject to an initial program load (IPL). Normally, a system is subject to one or more IPL's per day.

Much of the information is technical in nature; for example, the amount of time the computer is idle. The auditor might want to be certain that this information is being used by the data-processing department to achieve maximum system efficiency. Some information would be of particular interest to the auditor, since it records activity that takes place at some of the critical control points within the system. Some examples of this are: (a) date and time of all data set dumps, (b) records of each time a terminal logged on, and (c) records of each time a system halt command was initiated.

System use records provide data that would be helpful to auditors examining the operational aspects of a computer center. Some data in the records can be used when the auditor is performing an internal control review and evaluation.

5. *Subsystem records* Whenever a job requires a subsystem (subroutine, program, module) for some processing operation, that fact can

be recorded by SMF. This information is of value to the auditor for two reasons. First, it provides an audit trail of which subsystems are being utilized by which jobs. Second, it gives the auditor an opportunity to find out what activity is being entered by terminals and who is using those terminals.

One particular type of record is of interest to most auditors. This record is written whenever a sign-on attempt fails because of an invalid password. A limited number of invalid passwords are normally entered because of keying errors at the terminal. An abnormal number of such errors could indicate that someone is trying to break into the system. This error data may require audit investigation.

6. *User-written records* When needed information cannot be obtained from one of the categories described above, SMF provides the user with the option of incorporating his own analysis routines into the system. At specific points (user exits) within an SMF run, control can be transferred to user-written routines that will analyze events, record data for later review, or alter either the system or its data. This is an extremely flexible feature. It gives SMF an almost unlimited analytical capability, but at the same time it presents the opportunity for unauthorized manipulation of data.

The extensive capabilities for performing further analysis should provide the auditor with unlimited opportunities for evaluating data-processing. Auditors can build routines to review every transaction for conformity with organizational policies and procedures, to detect violations of systems standards, or to perform special analysis in support of audit objectives. In spite of this performance degradation, the use of analysis routines is an important technique, because it potentially allows the auditor to analyze the operation of a system during execution time without the specific knowledge of any other person or group. This could improve audit integrity, security, and independence in a computer environment.

The capability to alter the operating aspects of the system while it is being run must be exercised with caution. For instance, SMF can be used to delete certain records or even cancel a job running in production status. In his use of SMF, the auditor should be careful not to impede or alter normal production. On the other hand, the ability to delete records or cancel jobs might be an effective way for management to enforce its standards.

The auditor should determine if any systems in his organization are being altered during operation and, if so, why. Use of this capability should be well controlled, and the auditor should verify that such a control mechanism exists. SMF can be utilized to provide an audit trail that will record the use of such routines in production. This trail can then become the basis for reviewing such system alterations.

7. *Other user routines* Another type of user routine involves writing report programs for sorting, summarizing, accumulating, and editing SMF data to make it into useful audit information. To the largest possible extent, the user should try to employ the report-writing capability provided within SMF. It represents an easy and economical means of obtaining simple, analytical reports.[15]

The variety of audits that might be performed on the basis of SMF information is virtually unlimited. The following examples illustrate ways in which the auditor might use SMF information in performing audit reviews of the system of controls.[16]

1. *Determine users of data sets* The audit objective is to verify that all users of data sets are properly authorized and are utilizing these data sets only for valid purposes. Fields to be extracted from SMF records are date opened, job name, user identification field, and data set name. Primary sort is by data set name; the secondary sort on user identification field; and the final sort key is date. The report produced from this audit can be set up in a variety of formats. The simplest is to list each data access by user by date; however, an extremely long listing could result. It may be desirable to summarize the input and print one line for each user of each data set. A count of the total number of accesses by each user can be reported. For selected data sets, verify that all users are properly authorized. For example, confirmations showing all users for each data set can be prepared and sent to those responsible for the data sets. Any unauthorized users should be reported to the auditor for further investigation.

2. *Determine invalid passwords* The audit objective is to review accesses involving invalid passwords to ascertain whether they are caused by operator error or they involve attempts at unauthorized access. The fields to be extracted from SMF records are time of transaction, date of transaction, system identification, remote name (terminal), line name, and invalid password. The primary sort is by system identification; the secondary sort on remote name; and the final sort is invalid password. On the initial report all invalid access attempts should be listed. The general rule is that one or two invalid attempts from a remote terminal can be considered operator errors. Three or more invalid attempts warrant audit follow-up. This first analysis would show system identification, remote name, line name, invalid password, and date and time of transaction. Follow-up audits would report only three or more

---

[15]This presentation on SMF summarized from William E. Perry and Donald L. Adams, "SMF—An Untapped Audit Resource," *EDPACS*, September 1974, pp. 1–8; and "Using SMF as an Audit Tool—Accounting Information," *EDPACS*, January 1975, pp. 1–9; Donald L. Adams, "Evaluating Performance in Computer Auditing" *EDPACS*, February 1975; and Reader Feedback section of *EDPACS*, February 1975, pp. 1–17.

[16]Examples taken from William E. Perry, "Using SMF as an Audit Tool—Security," *EDPACS*, January 1976, pp. 1–8.

attempts to access a system from a remote terminal during the period being reviewed. Investigate excessive unauthorized attempts to enter secure systems. If distance or time is a factor, a confirmation approach can be used.

3. *Investigation of renamed data sets* In the normal course of operations, it should be unusual to rename a data set; this procedure, therefore, warrants occasional investigation. Fields extracted from SMF records are date renamed, job name, user identification field, old data set name, and new data set name. No sort of this information is required. Using this information, the auditor should review the users and the data sets renamed. If the data set is a sensitive one, the reasons for renaming should be established.

4. *Review of data set library* The data set library should have records for all active files in the organization. A representative sample of data sets can be selected from SMF records and checked against the library records. The fields to be extracted are date of activity, job name, user identification field, and data set name. The results should be sorted by data set name. The auditor should then check the data contained in the SMF records against the data set library. Both additions to and deletions from the library should be verified.

5. *Investigation of run frequency* One indication of a possible control problem is the excessive execution of a particular system. The auditor must verify that user application programs are not executed in excess of the normal schedule. This check applies only to periodic processing systems. However, where a hybrid system is used, this investigation can be important. The fields to be extracted from the SMF records are date job was executed, job name, job completion code, and programmer's name. The sort sequence should be on job name. For sensitive jobs, the auditor should determine that execution is in accordance with the normal schedule, for example, that daily jobs run five times per week, that weekly jobs run once a week, and so forth. Exceptions to these schedules should be thoroughly investigated.

Software Monitors

The ability to insure maximum performance and to optimize and safeguard resources is a prime concern of the auditor. Information needed to analyze CPU utilization, input/output utilization, and software efficiency is more accurately obtained by using software and hardware monitors.

Software monitors do a better job measuring software performance, and hardware monitors are best for measuring hardware activity. Both types of monitors overlap and intrude into the other's domain, but the levels of accuracy and degree of capability differ. For example, both hardware and software monitors can measure CPU activity, but the hardware monitor figure is more accurate because it does not degrade the system, and it can always take measurements, even when the operating system is running with interrupts disabled. Software monitors do not enjoy these advantages.[17] However, to evaluate the overall system performance, the software monitor can be used in conjunction with a hardware monitor and performance reports based on SMF data.

The software monitor is a program that is appended to the operating system or that runs as a high-priority problem program or system task. The software monitor can provide very accurate utilization data because it can read internal tables, operating system control blocks, status registers, memory maps, and so forth.[18]

The objectives of measuring system software components differ from those of measuring hardware components. Software component measurements are performed to determine utilization and hardware requirements, rather than levels and concurrency of hardware utilization. System software components commonly measured are operating systems, support software, and application programs.[19]

1. *Operating system* The operating system is a good place to look for performance improvement, because it is large and frequently used. Such measurements are done partly for information purposes and partly to evaluate operating performance.

These measurements tell data-processing management how much of the resources are devoted to the operating system, and they identify particularly inefficient sections of code. The existence of such sections could impel management to ask the vendor for improvement, or if this is not possible, commercially available software might be considered as a replacement.

The study might also indicate that the placement of certain routines should be altered. For example, the number of operating system subroutines supplied by the vendor may be so large that they cannot all be made core-resident. Therefore, some will be placed in secondary storage, usually disk. The decision as to which modules go where is usually based on the vendor's recommendations when the system is installed. The installation's workload has probably changed since that time.[20]

2. *Support software* Support software falls in the gray area between user programs and the operating system. Although run in the system much like user programs, support software are written by the vendor

---

[17]John J. Hunter, "Knowing ABC's of DP Monitoring Tools Vital Today," *Computerworld*, April 30, 1975, p. S/2.
[18]*Ibid.*
[19]*Ibid.*
[20]*Ibid.*

and appear to the ordinary computer user as part of the operating system. Examples are compilers, communications programs, and utilities.

With compilers and communications programs, the user is not seeking to modify the code of such complex programs, but rather to know what they cost in terms of resources. The aim is to ask the vendor to improve the program and/or to investigate using alternative software.

In the area of utilities, computer performance evaluation gives the user the most flexibility. Because utilities are frequently used, they offer high payoff potential. What additional measurements are usually taken for utilities? Basically, the same measurements as for user programs. The user can reasonably make changes to the actual utility code if the study indicates that such changes are necessary. Utilities can often be changed without vendor assistance and without fear of disturbing the operating system.[21]

3. *Application programs* User programs (application programs) are measured to determine resource utilization and code efficiency. Resource utilization measurements record and report the amount of time a program uses each of the resources it requests, such as core, tapes, and disk.

Sometimes the utilization is zero because the programmer allowed for the worst case. For example, the utility may request eight tape drives, even though it normally needs four. If the installation is short of tapes and the number of runs that need all eight tapes is one in thirty (monthly closing), the center may ask a programmer to change the utility.

Another important aspect of resource analysis is the determination if I/O activity and block sizes. Sometimes a program requires 10 more I/O's than necessary because the records were improperly blocked.

Code efficiency analysis involves measuring the amount of time spent in each identifiable section of code. In business it is often true that 20% of the customers account for 80% of the business volume. The same often holds true for programs.[22]

The software monitor can be used to isolate heavy page rate areas (in virtual storage systems) and to insure that all are being handled properly and in a timely manner. Application programs that use a number of IF statements incorrectly and do not contain a modular structure can cause a "thrashing" condition of pages where the CPU is spending a disproportionate time accessing from and storing pages upon magnetic disk. With some analysis and program rewrites, this program bottleneck can be reduced. Virtual storage systems have many overall advantages,

[21]*Ibid.*
[22]*Ibid.*

but they require a greater degree of sophisticated monitoring to insure that they provide those advantages in an efficient manner.[23]

Hardware Monitors

Many organizations have not had the time and, in some instances, the capability of obtaining and exploiting the full benefits of their present computer systems because of the rush to acquire newer technology. Many data-processing managers equate effective use of the computer with acquisition of a new one. The real test of management is to strike a balance between managing present systems effectively and exploiting the latest computer technology.[24]

With sufficient utilization statistics, properly evaluated, the overall computer equipment budget may be cut as much as 30 percent by changing the CPU, dropping channels, tapes, or disks, and at the same time improving overall efficiency. The broad purpose is to match the "horsepower" of the computer to the information system demands. To do this, the hardware monitor measures: CPU active, CPU wait, disk seek, disk data transfer, disk mount, tape active, tape rewind, and core storage timings and utilization.

Figure 13.5 outlines the elements of a hardware monitor. The main elements are as follows:[25]

1. *General probes* These probes are a set of signal sensors designed for minimum interference with the host computer and able to drive relatively long cables so that signals may be picked up from various points physically distant from each other and from the central monitor console.

2. *Logic circuits* These circuits accept signals from the general probes and allow logical combinations of the signals so that one may define events of interest.

3. *Counters* There are a group of counters that may be used to count the occurrence of various events, or to measure the time between events by counting the number of intervening clock pulses.

4. *Comparator probes* These probes are similar to the general probes, but they are used to sense a number of bits that appear in parallel, e.g., as in an address register.

5. *Comparator* This element provides the means for comparing the

---

[23]"Monitor Helps 'Insure' Applications, Monthly Tuning," *Computerworld*, April 30, 1975, p. S/3.

[24]Nathan Hod and John G. Burch, Jr., "Getting More from Your Computer," *Datamation*, November 1974, pp. 60–62.

[25]Jerre D. Noe, "Acquiring and Using a Hardware Monitor," *Datamation*, April 1974, pp. 89–95.

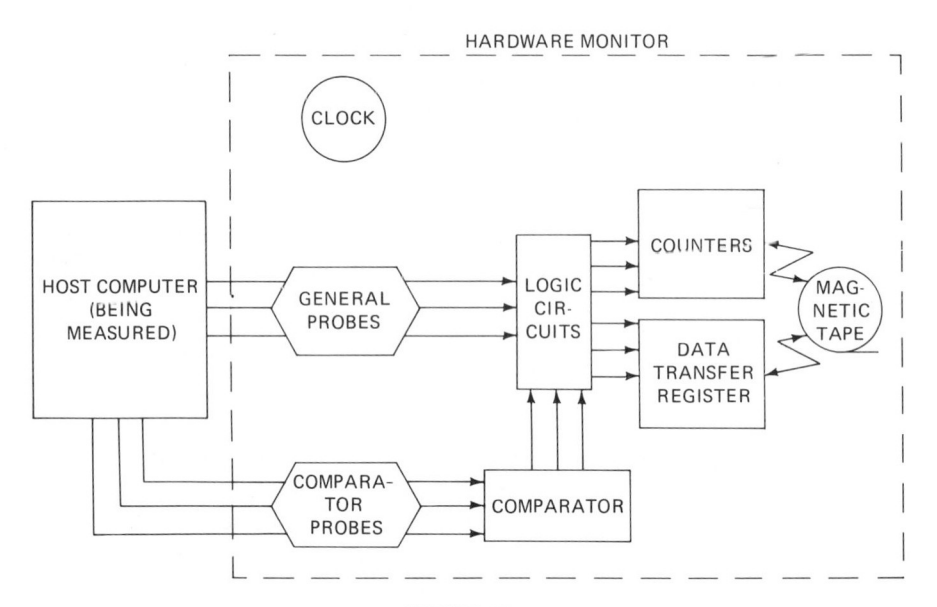

FIGURE 13.5.
Elements of a Hardware Monitor.

parallel bits with some present value at an instant defined by a signal on the comparator probes.

6. *Data transfer register* This element provides the means for passing utilization data directly from the host computer to the magnetic tape file. This register might be combined with the counter functions or with the comparator functions.[26]

7. *Magnetic tape* A single magnetic tape (can also be a disk) can hold several days of recorded data. The tape is later analyzed via the computer, just as any other job would be and reports are generated for analysis. Special programs generate numeric listings that show the exact percentage of time the measured components were active or inactive over a selected period. Other reports in graph form plot equipment activity against elapsed time.

The basic advantage of hardware monitors over software monitors is that hardware monitors require no systems overhead to run, and they operate independently of the system itself. No link-editing processes with the operating system are required, no core storage is required for the measurement software, and no other hardware except for the measurement devices is required. Hardware monitors measure activity much as electrocardiographs measures heart activity. Sensors are at-

[26]*Ibid.*

tached to the "patient," and the results are recorded for evaluation and diagnosis.[27]

With the use of hardware monitors, the following items can be investigated: (1) bottlenecks within I/O, (2) reduction of budget without diminishing throughout (throughput rate = data processing tasks successfully completed/system clock time to process the activities), (3) the necessity of upgrading to a larger CPU, and (4) potential improvements.

Event processing systems have the ability to compute input/output concurrently, and perform multiprogramming. There are four major ingredients to this functional capability: (1) CPU only when the compute functions are active and the I/O functions are inactive, (2) CPU and any I/O where both compute functions and some type of I/O are active concurrently, (3) I/O only where the CPU is idle while an I/O function is active commonly referred to as CPU wait time, and (4) system idle where both CPU and I/O functions are inactive.[28]

The hardware monitor can be an effective diagnostic package for comparing a present CPU with another to see if management should change. In Figure 13.6 is a comparison of the measured performance profile of an IBM 360/75 with an estimated IBM 370/155 profile. The results of the monitoring activity show that system throughput would be reduced if the 155 were installed. This reduction would occur because of an increase in processing time from 69.8 to 79.0 percent. A decision to change from one system to another is, of course, dependent upon the cost/performance trade-offs for each configuration. Particular situations may indicate that a reduced performance is acceptable because of a greatly reduced systems and operating cost.[29]

Many data-processing managers hypothesize that their system is channel-bound, i.e., they have an I/O bottleneck. A composite profile generated by the hardware monitor may show that the system is actually CPU-bound and that one or more channels can actually be eliminated and thus, cost savings be effected without compromising efficiency.

The utilization data produced by the hardware monitor can quantify the extent of additional capacity present in various parts of the system. Thus, the workload can be remixed and scheduled to provide quicker turnaround to critical jobs and better overall throughput. For example, the operations personnel can fit short CPU-time jobs (e.g., less than five minutes with a small amount of I/O) into time slots in the schedule. Such modifications can mean that short jobs that previously had a 24-hour

---

[27]Milton D. Sewald, Michael E. Rauch, Lyle Rodick, and Langston Wertz, "A Pragmatic Approach to Systems Measurement," *Computer Decisions*, July 1971, pp. 38–40.

[28]Stanley E. Robinson, "Strategy First Step in Successful Hardware Monitoring," *Computerworld*, April 30, 1975, p. S/6.

[29]Sewald et al, *op. cit.*, p. 39.

360/75:

TOTAL TIME	100%
CPU ACTIVE	34.2%
WAIT ON CHANNEL	35.6%
CPU AND CHANNELS INACTIVE	30.1%
CPU ACTIVE ONLY	15.3%
CPU AND INPUT/OUTPUT OVERLAP	18.9%

370/155:

TOTAL TIME	100%
CPU ACTIVE	55%
WAIT ON CHANNEL	24%
CPU AND CHANNELS INACTIVE	21%
CPU ACTIVE ONLY	24%
CPU AND INPUT/OUTPUT OVERLAP	31%

FIGURE 13.6.
A Comparison of the Measured Performance Profile of a 360/75 and an Estimated Profile of a 370/155.

turnaround now have an hour or less turnaround, and these jobs are essentially free, since they run in time slots that previously were unused.[30]

The General Accounting Office (GAO) has found the Social Security Administration (SSA) uses approximately 40% of the capacity of its 17 large-scale computers. . . .

The four IBM 370/168s the SSA now has on order and sitting in a warehouse "will represent an increase of more than 40% in large-scale computer capacity of SSA" if they are allowed to be installed, according to the programmer, Ferdinand Jung.[31]

13.7 THE AUDITOR'S INVOLVEMENT IN SYSTEMS DEVELOPMENT

It can readily be seen at this point that control and auditability of event processing systems require a great deal of preplanning. For example, it is difficult, if not impracticable in some situations, to change existing

---

[30]*Ibid.*
[31]Edith Holmes, "GAO Audit Finds SSA Uses Only 40% of CPU Capacity While Planning to Expand," *Computerworld*, April 26, 1976, p. 1.

programs to include tagging and tracing routines. To foresake the historical approach to auditing and employ concurrent auditing of transactions as they occur, the auditor must become involved in systems development to make sure that a system of controls and audit interfaces are designed into the system at the outset rather than tacked on afterwards.

> The auditor's participation in systems development and design will become more critical in the case of an advanced system. This involvement will enable the auditor to provide a valuable contribution, particularly from the control standpoint, to the company's new system and will, since audit requirements can be specified during the initial design phase, decrease the chance of an 'unauditable' system being developed.[32]

The Auditor's Objectives

Many computer systems personnel are still inclined to think in terms of computer equipment in isolation rather than in terms of sound management and business practices, system of controls, and systems auditability. There has to be a better rapport and channel of communications between these people and accounting and auditing personnel. In many cases, the auditor does not become aware of inadequacies in the controls and auditability of the system until it is "up and running." At this point, it is frequently quite difficult or not cost/effective to make extensive changes in the system to improve controls and auditing interfaces.

With the development of event processing systems with widespread networks of data communication systems and complex data bases, it has become imperative that the auditor play a key role in systems development. Since computer configurations and systems software of event processing systems are often inflexible, because of technological and budget constraints, the auditor no longer has the option of "playing it by ear" or beginning the review and testing of the system after it is operating only to conclude that significant inadequacies exist and must be corrected.

Many of the event processing systems require several years of planning, design, development, and testing before they can be implemented. The auditor should begin his involvement at the initiation of the systems project and remain throughout all phases (e.g., analysis, general design, evaluation, detail design, testing) of the systems development methodology.

---

[32]Task Force of the AICPA's Computer Auditing Subcommittee, "Auditing Advanced EDP Systems", *The Journal of Accountancy*, January 1975, p. 71.

Efficient and effective auditing of an electronic funds transfer system cannot occur unless the auditor's needs are met in the basic design of the system; therefore, both bankers and auditors would be well advised to become heavily involved in the system's design. . . .[33]

During the early phases, the auditor should make sure that the systems personnel are aware of controls, their application to systems, and audit objectives. The auditor wears two hats and must act both as consultant and as devil's advocate. He must give guidance and criticism.

During the design phase, the auditor should see to it that control and audit techniques (e.g., transaction logs, tagging and tracing) are embedded in the system and that standards (e.g., top-down structured programming, documentation) are followed. At critical points during systems development, the auditor should review all documentation and reports prepared to that point and make sure that there are no variances between what actually exists and what is reported. During evaluation, the auditor should make sure that sound cost/effective analysis is performed. He should review program listings to make sure that controls are in place. He should gauge overall development progress and make sure that the systems development methodology is being followed. He should determine where the systems project stands in relation to the schedule. The auditor must be alert to the fact that, in many instances, when a systems project is behind schedule, computer systems personnel will attempt to make the conversion deadline by cutting corners, especially in the testing phase. The auditor should perform a strong, conscientious review of all test data and testing procedures. He may also prepare independent test data and apply them for his own satisfaction.

The Auditor's Authority

The auditor should have the authority to delay implementation of the systems project, or any phase thereof, if he feels that significant inadequacies exist. At the very minimum, if the auditor's involvement is to be meaningful, he should have the option to alert top management that the implementation of the system or some part of it should be postponed. Management should be given the benefit of an independent review prior to systems implementation. Who else but the auditor can provide management with this independent review?

The output of the auditor should be a formal audit report which should be distributed to and reviewed by management (e.g., steering

---

[33]Kathryn Liebtag (ed.), "Heavy Involvement of Bankers, Auditors Advised in Development of EFT System," *American Banker*, April 14, 1976, p. 11.

committee). On an exception basis, it should report only significant findings. These audit reports should also include the current status of the project and an opinion and recommendations concerning the systems project and whether or not it is ready to progress to the next phase of development.

The Auditor's Independence

The auditing standard that states, "in all matters relating to the assignment an independence in mental attitude is to be maintained by the auditor," is perhaps the most important element in the auditor's work. If he assumes the role of a spokesman for computer systems personnel, or in fact becomes "part" of the systems development team, he sacrifices his independence and effectiveness as an auditor. The auditor's work must be based on an objective and disinterested viewpoint. This independent status of the auditor gives value and significance to his opinion and audit reports.

Playing the role of a quasi consultant and presenting guidelines and advice to the systems development team do not in and of themselves create a threat to the auditor's independence. If, however, the auditor becomes a part-time systems person and assumes a decision-making role, he is not in a position to make an independent analysis and review of the system he is working on. He should not, for example, allow the testing of systems controls and programs to become his responsibility. In such a situation, the auditor himself would be performing a critical portion of the systems development work rather than reviewing the testing procedures of the systems developers. What he should do is state what a control or technique must do. He does not do it or state how to do it. For example, he may state that "any transaction that changes the data base must be logged in a transaction file showing its origination, time, and date, identifying number, and so forth." Then he reviews the system to make sure that his guidelines have been followed. He performs this function for taxpayers, management, stockholders, government agencies, and others who rely on audited information. He also does it for himself to insure future integrity and auditability of the system. Otherwise, there would be no purpose to his involvement in systems development.[34]

---

[34] For further discussion on the auditor's involvement in systems development, see William E. Perry and Donald Adams, "Pre-implementation Audit Survey," *EDPACS*, November 1974, pp. 1–7; and "The Four Phases of EDP Auditing," *EDPACS*, May 1975, pp. 1–18; James R. Grimes, "The Auditor's Role in System Design," *EDPACS*, September 1975, pp. 1–7. Javier F. Kuong, *Computer Security, Auditing and Controls* (Wellesley Hills, Mass.: Management Advisory Publications, 1974), pp. 350–355.

13.8 SUMMARY

The effective way to audit event processing systems is to do it concurrently rather than periodically and after the fact. Transactions should be audited as they occur, and the key audit tool should be the computer. The system should automatically log all transactions on magnetic tape or disk for backup and for audit purposes. Tagging and tracing routines should be embedded in the programming logic to provide visible output of transactions as they flow through the system.

An integrated test facility (ITF) is one of the most powerful techniques that the auditor can use for concurrent auditing of the system. It provides not only evidential information about the controls and logic of the data-processing system, but also evidential information about the operations of the entire organization. Therefore, this technique can also be applied to operational auditing. A parallel test facility (PTF) has objectives that are similar to those of the ITF, but the test transactions do not flow through the "live" system. Rather, they are entered through a copy of the logic and partial data base of the system, or they are simulated.

Other techniques that can enhance the idea of concurrent auditing are: systems management facilities, software monitors, and hardware monitors. These are packages that have not been used extensively by auditors, but which appear to have strong audit application.

The last suggestion in this chapter is that the auditor should become involved in reviewing systems before, during, and after they are developed and implemented. The auditor can make a major contribution to the organization and its constituents by insuring that proper controls are designed into the system. Involvement of the auditor during the design phase makes the auditor's advice and expertise available throughout systems development and helps insure establishment of a well-controlled, auditable system. Because event processing systems are becoming so technologically complex, it is difficult, if not impracticable, to correct weaknesses after the fact.

REVIEW QUESTIONS

13.1 List and define at least two event processing systems with which you are familiar.
13.2 Define the transaction log and its purpose.
13.3 Define tagging and tracing. How is this technique implemented in a system?
13.4 List the significant SNAPSHOT points in a tagging and tracing routine.
13.5 List the tagging and tracing considerations.
13.6 Define an ITF and its purpose.

13.7 Compare an ITF with the test deck technique.
13.8 List the advantages and disadvantages of the ITF.
13.9 Define the two types of a PTF.
13.10 List the control and audit features of SMF.
13.11 List the control and audit features of hardware and software monitors.

DISCUSSION QUESTIONS

13.1 Discuss the differences between a preventive auditing philosophy and after-the-fact auditing.
13.2 Why is the term transaction trail used rather than audit trail?
13.3 "The audit trail has disappeared with the arrival of event processing systems." Discuss the merit of this statement.
13.4 "An ITF is the same thing as a test deck." Discuss.
13.5 Discuss the difference between an ITF and a PTF.
13.6 How can monitoring system packages increase the effectiveness of the auditor?
13.7 Why should the auditor become involved in systems development?

EXERCISES

13.1 Write a simple routine in a programming language of your choice to print out the results of a transaction when it is matched against a record in a master file and immediately after the master record has been changed by the transaction. Make your own assumptions.
13.2 Give an example of how you would go about setting up an ITF for a hypothetical company and the kinds of test transactions you would enter.

PROBLEMS

13.1 You are an auditor with "Big 8." The partner in charge of your office calls you in to see him. He has recently received a telephone call from the local district attorney's office. It appears that recent legislation concerning privacy may have an impact upon the "total court information system" recently installed by the state. Since much of the data on the system is very sensitive, you have been selected to perform an audit of the system.

The system's computer configuration is illustrated in Figure 13.7. The various files and queues are shown in the center with the telecommunication facilities to the left and the batch processing facilities to the right.

The three basic data files are the Case History File, Name and Identification Number File, and the Calendar File. Each basic file is separated into an active and inactive file to augment the online and batch oriented functions.

The remote terminal user has nine basic teleprocessing functions available. These consist of Remote Batch Input (RBI), Batch Output Reporting (REP), and seven online functions: CAS, NAM, NUM, ANM, PER, JAC, and CAL. These functions aid the user in the interrogation, retrieval, and updating of the basic data files via the remote terminals.

RBI allows for the input of batch data (via the remote terminals) by placing the input in a queue to be processed by the Batch Input Subsystem. REP allows the user to request batch output (from the remote terminals) by placing the requests on a queue to be processed by the Batch Output Subsystem. The seven online functions give terminal displays in reply to terminal inquiries, and are briefly described as follows:

CAS: allows the user to search, retrieve, and update the Case History File, and to display all associated transaction records at the terminal.

NAM: allows the user to search, retrieve, and update the Name File, and to display the desired records at the terminal.

NUM: allows the user to search, retrieve, and update the Identification Number File, and to display the desired records at the terminal.

ANM: allows the user to display all available identification numbers associated with a defendant.

PER: allows the user to display all available personal descriptor information associated with a defendant.

JAC: allows the user to display the arrest/conviction history of a defendant.

CAL: allows the user to search, retrieve, and update the Calendar File, and to display the docket of a court.[35]

You are specifically required to: (1) analyze and make recommendations concerning the system of controls, (2) your boss has recently been reading about the preventive audit philosophy and concurrent auditing and requests that you develop a report indicating the techniques that will support these concepts, and (3) describe techniques that have not been discussed in this chapter.

[35]John G. Burch, Jr., and Felix R. Strater, Jr., *Information Systems: Theory and Practice*, (Santa Barbara, Calif.: Hamilton Publishing Company, 1974), p. 97.

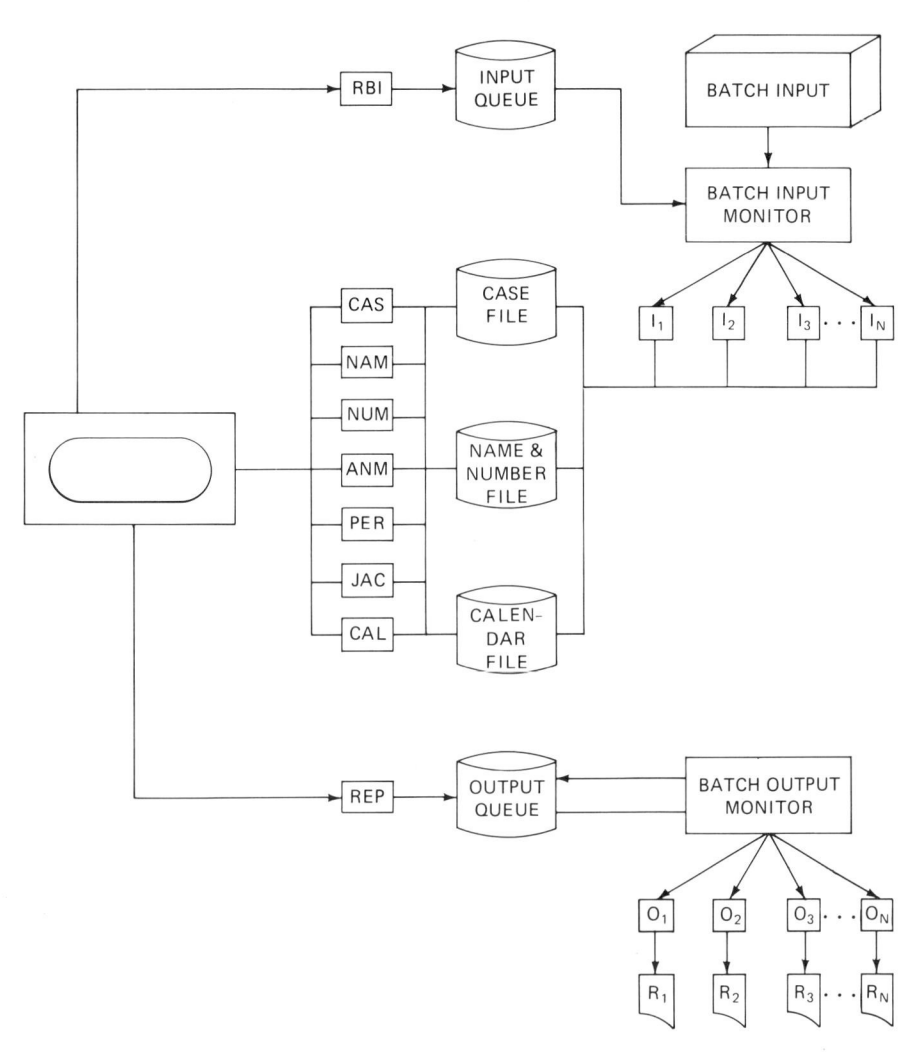

FIGURE 13.7.
Computer Configuration which Supports the Information System.

13.2 Super, Inc. (Sup) is a major retail chain throughout the United States. They have recently installed a point-of-sale integrated merchandising information system. The point-of-sale portion of the system is shown in Figure 13.8.

Sales transaction data entered through the point-of-sale registers supply the bulk of the input activity data to the integrated merchandising information system. Point-of-sale transaction data is input to the system by depressing selected keys according

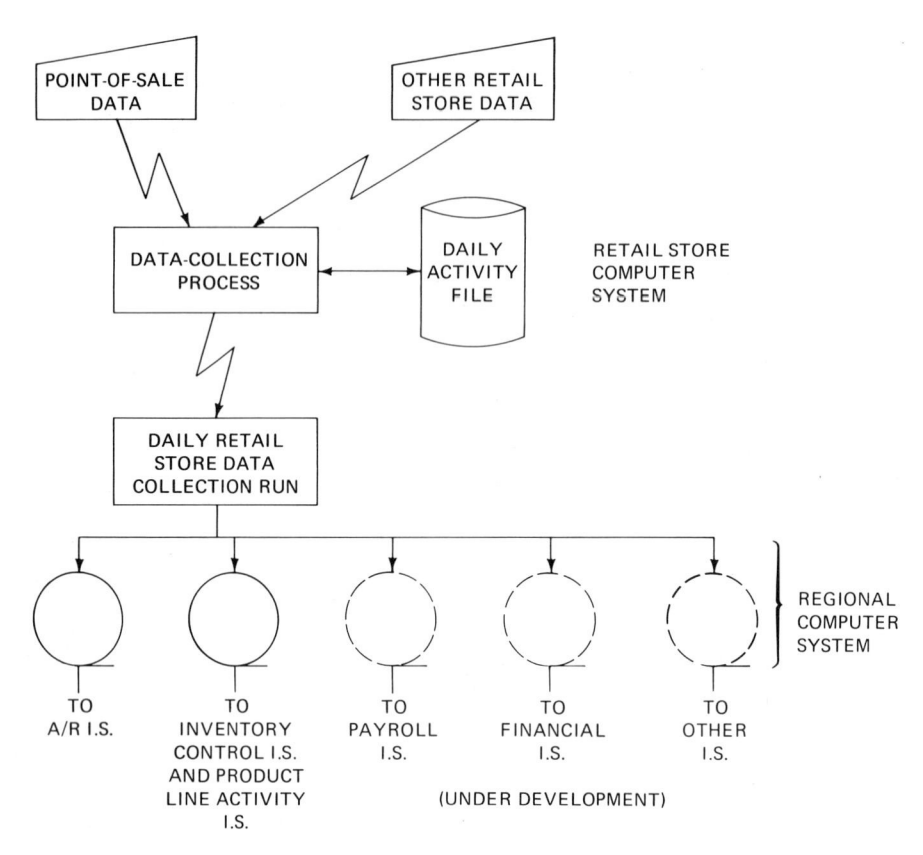

FIGURE 13.8.
Point-of-Sale Portion of Merchandising Information System.

to a specified sequence. Ordinarily the following descriptors are required for each sales transaction: employee identification number, merchandise division, item identification number, quantity, unit price, type of transaction (cash sale, credit sale, C.O.D., layaway, or return), and customer account number from the credit card (credit sale only). The register computes the extended price for each line item, sums the extended prices for all line items, and determines applicable taxes.

All of the point-of-sale registers in each retail store are connected online to a minicomputer located in the store. One of the principal functions of the minicomputer is to collect and temporarily store all point-of-sale transaction data accumulated during the store's operating hours each day. During the evening, all stored data are forwarded as a single batch to the regional computer center. The minicomputer also performs credit checks.

Goals, 77
Grandfather-father-son, 140

Hardware, 10
  typical configuration, 12
Hardware monitors, 79, 453–56
Hazards, 214, 249
  fires, 215
  fraud and unauthorized access, 215
  general hazards, 216
  malfunctions, 215
  natural disasters, 216
  power and communication failure, 215
  sabotage and riot, 216
Hybrid processing system, 384–85

Improve audit efficiency, 289
Independence, 275
Information systems, 3, 5–22, 402–409
Initial program load (IPL), 15
Input
  completeness, 102
  devices, 12
  preparation, 100
  verification, 101
Integrated systems, 407–409
Integrated Test Facility (ITF), 431–41
  case, 438–40
  definition, 432–34
  implementation, 434–38
Invasion of privacy, 43
Inventory, computer, 276

Job Control Language (JCL), 106, 137
  CSECT, 110
  JOBLIB, 109
  LET, 109
  NCAL, 109
  STEPLIB, 109
Job titles, 8
Josephson junction, 25
Judgment, 275

Key to
  card, 101
  disk, 101
  tape, 101

Large Scale Integration (LSI), 25
Laser, 25
Linkage editor, 108

Manager
  information systems, 7
  security, 10
Maxicomputers, 468–69
Message switching, 400
Microcomputers, 468–69
Microelectronics, 25

Microprogram, 27
Minicompany, see Integrated Test Facility, 431
Minicomputers, 468–69
Modems, 18, 396–97
Monitoring systems, 445–56
Monitors
  hardware, 79, 453–56
  software, 79, 450–53
MOSFET, 25
Multiplexers, 397–98
Multiprogramming, 387–88

No one way to audit, 466–68

Object module, 14, 107
Operating log, 133
Operating system processing, 105
Operating systems, 15, 21, 105–112, 387
  linkage editor, 108
  preprocessor stage, 107
  processor stage, 108
  supervisor, 15, 109, 110

Parallel processing, 441
Parallel simulation, 441–45
Parallel test facility, 441–45
Passwords, 449
Periodic systems, 377–80, 382–83
Personal attitudes, 287
Personnel
  exit procedures, 78
  functional areas, 77
  goals and policy of organization, 77
  screening and selection, 74
  training, 75
Personnel administration, 76–77
Physical controlled access, 217
  badges, 218
  cards, 218
  closed-circuit monitors, 218
  combination of control devices, 219
  double-door entry, 219
  guards and special escorts, 217
  one-way emerging doors, 219
  paper shredders, 218
  sign-in/sign-out register, 218
Physical location, 219
  backup facilities, 220
  carrier control, 220
  identification, 220
  remote, 219
  separate building, 219
Physical protection, 220
  coverings, 221
  drains and pumps, 220
  emergency power, 220
  fire control, 221
  general building safeguards, 221

Plan
  contingency, 72
  master, 69
  resources, 71
  specific projects, 71
  strategic, 71
Point of sale device (POS), 71, 98
Privacy, 37–44
  federal issues, 40–42
  invasion of, 43
  judicial process, 40
  state issues, 39–40
Procedures and models, 404
  automatic notification
  exception reporting, 404
  programmed decision making, 404
Processing controls, 112
Program aids, 120
  decision tables, 120
  librarian, 121
  shorthand, 120
  test data generators, 121
Program changes, 119
Program development, 117
  catalog, 118
  coding, 118
  implementation, 118
  logic design, 117
  test, 118
Program documentation, 118
Program operating controls, 116
Program status word, 110
Programmer
  application, 9
  maintenance, 9
  systems, 9
Programming languages, 14
Programs
  auditor written, 356–61
  client written, 354
  control, 314–16, 355
  service, 16
Project tasks, 81

Questionnaires, 278, 294–301
Questionnaires, preparation, 296–300

Records, 17
Read Only Memory (ROM), 26

Security goals
  detect, 217
  deter, 217
  investigate, 217
  minimize disorder, 217
  recovery, 217

Security program, 228
Security techniques, procedural, 221
  authentication, 228
  authorization, 227
  detect security violations, 229
  disconnection and separation, 223
  identification, 225
  exception reporting, 229
  integrity, 222
  isolation, 223
  monitoring, 229
  obfuscation, 224
  trend reporting, 229
Snapshot, 431
Software, 14
  monitors, 79–80, 450–53
Standards, 79
  computer operators, 79
Standards, general data processing, 81
  data definitions, 82
  modular programming, 82
  programming languages, 82
Standards system and programming, 81
  scheduling and controlling, 81
  time estimates, 81
Steering committee, 7
Substantive tests, 279, 290–91
Subsystems, 58
System Management Facilities (SMF), 445–450
System Modification Program (SMP), 111, 121
System of controls, see controls
Systems approach to auditing, 472–76
Systems concept, 403

Tagging and tracing, 424–31
Terminals, 18, 390–93
  intelligent, 391
  point of sale, 392–93
  telephone, 390
Test deck, 306–14
Total system, 18
Transaction codes, 95
Transaction controls, 409
Transaction log, 412–13, 421–24
Transaction record layout, 309
Transaction trail, 421–22

Uninterruptible Power Supply (UPS), 220
User programs, see application programs
Utility programs, 369

Virtual machine, 25
Virtual storage, 388–90